McCARTNEY

Books by Christopher Sandford

Fiction
Feasting With Panthers
Arcadian
We Don't Do Dogs

Sport
The Cornhill Centenary Test
Godfrey Evans
Tom Graveney

Film
Steve McQueen

Music
Mick Jagger
Eric Clapton
Kurt Cobain
David Bowie
Sting
Bruce Springsteen
Keith Richards

Christopher Sandford

McCARTNEY

CARROLL & GRAF PUBLISHERS
NEW YORK

To SRS

McCartney

Carroll & Graf Publishers
An Imprint of Avalon Publishing Group, Inc.
245 West 17th Street, 11th Floor
New York, NY 10011

AVALON
publishing group incorporated

First Carroll & Graf edition 2006
First Caroll & Graf trade paperback edition 2007

First published in the UK by Random House, 2006

Library of Congress Cataloging-in-Publication Data is available.

ISBN-13: 978-0-78671-871-9
ISBN-10: 0-7867-1871-4

9 8 7 6 5 4 3 2 1

Printed in the United States of America
Distributed by Publishers Group West

CONTENTS

List of Illustrations

Paul McCartney with four-year old brother Mike, 1948 (© *Keystone*).

Copy of Paul's birth certficate, 18 June 1942.

Paul's childhood home, 20 Forthlin Road (© *S. E. Sandford*).

St Peter's Church Hall, Woolton (© *S. E. Sandford*).

Paul with his father and brother Mike, circa 1960 (© *Keystone*).

McCartney in 1962 (© *Keystone*).

Paul with girlfriend Jane Asher at the London premiere of 'Here We Go Round the Mulberry Bush', 5 January 1968 (© *Central Press*).

Wimple Street, London, Paul's home for three years (© *S. E. Sandford*).

Paul relaxing in the Atlantic at Miami Beach with two fans during the Beatles inaugural US tour, 15 February 1964 (© *Bettmann/Corbis*).

The Beatles in America, 1964 (© *Hulton-Deutsch Collection/Corbis*).

Paul at the NME Poll-Winners Concert, Wembley 1965 (© *Peter Perchard*).

The Beatles arriving in London with manager Brian Epstein, 8 July 1966 (© *Bettmann/Corbis*).

The Beatles performing at Shea Stadium, 23 August 1966 (© *Bettmann/Corbis*).

A hand-written draft of a six-page letter from Lennon to McCartney, circa 1970 (*Reuters/Corbis*).

Paul and Linda McCartney with their band Wings, December 1971 (© *Hulton-Deutsch Collection/Corbis*).

Paul with Linda and daughters Stella, Mary and Heather at Heathrow Airport, circa 1973 (© *Express*).

Customs officer at New Tokyo International Airport with marijuana seized from Paul's luggage, 16 January 1980 (© *Bettmann/Corbis*).

Paul leaving Tokyo Detention Center, 25 January 1980 (© *Bettmann/Corbis*).

Paul at his home in Rye, Sussex, after his release from Tokyo, 28 January 1980 (© *Hulton-Deutsch Collection/Corbis*).

Paul and Linda at Ringo Starr's wedding to Barbara Bach, 27 April 1981 (© *Terry O'Neil*).

Paul and Linda at the British Video Awards, 1985.

Paul performing at the Live Aid concert at Wembley Stadium, 13 July 1985 (© *Neal Preston/Corbis*).

Paul during a performance at The Forum, 1989 (© *Neal Preston/Corbis*).

Exhibition of Paul's paintings at the Mark Matthews Gallery, 2 November 2000 (© *Mitchell Gerber/Corbis*).

Paul with Heather Mills at the Adopt-a-Minefield benefit gala dinner in Beverly Hills, 14 June 2001 (© *Reuters/Corbis*).

Paul with police officer at Concert for New York, 20 October 2001 (© *Reuters/Corbis*).

Stella McCartney receiving honorary degree from the University of Dundee, 8 July 2003 (© *Reuters/Corbis*).

Paul with Russian President Vladimir Putin at the Kremlin, 24 May 2003 (© *Reuters/Corbis*).

Paul performing at Superbowl XXXIX Halftime Show, Jacksonville, Florida, 6 February 2005 (© *David Drapkin*).

Acknowledgements

This is an 'unauthorised' biography so I'm particularly grateful to the 300 or so people who spoke to me, if only to vent. I would also like to acknowledge publicly and for all time my respect and admiration for Sir Paul McCartney's talent, drive, restless creativity, exquisite taste, eclecticism – especially the last, in tackling the worlds of children's film, poetry and abstract art. Nothing in the following pages is intended in any way as an attack or slur on him, his family or his fabulous body of work.

For recollections, input or advice I should thank, institutionally: Abacus, Amazon, Ananova, ASCAP, *Billboard*, Book Mail, Borders, the British Library, British Newspaper Library, Chapters, Companies House, *Daytrippin'*, FBI – Freedom of Information Division, Focus Fine Arts, Foyles, General Register Office, Helter Skelter, Liverpool Business Centre, Liverpool Tourist Information, London Beatles Store, Maltese Falcon, Merseyrail, MultiMap, the Music Box, Performing Right Society, Public Record Office, Rock and Roll Hall of Fame, St Peter's Church Woolton, Seattle Public Library, *The Times*, Vital Records, waronsex.

Professionally: Tim Andrews, Mark Booth, Jonathan Boyd, Randy Brecker, Ben Brierley, Gary Brooker, the late William

Burroughs, Chris Charlesworth, Noel Chelberg, Dan Chernow, Allan Clarke, Lucy Conlon, Lol Creme, Micky Dolenz, Paul Du Noyer, Rex Evans, the late Adam Faith, Chris Farlowe, Ros Fielden, Libby Fields, Judy Flanders, Alan Foulder, Lucy Gentry, Tony Gill, Charlie Gillett, Sarah Goldstein, Roger Greenaway, Jeff Griffin, Bob Harris, Alan Hazen, Dick Heckstall-Smith, David Henshaw, Jill Holmes, Tony Huss, David Jacobs, the Jaggers, Norman Jewison, Lenny Kaye, Joan Keylock, Tom Keylock, Max King, Alan Lane, Nichola Lee, Barbara Levy, Steve Loder, Nick Lowe, Angie McCartney, Ruth McCartney, Henry McCullough, Roger McGough, Kara McMahon, John Major, Robert Mann, Dave Mason, the late Mickie Most, Mark Noble, the late Jack Paar, Graham Paisley, Max Paley, May Pang, Graham Parker, Andy Partridge, Andy Peebles, Peter Perchard, Bruce Perret, Dave Peters, Harold Pinter, Ken Pitt, Jim Repard, Tim Rice, Neil Sedaka, Pete Seeger, Brian Setzer, Ravi Shankar, Ned Sherrin, Don Short, Pat Sims, Nancy Sinatra, David Sinclair, Grace Slick, Eric Stewart, Ed Strauss, Dick Taylor, Al Tilbrook, Kathy Ward, Adele Warlow, Christine Webster, Rusty West, Alan Weyer, Bobby Whitlock, Mark Wilson, Robert Wise, Tom Wolfe, David Wood, Glen Woodman, Tony Yeo, Irfan Zuberi. It's a pleasure to particularly thank Marshall Terrill, my co-worker on the biography chain gang and an indefatigable source of McCartney facts, figures and interviews over the past two years.

Personally: Adis, John Aeberhard, Amanuel, the Attic, Pete Barnes, Ray Bates, Benaroya Hall, Mihir Bose, Hilary and Robert Bruce, the late Alan Burrough, Changelink, Albert Clinton, Cocina, the late Doris Cohn, Ernst Cohn, Richard Cranfield, Cricketers Club of London, Deb K. Das, Mark Demos, Monty Dennison, the Dowdall family, John and Barbara Dungee, Fairmont Waterfront Hotel, Malcolm Galfe, the Gay Hussar, Gethsemane Lutheran Church, Audrey Godwin, James Graham, Peter Griffin, Richard Hill, Amy Hostetter, Ivar's, JCC, Jo Jacobius, Bill and Morgan

Johnson, Lincoln Kamell, Kinko's, the late Joan Lambert, Terry Lambert, Belinda Lawson, the late Daphne Lorimer, Vince Lorimer, Lee Mattson, Jim Meyersahm, Sheila Mohn, the Morgans, National Gallery room 34, Peter Oborne, Chuck Ogmund, Larry Olsen, Valya Page, Pan Pacific Hotel, the Parishes, Chris Pickrell, Prins family, Queen Anne Office Supply, Keith Richards, the late Peter Rushbrooke, St Paul's Hospital Vancouver, Debbie Saks, Delia Sandford, my father Sefton Sandford, Sue Sandford, Peter Scaramanga, Seattle CC, Kempton Segerhammar, Fred and Cindy Smith, the *Spectator*, Sportspages, the Stanleys, Subway 3674, Jack Surendranath, the Travel Team, Ben and Mary Tyvand, Valhalla Coffee Co of Tacoma, Wa., the Villars, Tony Vinter, Von's, John and Mary Wainwright, Jim Wheal, the Willis Flemings, Betty Wolstenholme. As usual my greatest debt is to Karen and Nicholas Sandford, who I hope will feel it's been worthwhile.

Thanks again, Fields family.

C.S.
2006

McCARTNEY

'The first string that the musician usually touches is the bass, when he intends to put all in tune. God plays this one Himself'

John Bunyan

'We were madmen'

Paul McCartney

CHAPTER ONE

Get Back

As far as rock music goes, Japan was the far side of the moon in 1980, long before the likes of the Stones blasted away its parochial charm and turned it into a virtual colony of Los Angeles. In those days it was a remote, enigmatic place, aloof and forbidding, of the sort ancient map-makers used to label 'here be dragons'. Paul McCartney had been applying for his work permit to tour here for nearly a decade, and was said to be ecstatic when the papers finally came through early that new year. The plan was to play eleven concerts, scheduled to run from 21 January to 2 February, raising both funds for McCartney's latest crusade – emergency relief for Kampuchea – and his own profile. On the way, he, his family and band enjoyed a three-day layover in New York, where Paul signed autographs and posed for pictures with scores of fans and well-wishers at the airport. Up until then, nobody had ever seen him unhappy in a crowd, even in those that ripped pieces of his clothes off as souvenirs.

On the evening of Monday 14 January, Paul put in a call from his suite at the Stanhope hotel to a number just across Central Park. As it happened, John Lennon (whom McCartney hadn't seen in nearly four years) had recently become more visible around town. Since flying back from his own family break in Japan the previous autumn,

Lennon had taken to walking the chilly Upper West Side streets, greeting all and sundry with a friendly if adenoidal hello, dressed in a fur coat, a fedora jammed down onto his thin nose that never seemed to get unstuffed. Of late, he and his wife Yoko Ono had both enthused about enjoying greater access to and from their many admirers in New York. The couple's welcome didn't, however, extend to McCartney, whom Yoko allegedly told, 'This isn't a good time. We're busy.'

'OK, listen. All I'm asking is to drop by, have a smoke and chew the fat with Himself.' There was a dubious silence. 'I can't stay,' McCartney stressed; it was the phrase he always used in delicate situations. 'We're off tomorrow to these gigs. Bring 'em on,' he added in a stagey, roll-right-up sort of way. 'I feel like kicking some ass again.'

'Oh, Paul, Paul. Is *not* a good time,' Yoko reiterated. 'We're busy on our houses.'

The call ended on a sour note when McCartney mentioned that he and his family were booked into the presidential suite of the Okura hotel, the Lennons' own semi-official residence when staying in Tokyo. There's no evidence that John was ever told that Paul had rung him.

The McCartneys' flight landed at Narita airport in the early afternoon of 16 January, Paul, dressed in a lime green suit, chugging into the Immigration hall holding his infant son James in one hand and a red women's make-up box – allegedly the property of wife Linda – in the other. Mysteriously, there were no reps from CBS Records immediately on hand to meet him. Japanese Customs, however, were there in force; their inspection quickly turned up a small plastic bag in Paul's hand luggage. It contained eight ounces of marijuana, with a street value of 600,000 yen or approximately £1,120. Relieving him of his son, two police officers informed McCartney that he was being arrested for possession. 'It's all a mistake,' he allowed as he was being handcuffed. 'A serious mistake.'

They flashed him a look and led him away.

The next three days were to be the worst of McCartney's life to date. First he was ushered to the airport's Drug Supervision Centre and grilled not only about the dope but also a statement he'd provided just weeks earlier, assuring the Japanese government that his pot-smoking days were behind him. From there McCartney (now known officially as Prisoner 22) was transferred to a four-by-eight-foot cell in Tokyo's metropolitan jail. His wedding ring and other personal effects were removed. Meanwhile, authorities impounded the jet freighter bringing in the band's twenty tons of sound equipment, each and every piece of which was stripped down and searched. The tour was cancelled. Turning the singer of Silly Love Songs back into a vice case and subversive, all of McCartney's music was banned by state radio. Around midnight on the 16th he was allowed his first two visitors, a public defender named Tasuko Matsuo and the British vice-consul, one Doland Warren-Knott. Both men advised him that he could get seven years.

Unable to sleep, McCartney spent much of his time sitting cross-legged with his back to the wall of his cell and gamely trying to sing a few show tunes like Baby Face, his favourite at moments of stress, for his fellow cons. His request for a guitar was denied. At dawn, breakfast was taken with a blunt spoon. After twenty-four hours in custody, Paul was ushered into a room furnished by a wooden table and three chairs, where two English-speaking interrogators announced that they meant to take him, step by step, over his entire life. 'What do you want to know?' he asked them.

The reply was equally blunt. 'Everything.' And for the next six hours McCartney gave them the lot: Liverpool; Hamburg; certain promoters with shotguns; Beatlemania; Eppy; the Maharishi; Apple. The old days. The narcs listened to this restless tale of social upheaval and culture-changing creativity in total silence, their faces deadpan. Following some perfunctory words of acknowledgement, they then attempted to march their prisoner – now manacled again –

outside and across a normally deserted back alley leading to the main cell block. This plan backfired dramatically when three to four hundred fans were found to be barring their way, accompanied by a gale-force squeal of 'Paul! Paul!' While McCartney himself appraised the scene calmly, his two jailers took him by the arms, lifted him up, and ran for it.

Next day and all that week, the 'MACCA IN CHAINS' headlines kept up a breathless drumbeat. Intense efforts were made to find larger significance in the bust, and the case brought together some unlikely allies. The 'straight' press spoke of McCartney's folly and arrogance, while most or all of his band (which would fold shortly thereafter) were similarly unimpressed. Meanwhile, a twenty-nine-year-old fan named Kenneth Lambert presented himself at Miami International airport, without money or a passport, and demanded a first-class ticket in order to fly to Tokyo to 'free Paul'. After debating the matter for some time, Lambert suddenly pulled a realistic-looking toy gun from his pocket and was shot dead by police. Other admirers saw McCartney's case as authority run amok, while in years ahead a story went round that the whole thing was actually the doing of a certain ex-colleague, who had spitefully tipped off a contact in Japanese Customs. The facts of Paul's ordeal could fit almost any agenda.

On the fourth day, McCartney was allowed writing paper, books and a first visit from Linda. After a week he enjoyed a communal bath, entertaining the murderers and rapists joining him there by bravely singing all five minutes of Mull Of Kintyre. Outside, the fans grew more vociferous in their support, and some ill-advisedly pelted the jail with stones. One teenaged girl wearing a *Help!* T-shirt would be shot and wounded by the police. An international media furore was also in full cry, putting pressure on the yen. Planeloads of lawyers began arriving from New York, demanding their client's release, and at that stage, after nine days inside, the Justice Ministry decided it would be in the public interest to set McCartney free. He was deported on the evening of 25 January, telling reporters on the flight home, 'I've been a fool. What I did was incredibly dumb . . . I'm never going to smoke pot again.'

Before touching down for a refuelling stop in Alaska, McCartney began to fret about the publicity the 'Jap thing' might bring, and quickly realised how much he'd underestimated it when two camera trucks raced up to meet him on the runway before his jet had even come to a stop. The bust only intensified interest in both him and the Beatles, those slightly poor relations of their own fame who, collectively, stood as tall and mythic as Stonehenge. George had sent his old oppo a 'Thinking of you' telegram to the Okura hotel. Ringo had nothing public to say on the matter, but, in a related development, found himself first taunted and then strip-searched when, a month later, he flew into Mexico City to begin filming *Caveman*. John, for his part, would continue to scoff at much of the Beatles legacy, if only for public consumption. He remained the most wildly changeable of the four. Indeed, it seemed to some in 1980 that Lennon was one of the many New York-area residents to have already had their identities stolen. Perhaps it was an old platinum card, carelessly tossed in a Dakota Building dustbin, which allowed the criminals to strike, or perhaps the purchase over the phone of a round-the-world air ticket. Whatever it was, it was difficult otherwise to reconcile the bouncy young turk of the 1960s with the beaky, 40-year-old contrarian so full of spit, vinegar and surprises. On 28 November, John gave a legal deposition as part of a suit against the producers of a Broadway show caricaturing Paul and himself. His affidavit, which would go unpublished for six years, began: 'I and the three other former Beatles have plans to stage a reunion concert, to be recorded, filmed and marketed around the world.'*

---

* This was in stark contrast to Lennon's remarks, two months earlier, in *Newsweek*: 'The four guys who used to be that group can never, ever be that group again, even if they wanted to be,' he said. 'What if Paul and I got together? It would be boring . . . I was never one for reunions. It's all over!'

For McCartney, the honours and rewards would roll on through the Eighties and right down to the present day. Back home that spring, he collected an Outstanding Music Personality award and won the Ivor Novello for International Achievement. He soon added a Grammy and on 16 May flew to Cannes, where Oscar Grillo's short film *Seaside Woman*, based on Paul and Linda's song of that name, took the Palme d'Or. He and his music seemed to be everywhere: when Lennon strolled in for tea at the Plaza hotel, the house violinist, as usual, serenaded him with Paul's Yesterday. Later that same week McCartney put out a solo album, about which the critics used terms like 'dumb', 'trite' and 'flat-out awful'. It went straight to number one.

Paul, Linda and their brood spent much of the summer on holiday in the Caribbean before moving to their beachfront home near Linda's family on Long Island. By then Lennon happened to be only ninety minutes away in the studio, cutting his own first album in four years. On Wednesday 13 August, McCartney rang John to suggest that he, Paul, 'drop by to help out on a few tracks. Just for a couple of hours . . . I can't stay,' he added. Just as she had seven months earlier, Yoko reportedly intercepted the call and made it very clear that both she and her husband were busy. Paul persisted; would she at least pass on his offer?

'Sure,' said Yoko, and hung up.

Every culture creates psychopaths in its own image: it's difficult to imagine transferring the typical British madman to America. Likewise, the 'lone nut with a gun' seems oddly indigenous to the US. While the two boyhood friends continued to circle one another, just such a character, a twenty-five-year-old flop named Mark David Chapman, working as a part-time security guard in Hawaii, began to entertain thoughts of murder. By early October, Chapman was reading everything he could get his hands on about the newly public John Lennon. At least one such profile, in *Esquire*, would speak of this 'conscience of his generation' re-emerging as 'a forty-year-old businessman worth $150 million.' There were other pieces extolling the percipience of John and Yoko's investments, the commercial boon of the whole comeback, and the goldmine of the Beatles back catalogue. Chapman began to denounce his one-time hero, complaining that he was a phony. When he left work for the last time on 23 October he signed the employees' log as 'John Lennon', before violently stabbing the name out.

Four days later in London, McCartney began cutting the soundtrack for a projected film about the beloved *Daily Express* children's character Rupert Bear, to which he owned the rights. Among the tunes recorded were Rupert Song (Parts 1 and 2), Tippi Tippi Toes and The Castle Of The King Of The Birds. A thirty-eight-piece orchestra and a boys' choir joined Paul to lay down both vocal and humming versions of the rousing We All Stand Together, which would be a British hit some four years later.

McCartney was sipping a Scotch and Coke when the young choristers filed out, in a reflective mood; the song had moved him. Around midnight, a Cinderella moment in the empty studio when the gear was being stowed, he turned to Linda and one or two friends and told them that it reminded him of the famously trippy session for All You Need Is Love. 'It was that same vibe. I just looked around, and there were all these flowers and happy faces smiling up at me.' Another sip or two, and he began murmuring huskily, 'John . . . John . . .' And Paul bent over chuckling, as though it had been yesterday rather than thirteen years before. At about that same moment Mark Chapman was in the J&S gunshop in Honolulu, where, for the equivalent of £65, he quickly concluded the purchase of a Charter Arms .38 calibre revolver.

On 4 November, a Tuesday, Ronald Reagan was elected the fortieth president of the US. John Lennon continued his now full-pelt media campaign prior to the release of his and Yoko's album

Double Fantasy. And McCartney made his third and last attempt of the year to reach his former partner by phone. By then Paul, too, was back in New York, overseeing the final edits of his concert film *Rockshow*, which would premier on 26 November. An employee at Lennon's home took the call and assured McCartney, 'OK, he'll get back to you.'

Five weeks passed. Then one day in December, McCartney was at AIR Studios in London, the phone rang and it was Lennon's people getting back to him. They wanted Paul to co-sign the deposition against the producers of the *Beatlemania* stage show, alleging that its sole purpose had been to commercially exploit the band even as its four members planned a major comeback concert. (This came as news to George and Ringo.) The lawyers were polite enough, and said that their client felt it might be a good idea for the Beatles' two 'capital generators' to present a united front on the issue, but John himself – already back at work on a new record, even as Chapman stalked him – never rang to discuss it.

Instead, in the early hours of Tuesday 9 December, Yoko phoned Paul's office, who in turn found him, with the unthinkable. John's assassination by Chapman would become the major news headline and talking point throughout the world for that week. The press immediately descended on McCartney's farm, cornering him among the sheep and goats, and got the shot everyone wanted, the *News* splashing it all over page two. And next day there he was, the so-called cute one, grizzled, puffy-eyed and surrounded by hairy animals. 'I can't take it in,' Paul announced. 'John was a great man who'll be remembered for his unique contributions to art, music and peace. He's going to be missed by [everyone] . . . He belongs to the world.'

The press thought both Lennon and McCartney still belonged to them, and in the hours and days ahead they doorstepped Paul wherever he went. (Many of these same papers who gave over entire editions to their editors' unbearable expressions of grief had ignored or panned *Double Fantasy* just three weeks earlier.) Around seven that Tuesday night, ducking out of the side door of AIR Studios towards his car, Paul was swarmed by a small mob of fans, reporters and TV cameramen. Amid the riot of upside-down faces mouthing 'How do you feel?' questions through his windscreen, he turned round and said, 'It's a drag, innit?' McCartney would come to rue the exact choice of words, which many in the media considered glib.

The cheeky Beatle became heartless. He 'shrugged off the news' one American music weekly wrote, 'as though bemoaning a light rain shower.' Actually McCartney was shaken to his core, and genuinely sad at how things had been left between the two of them. On the morning of 10 December, just twenty-four hours after hearing the news, Paul asked to meet Andy Peebles, the BBC DJ who interviewed Lennon the weekend before his death. Peebles went to AIR, where he found McCartney 'absolutely gutted . . . and like anyone in shock, totally fixated on a single issue. In this case, what had John said about him? How'd he really felt?'

McCartney's official statement on the tragedy, issued later that day, hinted at some of the same concerns:

> I've hidden myself in my work, but it keeps flashing into my mind. I feel shattered, angry and very sad. It's just ridiculous. [Lennon] was pretty rude about me sometimes, but I secretly admired him for it, and I always managed to stay in touch with him. There was no question that we weren't friends – I really loved the guy. John often looked a loony to many people. He had enemies, but he was fantastic . . . He made a lot of sense.

McCartney had suffered one other significant loss, when his mother Mary succumbed to breast cancer on 31 October 1956. For twenty-three years she'd been a hardworking maternity nurse, and for the last ten, on and off, the family's main breadwinner. Her husband Jim had come back from the hospital that dark Wednesday night and broken the news to his two bewildered sons. After a long silence, Paul had said, 'What are we going to do without her dosh?'

Fourteen years old. He'd had no real idea of how to cope and would soon turn to music as a release. Paul's 'It's a drag' observation of twenty-four years later may well have been fuelled by the fact that, as a child, he'd learnt to keep certain things to himself. So, too, his teenage concern about 'dosh' in time led to the shrewd, hard-headed businessman worth some £820 million.

It's somehow fitting, even if the facts are appalling, that McCartney should have survived Lennon. He was always the long-distance runner of the Beatles, an unabashed lover of his grannie's music, for whom aging gracefully was in the game plan all along. Unlike John, Paul's also enjoyed the ability to strike a sympathetic chord with a huge, worldwide public which feels him to be, at heart, 'just like us.' Of course, it's not true, but it's a rare gift that people should think it so. Like a Reagan or a Princess Diana, to name two, McCartney has gradually acquired special status as a much beloved Great Communicator.

The story that's led up to this began on that bleak Halloween in 1956, when overnight Paul became obsessive about playing music. Stewing over the awkwardness of the wake and the weeks that followed, he took refuge in his first guitar. In the fifty years since, he's done the following: become the most successful pop composer and recording artist in history, selling more than 140 million singles and roughly the same number of albums; scored at least eighty gold discs; acquired the copyright to over 1,000 other songs, including the works of Buddy Holly, Marvin Hamlisch, Sammy Cahn and Ira Gershwin, as well as the soundtracks to *Annie*, *Grease* and *A Chorus Line* (the list isn't exhaustive); collected an MBE, a knighthood and much else in-between, from Chile's Order of Merit to a fellowship of the Royal College of Music; been involved in at least four drugs busts; caused Billy Graham to fall to his knees to pray for his soul; flirted with various alternative lifestyles; had smash hits as a solo artist and also as a member of a duo, trio, quartet, quintet and sextet; casually written the most popular song of all time, Yesterday, since jazzed up, slowed down or otherwise mangled by 2,400 other artists, ranging from Elvis to Frank Sinatra. As a result, McCartney has enjoyed a virtual season ticket to the Novellos and the Grammys, and in 1992 was the first ever recipient of Sweden's Polar Music Award, sometimes known as the Nobel prize for the arts.

He's given his name to everything from a planet to a ground-breaking punk group (the Ramones, who were all big fans, especially of McCartney's old stage moniker, Paul Ramon). Snapped up the rights to such standards as Chopsticks, Sentimental Journey – and Happy Birthday. Written a chart-topping James Bond theme. Dabbled in, among other forms, electronica, classical, swing, ragtime, soul and disco. Compared himself to Bach. Starred in one of the best musical films of all time, and also in one of the worst. Published poetry and exhibited a painting called *The Queen After Her First Cigarette*. Graced the *Guinness Book of Records* for having played to the largest stadium audience in history, as well as for the fastest ticket sale in history. Generally soared far above the level of other Sixties pop stars with their vaudeville routines for the curious and the disturbed. Enjoyed the distinction of seeing a school in Cracow, Poland, teach eight-to-twelve-year-olds to speak English purely by studying his lyrics.

There are plenty of other prolific tunesmiths around, but none have touched McCartney at his peak. It'd be going too far to call him, as John Lennon once did, a ditty factory; going too far, but not going in totally the wrong direction. He was staggeringly productive. Whereas even Lennon would take two or three days to write a three-minute song, back then Paul actually took three minutes to write a three-minute song. He dreamt up hits-in-waiting while out walking his dog or sitting in the back of taxis. The melody of his most famous song came to him fully formed in his sleep. McCartney was *totally* musical; when not busy with his own career he found time to write for or produce everyone from Cilla Black to the Bonzo Dog Doo-Dah Band to the Everlys. Somewhere along the way, he became known, to Lennon and to millions of others, as the doe-eyed softy and perky melodist of breezy, lightweight fare like Hello, Goodbye, not to mention The Frog Chorus.

But like a stagnant pond, apparently calm to the naked eye, McCartney has always teemed with furious, invisible activity. As well as the Uncle Albert-style froth he's also been responsible for some of rock's more thrilling innovations. He was the first of the Beatles, and about the first pop star anywhere, to buck the old Tin Pan Alley convention of what a 'proper song' should sound like. That would have been legacy enough. But along with all the heady pranks involving wrong keys and tape loops and unsynchronised orchestras, McCartney was also restlessly shuffling styles and idioms right from the start. By the late Sixties he was regularly mixing old-fashioned showbiz 'oomph' with startling little novelties – for instance, the swampy bass lick, beloved of rap artists, he improvised on Come Together. He was 'into' Indian music before either Lennon or Harrison, and reggae fully a decade before chancers like the Police. Just turn on the radio. Every song harmonising in fourths and fifths rather than conventional thirds, that's McCartney. Every giddily vertical melody, that's McCartney. Jumping bass lines, wild octave leaps and yeah-yeah choruses – McCartney. Even in later years he never failed to take risks, whether pioneering the use of found sound or forgoing his brand name to trade under the aliases 'Thrills' Thrillington, the Fireman or plain Wacca, host of 1995's seminal *Oobu Joobu* radio show. No wonder his company logo shows a juggler keeping various planets aloft. McCartney himself often cites astrology when attempting to rationalise how an inveterate hoofer like him can also be an avant-gardist. 'I'm a Gemini, and we're supposed to be like this and that. We're quite schizo.'

★

Some, but not all of the McCartney story has grown threadbare through constant retelling. PhD theses about him have been accumulating for years, and there are whole books devoted to curating the exact dates and details of every song their subject ever recorded, and what he was wearing when he did so. Relatively few of them have challenged the McCartney stereotype: a happy-go-lucky, sweater-clad sort of bloke, more tuneful but not that much more hip than Val Doonican. That's the myth.

After finishing work in the studio shortly after John Lennon's death in December 1980, Paul and his family went back to the farm in Sussex. They'd remain in seclusion there, under armed guard, for the rest of the winter. He chose his occasional guests with care, refusing all interview requests and, not surprisingly, further enhancing security. One of his few visitors in the week before Christmas was an old Liverpool friend who remembers 'Paul talk[ing] a lot about the Fabs, and how John had always been the one of them to wear his heart on his sleeve.' Late one evening over a bottle of wine, McCartney said something that would stick in his friend's mind. It was something that might also have surprised the many fans who for twenty years had read about him in print or listened intently to his music, but it cut to the core of the man. What Paul said that night was, 'Nobody knows *me*, do they?'

CHAPTER TWO

A Sort of Presence

On the night of Christmas Eve 1936 Liverpool was in the grip of the worst thunderstorm in living memory. By seven o'clock the rain was so heavy that, for most of the short journey, none of the passengers huddled on the deck of the foot-ferry ploughing across the river Mersey to Wallasey could see the lights of either shore. Once docked, a few of these hardy souls made their way by bus up Liscard Road, past darkened houses and down a long lane bordered by pine trees and the town park, before alighting at a low, nondescript building, covered with peeling builders' tarpaulins, of about the size and feel of a scout hall, on which hung a sign: 'THE GROSVENOR BALLROOM & PARAMOUNT ENTERPRISES PROUDLY PRESENT – OLD TYME DANCING TO JIM MAC AND HIS BIG BAND'. Inside sixty or so customers milled around, discussing the weather.

When the headline act hit the stage, he was received like a king. 'Jim Mac' was actually a cotton broker and only a weekend musician, a lover of fast women and slow horses, but over the years he'd built up a loyal following. The lights dimmed and there was a big hand as he ran on, a chirpy-looking man in his mid-thirties with arched eyebrows, dressed in a dinner jacket, followed by the band. You'd never have known that he was suffering from arthritis, and could barely get out of his bed that morning. On their way in to Wallasey Jim's sister Milly had tried to talk him out of performing, but as soon as he got in his dressing room he'd turned to her and said, 'It's OK, love. I'm not sick any more. Let me give them what they want. I belong to them.'

He was right. For the next two hours Jim worked the small but increasingly vocal crowd, hammering at his piano, sometimes jumping up, both thumbs aloft, all the while keeping up a brisk repertoire of jazz and blues standards. In Jim's hands, the faster numbers were a riot. The midtempo, lovesick stuff, all plush vocals and brass, went down a treat. Once or twice, when introspection called, he sang while sitting quite still on a bar stool, stage centre, dragging on a cigarette. You could have heard a pin drop. Around ten that night, just as the church bells out on Manor Road began ringing for Christmas mass, Jim closed proceedings with the ever-popular Lullaby Of The Leaves:

Rustling of the leaves used to be my lullaby,
In the sunny south when I was a tot so high.
And now that I've grown
And myself alone,
Cradle me where southern skies can watch me with a million
    eyes . . .

Oh sing me to sleep
Lullaby of the leaves
Cover me with heaven's blue and let me dream a dream or two,
Oh sing me to sleep
Lullaby of the leaves.

It was spellbinding. You could see the Louisiana sky, and that lonesome train winding through the Dixie cotton fields. Those diehard fans who'd come on the ferry forgot all about the weather and the abdication crisis and the news from Germany, which, just a week earlier, had signed an anti-British axis with Italy. On the last note, there was a moment of awed silence, then cheers and applause. In a rapid gear shift, Jim and the band changed their minds about leaving and dashed off a Benny Goodman-style raver, which they brought to a runaway-truck climax. At the end of the number the shouts and whistles were as violent as a storm and lasted almost as long as the song.

It was wild. Jim and the boys came back for two more encores. He'd long since gotten over the arthritis and, after jogging back into the wings, reappeared sporting fake white whiskers and a Santa Claus hat which he doffed while jigging around and yelling, 'Merry Crimble!' After the final curtain the audience got to their feet and stood for two minutes, applauding that little man with gammy legs and bad teeth who'd made them all feel like shouting and dancing along with him.

'Milly timed them,' Jim would often recall in later years. 'Two minutes is long, you know. You have time to think. I listened to them . . . it was beautiful. It was so good it hurt! I went out there that night feeling like death, and I gave 'em everything. You can't imagine. It's the greatest feeling on earth!'

In time the lesson was well learned by Jim's son, who, twenty-four years later, would rock the same hall with his own band, then going under the name the Silver Beetles.

In fact, nobody could remember a time when the McCartneys didn't play music: the name comes from the old German for crate- or case-carrier, more often a strolling minstrel. For most of the nineteenth century the family were Protestants, builders and amateur performers in County Wicklow, before migrating across the water around 1867. There's some doubt of the actual date, but ample family folklore about the circumstances. At the docks Paul's grandfather Joe, then an infant, arrived with a tag around his neck asking that he be delivered, if lost, to the address of an Irish mission in the town centre. Not long afterwards, on his first day at school, one of the boy's teachers told him to set his sights high – 'don't try to wash dishes or be a waiter, we've got plenty of them' – but Joe himself seemed quietly ambitious. By his sixteenth birthday he was working as a tobacco cutter and occasional under-the-counter bookie along the seven-mile docks where tens of thousands of the failed, felonious or fed-up set sail for the Americas. After marrying in 1894 he and his wife Florence were able to put down £150 for their own terraced home in Fishguard Street, Everton, which they decorated 'like a chintz museum' according to one relative. Joe had an ear for a tune and on public holidays always played the tuba in his works brass band. The double bass was also a passion. He and Florence eventually had ten children, eight of whom survived.

The couple's second son James was born on 7 July 1902, and, after a token education, went into full-time employment at the age of fourteen as a sample boy for Hannay & Company, cotton brokers of Chapel Street, at a wage of 7/6 (37½p) a week. Jim was hardworking and sharp – the sort of man who could glance at a bolt of fabric from halfway across the room and come within a few pence of its price – and was soon promoted to sales. He'd also inherited his father's love of rhythm and (despite having ruptured an eardrum in a fall, leaving him part-deaf in his left ear) could nonchalantly pick up a guitar or anything else that happened to be lying around and bash out a riff with it. In later years Jim had to give up the trumpet because of dental problems, but that was the one and only instrument that ever defeated him.

Jim met Mary Mohin, a maternity nurse at Walton Hospital, shortly after the outbreak of the Second World War. Like him, she was of Liverpool Irish stock, though one of only four children and a practising Roman Catholic. The Luftwaffe chose the night they were introduced to carpet-bomb the Liverpool docks, and Jim and Mary spent their first date huddled together in a basement. The raid killed some 120 civilians that night. Many more were to follow. As Aneurin Bevan wrote, 'There'd never be a bleaker scene, or a worse day than any twenty-four hours on Merseyside under the Blitz.' The local refinery went up that same week, a black greasy pall shrouding the town centre. Incendiary bombs hit Liverpool on fifty-eight out of a possible ninety nights that winter. Gas masks were issued and blackout curtains hammered over windows. The war soon did for both the Jim Mac band and the Cotton Exchange, which closed its doors for the next four years. Although too old for the army, Jim was conscripted into a job turning out shells at a munitions factory and spent his nights as a volunteer fireman. The German attacks would continue on average twice a week from the summer of 1940 for the next eighteen months. Long before then the dead were being buried in mass graves in Anfield cemetery, and much of historic Liverpool lay in ruins. In these desperate circumstances Jim and Mary decided to marry, and exchanged vows in St Swithin's Roman Catholic chapel on 15 April 1941. The groom was thirty-eight, his bride thirty-one.

Five months after their wedding, Mary was pregnant. In what one account calls 'a flimsy slum that came with the job', she and Jim moved into two rooms at 10 Sunbury Road, within earshot of Liverpool football club. A more obvious benefit was that Mary was given the luxury of a private bed when her first son was born at Walton Hospital, shortly after two in the morning on 18 June 1942. He was baptised Catholic, and named James Paul McCartney.

Not long after that the family moved uphill but downmarket into a prefab bungalow on Liverpool's Knowsley estate. Paul would later conjecture that his 'chirpy, thumbs-up' side had its roots in the 1940s, a period he once called 'the best of my life'. He seems to have inherited his gift for happiness from his mother. As McCartney told the author Barry Miles, 'If ever you grazed your knee or anything it was amazingly taken care of because [Mary] was a nurse. She was very kind, very loving. There was a lot of sitting on laps and cuddling.' Yet by conventional standards McCartney had a tough early childhood: the family were hard up and there was a war on. While the worst of the German bombing was over by June 1942, the next few years in Britain were probably the hardest of the twentieth century. For Paul, the post-war decade would be one of icy nights in a bewildering variety of gaslit rooms, as the McCartneys moved to subsidised housing first in the town centre, then over the drink in Wallasey, and finally to different addresses around Speke, a 'new model town' dumped down some seven miles to the south. Clothing coupons and food queues remained a way of life. Paul would enjoy a diet rich in whale fat and tinned beef, and would wait until 1953 for the government to lift controls on chocolate and sweets. Jim Mac's career, too, never quite recovered its old lustre; the cotton market had virtually collapsed and it nagged at him, he admitted, that for the next ten years Mary would be the 'real earner'.

The boy was born on a Thursday morning, 'a screamer' according to his nurse, with hazel eyes and a lopsided mouth. 'He looked awful,' Jim was forced to concede. 'When I got home I cried, the first time for years and years . . . But the next day he looked more human. And every day after that he got better and better. He turned out a lovely kid in the end.'

In later years Paul would make much of his 'sign': Gemini, signifying change, novelty, trial and error. There are said to be profound mysteries about Geminis, the chief one being that they often seem to be several different people. These 'twin spirits' would be clearly recognisable in the Sixties, when the barefoot hippie became a company director and, ultimately, a multimillionaire tycoon.

Afterwards, everyone agreed that the birth had been the one bright spot of an otherwise dire summer. The news that June morning was of North Africa, where the British Eighth Army were falling back on

Tobruk, where they surrendered forty-eight hours later; of Washington DC, where Churchill arrived to discuss the deteriorating war situation with President Roosevelt; of Paris, where the Vichy government broadcast on the desirability of a Nazi victory and urged Frenchmen to work hard to that end; and of Liverpool itself, where the talk was of queues, protests and the bulldozing of bombed-out houses, which were unceremoniously dumped into the river.

Other than that, the setting of McCartney's birth was remarkable only for the grit and hue of the place, and for what it said of the people. By mid-1942 some 12,000 Liverpool homes had been destroyed from the air, and as many as 40,000 seriously damaged. 27,000 inhabitants had either left voluntarily or been evacuated out of town to North Wales. Most of those who remained were hardened, some of them unprincipled, but all of them, by now, tough, capable and self-sufficient. They were also famous for their stoical wit, which stood them in good stead during Merseyside's long decline. Of its kind, 'the Pool' followed a classic history among major British seaports: in the Thirties the Great Depression had set in like a chill Atlantic fog, and lifted just in time for the Luftwaffe. Much of the neoclassical city centre was already lost by 1942. The town planners soon finished the job, throwing up entire, prefabricated neighbourhoods on old bomb sites or green fields. 'Clearance' was the word, the result drab communities like Speke whose chief physical characteristics were endless one-way systems, roundabouts and mortuaries. Visiting Merseyside today one finds a Stalinist monstrosity built out of giant glass eggshells adjoining a handsome Georgian villa, which in turn sits next to a concrete slab. The incredible visual patisserie of Liverpool's baroque past and modern tat is symbolic of a town which seemingly lost its soul in the Fifties, and found itself on the wrong side of England, commercially speaking, when Britain discovered North Sea oil and then joined the Common Market some years later.

Down around the wharves, at least, Liverpool would remain one of those marginal places where cultures meet, English, Irish, Italians, Greeks, Poles and Chinese, to name a few, all jostling together spin-drier fashion. There were 'Chinky' takeaways and espresso bars on Merseyside before either became a London fashion. Liverpool's connections with America were profound, and it continued to be the main port of entry for cargo and passenger ships arriving from New York. 'Everyone knew someone on the boats . . . We were the first kids in Britain to get chewing gum and hear rock 'n' roll records,' John Lennon fondly recalled. The romance of the whole image grew with time, and in a Beatles nostalgia that provided both historical identity and tourist appeal for modern Liverpool. In reality, the action was confined to a few backstreets around the Pier Head, where women loitered in tight skirts and the smell of oil, coal, gas and horse dung, along with the shouted orders and grumbles of navvies, came up from the river. This was the place, full of noise, stench and rollicking seafarers, that fixed itself in the world's imagination.

Living out in Speke without a car, lugging groceries and a baby carriage, Mary kept fit. If you didn't die of a heart attack before you were thirty-five, she used to quip, you could live forever. Once or twice a week the family bundled onto a green, double-decker 'Corpy' bound for market, the beginning of Paul's love affair with the city bus.

The McCartneys' council house at 72 Western Avenue came with Mary's job, costing them only a few shillings a week in utilities. At bitter moments, Jim was prone to remark that, even so, it was over-priced. The place was a redbrick semi with a gas meter, no indoor plumbing, phone or fridge, and a few sticks of rickety furniture. There was a tiny garden, which pleased Jim, who had a green thumb and whose paper on the Care and Maintenance of the Lavender Bush had long been regarded as the seminal work on the subject in Liverpool horticultural circles. The view from the porch was of similar houses, as close-packed as dominoes ready to fall, of industrial stacks rising from the nearby textile mills and of estuary banks all but flattened by bombs. Mary, now working as a domiciliary midwife, was often thanked by her charges with little gifts of religious ornaments, plaster figurines and the like, and these were neatly displayed on the mantelpiece. From time to time, a particularly grateful patient would add a cake or a precious packet of Woodbines, which was more to Jim's taste. He lacked Mary's piety. After a glass or two, Jim was apt to note that he saw the world as a clock that God had wound up and left to run down. Although he'd agreed to his baptism, he didn't want Paul sent to a church-run school, with all its 'mumbo-jumbo'.

The McCartneys' second son, Michael, was born on 7 January 1944. Both boys were doted on by a large extended family including Jim's five married sisters, and were spoilt within the limits of the weekly budget. Mary's chief concern was that they should work hard, better themselves and grow up to 'talk posh', unlike their Speke neighbours. On the warmest days, she'd cycle around in her fur-collared coat, so that people could see that standards were kept up. From the start, Mike was the cheeky, back-chatting one. The saucer-eyed Paul seems to have grasped the importance of self-control even then. After once being walloped by Jim, he retaliated by creeping upstairs to his parents' bedroom, where with the aid of a ruler he carefully tore their lace curtains by exactly an inch. That inch was protest superbly contained. When the boys were sent to school, first two streets away in Stockton Road and then across town at Joseph Williams Primary, Paul came top of his class in English and Art, and second or third in everything else. Rain or shine, he seemed to arrive each day in what a teacher recalls as 'a freshly starched white shirt, neat sweater and polished shoes.' Although buses were infrequent because of the lack of petrol and of rubber for tyres, he invariably turned up on time and managed to remain spotless throughout the day. 'He always looked like his mother had scrubbed him from head to toe . . . The funny thing is, I can never remember him ever getting dirty.'

Paul's cleanliness was all the more virtuous as people were still exhorted to wash as little as possible, and to get the last possible ounce of wear from their clothes. 'Make Do and Mend' was the official slogan. While rationing continued, so did the Ministry of Food with its raft of regulations and popular ditties, such as the one reminding the public that:

> Those who have a will to win
> Cook potatoes in their skin
> Knowing that the sight of peelings
> Deeply hurts His Majesty's feelings.

Was it any wonder, John Lennon would ask, 'we all went raving mad in the Sixties'?

As the years passed, a certain routine developed: Paul would emerge each morning and stride confidently to that green bus somehow always waiting for him at the corner. His quiff was slicked down with Brylcreem and he could hang out of the window, giving a cheery wave to old ladies, and not put a hair out of place. His attention to detail, and particularly to his neat, fussy handwriting were striking for an eight-year-old. He was also starting to sing, prompting a classmate named Pat Sims to once jokingly suggest that he'd end up 'be[ing] a big name on stage and sneering at normal, ordinary people.' That was nonsense, said Paul. Performers were decent, hard-working folk, no different from anyone else. With that he looked up from the pen-and-ink drawing he happened to be doodling of St Aiden's Church (it won a school prize) while also speed-reading *Oliver Twist*. 'Just watch me,' he chuckled. By now Paul was spending his weekends either exploring the countryside to the south and west of Speke (near the present John Lennon Airport) or knocking on his neighbours' doors offering to do 'bob a job'. Instinct told Sims that 'that boy would go far.'

In 1949 the McCartneys had moved from Western Avenue to

another council house, at 12 Ardwick Road. 'Dynamic new communities spread their great, wide thoroughfares to the sea' is how Liverpool Corporation described Speke and its neighbouring towns at the time. The reality was less exotic. Paul was soon mugged while out on his bike there, and had his watch stolen by a couple of local toughs. He subsequently gave evidence against the young offenders in court. The way the story circulated, the pair then put it around the estate that 'that fookin' Macca' – the first known use of the nickname applied specifically to Paul – was dead meat. This version found its way to print in at least one biography, and was later recycled on various websites, but in actual fact Paul spent five relatively tranquil years on Ardwick, and particularly enjoyed rambling in the nearby woods with his *Observer Book of Birds*.

On 2 June 1953, the McCartneys, like millions of other British families, celebrated Coronation Day in front of their first, flickering television set. There were paper hats, and commemorative mugs and spoons all round. The ritual gave Paul added pleasure, since he was also clutching his leaving prize from Joseph Williams, a book on modern art he'd won for his essay on 'Why a monarchy?' Earlier that month he'd easily passed his eleven-plus exam, one of only four out of ninety-three in his year to win a place at the Liverpool Institute, or 'Inny', the city's top grammar school.

That same summer, Paul finally agreed to a standing request that he audition for the choir in Liverpool's Anglican cathedral. It was one of the most imposing, gothic-style churches in England – the ground-floor windows facing the graveyard were twice as high as he was – and suitably impressive even to a non-believer. 'Flipping heck!' said Jim, with that boyish enthusiasm that was one of his most engaging traits. His only advice on the matter was that Paul 'be himself' and not try to sing 'like one of them Yanks'.

Paul had always loved his father's music. Even then he had a decided weakness for 'fruity' vocalists like Fred Astaire, and wasn't above thrilling to Rudy Vallee and other Jazz Age crooners who worked with a megaphone. The vaudeville tradition ran deep in Ardwick Road. But a key generational clash had come one night when Paul casually mouthed the word 'yeah' instead of 'yes' when the whole family were gathered round the piano, to the profound distress of both Jim and Mary. There'd been a long pause. Jim had given up on the idea of performing, and the cotton business involved long hours and low pay. His boys were really all he had, and he wanted to be proud of them. He and Paul had discussed the issue and quickly reached an impasse that demanded the detached observer, the arbiter – Jim's youngest and best educated sister, Aunty Jin. Aunty Jin would solve the great 'yes' or 'yeah' debate. Strong tea was brewed, and everyone sat down in the tiny front room with the damp, brick-pattern wallpaper.

Aunty Jin listened to the pros and cons and sighed deeply. 'In the old days, who ever sang "yeah"? Bing Crosby? Impossible! Who would have dreamt it?'

Father and son waited patiently.

'But this is the Fifties,' Jin continued. 'Anything goes. And if God helped put kids on the earth, who says it's wrong for them to want their own music?'

'We're just talking about one word,' said Jim.

It was Mary, ironically, who settled the matter in Paul's favour, at least for the next ten years. And then one day in June 1963, Paul came into the front room of their next home and asked his father if he wanted to hear a new song that he and his mate John had just written, which they thought was quite good. Jim listened as they sat side by side and played She Loves You for the first time to an audience. 'That's very nice, son,' he said at length. 'But there's enough of these Americanisms around. Couldn't you sing "She loves you, yes, yes, yes"?'

In the end Paul flunked his audition at Liverpool Cathedral, his one and only failure of that summer. He apparently told friends that he'd deliberately spoilt his voice, not wanting to be accepted into something 'so BBC' and 'uptight'. Some time later, he did sing in St Chad's choir off Penny Lane, but soon dropped out, calling it, too, 'a real drag'.

These were about Paul's only forays into pre-teen dissidence. In later decades, various rock stars would put their names to whole books about childhood sexual abuse or their having been Satanic-cult victims. McCartney, by contrast, recalled even his motherless years as 'very homey . . . there was us, and there were always aunties around cooking nice meals.' Jim had a temper, true, 'but he never yelled at [Paul and Mike] cross,' Aunty Jin insisted. "Now boys, you know you mustn't do that . . . Now boys, it's time to wash the dishes." 'Toler[ation] and moder[ation] – that's me,' they heard him say repeatedly. For the next twenty years, the older McCartney would be content with his beer and fags, his piano and his odd flutter on the horses at Aintree. He still tended his garden, and a small sign occasionally seen outside the house proclaimed the presence of a 'consultant landscaper'. Jim liked nothing more than to lecture on the care of the humble shrub to his fellow enthusiasts, a passion he seems to have handed down to Paul. There was a sorry fall from grace on the estate in January 1954, when the South Liverpool Herbaceous Society admitted to purchasing half a ton of prime manure knowing it to have been stolen. Although Jim was a member of the club, there was no suggestion that he was tied up in this scandal.

Those little gifts left shyly at the McCartneys' back door seemed typical of the way people generally related to Mary. 'She was always out on her bike waving, well liked around town,' Pat Sims recalls. 'Mary was quite a looker. At the same time, I'd say some of us were just a bit wary of her. She was always telling her kids to "talk proper" and not like us.' Everyone agrees that Mary was the family mainstay and a tireless worker. Years later, Paul would still recall the snowy night when he'd peered down from his window and seen his mother set off on her bike, wearing her navy blue uniform, coat and hat, 'cycl[ing] off down the estate to deliver a baby somewhere.'

In October 1982, McCartney would send off a frosty, 200-word telegram to the prime minister of the day, urging her to 'give health workers a break' and warning that 'What the miners did to Ted Heath, the nurses will do to you.' It was left to his brother Mike to explain that the whole fuss was 'to do with our mum Mary, [who] was affectionately called "The Angel" by her patients.'

Most days after school, the two boys got on their own bikes or took a Crosville bus along Hale Road, then tramped through muddy fields down to the river. Around 1953 Paul got it into his head that, since he'd very likely do National Service one day, he should practise his killing skills on the local fauna. His first victims were the beetles and other bugs which scuttled around under the gorse bushes by Dungeon Lane. He soon graduated to frogs. Trawling their pond, he'd nimbly scoop up a pair of legs in one hand and wring the creature's neck with the other. The still-warm body was then impaled on a barbed-wire fence, and an eleven-year-old boy was royally entertained. Paul once took his brother to this grim spot and proudly showed him the seven or eight decaying corpses strung up there. Mike fled from the scene in hysterics.

Paul did well at the Institute, particularly flourishing under his English master Alan 'Dusty' Durband, doyen of Room 32 and bestselling author of *Shakespeare Made Easy*. At various times Durband's colleagues in the History, Art and Latin departments all recognised a similar talent. The consensus was that McCartney would one day make an excellent teacher himself. 'Our new lad with the intellectual look above the eyebrows', the staff magazine informally called him. Though there were far better-off students, Paul was always immaculately turned out in his dark blazer and flannels, a bit chubby, perky, and eager to please. Still, looking around that imposing, Victorian pile, you could have got long odds that the 'new lad' from the estate would one day return in triumph to the school hall, now named after him.

1955 was the first year anyone in England had heard the term 'rock 'n' roll'. Portly and cheroot-smoking, Bill Haley was the unlikely prophet whose grunted lyrics, set to a slapped double bass and a brisk backbeat, so outraged parents and thrilled their children. Above all, rock radiated the fragrance of escape. As a latchkey kid, Paul had often stolen off to the local Odeon to watch the adventures of Dick Barton or some similar action hero whose exploits he excitedly re-enacted at the family tea table. He found Haley even more alluring. Before long Paul would begin to 'sag off' from the Institute on sunny afternoons, crossing over Hope Street to sprawl in the vast Cathedral graveyard, smoking and writing lyrics.

In the summer of 1955 the McCartneys moved for the last time, a mile or two north-west to the altogether more twee neighbourhood ('a bit of posh' Mary called it) of Allerton, L18. 20 Forthlin Road was a terraced house with some pretensions to elegance: there was a lavender bush, a major selling point to Jim, at the freshly painted front door, inside plumbing and even a phone. The parlour of the little house was tidy, and the furniture commonplace but not shabby, with a floral sofa the most elegant piece, flanked by a sheepskin rug and two doilied armchairs. There were yellowed lace curtains at the windows, Chinese pagoda wallpaper and one of those boxy, wooden television sets that could have doubled as a coffin. On her first visit, a colleague of Mary's found 'a simple home . . . on a rather tight budget' and a pattern of life that was largely constant over the next twelve months. Paul rose early, wolfed a huge breakfast and left on the bus for the town centre, returning at dusk. After tea he might play some show tunes with Jim, or sit upstairs watching the action at the Mounted Police Training College next door. Forthlin Road boasted one or two other amenities. As well as the new television there was Jim's upright piano, a wireless and a set of the kind of encyclopedias one could buy on instalment at the Co-op. In later years Jim would rig up headphones connecting the radio to the boys' bedrooms, another key source of entertainment.

Mary's colleague never forgot Jim and his sons taking turns at the family joanna, challenging one another to write a song. Not surprisingly, their efforts were stilted at best – 'utter crap' in one frank assessment – but the friend remembers one day when Paul sat down and, amidst all the jingles 'did something blues-style, with his own lyrics . . . The first line was "He's just fourteen." The second was "The springtime of life." The third, which got a big laugh, was "But even in May, the sky can be grey." It wasn't much, but it stuck in your head.'

In the summer of 1956, impressed by all this activity, Jim bought his elder son a trumpet. *The Man With The Golden Arm*, with its memorable jazz score, was big in Britain at the time. Paul soon mastered the basics, but also came to know the very real difficulties of playing the instrument while simultaneously trying to sing. A few weeks later, he took the bus into town one Saturday and swapped the horn for a £15 acoustic Zenith guitar. Because he was left-handed, Paul had to do a carpentry job on it, moving the strings around, but immediately after that he was 'totally zonked . . . gone', if such conveys a process bordering on reincarnation. There was still the daily grind of school, and now looming O levels. McCartney's basic routine took place against a backdrop of gothic towers and draughty classrooms adorned by the motto NON NOBIS SOLUM, SED TOTI MUNDO NATI ('We're not born for ourselves, but for the good of the world'). Nonetheless, the essence of the act, from now on, involved Paul holing up somewhere with a notebook and his guitar. As Mike recalled, 'He didn't have time [for] anything else. He played it on the bog, in the bath, everywhere.'

Not coincidentally, 1956 was also the year Elvis first hit the British charts and teenagers everywhere thrilled to fabulous creatures like Chuck Berry and Little Richard, with their fast-moving songs about girls, high schools and cars. It was the year Paul, confirming Jim's worst fears about the decline of pop-music standards, invested his pocket money in a copy of Gene Vincent's Be-Bop-A-Lula. Before long there was the homegrown, or Scots figure of Lonnie Donegan, the inspiration for the skiffle boom with household utensils pressed into service as instruments, and a role model for British kids who, like him, took songs from the American South, dusted them off and shook them inside out until they were as clean and crisp – if not starchy – as a freshly laundered sheet. Paul was a skiffle fan, but his tastes covered the entire waterfront from the Swing Era to Elvis. Once he mastered the guitar, he quickly took on the qualities of a human jukebox, a compulsive mimic and performer who liked to hold forth even while sitting on the bus. During these ad hoc concerts, Paul, whose spoken free associations were a treat in themselves, connected the dots between seemingly unrelated subjects. While entertaining his fellow passengers with a sombre Memphis blues, he'd give a running five-minute seminar on the latest Dick Barton epic which included side-splitting impersonations of all the cast. A born showman, he was already socking it to people all over town. Pat Sims recalls that McCartney 'was as likely to sing to you as he was to talk.'

One morning Paul noticed another boy sitting on the upper deck of the 86 bus, also wearing the Institute's regulation dark blazer and tie. There were telltale signs, such as his mauve socks, that he, too, had fallen for Donegan, and even now he was doodling a picture of a guitar in his exercise book. Why hadn't he ever met this guy? Paul leant over, tapped him on the shoulder and asked his name. 'George Harrison.' Thick Scouse accent. He had something of a pale, queasy look and was eight months younger than Paul (George would later note that, 'Paul was always older than me; he still is'), who soon took to him as a 'lost kid brother'. Before long they were spending most of their free time crouched with guitars and gramophones in one or other of their parents' terraced houses. As Jim and Mary would note ruefully, Harrison was no great shakes at school and thus quite unlike their Paul. There were also striking sartorial contrasts. George adopted the rock and roller's ensemble of 'drainy' trousers and brothel creepers, except in winter, when he's said to have looked as if he were wearing a Russian peasant's smock under his baggy overcoat. Paul, on the other hand, dressed neatly in well-cut tweeds and always gave the impression of 'hav[ing] stepped straight out of the launderette.' Within a week or two of their meeting, it was clear that this odd couple had bonded over what Jim disdainfully called their 'jungle beat'. When Paul once ran a few pence short for his bus fare, George happily lent it to him. They wrote at least one song together, though this seems to have been mannered and trite – in Sims' verdict, 'basically Paul and George hollering at each other, at the top of their lungs, in a game of one-upmanship.'

Mary McCartney had been suffering from chest pains for some weeks, and finally admitted herself to hospital in late October that year. Breast cancer was diagnosed. She was forty-seven. Mary appears to have not wanted to 'bother anyone' with her condition, and thus wasn't treated until Jim and the doctors insisted. A mastectomy was performed, and soon afterwards Paul visited his mother in a wrenching scene 'with blood on the sheets somewhere' and rosary beads tied to her wrist.

'I would have liked to see the boys grow up,' Mary is quoted as having told a friend named Olive Johnson at the end.

Paul and Mike were spared the ordeal of the funeral three days later, held at Huyton's Yew Tree cemetery. Mary was buried as a Catholic, just as she'd asked Jim on her deathbed. Paul spent much of the next month being cared for at his aunt's house, where he 'slipped into a big chair and sat staring into space.'

Beyond the sorrow and self-reproach of the moment, the death of his mother was to become one of those pivotal events in McCartney's life, stirring ambitions and shaping decisions that might have been quite different had she lived. 'Aunty Jin's house was warm and lively,' insists one family friend, 'and the scene of many happy childhood days for the boys.' But with the resumption of school, Paul seemed to lose all interest in ever becoming a teacher, and instead threw himself more and more into music. 'I think it was Mary's passing that did that . . . One day he was bob-a-jobbing, and the next day he was practically a rock star.' It's arguable that losing his mother also made Paul particularly susceptible, in later life, to a certain kind of woman who (as both wives assuredly did) 'knew her mind'.

Eight months later, in the summer of 1957, Jim's worst fears about the 'jungle beat' were fully realised. Paul initially took just two O levels, passing in Spanish but failing Latin. He was supposed to sit four or five more in 1958 with a view towards the sixth form and, so Jim still hoped, a place at teacher training college. Meanwhile, his reports from the Institute made sorry reading: 'If he doesn't improve I shall punish him . . . Badly needs to apply himself . . . He is the biggest disappointment in the class.'

Paul was, however, learning fast on his new Rosetti's guitar, playing all the skiffle hits of the day and once actually catching a glimpse of Lonnie Donegan as he emerged from the stage door of the Empire theatre. The influence wasn't just musical: every British teenager had read the story of how Donegan had taken half an hour to record Rock Island Line, and his first quarterly royalty cheque had been for TWENTY-SEVEN THOUSAND POUNDS – always in capitals. Paul wanted some of that. Meanwhile, Jim could only wonder where it was all leading. On Saturdays, Paul took to lying in bed with the headphones before teasing his hair into a greasy DA (duck's arse) and sloping between Liverpool's bustling coffee bars and clothes shops. Eel and mash at Nemo's. A ciggy at the Pudding Bowl. Another pet haunt was the record department of Lewis's, where he regularly splurged on the latest Little Richard or Everly Brothers release. McCartney soon wrote his first full song that would be reproduced forty years later, I Lost My Little Girl – a homage to Mary.

On Saturday 6 July Paul varied his routine by cycling the short distance across the top of Allerton golf course to St Peter's parish church in Woolton. A friend from the Institute named Ivan Vaughan had raved about the summer fête taking place there, and more pointedly about the skiffle group scheduled to perform on a make-shift stage in the church meadow amidst all the rock cake and lemonade stalls. The Quarry Men, they were called. Vaughan told McCartney that the band were hot stuff, having a leader who could belt out classics like Cumberland Gap and, obviously not troubled by decorum, Maggie Mae – a ballad about a Liverpool hooker. Vaughan was insistent that Paul should meet this 'great fellow' who was both a poet and a hard nut, with a habit of confronting hecklers with his fist. 'Come on, mate. You'll have the time of your life.'

McCartney thought this a bit of a stretch. Who needed aggro? Besides, the Quarry Men weren't quite the phenomenon Vaughan suggested, playing chiefly at friends' birthday parties and the odd church dance. Just a month earlier, true, the lads had taken the bus to the Empire theatre to audition for a Carroll Levis talent show. The local star-maker had turned them down flat in favour of the Sunnyside Skiffle Group, a briefly popular Speke combo fronted by Nicky Cuff, the dwarf. After that, the Quarries' next engagement had been playing from the back of a parked coal lorry, an occasion marred by some local toughs who persuaded the band to hurriedly abandon the stage and leg it for a nearby semi.

Without bothering to hide his indifference, McCartney shrugged and said OK, he'd be there.

What Paul saw that warm Saturday afternoon was a six-piece group whose Teddy-boy pose rather jarred with their surroundings. Under the benign eye of Reverend Morris Pryce-Jones and his committee, there were flags, flashes of bunting, kiddie-kart rides, tombola and coconut shies, and smiling church ladies pouring tea. The Quarries' leader looked particularly arresting, being a septic mass of spots, Brylcreem and torn 'drainies', bobbing a greasy, Bill Haley forelock, and belting out his version of the Dell Vikings' hit Come Go With Me. Paul noticed that he was obviously having trouble remembering the words, but was 'busking it merrily.'

The Quarry Men played their first set at 4.15 that afternoon. At 5.15, there was a display by the City of Liverpool Police Dogs. At 5.45, more from the Quarries, who then packed up and humped their gear across Church Road to the parish hall where they were due to perform at the eight o'clock 'grand dance'. It was while they were setting up that Vaughan wandered over and made the four-word introduction that changed pop culture.

'Paul: this is John.'

As it turned out, McCartney and Lennon lived only a mile or so apart, separated by those suburban golf links. Twenty-five years after his death, new facts are still coming to light about the one-time leader of the Quarry Men. The classic images we all have of him – whether as the grinning moptop, the acid-gobbling surrealist or the bearded sage – are as easily accessible in the mind as family snaps in a wallet. The basic turn of events is that John Lennon was born in Liverpool on 9 October 1940, twenty months before McCartney; while his father was away at sea his mother, Julia, gave birth to a baby girl by a Welsh soldier. She then began to live with another man, Albert Dykins, with whom she had two more daughters. When John was five he was sent to stay with his mother's sister Mimi Smith and her husband in their agreeably large, bay-windowed villa at 251 Menlove Avenue, where there was a plant-filled conservatory and a lounge furnished by the complete works of Winston Churchill, bound in blue cloth. In the event, he remained there for fifteen years, sometimes visiting Julia, whom he appears to have loved as a sister, in her home nearby. In 1952, Lennon entered Quarry Bank Grammar School, where he did well at English and Art. Three years later the sudden death of Aunt Mimi's husband, coinciding with the onset of adolescence, seems to have changed John from a moderately studious boy into a juvenile delinquent. In late February or early March 1956 he heard Elvis singing Heartbreak Hotel. Not long after that, and much against her better judgement, Mimi had bought her nephew a £17 Spanish guitar at Hessy's in the town centre.

John's first group, the Black Jacks (illustrated by their uniform of sooty jeans and bootlace ties) were followed, in short order, by the Quarry Men.

McCartney's first act on meeting Lennon was to helpfully offer to tune his guitar. His second was to casually demonstrate note-perfect versions of Eddie Cochran's Twenty Flight Rock and Vincent's Be-Bop-A-Lula, to which he knew all the words. Shaking his head from side to side, he continued the one-man concert-audition with a screeching imitation of Little Richard. Paul then sat down on a bench, took out a cigarette and began to smoke it serenely.

'Fook me,' muttered Lennon.

A week or so later, Paul was again cycling across the golf course, somewhere near the Derby Arms, when he met John's friend Pete Shotton, the washboard player for the Quarries. The two chatted, and McCartney proficiently rolled them some 'loosies'. Then, over a smoke, came the proposition. John wanted Paul in the group and would cut him in on the action, provided there was any, as well as let him sing. He had a 'great set of pipes', Lennon had apparently noted. But before accepting, McCartney had one or two terms and conditions of his own. First, they should all get proper stage outfits, such as matching black flannels and white jackets. The band's player-manager, Nigel Whalley, didn't perform live and thus shouldn't receive equal dues. And the drummer was crap. McCartney had one final issue: he and his brother were going away to camp, and thus he couldn't join the Quarry Men for a booking they had that August at a new city-centre club, where Lennon would cause apoplexy among the folk fans present by singing an impossibly crude 'race' number. The song was called Hound Dog; the club was the Cavern.

The first time that Paul sang before an audience was at Butlin's holiday camp in Pwhelli, North Wales, late that summer. He and Mike did an Everly Brothers duet. The second time was on Friday

18 October, which marked his debut with the Quarry Men. This twenty-minute affair at the local Conservative Club (where Paul for once flubbed his guitar solo) began the strange, equivocal relationship between McCartney and Lennon. They were never 'close mates' John would claim. Where Lennon was direct, funny and sometimes castratingly rude, McCartney was a smooth operator and crowd-puller. While Paul was already exploring the avant-garde strains of Stockhausen and John Cage, John considered anything but the roots 'bullshit'. McCartney also proved better suited to the gerbil existence the daily slog of entertaining can be. He made no bones about his love of old-fashioned showbiz. It's fair to say that Lennon, by contrast, didn't much care for slick performers like Bruce Forsyth – the type who 'brushed his teeth and smile[d] into the lights' – though that doesn't make John exceptional. When it came to the contract between an artist and his public, it seemed Paul had read the fine print and John hadn't. Despite or because of their obvious differences, Lennon-McCartney soon became adept at writing songs together, eventually filling a school exercise book with unpretentious, two-minute tunes like Winston's Walk, Thinking Of Linking and One After 909. One afternoon they knocked off a toe-tapper called Love Me Do. Many of these numbers were worked up in the front room at Forthlin Road. Sitting knee to knee with their guitars, the two schoolboys would play old blues riffs – Paul's fretwork a mirror of the right-handed John's – and mumble some rhymes, moving words and music against each other to find new songs forged in the process. The sessions typically took between two and three hours, a formula that rarely varied right through the early days of the Beatles.

Not long after mangling his guitar solo at the Conservative Club, Paul suddenly remembered his friend George, the young rock and roller. John wasn't impressed – the kid didn't even *shave* yet – but eventually invited Harrison to a Quarry Men gig at Wilson Hall, after which he auditioned to John and Paul's satisfaction by playing

Bill Justis' hit Raunchy while sitting on the upper deck of the bus home.

Harrison was in. He joined the Quarry Men in March 1958, at about the time Paul was writing to Butlin's to ask for work for the group and himself over the summer holiday. Butlin's turned him down.

What with the Quarries and the sagging off to songwrite with John, Paul continued his downward spiral at school. By his sixteenth birthday he seems to have concluded that 'college and shit' wasn't for him. He'd discovered sex and was fast learning about birds, slags, judies, slappers, totty, red eye, finger-pie and other, more refined aspects of dating with local girls such as Julie Arthur (the niece of Ted Ray, the comedian) who would be serenaded with his guitar. His lovers in this period, who in later and less reticent decades yielded up a fair number of vivid details, agreed that Paul was striking in his energetic directness, his startling virility, his at times robust technique, as well as in his smooth patter. Forty-five years later, one young companion would recall how 'he sat me down in the front room [in] Forthlin Road with that funny floral and wavy wallpaper, not quite matching, and lovingly told me how the words were his experience and the music was his soul. Anything to get those knickers down.'

Paul's dream of pursuing music full-time took another leap forward on 20 March 1958, when he and John were on hand to see Buddy Holly at Liverpool's Philharmonic Hall. With the possible exceptions of Elvis (who never played in England) and Lonnie Donegan (whose star was descendant), there was no better role model around if you were a teenager and had any sort of ear for a tune. Just six days earlier, in fact, Holly had performed at the Woolwich Granada, where he made a lifelong fan of a fourteen-year-old grammar-school boy then calling himself Mike Jagger.

On 12 July that year, the Quarry Men entered Percy Phillips' Professional Studio – actually the back room of the seventy-year-old Phillips' semi at 53 Kensington, Liverpool – and paid 17/6 to cut a two-sided record. John sang Holly's That'll Be The Day on the A-side, and performed a McCartney-Harrison original, In Spite Of All The Danger, on the flip.

Tragedy struck three days later, when John's mother Julia was knocked down and killed while crossing Menlove Avenue after visiting her sister. The car that struck her was driven by an off-duty policeman who was later tried for manslaughter and acquitted. For seventeen-year-old John, this would be the 'ultra crap' moment of a childhood not untouched by shadow. He was at one point heard to say – and it's a convincing claim – that he was 'totally fucked'. The darkness would lift, but it would leave him deeply, some said permanently scarred. For the next two or three years Lennon suffered excruciating nightmares and was, as he put it, constantly 'drunk or angry'.

1959 would be a troubling year for Merseyside, whose long decline continued with the advent of commercial jet travel, and where the *Echo* began reviewing the puzzling new 'long players' alongside its redundancy notices and recipes involving powdered egg. It was also a lean time for the Quarry Men, who were stepping from skiffle to Holly-like pop in a not always graceful transition. A peak came on 29 August with the opening of a new teenagers' club, the Casbah, located in the basement of the Best family home in Liverpool's West Derby village. The 'Cas' would be painted over the next several weeks by anyone who dropped in, Paul adding some tasteful rainbow swirls to the ceiling. It also provided the Quarry Men with their first ever print review, in the local *Reporter*. From that relative high rock bottom followed on 15 November, when John, Paul and George appeared at Manchester's Hippodrome for Carroll Levis' latest 'TV Star Search'. By all accounts the actual performance went well enough. Unfortunately, the contest was judged largely on the basis of audience applause – the 'clapometer' – as each group reappeared at the end of the night for a final bow. By the time Levis came to call out the Quarries, it was too late. With no funds to stay overnight, the boys were already on the last tram home.

The Sixties: John's art-school friend Stuart Sutcliffe, a hip brunette they envied for his thinness, his shades and above all his luxuriously swept-back hair, reminiscent of James Dean's, joined on bass, an instrument he could barely play. This bugged Paul, who, admittedly, had helped recruit Stu in the first place, on several fronts. Things were going only moderately well for the Quarries, who currently had no drummer, no manager and no engagements.

'The truth is,' Lennon had observed with customary bluntness the last time he and McCartney had sagged off home together, 'we need Stu. The guy's a *star*.'

But Paul wasn't to be put off, here in this sun-baked parlour, awash in youthful confidence. 'Let's write one,' he smiled.

Sutcliffe quickly got them into matching black turtleneck sweaters and renamed them the Beatals, in homage to Buddy Holly's Crickets. He also began acting as the band's booking agent. Through Stu they met Allan Williams, the stocky, black-bearded owner of the Jacaranda club on Slater Street, where the Beatals liked to sit over a 'frothy coffee', talk shop, and gaze out the steamy window towards Chinatown. Paul and John hadn't even known of Williams at first, although they could hear him muttering 'yobbos' or catch a glimpse of his hands nimbly passing a plate of toast and jam through the serving hatch. The 'Jac', however, was but one of its owner's many interests around town. Williams also had ambitions to be a 'top-flight promoter', and in time became the group's first real agent.

McCartney was just seventeen, and notionally studying in the Institute sixth form for his A levels in English and Art. He in fact spent much of his time in that quarried graveyard next to the Cathedral, where he and John would pass most spring afternoons smoking and strumming their guitars. When it was wet or they fancied a change they caught the bus back to Forthlin Road. Arriving around two p.m. and fortified only by Typhoo, they'd have a new song written, rehearsed and the words neatly copied out in a schoolbook under the heading 'A Lennon-McCartney Original' before Jim returned at five. To aid the creative process, they sometimes rolled the tea into a pipe and smoked it. One day Paul plunked the vaudeville tune of When I'm Sixty-Four on his father's piano. Sitting in Forthlin Road about a year later, he similarly knocked off the lyric and first verse of a raver he called I Saw Her Standing There. More and more fans, particularly the young and female ones, were beginning to pay attention to the boyish charm, the banjo eyes and, above all, the sexiness and velvet power of the voice. For others, it was the sheer versatility that took the breath away. McCartney always had a wider, if not necessarily deeper range than Lennon, enjoying fruity old variety numbers and the likes of Sinatra and Peggy Lee, as well as gospel, jazz and classical. Stu would remember the time Paul played Lennon and him a 'straight blues he seemed to [have] made up on the spot, [which] he sang in a dead-on parody of John.' Everyone had the grace to laugh.

In November 1960, the Conservative government announced the phasing-out of National Service. This was just in time to allow groups like the Beatals at least the chance of a career, while the press now spoke the excited rhetoric of consumer demand. An election had just been fought and won on the slogan 'You never had it so good'. As well as the talent and the drive, McCartney also had impeccable timing. The introduction and rapid availability of the Pill ushered in, said Lennon, 'a whole new phenomenon . . . the chick wanting to get laid as quickly and often as possible.' So began Paul's decade-long reputation as a ladies man: after Julie Arthur there were Celia and Val and Layla and finally a pretty, soft-spoken girl called Dorothy Rhone. Her name was shortened to Dot by Paul, who further asked that she bleach her hair and adopt short skirts and fishnet stockings in tribute to his favourite actress, Brigitte Bardot. Some time later he wrote P.S. I Love You in Dot's honour.

Early that spring of 1960, McCartney had reapplied to Butlin's on behalf of the Beatals, a group, he added charitably, 'led by John Lennon'. The Redcoats again turned him down. During the Easter holidays, he and John did play together in a pub run by one of Paul's cousins in Caversham, Berks. Billing themselves as the Nerk Twins, they crooned country and western numbers while sitting on stools set perilously close to the dartboard. There was better news in the second week of May, when Allan Williams had the hurriedly styled Silver Beetles audition for Larry 'Parnes, Shillings and Pence' Parnes, the pop impresario with the stable of unfeasibly named singers like Billy Fury, Rory Storm, Duffy Power, Marty Wilde and Vince Eager. Somewhat to their chagrin, Paul and the lads were asked to go out on tour with a Johnny Gentle. In the spirit of the thing they all took handles of their own, McCartney becoming Paul Ramon. On Friday 20 May the Silver Beetles appeared as Gentle's backing band at the town hall in Alloa, Clackmannanshire.

The six shows that followed up and down Scotland were only a mixed success. Paul (who somehow persuaded Jim that two weeks off school immediately before his A levels would be 'good for revision') was set to earn a princely £35. Some twenty-two years later, McCartney happened to mention while on *Desert Island Discs* that neither he nor the band had ever been paid; Larry Parnes sued, and relented only after the BBC made a formal apology. The poverty format extended to rehearsals: there was little or no time to bond with Gentle, who just a few weeks earlier had been an apprentice carpenter, and was only slowly learning to sing as an alternative. Travel and hotel arrangements were basic. Still, the band managed to sweat up a nightly repertoire of Ricky Nelson and Little Richard hits, and had the beginnings of a real stage act. It was these hopped-up, forty-minute gigs in towns like Nairn and Forres that taught Paul and John how to 'put over' not only a song, but themselves. The trick involved more sleight of hand than either let on, and owed a lot to

Jim Mac's pre-war act with his showband. There was the little harlequinade when Gentle would shout 'It's all right!' and the band would holler back, 'Ariiight!' There was the jester Lennon and the cool and quiet Harrison, prone to Carl Perkins and, at this stage, apt to crank at his guitar. Above all there was the cute-looking one who sometimes stood stock still and sometimes broke into a little jig, all the while batting his brown eyes, which drove both the boys and girls wild.

'Someone actually asked me for my autograph,' Paul wrote home to his father from Inverness. 'I signed for them, too. Three times!'

From then on, Jim remarked, 'things were never quite the same.'

Within the fold, too, certain long-term dynamics were emerging; they soon settled into the small private rituals of the road. John was the wise guy. Paul seemed to be eternally 'on', a go-getter, and not troubled by self-doubt. To him, even bad times (as when Gentle wrapped their tour van around a car on the way to Fraserburgh) felt like initiation rites. George, as they sometimes reminded him, was the 'kid', already distant and inward. There were classic, Spinal Tap-like problems with drummers; a Tommy Moore had accompanied them to Scotland, but thereafter swiftly returned, broke and, thanks to the crash, missing his front teeth, to his old job at the Garston bottle works. Together with Stu, they made what McCartney called a 'great little band'.

In June, Paul turned eighteen. The night before he left the Institute, he had one too many in the course of saying his goodbyes and woke up on the sofa at Forthlin Road with his first serious hangover. It didn't stop him from celebrating his last day at school, an hour or two later, by jumping up on his desk to perform Good Golly Miss Molly. His climactic address to his colleagues, a paean to 'finger-pie', 'bevvies' and 'baccy' and the interaction between the three as a model for personal fulfilment, was a tour de force and at least on a par with the official speeches. A week later, the now-named

Silver Beatles resorted to backing a chorus line featuring Janice, the Belle of Bootle, and her Fabulous Front, on the postage stamp-sized stage of an illegal club in the red-light area of Toxteth. There was an audience of perhaps a dozen men scattered around wearing raincoats. As the band vamped *The Third Man* theme, Janice went through her paces, quickly stripping down to her sequinned G-string, which was the cue for Paul, John, George and Stu to hit a thunderous power chord and run. They were each paid ten bob.

The turn in the group's fortunes began a few weeks later, when Allan Williams stumbled down an ill-smelling flight of stairs in the notorious Reeperbahn district of Hamburg and into a club called the Kaiserkeller. Even by the standards of the place, its reputation stood low. Once down the steps, Williams was confronted with a small man of grim appearance, a former featherweight boxer who happened to have done time for manslaughter. His name was Horst Fascher, and he acted as security for the venue. As well as a few coloured lights in the rafters there was a vaguely nautical theme, with ropes and brass portholes, and a corresponding ambient stench of vomit. The owner, one Bruno Koschmider, was a squat ex-circus clown with a peg leg and an interest, he told Williams, in importing 'top rock and roll acts' like Tommy Steele to perform for his regular clientele of sailors, sexual deviants and art students. No deal was struck that night – Koschmider being preoccupied with a sudden bar fight – but the two soon met again at the famous 21's coffee bar (where Steele himself had been discovered) in London. Not for nothing had Williams once been dubbed the 'Colonel Parker of the North'. Seizing the moment, he swiftly arranged for his most promising act, Derry & the Seniors, to audition for Koschmider, who booked them for his club at a wage of thirty marks (about £3) each per day.

It was shortly after that that something like an exchange programme began. The specifics varied, but the essence of the deal was that Williams would have various teenagers cross the North Sea and travel Germany by minivan, alighting periodically to unleash loud,

American *negermusik*, in return for which Koschmider paid a generous finder's fee. Williams' was a pack mentality, and he already had several 'turns' at his disposal. After the Seniors, he planned to send over another of his favourites, Rory Storm and the Hurricanes, but they landed a coveted summer residency at Butlin's. His next choice was Gerry & the Pacemakers. To Williams' consternation, they turned him down, apparently not fancying the 'Krauts'. At this stage, a letter arrived from Koschmider requesting that the Colonel Parker of the North get a move on. Finally Williams thought of the sorry outfit, without even a steady drummer, just then eking out a few Saturday night dances in Wallasey, now calling themselves the plain 'Beatles'.

McCartney needed all his formidable charm to persuade his father that three months of playing rock music in the vice capital of Europe would be 'a good education'. Allan Williams called in person on the family at Forthlin Road, but seems to have rather spoilt his pitch by referring to Paul as 'John' throughout. The day was saved, instead, by brother Mike, who persuasively argued that Paul would be earning a weekly £15 (minus Williams' cut) for the duration, which was more than Jim made. On Tuesday 16 August, the Beatles were duly on the ferry to the Hook of Holland, from where Williams' battered green van wound its way to Hamburg. Just before leaving, the four-guitar group had wandered in to the Casbah club, where the owner's son, a shy, good-looking eighteen-year-old called Pete Best, chanced to be sitting at his shiny new drum kit. Paul and John exchanged glances. After a brisk audition, Best was in. The 'unluckiest man in showbusiness' had begun his two years of fame.

Just as McCartney made for Koschmider's second, 'more exclusive' establishment, the Indra, where the band were to play, his A level results reached Forthlin Road. He passed only one exam, in Art.

Wearing his two-tone shoes, black jacket and a deer-in-the-headlights expression, Paul looked around the Indra, which was chiefly a strip club. With Williams' help, Koschmider was about to relaunch it as a 'big beat' venue, but when McCartney and the band arrived, passing under the giant neon elephant at the door, it was still offering cabaret. No one paid much attention when the Beatles walked in. With brutal suddenness Paul realised that he was in one of those situations where it was necessary he keep his head. There was a group of butch sailors in one corner, and an American officer in uniform in another with his back pressed to the wall. He was sitting with two transvestites in powdered blonde wigs and a young black woman who was one of the Indra's performers. Seven or eight other customers were scattered around at tables each lit by a candle screwed into an empty wine bottle, feigning interest in an Asiatic-looking combo who, to a backdrop of black, red and yellow bedsheets, were singing Heartbreak Hotel in German. Presently the black woman stubbed out her cigarette and climbed up on the tiny stage to dance.

By now, John Lennon was laughing uncontrollably. 'This is it! What did I tell you, son? The toppermost of the poppermost!'

Paul just shook his head.

Not long after that there was apparently some misunderstanding between the American officer and the transvestites. Deftly pulling a spring-loaded cosh from his pocket, Koschmider excused himself from the Beatles and – with surprising agility – made with a low, scuttling gait to the corner. There he raked the three men with the choicest invective. When the officer shot back, 'Do you know who I am?', Koschmider told him in no uncertain terms who he was, and without further ado the entire party were escorted outside to Grosse Freiheit. Koschmider then returned to the Beatles, bowed stiffly, and announced that he would now show them their 'apartment'; this turned out to be a dank, two-room slum located immediately behind the screen of the Bambi Kino, an X-rated cinema he owned nearby. While in these dire surroundings, Paul slept under a tattered Union Jack as his sole bedding.

The Beatles were to play a total of 106 nights in Hamburg that year, initially at the Indra then, after noise complaints, upmarket in the Kaiserkeller. Paul would remark that the latter seemed to them 'like the fucking Albert Hall' by comparison. Fuelled by an inexhaustible supply of beer and Allan Williams' shouted demands that they 'Make a show, lads'*, the Beatles began to lose some of their native shyness. Both Paul and John would soon incorporate a series of lunges, lurches, shuffles, struts and wildly over-the-top impersonations into the act. The drugs may also have helped. In early 1960 McCartney had met the Beat poet Royston Ellis (supposedly the inspiration for Paperback Writer six years later), who allegedly showed him how to extract and swallow the Benzedrine strip from a common Vick's inhaler. During their manic stint at the Kaiserkeller, all the Beatles, bar Pete Best, enjoyed a multicoloured diet of Preludin and other amphetamines. As George Harrison would recall, 'We were frothing at the mouth . . . We used to be up there foaming, stomping away.' They were also attracting their first serious groupies. Much like Liverpool, Hamburg was 'ancient, raw, grimy, open all hours,' Sutcliffe wrote, with a 'tribal sense of community' that warmly embraced its entertainers. Most nights, the band left the stage at two a.m. At some point during the six hours between then and the Kino lights coming on, Paul would find his way home and sleep fitfully under the flag with one or more of his local fans. The 'sex gladiator', as John teasingly called him, was also a diplomat. All the time he was in Hamburg, Paul kept up a steady stream of postcards home, assuring both Jim and Dot Rhone that he was 'doing fine'. In the ten years ahead he would bed 'five or six hundred birds', and apparently came close to disaster on at least one occasion when a spurned lover named him in a paternity suit. By the late Sixties he'd settled down, as much as was in his nature, but this

---

* Echoed by the club manager, who encouraged the band by both hammering his one good leg up and down and yelling 'Mach Schau! Mach Schau!'

part of his reputation remained proverbial until his first marriage and the birth of his children.

Early in their Kaiserkeller stay the Beatles met a blonde, twentyish woman with a cropped, Mia Farrow cut, who wandered in with her leather-clad boyfriend. Ignoring John's muttered protests about his not fraternising with 'jerries', the couple introduced themselves as Astrid Kirchherr and Klaus Voorman. They were 'exis', or existentialists – art students who dressed alike, wore matching Ray-Bans and quickly fell in thrall to the pill-popping Britishers and their crazy *negermusik*. The glacially beautiful Astrid seems to have captivated all five Beatles, whom she began to photograph among the sub-surrealist props of the Hamburg fairground.

Astrid's eye fell, in particular, on the one Beatle who had hitherto been relatively quiet in the fräulein department – her fellow artist, Stuart Sutcliffe. Their relationship developed rapidly, offending not only Klaus Voorman but also McCartney. Paul: 'Stu and I used to have a deadly rivalry . . . He was older and a strong friend of John's. When I look back on it I think we were probably fighting for John's attention.' Another explanation was that McCartney himself fancied Astrid (whose Stravinsky records he regularly cadged), and thus resented his rival on a second level. Finally there was the fact that, spectrally cool as he looked, Stu was no musician. Paul would remark that both he and John had sometimes asked their bass player to turn away from the audience, so that they couldn't see that his fingers weren't in the right key.

Paul also had his issues with Pete Best. More and more, the pathologically shy drummer, never quite equal to the job, seemed the odd one out. In one memorable encounter, McCartney and Lennon had turned on Best one night at the Indra, accusing him of incompetence and, paradoxically, of 'being too good' for them. Their outburst was followed by silence. According to a firsthand witness to the scene, none of the other Beatles defended Best, not even Best himself. Seemingly unruffled, his thin face deadpan, he announced merely that he was 'going for a walk'. On 15 October 1960, a Saturday, the Beatles arranged to back Wally Eymond of Rory Storm's Hurricanes on two numbers they cut in a record-your-voice studio behind Hamburg's central rail station. Nobody bothered to tell Pete Best. The drummer for the session was another of the Hurricanes, a beagle-faced man called Ritchie Starkey, otherwise known as Ringo.

Things ended in some disarray for the Beatles that winter in Hamburg. Shortly after they began moonlighting at yet another club, the Top Ten, an indignant Koschmider drew their attention to the exclusivity clause in their contract and gave them a month's notice. Harrison was then deported for having lied to the German authorities about his age. Finally, McCartney and Pete Best managed to start a small fire at the Bambi Kino while vacating it for more luxurious digs above the Top Ten. When Paul arrived at the club an hour later, he found the police waiting for him. Arrested and charged with attempted arson, McCartney spent four hours under interrogation at St Pauli police station before being locked up for the night. His first experience of jail was followed, courtesy of the Bundesministerium des Innern, by his first plane trip. Paul arrived back at Heathrow on 1 December with just enough money in his pocket to catch a train to Liverpool.

McCartney would later speak of the winter of 1960–61 as a dark time. Monday 5 December was probably rock bottom: Jim sent him to the labour exchange, who arranged for him to work as an errand boy over the Christmas season, delivering parcels for the Speedy Prompt Messenger Service. Only a day or two later Paul was caught sleeping on the job, thus ending his career as a courier. A brief stint followed with the engineers Massey & Coggins, who paid him £1 for each eight-hour shift winding heavy electrical coils. The Beatles went back to the local dog-and-pony, which began paying dividends on 27 December, when they brought the house down at Litherland town hall. As the curtain rose the already festive crowd were met by Paul's hollered Little Richard impersonation and lusty swings of John's guitar, all amped up to the pain threshold. Their reaction was, understandably, a trifle demonstrative. Eighteen fainting cases.

Meanwhile, Stu was still in Hamburg, enjoying the holidays with Astrid Kirchherr. A friend of Best's named Chas Newby helped the band out with their Christmas gigs, but evidently decided that a working environment of girls first screaming, and then abandoning their upright posture wasn't for him. On New Year's Day McCartney at last decided to 'stop fucking about' and play the bass himself.

Six weeks later the Beatles first performed at the Cavern, the club where the Quarry Men had skiffled in the summer of 1957. The place was well named. To get to the now-legendary grotto (since demolished and rebuilt 'using the original bricks') you passed between rows of fruit and vegetable stalls trading to a backdrop of leprous Victorian warehouses, five storeys high, crossed a bomb site and entered a narrow door at 10 Mathew Street. A hatch gave on to eighteen greasy steps, the stone worn to the thinness of paper, leading down to a sort of crypt. There were three parallel vaults, each some ten feet wide, with a low wooden stage in the middle lit by bare bulbs. Nobody bothered much with things such as fire regulations or sanitation. During the more raucous numbers, flakes of wet plaster (or 'Cavern dandruff') poured down from the ceiling, which was both mouldy and daubed with graffiti. The whole place stank.

Over the course of the next two-and-a-half years, Paul and the Beatles came of age here. Arriving on foot, they gave their first lunchtime performance on 9 February 1961 for a fee of £5. By the time they vanished up Mathew Street in their Daimler on 3 August 1963, they were the biggest phenomenon in showbusiness. Those 273 shows in between, where the steam rose, girls swooned and Paul would *mach schau*, made even the Indra seem tame, and nobody present ever forgot them. It was a truly collective experience. There was no curtain between the Beatles and their public. The MC, Bob

Wooler, bawled a big circus intro and the band simply appeared, four figures in black caught in a jetblast of non-stop screaming. From the first note of Johnny B Goode, the place would go nuts. Everyone had sharpened up their act in Hamburg, and what Paul could do with a Little Richard riff wasn't to be believed. There were generous helpings of Elvis and Chuck Berry, as well as Chan Romero's show-stopping Hippy Hippy Shake. Sometimes McCartney and Lennon wheeled into a peak-decibel, clapalong version of What'd I Say. Or Paul might change gears with a treacly rendition of Over The Rainbow. The whole thing climaxed in a hell-for-leather raveup like Money, the signal for the audience to shake their fists and go into a synchronised 'Cavern stomp'. Clever, cocky and superbly versatile, the Beatles gave classic black R&B a facelift without smoothing the wrinkles.

Saturday night, 1 April, the group were back in Hamburg at Peter Eckhorn's Top Ten club. Allan Williams had persuaded the authorities to review McCartney's deportation order, chalking the arson up to an artistic temperament, duly lifted 'by special concession of the Bundesministerium'. (The Beatles repaid this favour by informing Williams that, having negotiated their own booking at the Top Ten, they were pocketing his fee.) Stuart Sutcliffe had effectively left the band and gone native, but he and Astrid frequently dropped by the club. Once or twice, Stu even climbed up on stage and noodled a bass for old times' sake. The boys were all struck by how pale he looked, and how dependent he now seemed on his girlfriend. On one such night, Paul made a tactless remark about 'the kraut' (Astrid) and he and Stu ended up rolling around under the piano, discussing the matter.

'"I'll kill you, you bastard!" I screamed at him. "I'll bloody get you!" he screamed back,' said McCartney, recalling the scene. 'I think they had to pour water on us in the end.'

To John, Paul was 'cute, and didn't he know it', a born hoofer who was also a 'thruster' and an 'operator' behind the scenes. The result, as Stu observed of the Lennon-McCartney axis, was 'some tension, some love and occasional shit.' Later in 1961, Paul would note that he'd composed 'about 70 numbers' with his partner. Lennon allowed only that they'd done 'a couple of things' together. In fact, their songwriting seems to have been only fitful during the early days at both the Top Ten and the Cavern, where the accent was on hustling out the oldies. If Paul was the more ambitious of the pair, he was the more inquisitive too, enjoying everything left-field from John Cage's 'Imaginary Landscapes' series to the early plays of Harold Pinter – all dismissed by the young Lennon as 'bullshit'. McCartney was also by far the most frugal of the Beatles. At some stage in the band's Hamburg residency, he borrowed £16 – equivalent to about a week's wages – from the long-suffering Allan Williams. Some thirty years later, Williams appeared at a McCartney concert in Seattle still clutching the IOU, which by then was worth many times its face value as a souvenir.

One of the first things Paul did with his Top Ten earnings was to buy a new Hofner 500/1 bass, lightweight and shaped like a violin, for which he paid in ten thirty-mark instalments. Another was to have dinner with a tow-haired young singer called Anthony McGinnity, better known as Tony Sheridan, who'd long struck Bruno Koschmider as being the most likely of all the English acts in Hamburg to become a 'second Elvis'. On 22 June Sheridan cut a record for Polydor and used the Beatles as his backing group. The studio was again basic, being the stage of a local infants' school, but it did the job. Two songs credited to Sheridan & the Beat Brothers were released on the German market and sold 112,000 copies that autumn. Back in Liverpool, a young record shop manager would take a box of imports, which he sold for six shillings a single. He ordered two more boxes.

At home the Beatles continued a fixture at the Cavern, with occasional gigs as far afield as Aintree, Knotty Ash, or, once, the deck of the MV *Royal Iris* crossing the Mersey. Local jive halls were busy switching from jazz to 'race', and Paul was heard to remark in a speech from the stage of Holyoake Hall that the estate of pop music was 'going fab'. It roused a special little cheer. On 6 July – exactly four years since McCartney had ambled to the Woolton church fête – a design student called Bill Harry launched a paper he christened *Mersey Beat*. The first issue carried a tale by Lennon entitled 'Being A Short Diversion on the Dubious Origins of Beatles'. Even Jim McCartney, occasionally dropping in to the Cavern on his lunch hour, was prepared to concede that the experience was 'a real eye-opener'. A slightly prim nineteen-year-old who was scrupulously polite to his aunts, Paul was an entirely different beast on stage. By now his act ran the gamut from the smoochy to the downright sexual. As Jim proudly noted, 'the birds were start[ing] to go potty'. A few of them were even making their way to Forthlin Road, where they left lipstick messages on the front door.

9 October: John Lennon turned twenty-one and, with a gift of £100, he and Paul decided to see something of Europe besides Hamburg. In Paris they promptly ran into Jürgen Vollmer, another of the exis, who happened to have just moved there to study photography. The Beatles all admired his design skills, which had included advising them to wear Ray-Bans on stage. One morning Vollmer took Paul and John up to his cheap hotel room in the Latin Quarter, washed the grease from their hair and combed it forwards in the style of his favourite actor, Jean Marais. In later years certain erudite pop critics liked to claim the look reminded them of the ancient Greeks, while to others the great templates were TV's Captain Kangaroo, or Moe of the Three Stooges. All parties soon agreed on a name, the moptop.

On Thursday 9 November, a twenty-seven-year-old, wavy-haired man wearing a dark, bespoke suit and carrying a briefcase made his way a trifle warily down the steps to the Cavern. His name was Brian Epstein, and he ran the record department of the family-owned music store around the corner at 12–14 Whitechapel. 'It was pretty much of a shock' said Epstein, recalling the scene, 'to go down into this darkened, dank, smoky cellar and see crowds and crowds of kids watching these four on stage . . . They had a rather untidy presentation, not terribly aware and not caring very much what they looked like. I immediately liked what I heard. They were fresh and they were honest, and they had what I thought was a sort of presence . . . a star quality. Whatever that is they had it, or I sensed they had it.'

Epstein had had a chequered career, having left school at sixteen and been discharged from the army on psychiatric grounds after he took to sitting in homosexual clubs pretending to be an officer. A year at drama school ended abruptly when he was arrested for 'importuning' in a public lavatory. There was another such incident when a young man in the Liverpool docks beat him up and later blackmailed him. On the other hand, Epstein proved himself a supremely efficient record retailer. He was hard-working, scrupulous and shrewd, with an infallible ear for a song and great personal style. A few minutes of archive footage exist in which, in wonderfully plummy tones, Epstein describes his discovery of these 'ill-clad' fellows and his subsequent decision to take them on because he 'rather liked their beat'. Next to some of the men the band had worked for in Hamburg, Eppy struck them as Merseyside's own Cary Grant, a titan of couth.

Nonetheless, as the weeks passed they all wondered about the fastidiously dressed 'queer' who now talked about managing them. Epstein, it seemed, suffered from wild mood swings and sometimes shocked Paul and John by cutting them off in midstream with a peremptory 'fuck' or 'shit'. Still, he always apologised profusely. Jim McCartney was the first to come around, telling Paul, 'You've got yourself a good Jewish gaffer there, son.' A day or two later the parties all met up in a local milk bar, where Eppy vouched that – for a modest twenty-five per cent of the action – he would personally ensure the Beatles never again played a gig for less than £15.

A number of further meetings ensued, in which Epstein carefully read the band his terms and conditions from copious, neatly typed notes at his elbow. He always seemed to give McCartney his best, eye-twinkling smile. They eventually agreed terms on 24 January 1962, though, for some reason, Eppy himself would wait another eight months to sign on the dotted line. By that stage everyone was talking excitedly about their becoming millionaires. Before the document was drawn up McCartney's father, with whom Paul still lived, had to give his legal consent, since Paul himself was nineteen, too young to be responsible.

Epstein appeared for the signing ceremony, which took place in his office on a Wednesday afternoon, immaculately turned out in his usual suit and tie, with a polka-dotted foulard scarf added for the occasion. He sat there fiddling with his monogrammed cufflinks. Something about the ensemble seemed to trouble him, because Eppy suddenly pushed the button on his office speaker and yelled, 'Get me tailor!' In a flash his whole face reddened, growing angrier, and he roared at the top of his lungs, 'Tailor! Now!'

There were heavy footsteps outside the door, which opened to admit a dapper young man with curly dark hair and sideburns: Alistair Taylor, Epstein's personal assistant. In a high-handed manner that was hard to watch, Eppy requested that he formally witness the contract and countersign it on each page. The efficient and likeable Taylor particularly impressed McCartney, who soon dubbed him 'Mr Jobworthy' for his willingness to do literally everything on behalf of Eppy and the boys it wasn't vital they do themselves.

Just how much the Beatles had needed Epstein was made clear on 9 December 1961, a month after they met him but before any new arrangements went into effect. A local promoter named Sam Leach had promised to break the band 'down South' – by which he meant Aldershot – and put on a Christmas revue certain to draw both 'thousands of kids' and the 'top London agents'. But when they arrived after a nine-hour van journey, the Beatles found exactly eighteen customers waiting for them.

'The guys said it wasn't worth playing,' Leach recalled, 'but Paul persuaded them. "Come on," he said. "Let's show we're professionals."'

That thin, rustic audience would enjoy a full-throttle Beatles concert, complete with McCartney's Little Richard turn, the first of what would be several forays 'down South' by the band over the next four years. At midnight, as the last of the revellers shuffled off, Paul, John and George took to the floor and danced with one another. After that, owing to noise complaints, a policeman arrived and told them to 'piss off home'.

The Beatles were a tough sell for Epstein, who would find only lukewarm interest in his boys among the London showbiz establishment. To the scouts and sinister 'market penetration' men down South, Liverpool wasn't good enough: hopelessly provincial, crude, lewd and stinking of fish and chips. By now the 'Merseybeat' bands were attracting a few enterprising reporters, who recorded their behaviour as if they were animals in a wildlife documentary. Epstein soon put his charges in cutesy grey tweed suits and impressed on them the need for punctuality. For the first time, their sets were prearranged and rehearsed. On New Year's Day 1962 the Beatles auditioned for Decca, pioneers of both the wind-up gramophone and long-player, who famously turned them down. Guitar groups, in the assessment of Dick Rowe (head of A&R) and Sidney Beecher-Stevens (sales manager) were 'on the way out'. The two seers concluded the interview by telling Epstein, 'The Beatles won't go. We know these things. You have a good little shop in Liverpool, why not stick to that?' As the door was closing behind him, Eppy retorted that his boys would, on the contrary, be bigger than Elvis.

8 February, Thursday afternoon, Epstein wandered in out of the rain to the HMV store in London's Oxford Street, still clutching his reel-to-reel audition tapes. Having been turned down in short order

by both Pye and Oriole, with only the Woolie's label to go, he was
wet, bedraggled and 'thoroughly brassed off' lugging the two heavy
metal canisters around town. Some of his habitual cool seemed to
have wilted. On the first floor of the shop was a small studio, little
more than a record-your-voice booth, where customers could cut
their own, lightweight discs, which struck Eppy as a fair plan. As the
engineer on duty was making the transfer he casually remarked that
some of the stuff wasn't too bad, and that there was a music
publisher named Ardmore and Beechwood on the top floor. Their
manager, Syd Coleman, in turn listened to the newly minted demo
and asked Epstein whether he was at all interested in speaking to
their affiliated record company.

Eppy replied that he was, rather.

'I'll call someone,' said Coleman.

'What's his name?' asked Epstein, taking out a finely bound
notebook and a gold fountain pen.

'George Martin.'

On 11 April the Beatles flew to Hamburg, where they logged another
180 hours stage time over the next seven weeks. Astrid Kirchherr was
waiting for them at the airport with terrible news. The day before,
Stuart Sutcliffe, who'd long complained of crippling headaches, had
collapsed and been rushed to hospital. He died before they got there,
in Astrid's arms. He was twenty-one. The postmortem would show
that Stu had suffered a brain haemorrhage, allegedly the result of a
beating he took from a gang of thugs after a concert some two years
earlier. Tears welled up in Paul's eyes, while John, doubtless in
shock, is said to have laughed hysterically. Despite their loss, the
Beatles went on as scheduled and scored an opening night triumph
at the new Star Club. Eleven arrests for disorderly conduct.

At this point, McCartney began a brief but intense relationship
with a young blonde named Erika Heubers, who worked as a waitress
in a Reeperbahn nightclub. A friend there would remember her

saying, 'Paul and I were truly in love . . . It was a beautiful, beautiful thing. I gave him my heart.'

That the affair lasted only a week in no way diminished its romance for Erika. Nor its significance: on 18 December she gave birth to a baby girl, Bettina, and claimed that Paul was the father. He vehemently denied it, although three years later McCartney settled a suit brought in the German courts, paying £2,700 (while not admitting paternity) towards the child's welfare. Bettina herself would resurface in April 1983, requesting a monthly maintenance grant of £375 to augment her earnings as a fuse-stuffer in a Hamburg fireworks factory. The twenty-year-old then attempted to launch herself as a singer, but her career in showbusiness was short-lived. Not long after that, Bettina was pictured in *High Society* magazine wearing only a pair of black leather gloves and wielding a clear plastic guitar. She went on to lose two further maintenance hearings against McCartney, who agreed to waive his right to costs.

Eppy, meanwhile, had now made the better acquaintance of George Martin, the soigné, thirty-six-year-old head of EMI's Parlophone label, low if not the absolute dregs of recorded sound, with a bent for easy listening and comic-dialogue LPs. Martin liked the demo, and shook hands over a sherry with Epstein late in the morning of 9 May. Representing the barest of investments by EMI, the deal agreed merely to offer Paul, John, George and Pete a provisional contract, subject to their satisfying Martin at Abbey Road studios. He hadn't yet met the Beatles. Eppy then stepped around the corner to the post office and sent a telegram to Hamburg: 'CONGRATULATIONS BOYS. EMI REQUEST RECORDING SESSION. PLEASE REHEARSE NEW MATERIAL.'

McCartney's reply to Epstein read, 'WIRE £10,000 ADVANCE ROYALTIES.'

Back in Forthlin Road, Jim now found his son's name in print almost every week and called it to Paul's attention with a throaty chuckle. The older McCartney seemed genuinely proud that his own showbiz ambitions were to be fulfilled by 'our kid'. He was even proud when some of the press belatedly discovered and occasionally wrote about the Jim Mac band. For the rest of his life Jim spent his time on the lookout for either of their pictures in the paper, until, shortly before the end – he was then seventy-three – he took Paul's hands in his and gravely asked him, 'Do you look like me or do I look like you?'

6 June 1962: Around lunchtime, the *Evening News* vendor at the foot of prim, tree-lined Abbey Road set up his stall behind a poster promising 'D-DAY SOUVENIR SPECIAL'. The Beatles arrived on the scene shortly thereafter. They went in the tradesmen's entrance and made their way to Studio 2, where they performed to the satisfaction of Martin's assistant Ron Richards and an engineer. Around seven that evening, on hearing a number called Love Me Do, Richards was moved to fetch his boss. Martin thought the Beatles, dressed up as provincial moppets, 'very clean' – Eppy's influence – and McCartney, in particular, a true pro. In those days of crude, two-track recording, the bass typically sounded like a weakly snapped rubber band. Yet there was Paul with his weird-looking contraption, somewhere between a gamba and a violin, making the room jump up and down the block. Martin was less impressed with Pete Best. At the end of the session, he took Epstein to one side and told him, in so many words, his drummer would have to go. There appears to have been some behind-the-scenes debate about this over the next two months. In early August, Best arrived for a rehearsal one morning and excitedly announced plans to buy a new Ford Capri once his 'EMI dosh' came in. McCartney looked uneasy and said, 'Take my advice, Pete. Don't do it. You'd be better off saving your money.'

The 'EMI dosh' amounted to a one-year deal, with four further annual options, in which the label undertook to pay the Beatles (who in turn paid Epstein and his staff) one penny for every single sold. A million-seller would net each band member roughly £600. The company brass had fallen about laughing when Martin told them the name of his new signing, assuming that the man behind such fare as Peter Sellers' *Songs For Swinging Sellers* was having another one of his 'Goon jokes'. In the event, EMI scheduled Love Me Do for release third in line behind their 'autumn blockbuster' (Nicky Hilton's Your Nose Is Gonna Grow), crediting its composers in their catalogue as 'Lennon-McArtney'. Epstein was also busy booking the boys onto the Top Rank ballroom circuit, as well as renegotiating their regular spot at the Cavern. On Friday nights, each musician was now handed a typed 'accounts statement' along with a detailed memo from Eppy explaining why a particular show was important, and stressing the need for punctuality and decorum.

Paul's twentieth birthday coincided with EMI formally inking their contract. He was doing better than any McCartney ever had, better than most had even dreamed of, and he was doing it by playing music. He had a rent-free room, an old Ford Classic and a weekly envelope containing £20 or £30. After forty-five years of full-time work, Jim Mac was earning at best half as much.

Paul and John finally agreed to fire Pete Best in the middle of August. Two years earlier, Best had stepped in to help, if not save the Silver Beatles and, if free of their manic wit, had kept the show on the road – even making the band's bookings for them before management intervened. Now he was out. McCartney and Lennon (who may have been preoccupied by his wedding on the 23rd to Cynthia Powell) entrusted the job to Eppy, who hired on their Hamburg friend Ringo Starr. Best was distraught and spent some time over the next week trying to speak to McCartney, who wasn't available to take his call.

On 4 September the Beatles flew to London and recorded Love Me Do for George Martin. Ringo proved an only so-so idea, and Martin booked a house drummer, Andy White, for yet another session at Abbey Road a week later. In this patient, bricklaying fashion a two-minute single, described as 'George Formby doing the blues', was finally cut and released, hitting number seventeen in a chart dominated by the likes of Cliff, Rolf Harris and Bernard Cribbins warbling Gossip Calypso.

The ultimate verdict, however, belonged to EMI. Following the modest profit shown by Love Me Do, the Beatles were again summoned to Abbey Road on 26 November. They arrived around 6.30p.m. and worked until ten, with a thirty-minute break for dinner in the canteen, which they paid for themselves. The whole thing, they concluded, was more like a factory than a studio, with technicians in white coats and ties, and managers who made a point of clocking everyone in and calling 'Time' at night. In the course of those three hours, the band recorded Please Please Me, Ask Me Why, and a third McCartney-Lennon original they called Tip Of My Tongue. The first of these managed to combine the vocal styles of Roy Orbison and both Everly brothers with a bluesy dockyard harp and a throbbing Motown bass. At the end of this stylistic pile-up the four Beatles sat there, grinning sheepishly, until George Martin pushed the button on the studio intercom and calmly announced, 'Gentlemen, you have just made your first number one.'

They went back to Liverpool, where McCartney strolled across Mathew Street one lunchtime to The Grapes and ordered a pint and a sandwich. He was a penny short. Just then, the impressive figure of Paddy Delaney, the tuxedo-clad former Guardsman who kept order at the Cavern, walked through the door. 'I'll make you a loan,' he told him. 'Remember me when you're famous, son.'

'I will,' said Paul.

CHAPTER THREE

The Toppermost

On the night of 19 January 1963, a bitterly cold Saturday lashed by alternating rain and snow, seven million British viewers tuned in to watch the Beatles perform Please Please Me on *Thank Your Lucky Stars*. From out of the Dickensian gloom came a startling image of four young bucks wearing matching high-collared suits and smiling broadly throughout. When Paul and John stepped smartly to the mike for the 'Whoa yeah' chorus, which they sang in falsetto, both shook their pudding-bowl hair. At that precise moment the dominant noise in the studio changed from one of polite applause to frenzied screaming. Although bottom of the seven-act bill, the band and their half-audible 'turn' were the first point of order when offices, factories and, more to the point, schools opened the following Monday morning.

McCartney was just twenty years old, and he was famous.

The show was doubly significant because it consummated affairs between the Beatles and one Dick James, the former yodeller of TV's *Robin Hood* theme tune and now a semi-successful music plugger. James had secured the band's *Lucky Stars* appearance through an old friend who happened to be the show's producer. On the morning of 22 February, Paul and John were driven to a dank Toxteth basement flat Eppy sometimes used and there presented with a contract. Effective immediately, the deal established Northern Songs, an entity controlled fifty per cent by James and his partner and fifty per cent by Paul, John and Brian Epstein. All future Lennon-McCartney copyrights would be vested in the company, which James agreed to manage for ten per cent of the gross action.

Paul: 'And that was the deal I'm still under. That little murky signing in the dark mews in Liverpool is it . . . We just didn't understand it. We didn't know what was going on at all. We enjoyed writing the stuff and we just hoped someone was looking after our interests.'

Dick James, they learnt, had a fairly colourful CV. Born Richard Leon Vapnick in East London, he'd worked as a crooner in a pre-war dance band, served in the army and found time to write on the side; James was the creative force behind Max Bygraves' seminal hit I'm A Pink Toothbrush, I'm A Blue Toothbrush which Paul had liked to whistle in the bath back in Ardwick Road. After the success of his (George Martin-produced) *Robin Hood*, he'd given up full-time singing and decided to set up shop in Tin Pan Alley. At forty-one James was bespectacled and wiry, though thickening around the middle, with the look of a prematurely hatched bird, Adam's apple darting up and down his narrow neck. What he had of hair was frizzy and set off by bushy sideburns. Like Epstein, he was a famously sharp dresser and a stickler for presentation and punctuality. He was also a smooth operator; on their first meeting, James had taken one look at Lennon and McCartney and vowed to make them 'bigger than Rogers and Hammerstein'.

'We're partners, we're pals,' he assured them. Paul and John nudged one another and rolled their eyes upward.

Along with Lennon, Epstein and Martin, James would be a, or *the* key figure in McCartney's life in years ahead. Rounding out the entourage were Neil Aspinall, the band's road manager, 'Big Mal' Evans, the muscle, and Peter Brown, Eppy's other assistant and long-time confidant. This was a fanatically loyal and distinctly Liverpudlian crew. Everyone from their part of the world somehow seemed to know everyone else, and outsiders weren't welcomed.

It's hard to say exactly when the Beatles arrived at the dangerously combustible centre of the pop universe. How they got there, however, is no mystery.

There was the year that began on 11 February 1963, the day they cut their entire first album, and ended on 11 February 1964, the day they gave their first paying performance in North America. There were wild concerts, full of smoke, chrome and pungently damp seats, everywhere from the Cavern to the Royal Albert Hall. There was a precedent-setting appearance in front of the Queen Mum. There were EPs, LPs and singles, in-between which Paul casually provided hits for various friends from Tony Newley to the Rolling Stones. Finally, there was Richard Buckle, the veteran music critic of the *Sunday Times*, proclaiming McCartney and Lennon 'the greatest composers since Beethoven.'

When not on tour Paul spent much of his time in the elegant villa at 3 Abbey Road, perched on a stool in the big, sparsely furnished room, built to accommodate a symphony orchestra, where the Beatles did their work. George Martin's excellent bedside manner brought out the best in him: McCartney was growing increasingly adventurous on the bass, lofting off on melodies rather than just plunking the root notes. Witness the bluesy hooting on a Lucille or Long Tall Sally – both stage favourites – he was also capable of mixing a bit of rough with the smooth; Paul's vocal on I Saw Her Standing There, nailed in two takes on 11 February 1963, had a swagger even Lennon admired.

After the Beatles meekly picked up their equipment and left, Martin would recall listening to the tapes and thinking, 'There's nothing bad here! Normally, you can cut one or two things right away, and there was nothing bad.'

The band were on the road most of that spring and summer, dolled up in their burgundy, velvet-collared suits and pink shirts (selected by Paul) and caked in Max Factor make-up. Travelling arrangements were still spartan, though Eppy and his well-spoken associates ensured that there was a steady supply of freshly laundered gear as well as the boys' favourite foods, books and magazines (including *Investors' Guide* in Paul's case), with side trips to local art galleries wherever they went. Compared to Frank Sinatra's clan, the Beatles' looked like the Bloomsbury Group. John, George and Ringo, reasonably enough, appeared to ignore the entourage except when bawling them out if something went wrong. Paul, by contrast, took pains to endear himself to everyone on a personal level. Late one Sunday night after singing himself hoarse at a 'Rhythm & Blues Marathon' at the Cavern, McCartney noticed Epstein standing off by himself and wandered over to ask whether he fancied a meal.

Eppy seemed startled by the offer. 'Really, Paul,' he stammered, 'that's very sweet of you. Of course, I should love it. I can't remember when I was invited to dinner last. Not by someone I like.'

And, much to McCartney's embarrassment, Eppy took out a silk handkerchief and dabbed away a tear that had welled up in each eye.

On 14 April the Beatles taped another *Thank Your Lucky Stars* and drove across South London to the back room of Richmond's Station Hotel – now dubbed the Crawdaddy Club – where the Rolling Stones were in residence.

They stood right at the front, in their matching German overcoats and suede 'twat' hats, with just a few feet between them and the Stones. Mick Jagger would remember thinking, 'Fuckin' hell! I want one of those coats!', a key moment in his decision to rapidly abandon the blues and launch his band on the hit parade.

Meanwhile, the Beatles put out their *Please Please Me* album. Recorded in ten hours, it spent thirty weeks at number one and eighteen months on the chart. This was the great leap forward, with

Paul and (a fast improved) Ringo doing the locomotion on ravers like Twist And Shout, some seductive pop moments and rich, Motown-tinged harmonies throughout. I Saw Her Standing There blazed with the zeal of live instrumentation and the classic, streetwise lines, courtesy of John, 'She was just seventeen/You know what I mean'. Under Martin's baton, *Please Please Me* retained trace elements of the band's booming, knockabout live act alongside the mood pieces like A Taste Of Honey. Everything was infused with a sense of frenetic, primal energy and passion that went far beyond mere homage. The result was a sparkling, unselfconscious celebration of R&B – a last chance to get into the Beatles at entry level before they became an institution.

Out the following month, a third single, From Me To You: a perky act of retro conjuring, mixing some Frankie Valli falsetto and bluesy harp with Lennon's abrasive vocal. Written in thirty minutes in the back of a tour bus, it, too, went straight to the top.

On Thursday 18 April, London and South-East England began to emerge from the worst winter in 200 years. It was a bright, cold day, dry for once, when the Beatles pulled up outside the Albert Hall at ten sharp that morning. They spent most of the next few hours either rehearsing or fooling around in their dressing room with their new friends Jagger and Richards. The two Stones helped set up their gear for them, then watched in awe as the Beatles calmly applied their make-up and triggered a riot the instant they walked on stage, which came under a non-stop barrage of bras and undies sailing over the footlights. Paul noted that, when he next saw the Stones, Mick was 'made up like a tart'.

Milling around backstage with Jim Mac and his sisters was an attractive, flame-haired actress whom *Radio Times* posed for a shot with Paul and John. She was just seventeen and her name was Jane Asher. McCartney spent some time with her later that night at the Beatles' hotel, and soon afterwards they were officially an item.

'We'd never met anyone like her,' Lennon recalled fondly. Despite

Jane's youth, she seemed to have been everywhere and done everything. Encouraged by an arty mother, she'd first enrolled with a theatrical agency aged seven and had since graced several British films and starred in the West End stage version of *Peter Pan*, as well as – the ultimate accolade – having guested on *Juke Box Jury*. In Lennon's view, she was 'smart, dead sexy and fun'. John's wife Cynthia adds that McCartney 'fell like a ton of bricks for Jane. The first time I was introduced to her was at her home and she was sitting on Paul's knee . . . He was obviously as proud as a peacock. She was a great prize.'

Later in April, McCartney, George and Ringo left for a twelve-day holiday in Tenerife. The first afternoon, Paul nearly drowned while swimming in the Atlantic, after which he stuck to the hotel pool. John and Eppy went off alone to Spain, where they allegedly had sex and, more plausibly, thrashed out future plans for the Beatles.

Soon after everyone got home, Epstein invited Paul and John to a working lunch at his accountants' office in Albermarle Street, Mayfair. McCartney arrived late, to be met by Eppy and several men in dark suits sitting around the boardroom table. They informed him that they'd thought it over and decided the creative team should no longer be billed as McCartney-Lennon, but Lennon-McCartney. When Paul asked why he was told that it sounded better.

'Not to me it doesn't,' he said.

Please Please Me, the first and last album featuring the old credit, remained a fact of life that summer. More was to come: more concerts (235 during 1963), more radio and TV (including the Royal Variety Performance) and, everywhere, more Beatles. Some of those primitive gigs looked like a Hieronymous Bosch painting of hell: waves of girls swarmed across the footlights to clutch at Paul or John, who were content to yell back into the din for twenty minutes before exiting the building, often by means of clambering up fire escapes or diving down laundry chutes, to relative safety. Around McCartney in

'63 there was always the sound of fans braying and squealing, MCs sternly asking for order and police chiefs rumbling 'Disgraceful!' It was one great headline after another.

In June, Paul turned twenty-one. Forthlin Road now resembling the Alamo, the party was held at his Aunty Jin's house in Huyton. It was a characteristic McCartney affair – large, loud, happy, with children playing underfoot and Jim bashing out old show tunes on the piano. Only Lennon departed from the prevailing mood. He's remembered as having introduced his wife as 'my bird' before taking violent exception to Bob Wooler's tactless remark, 'Hello, John. How was the honeymoon?' Apparently believing 'the cunt was saying I was a bloody queer' – the reference being to his recent holiday with Eppy – Lennon beat his old Cavern friend to a pulp. A claim for damages followed, which Wooler settled in return for an apology and a lump sum of £200.

By now John and Paul were banking that amount, or more, a week, nothing to sneeze at at a time when the average UK per capita income was still under a grand a year. Seemingly confirming the group's new-found prosperity, the entire Beatles organisation would soon move from Liverpool to London. Eppy and his North End Road Music Stores Enterprises (NEMS) set up shop at 5–6 Argyll Street, next door to the Palladium. The band were installed in a flat at 57 Green Street, Mayfair, though this seems to have been a crash pad – somewhere to pour themselves a drink and change gear. Paul spent much of his time at Jane Asher's parents' house a mile or so away, in a neighbourhood favoured by the smarter end of the British medical profession. By now, it was official that McCartney had a 'bird'. And not just any bird, but Britain's sweetheart, one of the youngest actresses ever to star in the West End. Before long he and Jane were a daily item in the gossip columns and Jim Mac, back in Liverpool, let it be known he was 'dead chuffed' by all the wedding rumours.

The Beatles' success had achieved the seemingly impossible in making Merseyside fashionable, and Epstein was now fast grooming a stable of supporting acts. Having been an impoverished backwater, Liverpool suddenly seemed set to become the cultural centre of gravity in Europe. Every NEMS press release and poster was designed so that, after the Fab Four, came the 'top rising stars': Gerry & the Pacemakers, Billy J. Kramer and Cilla Black. This was astronomy according to Eppy, who relied on Lennon-McCartney tunes to provide everyone with hits. A Beatles fan club was also being organised. Of the five or six daily sacks of letters pouring into Whitechapel, up North, and Argyll Street, down South, roughly half were addressed to Paul.

26 June, the Majestic, Newcastle-upon-Tyne. The Beatles got through their last ever ballroom blitz, accompanied by peak-decibel screaming and a volley of soft toys and other Paul-inspired gifts. It was the city's first real pop concert: the words entered the language, alongside FAB and YEAH! in the next day's *Chronicle*.

Back to the Turk's hotel. A suddenly quiet late Wednesday night, with McCartney and Lennon sitting facing each other on the twin beds of their third-floor room. Here, the necks of their guitars banging if they leant forward even an inch, they wound down by writing a song. The Beatles' fourth and, as Eppy's PR had it, 'long awaited' 45 existed in several spurts of inspiration. McCartney lit a cigarette, then hit a bluesy chord on his Gibson. The rest of the first verse, which largely followed speech inflections, was Lennon's. He and Paul then began swapping phrases, some debate ensuing about whether to proceed in the third person rather than their usual first or second.

Paul's smooth face, still rosy with stage make-up, hardened in intellectual engagement. 'Everyone likes a good story,' he insisted. John shrugged at that, merely noting that they weren't 'fucking novelists,' were they?

Five days later, after bouncing the tune off Jim Mac, the boys were ready to record She Loves You. Back in Abbey Road, George Martin listened to the run-through and politely suggested they snap it up by going directly into Paul's 'yeah, yeah, yeah' chorus. Featuring the trademark harmonies and some jazzy guitar on a bed of Ringo, the band's new single, released on 23 August, spent eight weeks at number one. Nothing could stop them now.

On 26 August, McCartney was fined £25 at Wallasey Crown Court and banned from driving for twelve months following his third speeding conviction of the year. A fortnight later, he was back on Merseyside as one of the judges of the 'Miss Imperial '63' beauty pageant. In mid-September he and Jane, along with Ringo and his girlfriend Maureen, went on holiday to Greece. They got back to Heathrow late in the evening of 2 October, and Jane's mother Margaret made the broad-minded suggestion that Paul spend the night at their place. Number 57 Wimpole Street was a five-storey Georgian house with a small music room in the basement where Mrs Asher gave oboe lessons. There were also bookcases full of first editions, fine paintings on the walls, photographs displayed in silver frames and an enormous, stone-flagged kitchen where meals would be served up at any time of the day or night. McCartney would soon pronounce Wimpole Street a 'cool scene'. On and off, he lived there for the next three years.

Andrew Loog Oldham, the self-coined 'teen tycoon shit' who ran the Stones, happened to share a long car journey with McCartney and Lennon that autumn. 'All very weird,' Loog says. 'They spent three hours talking about getting themselves disfigured so that the fans wouldn't recognise them.' 'We could have our faces cut up,' Paul mused. 'Walk around like Frankenstein with stitches and oozing pus,' he added suavely.

Paul and John had a gift for Oldham, a Jurassic rock song with a lilt of Bo Diddley, called I Wanna Be Your Man. Whether first presented in the car or – memories are vague, even by the fuzzy standards of the Sixties – the basement of Studio 51, it required only thirty or forty minutes to write, and an hour more to run it through for the Stones. Released as a single on 1 November, it made number twelve. Mick and Keith were awestruck by this ready-made hit, which the press agreed to be 'absolutely, completely wonderful' in every way. *Disc* gave it five stars. Lennon and McCartney thought so much of I Wanna Be Your Man that they gave the Beatles' own version of it to Ringo to sing.

Sunday 13 October, the London Palladium. A TV audience of fifteen million watched the Beatles bring the house down. The decibel level of screams and cracking seat fixtures exceeded that of the music, which 'might as well have been us farting,' Lennon noted. In a shocking breach of Palladium protocol, fans had kept the theatre under siege all day. After the show, the cameras caught Paul as he ran for the band's car, eyes bulging in a moment of frozen shock, a girl clinging to each arm. In its review, the *Daily Mirror* remarked that 'police fought to hold back 1,000 squealing teens' – something of a stretch – and the front page splash both there and in the *Daily Mail* and *Daily Express* marked the official birth of Beatlemania. Paul and the boys had woken a sleeping generation. Ironically, the real frenzy began just as the banshee stage act sank into self-parody, with manic, off-key songs no one could hear each followed by a stiff, theatrical bow. After the Palladium riot, the band went back to their hotel, rang some girls, had a few drinks and laughed about how they'd played out of tune. The reviews were still terrific.

Paul always remembered his father telling him how to 'make a show', packing it tight without a single dull moment. Aside from the stagecraft, the Beatles appealed to some very basic instincts. First, they were a *group*, with their matching halter-neck suits and twin moptops. Handled properly, as Jim said, a team could always rise to a level of shtick denied the solo act. Then there was the fact that Britain had just endured a long summer of upper-class buffoonery in the Profumo affair, with its cast of the Conservative Minister for War, sundry models, a society osteopath and the Soviet naval attaché; this reached its nadir when the osteopath, Stephen Ward, committed suicide on the eve of his trial for 'living off immoral earnings', a turn of events which seemed to slake even Fleet Street's appetite for scandal. Harold Macmillan had resigned as prime minister on 10 October – the week the Beatles played the Palladium – and been replaced by the Earl of Home, a Scottish laird who made his predecessor look like Elvis. Critics noted the gentlemanly self-deprecation, the faint suggestion of bumbling and the general air of one born to the 'incestuous bartering-house for vested interests' as John Osborne termed the ruling class, in a hint of the coming end of deference. By late 1963, the old, pre-war Establishment was still – just about – running the show; a post-war generation was coming up behind, fast. There was a definite mood about that that dismal time and place, Britain under Sir Alec Douglas-Home (as he became), needed a lift.

On 22 November 1963, Parlophone released *With The Beatles*. Recorded in the relative luxury of thirty hours, the band's second LP proves the definitive mix of big beats, teary ballads and slick, in-the-pocket grooves. Paul sprinkles his relationship songs like All My Loving with some free-swinging chord changes and typical harmonic skill. Continuing the stylistic hopscotch, the Beatles give the full boogie-woogie treatment to Chuck Berry's Roll Over Beethoven. There are playful renderings of Broadway tunes (Till There Was You) and Motown chestnuts (You Really Got A Hold On Me, Please Mr Postman). George and Ringo even get to do one each. *With The Beatles* showcases not only the creative talent but the group's cohesion, all pounded into place by Martin's intimate-sounding production. An album that lives up to its title.

Late on a summer morning in the dining room of the Palace Court hotel, Bournemouth, the photographer Robert Freeman took the famous 'half shadow' shot for the cover. That one image would be so widely studied, reinterpreted, sampled and stolen by so many acts, in so many different styles, that it truly revolutionised pop art. You had to hand it to the Beatles; even their album sleeves were incendiary.

Along with millions of others, McCartney loved *With The Beatles*, which Lennon came to see as a 'cop-out'. The inscrutable nature of the duo's creative pact – John as the famously sarky observer of 'real life', Paul as the chirpy, tell-a-story one – was fast becoming an issue. With a few notable exceptions, they rarely collaborated again as equals. The pattern from now on was that one man would turn out the main feature and the other would add focus. Around the time of *With The Beatles*, McCartney first admitted thinking that he could almost certainly write a number-one hit without any help at all. But he wasn't quite ready for that, not yet.

McCartney still went up to Liverpool every chance he got, though nowadays this took military planning. Jim would typically get a call around nine at night, telling him to turn off all the lights in the house as if he were going to bed. With luck, the doorstep girls would fold camp for the day. Thirty minutes later, in scenes reminiscent of *Mission: Impossible*, a decoy car would drive up Forthlin Road while a second vehicle with smoked windows pulled up in the rear, Paul and Jane, both dressed in black, scurrying through the back door, which was then bolted behind them. Since neither of them could step out in daylight without being mobbed, they tended to leave again before breakfast.

Back at Wimpole Street, the Ashers always remembered the wet night when John Lennon came over and he and Paul politely asked to borrow their music room. In a final flourish of the old fifty-fifty style, they sat side by side at the piano, 'playing into each other's noses' in John's phrase, before returning upstairs to ask the family if they fancied hearing a 'wee tune', actually one of the birth cries of rock and roll. It was called I Want To Hold Your Hand. Featuring a plunging, dive-bomber bass, those twin-octave vocals – and several other dazzling effects – the Beatles' fifth single brought off the rare trick of mixing experimentation with sales.

Big sales. I Want To Hold Your Hand took *advance* orders of over a million copies, and stayed at number one for six weeks. Meanwhile, *Please Please Me* was knocked off the top of the LP charts by the Beatles' own follow-up, and various EPs were going gold. All in all, the British public would pay £6,250,000 for Beatles discs during 1963.

Only one thing troubled Eppy and the boys as they turned the pages of *Record Retailer*. America had so far remained immune to Beatlemania. In a Dick Rowe moment, Jay Livingstone, the head of EMI's sister company Capitol, had passed on Please Please Me with the curt note, 'We don't think the Beetles [sic] will do anything in this market.' He much preferred the Beach Boys. A small Chicago label named Vee Jay eventually released the single, which did nothing. In May, Vee Jay issued From Me To You. It did nothing. The Swan label tried next, releasing She Loves You in August. It also did nothing. (*Billboard* finally gave it a small mention on page thirty-two, next to their 'help wanted' ads.) The record industry, like much of the country, would then go into a tailspin as a result of events that autumn in Dallas. Having seen their young president assassinated on the very day home fans queued in their thousands to buy *With The Beatles*, the US was in no very good mood to welcome four goofy Brits with nutty haircuts.

Early on the morning of 31 October, the Beatles had flown back to Heathrow from a short tour of Sweden. The scene that greeted them that wet Thursday had lifted even Paul, who was in the dumps about his mother on the seventh anniversary of her death. Five to six hundred fans (many of them now sporting Beatles moptops) were jam-packed onto the Queens Building balconies, screaming and tearing at their clothes. Intrigued, a small, jowly man, dressed like a funeral director, who happened to be in the terminal changing planes, ventured upstairs to see what all the fuss was about. His name was Ed Sullivan, and for the past fifteen years he'd hosted a top-rated Sunday night variety hour on American TV. For most of that time 'Uncle Ed's' show had consisted of the most familiar, family-oriented fare, with one or two mild concessions to youth: back in 1956, he'd introduced the viewing public to the 'singing truck driver' Elvis Presley, whom the cameras showed only from the waist up. Like most Americans, the middle-aged Sullivan had never heard of the Beatles. He did, however, recognise mass hysteria when he saw it, and rapidly sought out Epstein to talk about having the boys on his show.

A day or two later, Paul informed Eppy with great dignity that 'I'm not going to the States until we're number one there.' After the laughter died down, McCartney was reminded that even a big name like Cliff Richard had bombed on his one American tour, while She Loves You was just now being played on a few college radio stations, to deafening indifference. Paul wasn't the slightest bit fazed, assuring everyone that the Beatles would conquer the biggest and toughest market in the world within a couple of months. Actually it took three.

On 5 November, the morning after the Royal Variety show*, Epstein flew to New York with his twenty-year-old travelling companion Billy J. Kramer. Eppy's first port of call was the dark-panelled Capitol Records office on Sixth Avenue. By mid-afternoon he was busy haranguing Livingstone's colleague Brown Meggs, the Director of Eastern Operations, assuring him that the Beatles were, truly, the Next Big Thing. As proof Epstein brought out a reel-to-reel recording of the song Paul and John had knocked off a month earlier in the Ashers' basement. Meggs flipped on the tape with no visible sign of excitement. His idea of a hit was Surfin' USA, or, more recently, the 'Jiving Jap' Kyu Sakamoto warbling Sukiyaki. Two and a half minutes later, he slowly crushed his cigar, shrugged in despair and finally muttered, 'Well, we'll do our best.' A release date for I Want To Hold Your Hand was set for mid-January 1964. Hopping

* Asked by the Queen Mother where he was performing next, McCartney had bowed and mumbled, 'Slough'. Her Majesty – in a Beatlesque quip of her own – had replied, 'Oh, near us.'

a cab to the Delmonico hotel, Epstein rapidly agreed with Ed Sullivan that the Beatles would appear on two shows in February at $3,500 a shot. (Seven years earlier, Sullivan had paid Colonel Parker and his truck-driving protégé five times as much.) Eppy then hurriedly changed into full evening dress and an opera cloak to enjoy a night out on Broadway, before flying home a day later. Everyone agreed he cut quite a dash.

Epstein and his men were hard at work the rest of that winter selling the Beatles. Activities included writing long letters to the BBC, drafting press releases and arranging for the occasional reporter to go backstage. Their frame of reference began with a photo spread in *Melody Maker* and ended with a polite review in *The Times*.

In other words, compared to an American PR campaign, they did next to nothing.

If 1963 was the year a mass market discovered the Beatles, then '64 would go down as the year the Beatles discovered mass marketing. Paul Russell, the Capitol merchandising boss, reacted to I Want To Hold Your Hand with a blitz that owed as much to Sullivan's patronage and word of mouth as to any corporate acumen. As well as trade ads in *Billboard* and *Cash Box*, there would be media kits, photos, badges, buttons, banners, decals, posters, stickers and 'exclusive accessories' – everything from socks to Beatle wigs. If a teenager could wear it, Paul and the boys were on it.

Thanks to NEMS the band itself was keeping a tight schedule, fulfilling a thirty-seven-date tour of old art deco fleapits from Carlisle to Portsmouth. It was one wild night after another. At each stop a ruffle-shirted MC would bound on stage and ask, 'Do you want to see John?' (Roars). 'George?' (Roars). 'Ringo?' (Roars). 'Paul?' (Mayhem). A frantic pop party then followed, with stretcher cases and arrests. As the curtain came down there was generally a full-scale riot in progress, suddenly ended, as if by a thrown switch, by everyone freezing in place for the national anthem. The year closed with a sixteen-night Beatles Christmas Show, devised by Eppy, complete with panto, comedy routines and a little music.

For a couple of hours after each gig, John would mutter darkly about having to dress up in a topper and cloak to 'fook around' in some farce in which he invariably played the role of the villain. Paul, by contrast (invariably the hero), did whatever it took, cheerfully getting into the spirit of the thing and repeatedly thanking the audience on the band's behalf. He remained every mother's nomination for son-in-law. Even now he was endlessly accommodating, posing for as many snaps and signing as many autographs as time and energy allowed. Unlike John, he never considered himself off duty.

As Capitol rallied its sales force into 'Beatles Are Coming' mode that new year, McCartney and the band trained their sights on Paris. Opening night at the Olympia theatre was a flop, with a chaotic, ten-act bill including jugglers, clowns and other, less easily classified turns, several equipment failures and a backstage brawl involving both French and Italian paparazzi. During breaks in the nineteen-day residency, McCartney might stretch out in his suite at the George V with a bottle of wine and a couple of fetching local fans or, when she was in town, don a false beard and stroll down the Champs-Elysées with Jane. There were trips to the Follies-Bergère and the Louvre, and several sittings for his own portrait and bust. Somehow, he was also writing throughout. On 29 January, the Beatles were woken early by George Martin, who was under orders to take them into Pathé-Marconi studios to cut German-language versions of She Loves You (*Sie Liebt Dich*) and its follow-up, *Komm, Gib Mir Deine Hand*. This ordeal over, Paul then announced that he had a 'new one' ready. Everyone stared at him. Was the guy for real? Strapping on his Gibson acoustic, McCartney settled on a stool and ran through the tune, which even John greeted with a spluttering puff of cigarette smoke and the word 'Yeah!' Martin loved it too, but again suggested that they gas it up by going straight into the chorus – 'Can't buy me love'.

When Paul got back to the hotel he had them send up a grand piano, the better to work on some of the songs that became *A Hard Day's Night*. That he was now reportedly making £500 a week didn't slow him down. Just the reverse. Later that winter McCartney turned up for a brainstorming session at Lennon's home with the words, 'Let's write ourselves a swimming pool.' Meanwhile, George Harrison was worried about keeping up payments on his new car, and Ringo just wanted to make enough to open his own hair salon.

The next weekend in Paris, Jane Asher was still trying to persuade Paul to get up from the piano and take her shopping. 'She went down on one knee, literally begging him,' says Dezo Hoffman, one of Eppy's photographers. 'No good. When Paul wanted to do something, he did it.' A night or two later, Hoffman and his rival Harry Benson both got an urgent call to come up to the hotel and take some shots. The Beatles had just heard that I Want To Hold Your Hand was number one in America, and they wanted to celebrate.

Back in New York, Capitol Records had seen dramatic returns on its marketing strategy. A few radio stations had gotten hold of advance copies of the single, and were being flooded by calls asking about the Beatles. With Ed Sullivan's encouragement, Capitol's sales jihad swung into top gear over that holiday season. By Christmas Day, two entire factories in New Jersey were working round the clock to turn out all the T-shirts and wigs. The record and the merchandise were soon selling one another. Capitol had thought that I Want To Hold Your Hand might shift a total of between 200–220,000 throughout the US and Canada. From early January, they were busy selling in half a million copies a week, and ordering more just as soon as the plant could press them.

On 3 February, the Beatles visited the American embassy in Paris to obtain their H-2 work permits, strictly contingent on there being 'no unemployed US citizens capable of performing the job themselves.' Four days later they were safely aboard Pan Am flight 101, bound for New York. Also on hand were Eppy, Neil Aspinall and Mal Evans (all busily forging 'Love ya, Paul' on thousands of glossy photos), a few lucky journalists and sundry British and American entrepreneurs who, one by one, thrust themselves before Eppy throughout the seven-hour journey with their foolproof schemes for more Beatle boots, shirts, jackets, hankies, aprons, masks, lunch-boxes, chewing gum and dolls. Meanwhile, nervously pacing the first-class cabin was a tiny, frizzy-haired man in shades who occasionally bent down for a word with Paul or John: the producer Phil Spector, whose reign as America's 'tycoon of teen' would suffer a sharp reverse due to events over the next fortnight. Spector was so uptight about flying that on one of his passes he looked down at the card game McCartney was playing and groaned, 'Fuck me. Ace and queen of spades. The death hand!'

At 1.20p.m. local time, the Beatles' plane – the *Clipper Defiance* – landed in a light snowstorm at the recently christened John F. Kennedy airport. Everyone sat and waited, and waited. There was no chit-chat, just increasing nervous anticipation and repeated whispers that a big crowd was there to meet them. Finally the cabin door swung open, admitting a blast of arctic air, and even the Beatles gaped: 4,000 screaming, banner-waving fans were packed onto the Arrivals building balcony.

Gazing at this scene, Paul, first out of his seat, smiled at John and murmured, 'This is the business.'

The author Tom Wolfe, then a cub reporter for the *Herald Tribune*, would long remember the stampede that followed. 'There were hundreds of boys, high-school students, running down the Terminal hallway with their combs out, converting their ducktail hairdos into bangs. They'd just seen the Beatles . . . They saw these haircuts, and they started combing their hair forward so it would fall over their foreheads like the Beatles . . . I'll never forget that scene. That was symbolic of a big change; the last semblance of adult control of music *vanished* at that moment.'

After the formalities, the Beatles were hustled into the airport's press room, where 200 reporters and cameramen were waiting for them. Epstein's friend Brian Sommerville, a lantern-jawed ex-Navy officer-turned-journalist was there to 'handle' the media. A stern taskmaster at the best of times, the next few minutes would put unbearable strain on his fragile PR sense. When Sommerville appeared at the podium, he snapped on a pair of thick, horn-rimmed glasses and took a good look around. The sight must have jolted him: he snatched them off again at once and started to polish the lenses. When his requests for 'Silence, please' were repeatedly ignored, Sommerville yelled 'Belt up! Just belt up!' before recovering himself.

'Good afternoon,' he said at length, giving a brisk salute. 'My name is Sommerville. Mr Sommerville,' and he chalked up SOMMERVILLE in big letters on a blackboard, to make sure they'd understood. While the Beatles stood quietly behind him, smoking and smiling, the press corps were busy hollering, 'Down in front . . . Gimme some room . . . Whatsa matter . . . Hey, guys, lookie over here!' After several angry chops of his hand, Sommerville at last managed to start a Q&A session, which brought a revelation. The Beatles were *funny*.

Reporter: 'Will you sing something for us?'

John: 'We need money first.'

Reporter: 'Was your family in showbusiness?'

John: 'Well, me dad used to say me mother was a great performer.'

Reporter: 'What do you think of the campaign in Detroit to stamp out the Beatles?'

Paul: 'We've got a campaign of our own to stamp out Detroit.'

Everyone guffawed. Gazing down on an audience whose own heads strained upwards, McCartney beamed. 'We have a message,' he said.

Suddenly there was a moment of silence. 'Our message is,' he began, 'buy more Beatles records!'

Paul and John were brilliant at this sort of thing, and happy to do whatever it took to win American hearts and minds. They may have been pushing on an open door. The country had been in a state of shock for eleven weeks – the day the Beatles arrived there were pictures in the paper of a grim-faced sheriff holding up the rifle used to assassinate President Kennedy – and thus about ready for the band's inoffensive thrills. You could argue that the 'whole Beatle fantasy' (Lennon's words), about equal parts escapism and therapy, was so spirited, and so successful, because it had so much real unpleasantness to fend off. Paul himself believed that 'we bit America and it went mad.'

Epstein had done his part in setting up the Sullivan show, but otherwise appeared at a loss during the next two weeks. They were an educational experience for him. Eppy seems to have only half understood the Beatles' dollar potential, and had entrusted the US marketing rights to one Nicky Byrne, a man he'd met at a cocktail party in Chelsea. Byrne then formed a company called Seltaeb ('Beatles' backwards), to which Epstein agreed to give ninety per cent of the American spinoffs. Seltaeb's first act was to co-ordinate its efforts with Capitol Records. Its second was to meet with the Reliant Corporation, which paid $25,000 against ten per cent royalties for the rights to manufacture a Beatles T-shirt. In the week of 7 February, two million were sold. The band's accessory-heavy tour would soon create a phenomenon in which a cheap wig became, in and of itself, a cultural icon. Six months later, Nicky Byrne's partners in Seltaeb began proceedings against him, alleging $150,000 had been spent on his own 'comfort and benefit', specifically including round-the-clock limos, private planes and Tiffany's jewellery for his girlfriends. At that stage Epstein also sued Seltaeb and Byrne launched a countersuit against NEMS. Millions of dollars of business was lost while the Beatles brains trust tore itself to shreds.

★

Home for the next week was the venerable Plaza hotel, with two or three hundred fans prowling the corridors and at least five times as many on the street. A one-time candidate and future president, Richard Nixon, had stayed there just the night before, without incident. He even joked about buying himself a wig. As McCartney, by contrast, appeared in the Plaza's marbled lobby, pandemonium broke out. Appraising the mob, two large New York Irish policemen grabbed an arm and a leg each and carried him like a tailor's dummy to the relative safety of the elevator. Paul got up to his suite on the twelfth floor, poured himself a drink and turned on the first colour TV set he'd ever seen. All three networks were showing wall-to-wall Beatles.

'The Civil Rights Bill gets less attention than a freak show!' the NBC commentator shouted. 'What's going on in America?'

Responding to dozens of invitations, three of the four boys (George had flu) eventually managed some New York nightlife. Paul was smuggled out the back entrance, wearing his standard disguise (hat, false beard, shades) and his standard expression (big tipsy smile lighting up his face). His destination was the Playboy club, which he left some hours later with a bunny girl.

Meanwhile, the Ed Sullivan Theatre had received 56,000 ticket applications – well subscribed, for a room seating 700. On 8 February the Beatles rehearsed on a set consisting of large white arrows pointing in at them, their sponsor 'want[ing] to symbolise the fact, they're here.' Sullivan himself soon appeared, a dead ringer for Nixon, whirring around with his stiff, robotic walk. 'Who sings the songs?' he barked at Epstein, watching nervously from the wings.

'That one,' Eppy said, pointing at Paul.

Elsewhere in New York, the generational clash started the moment the band arrived, and continued through their wisecracking performance at a photo shoot in Central Park. This was the era of sanitised 'rock 'n' roll' on such safe, Saturday afternoon shows as

American Bandstand, and Ricky Nelson's forays in *The Adventures of Ozzie and Harriet.* Young performers weren't meant to talk or act like the Beatles, who showed distinct signs of intelligence beneath their bangs. With half the city now going nuts, the other half became tetchy, making it a point of honour to show their independence by griping. One wag at Radio WNEW announced that I Want To Hold Your Hand ought to be titled We Want To Hold Our Noses. The *New York Times* judged the Beatles a 'fine mass placebo' and 'preposterous', mild stuff compared to the band's anonymous critics who offered to tar and feather them, if not bash their fucking skulls in. Paul, who got his very own first death threats, would later remark to Jim Mac how so many people in America had seemed so strangely uptight. For all its size and sweep, there was 'nothing that hip' about a society whose choice of presidency lay between Lyndon Johnson and Barry Goldwater.

It was now the Sunday evening of 9 February; the Beatles were back at the Sullivan Theatre, where their host clanked around his dressing room, trying to memorise all their names. Perhaps rashly, Eppy chose that moment to walk in and announce, 'I'd like to know the exact wording of your introduction.'

First Sullivan reddened. Then he said, 'I'd like for *you* to get lost.'

When the moment came, around eight that night, Ed kept it short. '*Lezz 'n gennlemun, the Beatles. Let's bring 'em on!*' It wouldn't have mattered if he'd been reciting the Black Panther Party manifesto, because the words were lost in a cyclotron of hormonal abandon. Amid ear-splitting screams in the studio audience, the band did All My Loving, Till There Was You and She Loves You. After an interlude from the banjoist Tessie O'Shea, they returned for I Saw Her Standing There and I Want To Hold Your Hand. Five songs, three led by Paul. Several papers were already referring to him as 'the cute one' and 'the star'. John sometimes used the same terms, not affectionately.

The Beatles enjoyed mixed reviews for their first Sullivan appearance. They got a Trendex rating of seventy-three-and-a-half million viewers, then easily the largest in television history.

As Jim later noted, that snowy Sunday night changed everything for 'our kid'. It was now that he transcended the label of mere pop star and became, once and for all, *Paul McCartney*, the lead in a forty-year melodrama of fame, feuds and frequent dunks in the tabloid trough. It also provided something of a turning point for Sullivan, whose show would come to vary its standard line-up of elderly Broadway stars and acrobats with the likes of the Stones, the Doors and Janis Joplin. A final beneficiary were bands such as the Dave Clark Five and Herman's Hermits, who enjoyed a shocking American chart success in the year or two ahead.

On 11 February, the Beatles played their first US concert, at the Washington Coliseum. 8,000 fans lapped up the tightly choreographed package of big ballads, jubilant harmonies and flying pudding-bowl haircuts. On Valentine's Day, America fell more in love with McCartney than ever, as snatches of Coliseum footage were aired in between news of the Warren Commission and the first, curt reports from Vietnam. The broadcasts showed a man on top of his game, smiling broadly and, every few bars, snapping his left hand off the bass to shake it aloft. He'd since added a cute touch to the Beatles' Carnegie Hall gig (ninety per cent female clientele) on 12 February. After twenty minutes of sustained audience baying, with rowdy whoops of 'Paul!' and 'Ringo!', McCartney gained a semblance of order by stepping forward as if to speak.

He did. He invited everyone to join in on the next song and make some noise.

Meanwhile, Sir Alec Douglas-Home, in town for talks with President Johnson, found himself being asked more questions about the Beatles than about South-East Asia. The US Attorney-General had some trouble getting into the Plaza for lunch with his family because of the thousand or so screaming girls at the door. 'We've never seen or heard anything like it,' he reported. His name was Robert Kennedy.

The Beatles had one final treat ahead. Everyone flew down to the Deauville hotel in Miami (from where they did another Sullivan show) for some much-needed R&R. The scenes that greeted them made New York look Anglophobic by comparison. A girl in a polka-dot bikini immediately attached herself to McCartney at the airport and rarely left his side for the rest of the week. Next in the receiving line was a rep from MG Motors, who turned over the keys to a red convertible for Paul's use while in Florida. No charge. If there was a moment when McCartney was at his happiest in America, it was in this car. His only complaint? That the MG wasn't large enough to take all the birds he wanted to invite out for a spin. Once decanted into his room Paul ordered up a steak and lobster dinner, Mal Evans acting as a kind of turnstile against the non-stop, all-female siege at the door. One enterprising local girl, Lucy Gentry, queue-jumped by coiling up under the room-service trolley and, once inside, telling Paul she loved every one of his songs, which was good. He, in turn, loved her speedy, romantic pledge to make no demands on him the minute after they parted, which was better. The evening ended with Paul, Lucy and the girl in the polka-dot bikini allegedly lying in a king-size bed, each one with a glass of champagne, looking down on the ocean.

McCartney: 'You kidding? It should have been Can Buy Me Love, actually.'

Having conquered America, Paul was back in the Ashers' house in Wimpole Street. As well as being 'a bit of posh' the place had the bonus of being a *salon*: Jane was busy filming *The Masque of the Red Death*, and guest-starring in *The Saint*, while writing pop reviews, opening village fêtes and generally being the It Girl of 1964. Her sister Clare was also in showbiz, appearing on the radio soap opera *Mrs Dale's Diary*. Their brother Peter, a bespectacled nineteen-year-old with red hair that he brushed forward in a Beatle cut, formed an Everlys-style pop duo with his schoolfriend Gordon Waller. That May they had a number-one hit with World Without Love, a song Paul wrote for them. Their mother Margaret was a vivacious ex-conservatory musician and latterly teacher, one of whose students had been George Martin. Not surprisingly, the family's table talk tended to the stage and the arts scene in general. 'Everyone was always shrieking and doing impersonations' is one fond memory. Presiding over it all was the brilliant and voluble figure of Dr Richard Asher, artist, collector, and world-renowned consultant in blood and mental diseases (himself a manic-depressive), co-discoverer of Munchausen's syndrome, best-selling author of *Nerves Explained*, and of a scholarly paper on mass hysteria. The single greatest cause of which now happened to be living directly above Dr Asher's study, in a room furnished by a bed, a guitar, a piano, two Cocteau sketches, and a hand-drawn sign over the door saying 'Paul's Place'.*

There was square and there was hip, and then there was the world in which the Ashers and their house guest lived. Before long, the place could have doubled as the set for a rather heavy-handed Beatles biopic, with herbally scented rooms and flowery murals, crossed with some of the shrill dottiness of P.G. Wodehouse. The family regularly sat down with ten guests to lunch, fifteen to dinner. Jane thought nothing of taking twenty or thirty phone calls a day from giggling girls, to whom she was heroically polite. Dr Asher explained that he had to keep the number public because of his medical practice. There were generally a dozen or so fans at the front door, though Paul sometimes made his escape by climbing out of his attic room, shinning along the parapet, jumping onto the roof next door, knocking on his neighbour's window and going down in his lift to the

* On 26 April 1969, Dr Asher's body was found lying at the foot of his house, in the doorway of the room where Paul and John wrote I Want To Hold Your Hand, an empty bottle of Scotch nearby. The cause of death was given as a mixture of alcohol and barbiturates.

cobbled mews behind Wimpole Street, where the Beatles' chauffeur would pick him up in a black Austin Princess. It was all a long way from the Speke council estate.

On 2 March, McCartney and the Beatles began shooting *A Hard Day's Night*. The original idea was to turn out a cheesy, Elvis-style romp and a matching album. Paul then brought in the scriptwriter Alun Owen (*No Trams to Lime Street, The Concrete Jungle*), and the sharp-talking Dick Lester, of Goon Show fame, was hired to direct. The studio deal, even after haggling, was far below even the modest norm of a 1964 feature-length movie. *A Hard Day's Night* would be shot for £180,000 (of which the band were paid a flat fee of £25,000), or roughly what a B-list star today makes in perks. But it was enough. Cavorting around various locations in London and the South-East over the next six weeks, the Beatles made that rare thing – a day-in-the-life story that was fresh, funny, and with a snappy beat.

On 27 March, Paul and Jane Asher were at a sixteenth birthday party for the singer Adrienne Posta. Also present was their friend John Dunbar, a young Cambridge graduate who wrote art reviews, and Dunbar's 'chick', a thin, tooth-white girl who looked like something out of a Scott Fitzgerald novel: Marianne Faithfull. Appraising her blonde hair and stunning face, modestly turned, Andy Oldham had a vision of 'an angel with big tits' and duly signed her. Faithfull had a Top Ten hit that summer with As Tears Go By, but, like Peter Asher, proved sadly short-lived as a pop star.

Fresh from wrapping *A Hard Day's Night*, the Beatles brought down the house at the annual *NME* Poll-Winners' concert at Wembley. Bottom of the bill was a Mancunian group called the Mindbenders, featuring a future member of 10CC, and McCartney collaborator, Eric Stewart:

It was a weird scene . . . I'm backstage and Paul comes out of his dressing room, throws his arm around me and says 'Wotcher'. Smashing bloke, very down to earth. John was a very uptight guy I didn't like too much. George and Ringo sort of grunted.

Later in the spring the Beatles were forced to play in Hong Kong and Australasia with the session drummer Jimmy Nicol, after Ringo came down with tonsillitis. Nicol found John friendly and George not. McCartney was the 'detail guy', fussing about whether Nicol had the right clothes and boots, telling him what to do on stage, and offering various bits of fan-management advice once back at the hotel.

He was always 'there' for you, whether you wanted him there or not.

A Hard Day's Night. Single and album hit in July: from the opening bolt of the title tune to the tick-tocking fadeout of I'll Be Back, these were songs that soared far above being merely a movie spin-off. In fact the first thing you noticed, once past the checker-board cover, was how the titles sounded angry: I Should Have Known Better, You Can't Do That, Tell Me Why. These were wry self-assessments by John, who went on to write I'm A Loser a few weeks later. Balancing it all was McCartney's collegial enthusiasm and peerless bass playing. Can't Buy Me Love was the most fun that anyone could have with four strings. Paul's Things We Said Today set the seal on a gamut-running LP that spent nine months in the chart.

The film, too, got rave reviews ('the *Citizen Kane* of jukebox musicals' said *Village Voice*) and a premiere at the London Pavilion. Many arts critics came to scoff, but were forced to concede that it was 'fresh, irreverent', with 'daring camerawork, fast cuts and breezy improvisation', all in all 'a blast of propaganda not only for the Beatles but for the much vaunted "younger generation".' Jim Mac was there, dolled up in his old dinner jacket, on the eve of his sixty-second birthday. Later there was a small party back at the Dorchester hotel, just the Beatles, their families, and Princess Margaret. At midnight Paul toasted his father with champagne and handed him a painting of a racehorse; the horse itself, called Drake's Drum, followed the next day. A year later it romped home at 20–1 to win the Hylton Plate at Aintree, earning its proud owner £6,000 – 'the only money I ever made on [the] nags.' Jim sat down for a Q&A session with *Sporting Life* immediately following the race. His occupation, he said, was 'retired salesman'. And then he added, with a deep chuckle, 'I just retired.'

By then Jim was living in Heswall, Cheshire, in a mock-Tudor villa called Rembrandt also bought by Paul. Mike McCartney had trained as a hairdresser but was now launching his own group, a surrealist prank he called Scaffold. Jim vividly recalled the day in 1963 his younger son quietly announced that he meant to go under an alias. If he wanted to change his name, Jim had said, why not change it to something as far from 'McCartney' as possible, say 'Smith' or 'Jones', rather than 'McGear', which was Mike's choice. It was a fair point. What it may have missed, however, is the underlying psychology. McCartney. McGear. Mike wanted only to 'retain a little dignity amongst the chaos', and never meant for a clean break.

Paul, meanwhile, was busy defending the family name from a second woman claiming to have borne his child. In late 1963, Anita Cochrane, a nineteen-year-old from Liverpool, had begun writing hurt letters to NEMS. At this point, the conflict, if there was one, was still just a 'girlfriend problem' as Epstein termed it. When McCartney declined to answer, Cochrane took to sending the office various maintenance claims on behalf of her son, whom she called Philip Paul. The following spring Eppy allegedly made a 'full and final' settlement of the affair, involving a small payment and no admission of liability, though this seems not to have pacified the girl's uncle. He rather spoiled the *Hard Day's Night* premiere by parading up and down the street, distributing thousands of leaflets accusing Paul of being a delinquent father. Mal Evans was delegated to quietly remove him.

Others saw the Cochrane affair as less a paternity suit than a warning sign for Jane. To them, it was the same Paul who slept with dozens of women while on tour and told those who asked what his chick thought, 'I don't care what she thinks. We're not married.' Around the Beatles in '64 gossip had it that McCartney was, in so many words, a randy sod. What struck them was how much he seemed to love the whole Asher set-up, with its heady mix of good conversation and free food, more than he loved Jane herself. Things We Said Today, a tune he wrote for her, may have sounded on the surface like yet another big, brown-eyed ballad. But to insiders it was Paul taking stock ('You say you will love me/If I have to go') and predicting the worst. 'Jane was very naïve,' says a friend.

From the time *A Hard Day's Night* hit the screens, Epstein was working his boys to the brink. On 12 July the Beatles played the Hippodrome, Brighton, the first in a series of summer concert parties at traditional seaside resorts. Later in the month they did back-to-back sessions for BBC Radio, headlined an all-star revue at the Palladium, toured Sweden for the second time in nine months and, on 11 August, began work on a new album with a view to a pre-Christmas release. Even the chirpy Paul was beginning to feel the strain, particularly now the gigs had plunged into orgiastic chaos, dinned out by young fans who howled their way through most numbers. They also shrieked, squealed, wailed and cooed, and there were long stretches in many songs when they did little else. McCartney's public performances took place in a gale of shoes and handbags sailing over the footlights, love notes, often pinned to bras and underpants, and the occasional well-thrown bottle or chair leg. He once took a full carton of cigarettes to the face, not to mention the usual quota of fruit, veg and other missiles. During an appearance in Sydney, Paul had to stop the show twice because the group were being pelted with jelly beans.

Late one night McCartney was sitting on a stool in Abbey Road after the fourteenth take of a new song, Baby's In Black, when George Martin walked by and affectionately squeezed his arm. 'Not so hard, OK, mate?' Paul said, squirming a little. 'I've got so many bruises I look like I've gone twelve rounds with Cassius Clay.' He was half joking, but only half.

On 19 August, the Beatles began their first full American tour at the Cow Palace, San Francisco. The mad geography and one-paced, wham-bam rocking of the shows were matched by the decadent lunacy backstage. Paul and John, in particular, were regularly presented with wheelchair-bound children, whose hysterical parents shouted, 'Go on, kiss him! Make him walk again!' In California, a brisk street trade was done in the band's used bed linen, as well as in hairs allegedly pulled from their combs. Vegas followed, then Seattle's Coliseum. All afternoon the joint was rocking to a lusty chant of 'Paul! Ringo!' which soared up to the pain threshold as showtime approached, and went on from there to get rowdy. Sweating profusely, McCartney paused for a moment before running on. The famous eyebrows arched when he saw the sheer scale of it: 14,045 customers, 600 stretcher cases. Frantic girls bounced up and down on their chairs like popcorn. After twenty-five minutes the Beatles were spirited away in an ambulance while several hundred fans finally managed to rush the stage, which they then kicked to matchwood. Back at the hotel, it transpired the local promoter had arranged to buy the carpet in the band's suite (number 272, today a shrine), cut it up and sell squares of it as souvenirs. The boys put paid to this plan by pissing all over it.

After barnstorming around America for a week or two, McCartney knew that his life had changed forever. So did his security people.

Death threats now came in daily for all the Beatles, particularly the two cute ones. When pop critics opined weightily on Ringo's unique 'low' style (crouched down over his drums, cymbals raised high) few could have known that this was to minimise the risk from snipers. By now the *Washington Post* had referred to the four Scousers, who a year or so earlier had all been broke and living with their mums and dads, as 'the most powerful agent for positive change' on earth. And, as the band knew from their viewing of *Superman*, their favourite American TV show, with great power came great risks and responsibilities. As ever, Paul was the calm centre of the storm. One paper called him 'a charmer, coquettish . . . almost the girl of the group' in his eagerness to please. This went over well with the female members of the audience, but won a few churlish reviews (such as 'GO HOME, LIMEY FAG!') from the men. Every action has a reaction, and Beatlemania would find its counterpoint in Beatlephobia. Lennon, too, was evidently beginning to have second thoughts about both the band and McCartney. At the crux of their ongoing debate, even more than Paul's feeling that John could be more positive, was the fact that Paul believed, actually he *knew*, it was all worthwhile, as in: 'Fuckin' 'ell, lads. It's showbiz!'

In New York the Beatles first met the tousle-haired, somewhat vacant figure of Bob Dylan, who came bearing marijuana. McCartney put his introductory roach in his mouth, lit it and slipped *The Times They Are A-Changin'* on the turntable. A toke or two later, Paul suddenly discovered the meaning of life, which he had the presence of mind to jot down on a scrap of paper. Squinting at his notes in the cold light of dawn, he read, 'There are seven levels.' In scenes out of *A Hard Day's Night*, the band made their post-gig getaway next night in Atlantic City by jumping off a pier into a speedboat, which took them offshore to a waiting hospital ship. Several hours later, back in the Lafayette hotel, Mal Evans opened a door to usher in a conga line of scantily clad women, who briskly fanned out, sat in people's laps and lit cigarettes. 'Help yourselves, lads,' he announced, rather unnecessarily. On 31 August, Paul managed a brief phone conversation with Elvis, who was stoned. All the Beatles were uptight about playing Dallas ('Lorra guns here, are there?'), and appalled by the public facilities, still marked 'White' and 'Colored'. The shows as a whole seemed to lose a little zing down South. McCartney refused to go on in Jacksonville until Eppy came backstage to personally assure him that the audience wouldn't be segregated.

On 22 September, the *New York Times* reported:

> The Beatles flew home to England yesterday with the rings of girlish shrieks and more than $1 million in receipts as the echoes of their month-long tour . . . It was considered one of the most successful of its kind in profit, attendance and attention.

The paper added that, though they left in relative quiet, 'four thousand screaming fans gave them an uproarious welcome when they landed early in the morning at London airport.'

A few hours after the big reunion, Jane found herself sitting in the kitchen at Wimpole Street, rapt, as Paul spun tales of the road. These were both funny and dramatic, if also selective. There was a bottle of wine and music from Margaret's pile of records – Handel, Stravinsky, Cage – to fill the lulls. McCartney seemingly told his girlfriend that he'd behaved himself immaculately, and she had 'nothing to worry about'.

And Jane did, by and large, buy Paul's line. Even when gossip about all the groupies and love children began to surface, says a friend, 'she thought the sun rose and set on him.' A more serious issue, by far, was Asher's blunt refusal to give up her job. Paul liked a fixed routine and his 'old lady' there to cook and clean for him. Jane wanted what she'd had since the age of twelve – the chance to perform for her public. The spate of songs McCartney wrote about Asher in 1964–5 would offer a good chance to study their ups and downs: She's A Woman – exuberant, with vocal and bass lines both pushed to their limit; Another Girl – trouble ahead; I'm Looking Through You – self-explanatory. Meanwhile, You Won't See Me (a straight Motown lift) kept it as short and sharp as a ransom note. While it was admirable McCartney chose to exorcise his personal demons through work instead of wallowing in self-pity, Jane's friends could only wonder. She remained Paul's genial cheerleader.

On 9 October, the Beatles began yet another tour, fifty-five shows in twenty-five towns in thirty-two days. No wonder the next American number one Paul knocked off with John seemed a trifle harried. After *A Hard Day's Night*, it was realised that the band had a major tax problem – as well as the tour fees and royalties, Northern Songs was being floated on the stock exchange – and Eppy advised everyone to buy property. To that end, Lennon paid £60,000 for a twenty-seven-room mock-Tudor pile next to a golf course in Weybridge, Surrey, with Queen Anne furniture and a baronial fireplace. On a rare morning off that autumn, McCartney was chauffeured down for a songwriting session. As they turned into the lane Paul looked up from his *Daily Mail* and asked the driver whether he was keeping busy. 'Busy?' he said. 'I've been working eight days a week.' McCartney walked into John's all-black study, sat down and told him, 'I've got a great title.'

Meanwhile, Jim McCartney, after eight years of widowhood, had met a Kirby woman twenty-eight years his junior named Angela Williams. After three or four nights out together, Jim invited her back to Rembrandt, casually put his hand on her shoulder and said, 'I've got something to ask you. I'm rattling around this place all on my own. Do you want to be my housekeeper or my wife?'

Angela gave it a second, then chose the latter.

The recently widowed Angie was in many ways a perfect applicant for the role they had in mind. She and Jim had friends in common, both enjoyed a drink and a laugh, and liked to potter around the Rembrandt garden. Angie was attractive (a former 'lovely legs' winner at Butlin's), well spoken and discreet. What's more, she had a five-year-old daughter, Ruth, whom Jim adored. A few months later, the three of them heard their names called out over an airport tannoy as 'Mr and Mrs McCartney, accompanied by Ruth Williams.' Jim turned to the girl there and then and said, 'I'm going to adopt you.'

After Angie agreed to his marriage proposal, Jim got on the phone and rang Paul at Wimpole Street. Five hours later the younger McCartney appeared at Rembrandt in his midnight blue Aston Martin, having found a service station willing to sell him two dozen red roses. There was an awkward moment as he and Angie looked each other up and down, but for the most part it was a happy and quite emotional occasion. After a glass of champagne Paul asked to meet Ruth, asleep upstairs, who recalls:

Angie brought me down in my Tesco's flannelette pyjamas and put me in this guy's lap. What's this, I thought, and looked up into the most famous pair of eyes in Britain. Paul was great . . . I remember showing him my scar where I had a kidney removed and him saying, 'You should see our Ringo. He's *covered* in scars.' Lovely bloke, at least in those days. Smashing with kids.

Jim and Angie were married on 24 November 1964 at St Bridget's Church in Carrog, North Wales. Both McCartney brothers attended, Paul leaving early in the Aston Martin to record for BBC Radio's *Saturday Club* – coincidentally his favourite programme while living at Forthlin Road. The service was conducted by a former hospital colleague of Mary's, and, due to administrative error, the hurriedly delegated best man was Griff, the gravedigger.

Meanwhile, *Beatles For Sale* was released in Britain and America, on different dates and by different names. An oddity, there were a few clunkers: I'll Follow The Sun (also from Forthlin Road days) was vaudeville meets pop, but not in a good way; and much of the rest was a mooch through the old Hamburg stage act, with Ringo, for some compelling reason, assuming lead vocals on Honey Don't. Set against the turgid country and western workouts were the witty and tuneful novelties, all McCartney's: the pioneering fade-in and walking bass to Eight Days A Week, not to mention the effects-laden What You're Doing. While Paul and John both laughed at their music publisher Dick James with his *Robin Hood* past, they privately agreed he sometimes had a point. James often told them they needed to write more 'proper songs' that had a beginning, middle and end to them. He thought the stuff on *Beatles For Sale* 'all over the shop'.

That album lived up to its title, too, with a year on the chart.

1965 began with the jangly electric guitar and rumbling tom-toms of Ticket To Ride. Here some discrepancy exists between McCartney's version of events ('We sat down and worked on it together for a full three-hour session') and Lennon's – 'Paul's contribution was the way Ringo plays the drums.' Whatever its true authorship, Ticket was proof of the Beatles' ability to have it all: to entertain their audience and challenge them, too. Released as a single on 9 April, it ushered in a new era in which Paul and John would focus more on the studio than what a critic had dubbed the 'wet panty hysteria' of the gigs.

In tangible recognition of the creative team, in February that year Northern Songs went public. Dick James retained 37.5 per cent of the shares, Paul and John fifteen per cent each. Shortly after the successful launch, Lenmac Enterprises – a private company owning the copyrights, controlled eighty per cent by Paul and John and twenty per cent by Epstein – was sold to Northern for £365,000. The first result was the freeing up of a tidy lump sum for McCartney, who now had an account at Coutt's from which both he and Jim could draw a few thousand whenever they felt like it. The second, unforeseen result was the disastrous loss of his own songs. When, in 1969, Northern was sold to Lew Grade's Associated TeleVision, Lenmac went with it.

On 22 February the Beatles began work, if it could be called that, on their second film. This was a sorry farce called *Eight Arms to Hold You*, eventually retitled *Help!* Partly for tax purposes shooting began in the Bahamas, where, possibly thanks to the collective ganja intake, Paul was directed to spend a day swimming, fully clothed, in the pool of his Nassau hotel. Three weeks later the action moved to the Austrian Alps. As usual, McCartney was busy writing throughout.

Lennon came in to the band's suite one night for a drink and stayed to listen to a tape of the new album-in-progress. After Paul's Another Girl and two or three others, John muttered, 'I probably like your stuff better than mine.'

In those days, McCartney still valued Lennon's opinion; with a combination of bemused pride and trepidation, the older man had watched him assume the songwriting role as if watching a baby take its first hesitant steps. As with his own child, John also tended to be blunt. From the start he'd been the one to tell Paul 'That line sucks.' The result was a true and time-tested partnership. Yet, by 1965, the old firm's days were clearly already numbered. Ferociously competitive, each man typically had both a title and melody in hand before calling in the other. Only then would they go down into the music room, smoke, yawn, joke a bit and get to work. The end product was popularly known, not least of all by them, as 'Paul's song' or 'John's song'. It was sadly symbolic that a number of early McCartney-Lennon originals, all co-creations, were lost forever when, spring-cleaning about that same time back in Wimpole Street, Jane threw away a notebook she took for 'junk'.

Walking around the streets of St John's Wood between sessions late one afternoon, McCartney had begun to hum the bluesy riff of She's A Woman. Turning the corner to the studio he played the song through on his guitar, start to finish, and asked John what he thought.

Lennon peered at him for a moment over his glasses. The same terse qualities that made John so good in interviews came into play here, as he searched for the words with most telling effect. 'Fook me,' he said, at length; and that completed the creative exchange. She's A Woman was recorded on the spot and released as the B-side of Lennon's own I Feel Fine.

McCartney seemed to be quarrying his work night and day, whether on holiday in Tunisia (where he dreamt up Another Girl) or sitting in the basement at Wimpole Street, where he startled the

Ashers one afternoon by breaking into a sound like a hollering, half-slaughtered hog, which became the rock 'n' roll classic I'm Down. A mutual friend remembers sharing a smoke with Paul and Jane at the opening of the Pickwick club in London that Easter. 'There's nothing like the eureka moment of knocking off a song that didn't exist before – I won't compare it to sex, but it lasts longer,' McCartney explained cheerfully. The reference was vintage Paul: 'You could be fooled by the fact that he was the big, money-making machine,' said the comedian Frankie Howerd, who shot a few scenes for *Help!* 'Underneath all that, he was just a guy. And a very horny one, too.'

Between clubbing and recording Paul still headed north whenever he could, which these days was about twice a month. He obviously doted on young Ruth, his stepsister, who remembers him taking her to Chester by bus, and driving her to London for the latest Carnaby Street gear. This was in notable contrast to his adult relationships. On one overnight visit McCartney had a misunderstanding with Jim about the latter's policy on drug use in the house. Another bone of contention was Paul's hard and fast rule that no other guests be present when he stayed at Rembrandt. Angie once forgot herself after the sudden death of her sister and invited over a few friends on a weekend her stepson also happened to arrive.

Paul wasn't happy. When Angie began to apologise McCartney turned on her and reportedly noted, 'This is my house! Don't forget I put the food in your mouth! If it wasn't for me, you'd all be on the street!'

'No one,' adds Angie, 'ever broke Paul's rule again.'

Many column inches have been devoted to the Beatles' next great move. It began life one morning in mid-May, when McCartney woke up in his room at Wimpole Street with a melody running through his head. With its rich, yearning tones and intricate 'leaning' notes, this was a pretty superior kind of dream. Paul stumbled over to the small piano he kept by his bed to capture such moments, ran through the tune, jotted down a few lyrics, then fell asleep again. Over the next week or two he tinkered with the song – now going under the title Scrambled Eggs – before flying to the Algarve for a short working holiday as a guest of the Shadows' Bruce Welch. Immediately he arrived, McCartney asked Welch if he could borrow a guitar. He spent the next three days strumming and toking out on the terrace overlooking the sea, returning to London in response to a news flash that the Queen had awarded John, George, Ringo and himself the MBE. It was a typical manipulation of the honours system by Harold Wilson, though one the Beatles deserved more than most, and which thrilled Paul. Once back at Wimpole Street he excitedly rang Jim and issued a statement confirming that he and his father both thought it 'cool', and that Mary, too, would have been proud. Scrambled Eggs became Yesterday.

The basic track was cut at Abbey Road on 14 June, George Martin adding the then unheard-of classical touch by way of a string quartet, each paid around £5 for their labours. (McCartney's own preference had been for an electronic backing supplied by twenty-eight-year-old Delia Derbyshire, the avant-garde force behind the *Doctor Who* theme music.) Yesterday was finished in a two-hour session on 17 June, mixed into mono, and released as an album track seven weeks later. It was the perfect ballad, and McCartney knew it: 'Now it looks as if *we're* here to stay' the Beatles sang in their next Christmas message to members of their fan club. 'Of the gods!' the weekly *Review* screamed after Paul performed Yesterday on American TV.

John Lennon, by contrast, was never quite sure about the song, privately referring to it by the slightly extended title of Yester-fuckin-day and calling it a 'good tune for Matt Monro'. (The venerable crooner did, in fact, have a British hit with it.) Lennon was said to have ground his teeth when McCartney played the song on the *Ed Sullivan Show*, to a coast-to-coast audience of seventy-two million, backed only by members of Sullivan's orchestra. The haunting quality of his performance left the teenage girls in the studio audience apparently unsure of how they were supposed to react. The Beatles knew how they felt. Neither John, George nor Ringo contributed a note to Yesterday, and legend insists weren't even present when it was recorded. The matter would rankle even beyond the grave: some thirty-five years later Paul sought to reverse the song's credit to 'McCartney-Lennon' on his own albums, a move John's widow resisted. The London *Evening Standard* quoted a source close to McCartney as saying, 'He thought they had sorted everything out. He's really angry that she's chosen to do something this petty.'

In 1965 Paul's attitude to John was very much that of one who happened to live in the shadow of an active volcano. He tried to stay out of the way of Lennon's periodic eruptions, but if he cursed the 'old git' at times, he was also proud and fiercely protective of the man who, when not on the road, spent much of his time stoned out of his head in his stockbroker-belt villa. The journalist Maureen Cleave would characterise John just then as the 'laziest person in England'. Even in the frantic, beat-the-clock sessions that produced *Help!*, McCartney demonstrated an unerring knack of zooming in on a song's weaknesses – ones Lennon might sense as he sat around the studio, but rarely bothered with. Paul always did. He made both fans and a few enemies by his professionalism and inability to suffer fools gladly – an issue, particularly, when the fools happened to be his fellow Beatles. Various minor tensions also surfaced while off duty. McCartney sometimes took Lennon with him to visit Rembrandt, where he's remembered as once having nodded off at the dinner table and, on another occasion, asking the sixty-three-year-old Jim, 'Are you a tit man?' John also complained that Paul, with his roguish charm, seemed to be coming on a bit strong to his wife Cyn. Behind the suavity, Lennon noted, hid 'a randy sod'.

Early August, *Help!*: The first Beatles LP to thrill and amuse their public, and educate them as well. (In America, where the disc came padded by six 'golden greats' from the George Martin Orchestra, consumer reaction was more mixed.) By now even the most naïve fan could distinguish between songs, which break down here along party lines: Paul's, tuneful and sometimes childishly simple; and John's, which tend to hard-bitten Dylan pastiches. With their fifth album, the boys establish themselves for all time as deeper, more cynical and more varied than the yeah-yeah stereotype. Admittedly, there are a couple of false starts: McCartney's The Night Before retreats to the stark, two-chord territory of Love Me Do, and Harrison's I Need You runs out of steam halfway through. But then, with the fat beat of Ticket To Ride, things take a dramatic turn for the better, indeed for the stupendous: *Help!*'s flip side packs in Act Naturally, with Ringo's infectious hooting, Paul's folk-rock I've Just Seen A Face – and Yesterday. Other delights include the title track, a frazzled take of Dizzy Miss Lizzy, and, thanks to John, some distinctly tougher lyrics of sadness, frustration and bile. *Help!*'s release that summer coincided with a marketing initiative successfully aimed at selling the Beatles as serious musicians: it spent thirty-seven weeks on the chart and proved what a waste of time, and of remarkable talent, the film of the same name was.

Throughout the spring and early summer Epstein had been planning a second full-scale US tour in conjunction with General Artists Corporation (GAC), America's largest theatrical agency. The hard-nosed men at GAC were amazed at how little the foppishly clad 'Queen of England' (as one memo called him) seemed to know of the business. In fact, at thirty Eppy's best days, personal and professional, were already behind him. His once-flourishing stable of Liverpool talent had failed to move with the times, he was staying up all night and sleeping all day, fuelled by a mixture of hog tranquillizers and brandy, on top of which there were gambling debts and blackmail. Paul was sufficiently alarmed to seek out the Rolling Stones' new American business manager, one Allen Klein, to negotiate with EMI on the band's behalf. Eppy saw off the challenge, but it was all he could do to get the boys on the plane to New York, that Friday 13 August, without a mutiny.

As for the performances: on the 15th the Beatles set an attendance record of 55,600 (paying $305,000) at Shea Stadium, under the steely gaze of the *New York Times* critic Murray Schumach:

> Magnificent and terrifying . . . At the end of the concert the group rushed into a car that had been driven onto the field near their stand and sped off amid shattering cries of vexation and adoration . . . For more than an hour afterwards, fans were being rounded up in the stands and carried and pulled away. The police were so upset by the event many forgot to remove the cotton they had placed in their ears after the first shrill outbursts.

In Atlanta, Paul and John at times seemed to be singing two entirely different songs. Station-tannoy acoustics. Fawn-coloured army tunics, apparently tailored by a blind military fetishist. Minneapolis, where there were 'LIMEY FAG' banners and the police arrived at the band's hotel in response to complaints about scores of naked girls running amok through the lobby, inappropriate here in the Midwest. The chief of police informed the press, 'Those people are the worst I've ever seen visit the city.' A blonde young guest named Judy Flanders, flushed from McCartney's room, produced a driver's licence establishing her age as twenty-one. 'I doubt she was older than sixteen,' the chief told the reporters.

Portland: After ten minutes of pneumatic drums and ropey harmonies, it was borne in on Memorial Coliseum that it wasn't to be one of those nights of virtuoso musicianship. McCartney, at least, gave it everything he had, tossing his head around, his mouth twitching open and shut like a small valve. For those high up in the stands, the band looked like a distant Punch and Judy show, with Paul and John circling each other and bopping up and down.

Meanwhile, Eppy and Colonel Tom Parker had spent the best part

of a month negotiating the 'terms of engagement' for a meeting
between the Beatles and Elvis Presley. This historic Sixties scene took
place at Elvis' pink, doughnut-shaped pad in the Hollywood Hills late
on 27 August. There was the sense of a momentous encounter that
warm Friday night, a rock 'n' roll version of the Allied leaders
converging at Yalta, if sadly less productive. When the moment came
the five musicians sat around, amid several medallion-clad handlers,
with nothing, apparently, to say to one another. McCartney tried hard
not to stare at the house, which had been furnished in a one-hour
whirlwind trip to the Miracle Antique Mile in Pasadena, though he
openly admired his host's new-fangled TV remote control. Eventually
a jam session broke out, but this rather fizzled when Paul good-
naturedly advised Elvis to 'make more records like the old ones'.
Elvis, despite one or two public statements to the contrary, despised
the Beatles. Eppy was distraught that an event into which he put such
high hopes should have turned into such a fiasco.

Five years later, a pilled-up Elvis – then just entering his rhine-
stone phase – invited himself to the White House in order to debate
'youth culture' with Richard Nixon. Once inside the Oval Office,
Elvis sat down and began a long diatribe against drugs in general and
the Beatles in particular. 'Those guys are a major force for the anti-
American spirit,' he announced. 'They came over here, made their
money and went back to England.'

This summit, too, ended badly, when the shrill, giggly tones of two
secretaries in Nixon's outer office came over the intercom – 'Did you
see Liberace?' were the exact words – killing the conversation. The
president hadn't troubled to flick the 'off' switch.

Elvis' was precisely the fate McCartney would go out of his way to
avoid. Despite a taste for uncomplicated sex and recreational drugs,
he was always the most self-disciplined of Beatles; as Maureen
Cleave would remark, he was the 'only one of them who [could] tell
you what the date was. The other three barely knew what year it was.'

The sixteenth and last American gig, in San Francisco, was the familiar riot, with a few boos echoing from the bleachers for the chaotic performance. After three weeks on the road, even McCartney was a bit wan around the edges. But all he had to do was flash that killer smile and he was irresistible – something his US fans had known ever since Paul burst onto the scene as the impish good-timer on that first *Sullivan* show. As he flew home to a typically lusty reception, he was able to boast an impressive CV for the summer. He'd played live to some 340,000 customers; performed Yesterday to a TV audience 200 times as large; entertained everyone from Bob Dylan and Brian Wilson to the Mayor of Chicago; stayed in some of the world's best hotels, as well as some of the worst; had a bullet-filled envelope anonymously sent to him through the post; charmed innumerable press conferences, signed thousands of autographs, 'rooted himself silly', according to Judy Flanders – and been described as a 'dedicated hoofer', which Paul said he didn't mind at all.

And yes: now and again he'd also worked on his songwriting.

A lot was riding on the result – financially for EMI, which was still paying the Beatles the grand sum of sixpence (2½p) for every LP sold, and thus earning the company and its suppliers an incredible ninety-five per cent of the action, and creatively and personally for the ambitious Paul.

The result, *Rubber Soul*, was the Beatles' great breakthrough from – John's phrase – their 'knicker-wetter' days into the acid-fuelled adventures to come. McCartney's legendary work ethic (virtually a song a day) entered a new phase, an era of herbally tinged cigarettes, convivial be-ins, freakouts and happenings, and late-night readings from the *I-Ching*. He even began to dress the part, experimenting with paisley shirts and flares in-between tasteful bouts with Eppy's Savile Row tailors. Most nights after recording, he was at one of the new ultra-hip London clubs, like the Ad Lib, that somehow packed in three or four hundred people – throbbing, sweating, dancing the conga and crashing into the laps of strangers. (Much how Paul bonded with his first wife.) Then it was typically on to Wimpole Street, where steak and chips were served at five a.m.

He and Jane broke up several times that autumn. She packed a bag and went off to stay with a girlfriend, or perform in some provincial theatre, leaving him behind with her mum and dad. Talking to friends like Allan Clarke in the Ad Lib, Paul complained that he wanted his bird at home with him, while Jane insisted she work; that he'd seen his own mother flog herself back in the bad old days, and couldn't understand why a woman would want to do that when she didn't have to.

There were times when his unhappiness was also a source of inspiration. After one furious lovers' tiff McCartney went upstairs to his room and fired off the lyric and tune to I'm Looking Through You, adding a chorus he yelled at the top of his lungs. When, that October, Jane 'again pissed off', he complained, to work in rep, he wrote the snappy riff and suicidal words of You Won't See Me. Both these songs would go through a series of agonizing redrafts before Paul deemed them fit for recording. He was 'drained emotionally', Judy Flanders says. '"My chick doesn't understand me. Help." That sort of thing. He was crying, really crying.'

The self-pity didn't last.

Paul was up at Rembrandt one sunny weekend, strumming a guitar under the beeches in the back garden, when he hit on a catchy verse/chorus that, inside twenty minutes, became We Can Work It Out. The next day he and Lennon added the brisk middle eight ('Life is very short . . .') and brought it into the studio on 20 October. The standard critical line has John's dry realism countering Paul's rampant affability, though the original lyrics are rather darker than the title suggests. Jane's reaction was, by all accounts, effusive. Something about the song moved her. 'No, I'm not Paul's wife,' she told the Sunday press. 'But, yes, we're going to get married.'

*

As it happened, just a week earlier Paul and John had knocked together a larky, Stax-like tune called Day Tripper. Lennon sang the lead, and while agreeing it was 'nothing great' wanted it as the Beatles' next single. McCartney, backed by Harrison, Starr and Martin, lobbied actively for We Can Work It Out. There was a stand-off, with John muttering in his cups about Mr Showbiz ('his voice could put babies to sleep') and vowing revenge – somewhat surprising, seeing that the band's public profile just now swung to an all-time high: on 26 October the boys were driven to Buckingham Palace, amid VE Day-type mob frenzy, and led to the state ballroom to be invested by the Queen. Next day Paul happily pronounced the place a 'keen pad', and later let slip a more private detail. The four of them had been gently stoned, having slipped their escort long enough to enjoy a crafty drag in one of the royal washrooms.

A day or two later, EMI decided to market Day Tripper and We Can Work It Out as a double A-side. Lennon wasn't happy with the compromise. By now he was brooding about his being a wage slave, and blamed the pressure for his frequent bouts of depression. One day Paul wondered aloud, in one of his regular philosophical asides, what the world would be like if everyone were a genius – what if every tea lady or navvy were born with the brains of a Bertrand Russell? John considered the question and remarked that on the whole, the world would be a better place: 'But – a lot of people would have to die at EMI first.'

By October 1965, McCartney had lived in the Ashers' upstairs box room for two years, rent free, though he'd arranged to have the outside of the house painted for them. He and Jane remained a public item, beloved of the London 'in crowd', even as they squabbled behind the scenes. Aside from Jane's career there was the fact that Paul, with his singular charm and fame, inevitably acted as a lightning rod for a certain degree of female affection. Cynthia Lennon would characterise him as the 'town bull', while to Judy

Flanders he was 'one cool customer . . . Champagne and roses at night, a pat on the ass in the morning.'

Nonetheless, when McCartney bought his first property, a three-storey Regency house at 7 Cavendish Avenue, just east of Abbey Road, Jane joined him there. The place cost him £40,000 and £20,000 to decorate, which 'took forever'. McCartney installed a Victorian coaching lamp in the drive and, within, brightly coloured bean bags, a formal dining table, Porthault bed linen that he had changed daily, two oil paintings by Magritte and a sheepdog of uncertain pedigree named Martha, all bathed by special 'trippy' lighting. The overall impression was of a Sixties art gallery with submerged Olde English charm. Cavendish Avenue also came to feature an outdoor 'meditation chapel' in the shape of a glass dome, for 'getting in touch with your karma'. It was a rich irony, perhaps, that Paul chose to install a huge round bed, once owned by Groucho Marx, bang in the centre of it.

Meanwhile the house, discreetly hidden by an eye-level wall, became something of a rock star crash pad. Since the other Beatles all lived in suburbia they frequently gathered at Cavendish Avenue before being chauffeured the two-minute journey to Abbey Road. Over the years, various other musicians, artists and poets came to be entertained to tea and a smoke, often joining McCartney for a sing-song around his psychedelic-painted piano. Paul later remarked that he'd 'turned Mick Jagger on to pot' on such an occasion. 'Which is funny, because you'd have thought it would be the other way round.'

On 11 November the Beatles removed the joints from their mouths long enough to finish the vocals for *Rubber Soul*, an LP of no little charm which duly hit the top by Christmas. For an album said to be inspired by various relationship woes, it was decidedly light-hearted: the opening romp, Drive My Car, wrapped an Otis Redding groove around a sassy lyric that was about far more than being chauffeured. Some of the same gag stole into Norwegian Wood, where, in a neat role reversal, it was John who wrote the moving stanza about a love affair and Paul who added the pay-off line about burning the girl's house down. Elsewhere there were various pranks involving Goon Show-type piano (The Word), plaintive French warbling (Michelle) and chanted backing vocals consisting of 'tit-tit-tit' (Girl). The lame pun of the album title was McCartney at his most waggish, if not inspired.

If more wordy than its predecessors, *Rubber Soul* was a typically well crafted affair, relying on a bubbling Ringo beat, basslines that refused to leave you alone and, on In My Life, a baroque piano fill courtesy of George Martin. Several tracks saw the Beatles bring folk and jazz stylings to bear on their old friend the pop melody. McCartney's Michelle was one of his lusher moments, an all-but solo turn with the band padding discreetly behind, and a chorus that sounded ominously like Nina Simone. Perhaps wisely, Lennon vetoed it as a single. Oddly enough, a tune American critics would hail as an instant classic had actually existed, in one form or another, for seven years. Paul had fished Michelle out of his grab bag, working it up from an old party piece he used to perform back in Liverpool Institute days, his friend Ivan Vaughan's wife, a French teacher, adding the '*Ma belle*' lyrics.

'Years later,' says McCartney, 'I sent her a cheque around. I thought I'd better, because she's virtually a co-writer on it.' Michelle, too, got the Matt Monro treatment, won a Grammy, and quickly became one of those standards that works its way under the skin, shedding spin-offs and a slew of re-releases and covers until it stopped being a song and turned into an industry. In the early days of 1966, Epstein called a group meeting in which he revealed that Michelle was enjoying some 6,000 plays on US radio every week, making it second in popularity only to Yesterday. He and Paul were ecstatic, gossiping and smiling to one another on the sofa. John, George and Ringo sat around yawning and fiddling with their beads.

★

The Beatles couldn't get any bigger than they already were. They could only get better, and more frustrated, chafing at their moppets' public image. The cutesy uniforms Eppy still insisted on in concert jarred badly against the shaggy Afghan garb, patched, multicoloured jeans and grannie glasses the four of them increasingly favoured at home. Paul, in particular, was also beginning to experiment with sound techniques, making collages of revved-up guitar and distorted violins that sounded like shrieking seagulls, or performing on non-traditional instruments – fresh vegetables, for instance, in which he was something of a pioneer. (McCartney once turned up for a *Rubber Soul* session bearing a tape-loop consisting of wild tribal chanting mixed in with snatches of Benjamin Britten's opera *Gloriana*, a fusion suggesting that his wasn't a typical Tin Pan Alley sensibility.) The sunny tunesmith with the 'parent style', the switched-on artist dabbling in *musique concrète*; both were Paul. One way or another, he was becoming a being apart from the other Fabs.

The irony of the situation wasn't lost on McCartney himself.

'I was into a lot of those things,' he told Barry Miles. 'Which is very strange because I was known as the cute Beatle, the ballad Beatle or whatever . . . John was the cynical one, the intellectual. In fact at that time it was wildly in reverse. John would be coming in from Weybridge; he'd sit and tell me he was fucking jealous.'

McCartney and Lennon were agreed on one thing: the days of their hollering out hits while simultaneously being pelted with their fans' underwear were fast drawing to a close. The only ones who didn't ever enjoy Beatles gigs, it seemed, were the Beatles: their renown was such, John had noted, that 'we could send out four waxwork dummies of ourselves and get a reaction.' Both he and Paul, in particular, were exhausted, having aged far more than two years since 1963. Eppy, after wiring the group an itinerary for yet another Christmas tour, was coolly informed by all four of them that they weren't interested. He soon talked them into it, but, as the curtain rose in Glasgow on 3 December, even he must have sensed the obvious. Nine days later, the Beatles gave a deep, ironic bow, waved, and ran off stage at the Capitol cinema, Cardiff. At least in Britain, they'd heard the screams for the last time.

CHAPTER FOUR
'I Got My Thick Cardboard'

On Thursday night, 24 February 1966, McCartney stepped out of a car in London's Belgrave Square. His destination was the Italian Cultural Institute, where he sat in a folding school-chair at the feet of the world's first travelling professor in 'electro-acoustics', Luciano Berio, forty, who had a new work to stage for his invited audience. According to Berio, one of the most important features in the artistic process is repetition. So a good part of his performance that night consisted of a recurrent tape-loop, *Laborintus 2*, which combined readings from Dante with various droning sound effects. Then came an even more striking recording, featuring an orchestra playing at peak volume, and backwards, accompanying more or less the complete spoken works of T.S. Eliot. This went on for some ninety minutes. Then it was repeated.

McCartney, the author of Yesterday and Michelle, was entranced. A week or so later he made his way to the basement of the Royal College of Art for a world premiere (live performance, this time) by the composer Cornelius Cardew, twenty-nine, a one-time protégé of Stockhausen and Cage and later founder of the Scratch Orchestra. When Paul arrived Cardew's group were settling into a semicircle on the floor, unpacking their instruments – hammers, saws, electric drills, a cello, vibes and other percussion. To start proceedings off, one of the musicians blew a whistle while another drummed on a metal tea tray. Cardew, seated at the keyboard of a piano he never touched, muttered, 'Encore, encore', patting his sides with pleasure. The whistler and the drummer obliged. One of the other band members produced an old car horn and gave it a toot. A fifth musician then played a solo passage involving a tape deck and a signal-gathering device that emitted a 'ping' like a ship's sonar. McCartney himself, smiling and nodding his head, tapped vigorously with a coin on the edge of his pint mug, occasionally chanting 'Yeah, yeah . . .' The process was repeated for the next two hours.

The next morning, McCartney was driven in to a meeting at Dick James' Soho office. James had loved Michelle, a song from which he was making a small fortune. Before everyone got down to business, Paul excitedly related the events of the night before, adding that he fancied doing 'some of that Concept shit' on the next Beatles album.

James knew that he was dealing with a creative soul, but he'd never thought of him as nuts. He was inclined to think being 'arty' worse than that.

'Paul, why klutz around?' he asked him. 'We got a good thing going. Blow me! Stick to what you do best!'

McCartney just shook his head.

Yesterday was widely tipped to feature in the Grammys that spring, but lost out as Record of the Year to A Taste of Honey by Herb Alpert and the Tijuana Brass. McCartney expressed mild indignation. (His song did go on to score an Ivor Novello award in July.) There was mixed news for him, too, on the broader commercial front. A year earlier, Dick James had defied convention and taken Northern Songs public. Less successful, from McCartney's point of view, was the subsequent sale of Lenmac Ltd., which made John and himself £140,000 each – welcome at the time, but a woeful under-valuation of their songs' true worth. By a complicated series of

subpublishing deals, James also succeeded in holding on to
seventy-five per cent of McCartney and Lennon's royalty income
from North America and other foreign markets. Meanwhile, the
long-running feud between Epstein and his former merchandising
manager Nicky Byrne – who denied any wrongdoing – was
crawling through the New York courts, where in time it attracted
the attention of the Internal Revenue Service. The IRS now
attached $1 million of the Beatles' 1966 concert earnings, holding
the money, interest free, until 1976. On top of that, Eppy was still
agonisingly re-negotiating the group's deals with EMI and Capitol,
who from 1963–7 continued to pay their star corporate assets at
rock-bottom rates. Finally, no matter how much or little he
earned, McCartney was subject to Britain's then swingeing income
tax. Top whack, ninety-five per cent.

One way or another, those weekly meetings around James'
boardroom table were just barely civil. And who was paying, the
Beatles wondered, for all the Regency furniture and gold plate? With
so much at stake, friction was inevitable and hurt feelings the rule.

When McCartney slipped up to Liverpool (where he was on hand
to see his racehorse win the Hylton Plate on 26 March) there were
issues, too, with Jim and his wife. The years had transformed Paul's
father into a gaunt, grey-faced old gentleman increasingly crippled
by arthritis. A reporter named Alan Weyer, who tracked him down
at Rembrandt, found Jim 'slightly dotty'. He knew all the old dance
hall songs and with the slightest encouragement could sing them in
tune without benefit of an accompaniment. 'He was a little lost,'
Weyer adds, 'and, what sticks in my mind, kept referring to his
second wife [Angie] as Mary.'

Ruth McCartney: 'Sometime that spring there was a crisis. Jim sat
Angie down one morning and said, "Our Paul doesn't think this is
working out. He's told me we should pack it in. I'll buy you both a
flat or a little shop. What do you want?" "I want you," she told him.'

If Paul feared the worst for his father's marriage, as he said, he

Mother Nature's Son: Paul in 1948, aged six,
with four-year-old brother Mike.

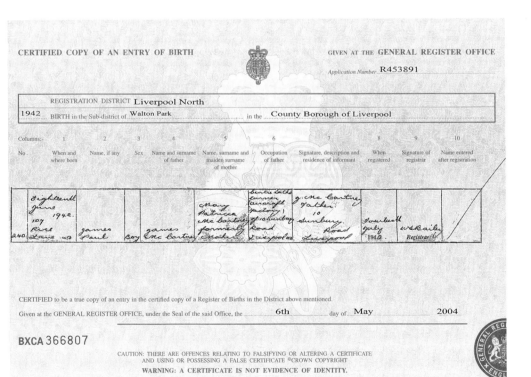

18th June, 1942 (Waterloo Day, traditionally a lucky day to be born): McCartney's birthday.

20 Forthlin Road, McCartney's boyhood home and scene of his early collaborations with John Lennon.

St Peter's Church Hall, Woolton, where the teenage McCartney and John Lennon first met.

Just before Beatlemania struck, with father Jim and brother Mike.

Love Me Do:
McCartney in 1962,
the year it all began
happening for the Beatles.

Jane Asher, the on-and-off future Mrs McCartney from 1963 to 1968. Cynthia Lennon says that 'The first time I was introduced to her was at her home and she was sitting on Paul's knee… He was obviously as proud as a peacock. She was a great prize.'

(Middle House) Wimpole Street, London, McCartney's home for three years, where he lived in a room 'furnished by a bed, a guitar, a piano, two Cocteau drawings and a hand-drawn sign over the door saying "Paul's Place".'

Miami Beach, February 15, 1964.
'You kidding? It should have been Can Buy Me Love, actually' McCartney was later to quip.

The Beatles in a rare off-duty moment in the US in '64, during the tour
that changed pop music forever.

Backstage at the NME Poll-Winners Concert, Wembley 1965 – Peter Noone (*right*) gestures to the camera.

Despite the smiles on their faces, the Beatles were about to cause a moral outrage thanks to Lennon's 'We're more popular than Jesus now' remarks. Just over a year later, their mentor and manager, Brian Epstein (*left*) would be dead.

Paul, George, John and Ringo at Shea Stadium, New York, 1966. One of the last concerts the Beatles ever gave.

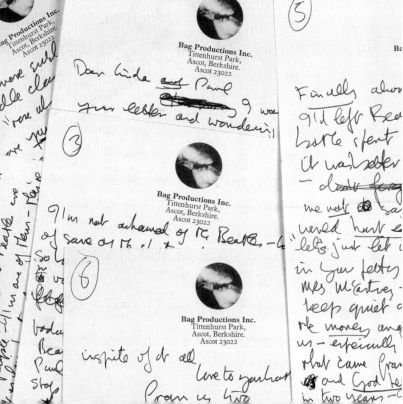

In the bitter Beatles' fall-out, Lennon expressed his views on McCartney and the band in a six-page letter; he gave Paul and Linda's marriage 'about two years'.

needn't have. Jim's relationship with Angie would survive for the next ten years. A subtle shift of balance would take place as Jim became a semi-invalid, and his wife assumed more day-to-day responsibility for running the house. As a result, it's possible Paul no longer enjoyed his trips north quite as much as he once had. More and more, he sought out other places where the battles of the overwrought, overtaxing Sixties could be left behind.

Cavendish Avenue kept McCartney waiting. At one point he was supposed to move in before Christmas, which slipped back to February. In the end, owing to the usual delays, the builders finished the new house to his satisfaction only in April 1966. Not long before he left, Paul wandered down to the Ashers' basement music room one last time. Jane's mother had recently arranged for a well-respected professional from the Guildhall School to give her house-guest piano lessons. She thought he might possibly benefit from the discipline. Waiting for his tutor to appear that wet morning, McCartney, confirming some of Margaret's views, began doodling an E-minor vamp on the keyboard, adding some gibberish words about 'Ola na tungee/With a head full of clay/No one can say.' At that stage the man from the Guildhall came in and Paul played him the tune, making some more of it up as he went along.

'The time jumps are crude, the melody naïve' was the verdict. 'It could be a big hit. What are your plans?'

'It's just something I'm working on,' said McCartney, vowing there and then never to take another piano lesson. Ola Na Tungee became Eleanor Rigby.

On Wednesday 6 April the Beatles drifted in to Abbey Road and began recording their follow-up to *Rubber Soul*. It would be the one in which the mind-altering drugs fully kicked in. The first track in the can, on which Lennon said he wanted to sound like the Dalai Lama singing from a mountain top, gave due warning that this was to be something more than all-round family entertainment. The next afternoon, McCartney appeared in the studio with the defining effect – a Co-op bag full of tape-loops, which were mixed in with John's alpine vocal, a sitar drone by George and Ringo's thunderously echoing drums. Tomorrow Never Knows, they called it, less than a year since Yesterday. It wasn't quite Lord Clark talking about world civilisation, but it was smart, fluent and well ahead of its time.*

The gap between how McCartney was seen in public and how he behaved in private wasn't just wide, but yawningly so. It was obvious now to insiders that this doe-eyed lover of sheepdogs and show tunes was a left-fielder who, so he told Lennon, planned to put out a whole album of loops – *Paul McCartney Goes Too Far*, he called it. In fact the sound collages were only the half of it. McCartney was also the first customer into London's new underground bookshop and gallery, Indica, to which he brought dozens of friends, including the other Beatles, and donated some £5,000. He was up to his neck in the proto-surreal generally, whether collecting pieces by Magritte or thrilling to the avant-garde playwright Alfred Jarry. Not coincidentally, Paul was also ever more in thrall to pot, to which he wrote an ode on the next Beatles album, and soon fell in with the Tara Browne set, a collective of Swinging London's beautiful people, who offered him the finest LSD and cocaine. He didn't need a subpoena. McCartney later remembered Lennon remarking, '"You're never the same after [taking] acid", and I don't think any of us ever were.'

A good many other musicians were coming to the same conclusion. The magnificently hip singer-songwriter Grace Slick, for one, 'spent the year loaded', cranking out the dazzling songs that became Jefferson Airplane's *Surrealistic Pillow* LP. She remembers McCartney, whom she got to know in San Francisco, as a 'real sharp guy . . . I was quite taken. Even though John was meant to be the

---

*The song, which was initially called 'Mark I', 'The Void' or 'The Psychedelic Thing', actually took its title from one of Ringo's quips, which Paul and John were sharp enough to pick up on.

turned-on one and Paul the pop one, some of us had the sense it was switched around.' Another artist enamoured of McCartney was the celebrated Beat author William Burroughs. 'When I first met him, part of what interested me was the dichotomy. Here was this sweet-looking young kid who wanted to talk about tape-loops and putting animal sounds on his records. When I saw that, I said, "I gotta listen more to the Beatles."'

Sometimes, McCartney's dash for artistic growth backfired. In hindsight, album-cover photos of him and the boys wearing bloody white coats and holding up decapitated dolls were probably only a so-so idea. The whole image was so hideous, or incongruous, that an EMI director's wife vomited over her advance copy and the entire pressing of 800,000 sleeves had to be withdrawn.

The 'butcher shot' was then shelved for twenty years.

On 25 May McCartney met up with Bob Dylan, who was touring Britain and granting private audiences in his suite at London's Mayfair hotel. The two men enjoyed a toke and several cocktails before Paul, at his host's request, put on a tape of Tomorrow Never Knows. Dylan listened through to the final shrieking seagull effect and slowly exhaled a cloud of smoke. 'Oh, I get it,' he said at length. 'You don't want to be cute any more.'

'Yeah, that's it,' said McCartney.

On 10 June, the Beatles released Paul's song Paperback Writer, another novelty tune (he'd just written Yellow Submarine) with some deep-pile harmonies modelled on the Beach Boys. Like the previous ten Lennon-McCartney singles, it went to number one. In these new sessions, Paul appeared to be running in the same direction as John, George and Ringo, but he was also out ahead of them. Nowadays he often skipped the band rendezvous and drove himself to the studio before the others, presenting them with his ideas, and exactly how he wanted them played, when they straggled in later. One such was the lushly textured Here, There And Everywhere – another response, apparently, to Brian Wilson's songs. McCartney and Wilson formed a mutual admiration society, each speaking of the other as the 'greatest writer alive' and a 'soul twin'. (Among other coincidental similarities, their birthdates were only two days apart.) One way or another, McCartney was working all hours at Abbey Road, not only recording but now also sallying upstairs to the control room, previously the domain of George Martin and his boffins, for some technical exchange. Sessions for the band's seventh album ended on 21 June, with a release date set for August. Until then, except for a handful of devoted aides and a few lucky peers, the new music Paul and co. were developing remained a secret.

A hint that something might be in the air came with the quick follow-up single, Eleanor Rigby. That name famously appears on a gravestone in the Woolton churchyard where Paul met John, though the title seems to have been inspired more by the actress Eleanor Bron and Rigby's shop in Bristol, which McCartney passed one morning when visiting Jane Asher. Musically, the song owes a debt to Martin's wintry string arrangement, itself bridging the previously diverse worlds of Vivaldi and Bernard Herrmann's *Psycho* score. Lyrically, too, it was a breakthrough, putting death on the charts some thirty years before Marilyn Manson. All intoxicating stuff, and a wake-up call for pop music generally.

It, too, went to number one.

26 June, the Ernst Merck Halle, Hamburg. Just four years earlier, the Beatles had left town after a Star Club residency for which they were each paid £65 a week. Now they went back for a one-day fee of £8,000 split between them. After the second and final show, McCartney announced his intention to put on a hat and shades and make a nostalgic tour of his old haunts.

'Don't be silly,' tutted Epstein. 'You'll be mobbed.'

Paul laughed calmly. 'What the fuck do you mean, mobbed?' he asked with a smile, and pushed open the door. 'I'm only recognised when I want to be.'

Paul started whistling Yesterday and strolled up the Reeperbahn. No one bothered him.

Nine days later the Beatles were all but lynched in Manila, having declined to appear for a semi-official reception hosted by Imelda Marcos. Suddenly deserted by their local security detail, the four of them picked up their bags and ran, as best they could, through a jeering mob at the airport, Epstein taking a blow to the face and Mal Evans going down under a hail of fists. Once aboard their plane, the band were then required to part with half their concert fee in order to pay local 'taxes'. By the time the flight landed for a fuelling stop in Delhi, Eppy's face had welled up with angry red welts, everyone was cursing everyone else, and even Paul was muttering about chucking it all in. 'People were yelling . . . So was I. The Monkees days were over.'

London swung to its peak that summer, with McCartney joining men like the army officer-turned-art-dealer-cum-junkie Robert Fraser, Indica's Barry Miles and John Dunbar, the designer Christopher Gibbs, Tara Browne, David Bailey and sundry Stones and Animals at the heart of a scene headquartered in the Ad Lib club. A more general revolution was underway against the Britain of *Hancock's Half Hour*, with its grinding conformity and identical redbrick semis furnished just like grandmother's. After the drab years of rationing and austerity, Terence Conran's brightly coloured, brilliantly packaged Habitat became a flagship of hip, officially declaring the three-piece suite 'grotty' and 'far too boring' a concept. Instead customers would be buying a basic cotton-covered Larnaca sofa with a couple of related armchairs. Other, similarly enterprising retailers competed to introduce the UK to such exotic commodities as fresh fruit and shops that stayed open until after five in the afternoon. John Stephen and Mary Quant were showing that you didn't need to go to Savile Row or Bond Street for fashionable tailoring; out went old fogies in sensible suits, in came 'with it' young professionals in flares and miniskirts. Finally, and by a lucky bit of timing, the rapid availability of the Pill happened to coincide with the arrival of that other defining symbol of swinging bedroom etiquette, the duvet.

An air of sexual possibility charged McCartney's pad, too. Apart from three weeks or so on the road, he spent much of the summer at his new London home. Activities included strumming a guitar, making cut-ups, rolling joints, tinkering with his free-form sculptures in the basement and squiring around a prodigious number of actresses and models. In fairness, however, it should be noted that, for Paul, a lack of conventional beauty wasn't necessarily a handicap. It was enough that his companion be 'arty', or enjoyed a concomitant morality. Such women fairly threw themselves at him whenever Jane wasn't around, and once or twice even when she was. A businessman calling by appointment at Cavendish Avenue was struck by his meeting a young brunette dressed in what appeared to be a swimsuit, 'sitting demurely on a chair in the hallway [like] a job applicant.' Mal Evans, it's said, always recalled arranging a shift system on Paul's behalf, as well as the inevitable moment when, owing to sheer weight of numbers, one girl on her way in met another one on her way out. McCartney tolerated the administrative lapse with composure. 'He laughed and told them both to leg it upstairs and wait for him. They did.'

That summer, McCartney also purchased High Park Farm, set in 180 acres of rolling hills outside Campbeltown on a remote stretch of western Scotland. The place was an escape from the pressures of Beatlemania. It was also a 'total knocking shop' says one guest, a minor and notably unstuffy royal, who remembers she excited Paul's interest by going about braless. In time McCartney and his wife would decorate the place, but for now it remained semi-derelict – peeling wallpaper, bare boards, a smell of damp, peat, stale food – furnished with packing-case tables, chairs apparently made out of antlers and a couple of boxes thrown together as a bed. The bath was a rusty dairy trough set on a concrete slab outside the front door.

Back in March, Maureen Cleave had talked to Lennon about his new, switched-on view of life, which gave him an opportunity to share some thoughts on religion. 'Christianity will go,' John announced. 'It will vanish and shrink . . . I'm right and I will be proved right. We're more popular than Jesus now.'

No one batted an eye at the time these remarks were published in the London *Evening Standard*. But when, on 29 July, they appeared in the American teen magazine *Datebook*, something like a holy war broke out. With another US tour due to start on 12 August – including some dates in the Bible Belt – radio stations began banning Beatles records and, in several cases, organising their public burning. Death threats came in against both Lennon and McCartney, and Epstein, bombed on pills and still badly shaken by Manila, considered cancelling the whole thing at a loss to the band and himself of a million bucks.

Eppy pulled himself together, John apologised. But still they came, wave upon daily wave of hate mail and barely coherent promises to kill the evil Limey bastards: hack the cocksuckers' heads off, or something just as charming. Nor were the band's immediate families spared. In early August, Paul rang his father and stepmother, who happened to be on holiday in the South of France, to prepare them for the worst. The warning was as well; sure enough, the next two weeks were a nightmare. A bored agency reporter picked up the story in Nice and soon the forces of news-gathering were all over the frail Jim, who could mutter only, '*Non. Non. Pas de* comment.' On 11 August the Beatles themselves flew to Boston, where 400 police and plainclothesmen were deployed to keep them apart from the angry crowds at the airport. Their arrival later that day in Chicago knocked both the city's current race riots and the Vietnam war out of the headlines.

Now all that remained was the tour, which did not go well.

The Beatles' US audiences had always been quite effusive, but only now had they got down to mass psychosis. Every show was a multi-layered riot, with, typically, young fans up front with their hands stuffed down their briefs, behind them burr-haired men in their thirties and forties bawling obscenities, some dressed in the distinctive garb of the Ku Klux Klan, and, scattered throughout, the band's locally hired muscle advising all and sundry to shut the fuck up. The Olympia, Detroit, rapidly degenerated into a mob orgy, with punch-ups and arrests. Hysterical girls, sweaters customised with slogans indicating how positively they'd respond to any amorous move Paul might make towards them, stretchered out. Not a dry seat in the house. As the boys abandoned their instruments and ran, Mal Evans heard McCartney muttering under his breath, 'It means nothing. Nothing.' He wanted to play Tomorrow Never Knows; the kids wanted to hear She Loves You. The next day's show, in Cleveland, was delayed for thirty minutes when two to three thousand fans attempted to storm the stage. Two nights later someone tossed a firecracker at Paul just as he wheeled into Yesterday, causing him to fluff the first line. In Seattle the band came under a barrage not of bras and knickers but of insults and shaken fists, some of which held bottles, until the whole playing area was a war zone strewn with broken glass, twisted cables and mikes that cut in and out, leaving the Beatles barely audible. They got rave reviews, anyway.

Conversely, in both New York and LA the band (who phoned the shows in) played to thousands of empty seats. When they failed to fill Shea Stadium, *Variety* reported that the box office was 'solid, if not as spectacular as in previous years.' Putting it mildly. Even so, the Beatles were picking up sixty-five per cent of the gross, which translated into roughly $190,000 per stadium, or $6,000 for every minute they stood on stage. Paul: 'It was run on, take the money, run off.' Now even he was arguing that the 'freak show' gigs were ruining them as musicians.

He'd reached this conclusion after a nightmarish concert in St Louis, where 'it was raining and we had a couple of bits of corrugated iron over us. It looked like a mud hut in the middle of somewhere and there were people miles away cheering . . . We did the show and piled into the back of one of those panel trucks, like a removal van. We were sliding around trying to hold on to something . . . I swore a bit and said, "I've fucking had it." And the guys said, "Well, we've been telling you for weeks, man!" But finally they had my vote.'

Monday 29 August, San Francisco. It all ground down in a frantic hits party, which the Beatles sang through gritted teeth, and which they could barely hear. Real indignity befell the closer; while John did Day Tripper, Paul did Long Tall Sally. In a neat frame, the first date of the band's first American tour had taken place only a mile or two away. Everyone sprinted for the armoured car backstage and headed for the airport, where a young Catholic priest with a collecting box waylaid McCartney and asked him if he really thought he was bigger than Jesus. Paul said no, he didn't, and after chatting some more gave the man all the money he had on him, a ten dollar bill. On it he wrote, 'Love ya, xx'. The priest gave McCartney his blessing in return. His last question was whether Paul ever felt for the kids in the audience, or were they all just a ticket?

'Of course I feel,' McCartney said. 'I'm human.'

The Beatles then disappeared.

Other records had hinted at what was to come, and, thanks largely to Eleanor Rigby, a number of bands were busy adding touches of the baroque. But *Revolver*, out that August, had something else – intricate unison themes, dissonant chords, backwards tape-loops, and songs that ran the gamut from pop's crown jewels to 'Concept shit'. The Beatles' secret was out.

Forty years on, McCartney's name may have become a byword for middle-of-the-road craftsmanship. Blandness was not what came to mind when you listened to *Revolver*. As well as Eleanor Rigby and the big 'n' brassy Got To Get You Into My Life (a paean to pot) there was Good Day Sunshine, the best of dozens of songs celebrating that World Cup-winning summer. Slivers of folk, rock, blues and 4/4 waltz all rattled around in For No One, as befitted a man whose influences ran from the Fugs to Debussy. Even the smoochy stuff like Here, There And Everywhere took the melodic route less travelled. With Tomorrow Never Knows (mellotrons, seagulls and sitars to the fore, and thus problematical to reproduce on stage), the happy wackers from Liverpool turned into the time bandits who could do chamber music one minute, futuristic rave-ups the next.

Revolver hit the chart on 13 August. A week later, it replaced *The Sound of Music* at number one.

It was a long way from the baseball parks of California and New York to 7 Cavendish Avenue, where McCartney returned late that summer. Despite, or because of, all the refurbishment, it's remembered as a slightly gloomy spot that reeked of both animals and dope. These were the days of seeded marijuana; castaway seeds sprouted in the spongy rot of what had been the basement rug, and both main floors were crammed with a variety of antique cocktail cabinets, ashtrays, spittoons, bookcases, musical instruments, televisions and a huge, production-model VCR. No one ever saw much natural light. McCartney awoke late, and even then the windows and curtains remained shut against the dozens of fans hanging around outside day and night in the hope of catching a glimpse of him. Meanwhile, there were problems with the husband and wife domestic couple, the Kellys, who looked after the place. They were used to 'something better'. From time to time, McCartney had to restrain them from giving away some of his comfier clothes to charity. His table manners – which tended to the casual – drew muffled tuts of disparagement. There was a frosty scene whenever one of the Kellys met an overnight guest tiptoeing up or down the stairs. Eventually, Paul fired them for selling their story to a magazine.

McCartney had a distaste for being cooped up, and seems to have chafed against the idea of his 'be[ing] the squire of St John's Wood.' Compounding his restlessness, the 'old lady' – Jane Asher – was again off on location. Paul was clearly frustrated by this, and there was the added stress of knowing that, when Jane did appear, he was expected to talk about commitment and marriage. Only a week after coming off the road, McCartney summoned Mal Evans and told him he wanted to 'pack, lock up and drop out' in a foreign country. Any country. He wasn't fussy.

Paul and the Aston Martin set off late one morning to Lydd airport, where a cargo plane took them across the Channel. From Calais, he drove on to Paris. To fool the fans, McCartney had donned Coke-bottle glasses, slicked back his hair with Vaseline, then chosen a rather grubby mac to round off the cover, hoping to pass for a 'normal young Frenchie'. The country cops of the highways and byways, however, took him for a lunatic, and waved him through one town after another. Eventually he made it as far as Bordeaux, keeping a diary and a home movie of his experiences along the way. Mal Evans would remember that, in the end, 'Paul couldn't get back fast enough to wash his hair, ditch the specs and become a Beatle again.'

McCartney was changing so fast and so many mental connections were being made by him on the high tides of pot, that he decided to keep the docu-diary going, just for a lark. This wasn't to be your average litany of birthday parties and weddings. Typically, the films involved a collage of fast cuts, swirling camerawork, blinding lights and surrealistic studies of a ticking clock. Paul then synched it all up to a tape-loop symphony.

McCartney also lavished enormous attention on his social life. He remained a fixture at all-hours clubs like the Ad Lib and the UFO, where, a patron recalls, 'he went through the Young Things like a knife through butter.' Paul's taste in women ignored all considerations of age and appearance, and also spanned the class structure. There were debs and domestics, dolly birds and shopgirls, and one 'fantastic bit' whom he wanted to take on holiday, he once told Alistair Taylor, only he couldn't for the life of him remember either her name or address. (Taylor, by dint of detective work, tracked her down: Maggie McGivern.) Later that winter, Bill Wyman and his partner Astrid Lundström walked into a London nightspot, where they met McCartney and Neil Aspinall. After a while Wyman realised that 'Paul was playing footsie with Astrid . . . Later as we sat talking in the car near her flat we saw McCartney arrive. He spotted us and drove around and around her flat until he finally gave up and left.'

For then.

'What did Wyman expect?' asks a mutual friend. 'Paul was the most charming man. Paul was kind of irresistible. Bill was resistible.'

McCartney also found time, that autumn, to compose the sound-track to the Boulting brothers' feature *The Family Way*. It was an unchallenging commission, consisting of thirteen variations of a single song, but it seems to have had an inordinate effect on Lennon, who donned a false beard and hat to buy himself a ticket to the film, despite the disguise, 'one of the more embarrassing [purchases] I ever made, well on a par with my first packet of Durex.'

With the Beatles on hold, McCartney himself often traded in his famous brand name for an alias. Posing as Ian Iachimoe, the 'Polish new wave film director', he used the pages of *Long Hair Times* ('Global Moon' edition) to offer cash prizes for interesting scripts. One such involved an egg falling, in extreme slow-mo, into a dirty ashtray, and won its author twenty guineas. McCartney was also an enthusiastic backer of Britain's new underground paper, *International Times*, launched that October. The restless explorations continued with free-form 'soundscapes' and tapes of tribal drums 'n' pipes he recorded while on holiday with Jane Asher in Kenya. Later in the year McCartney, cloaked in flowing Arab robes, sat happily through a four-hour event at London's Roundhouse, where various slide projections were accompanied by screeching feedback effects courtesy of Pink Floyd.

Finally, in January 1967, Paul booked Abbey Road to record a subversively weird collage he called Carnival Of Light. Close on fifteen minutes of 'randomised freakout' ensued, with reverse tapes, distorted guitar and a sound like someone gargling all mixed in with Lennon yelling 'Barcelona!' Although performed twice at the Roundhouse, the piece was never commercially released. McCartney laid it aside to concentrate on yet another new work, named Penny Lane.

On the morning of 1 September 1966, a small, thirty-three-year-old woman dressed in black and surrounded by her collection of clay dolls and abstract tinfoil sculptures passed through Customs at Southampton docks, where she was hailed as a 'Nip' and asked, 'Off to the Continent, are we?' Her name was Yoko Ono, and her destination, she replied, was London.

Yoko's past, even by the standards of the day, was exotic. She was the daughter of a Tokyo banking family which abandoned her to a nanny and then emigrated to America after the war. There Yoko attended the upper-crust Sarah Lawrence College, eloped with an avant-garde musician, and settled with him in a garret in New York. When her parents disinherited her for this act of rebellion, she sent them a bottle filled with urine. Returning to Tokyo, she divorced her husband and married an American film-maker named Tony Cox, with whom she had a daughter. In time the Coxes moved back to New York, where Yoko achieved fame, of sorts, for a series of Warholian pranks – for instance, publishing a manifesto and another book, *Grapefruit*, consisting entirely of one-line 'instructional poems'. Over the years there would also be paintings, lithographs and Yoko's much admired 'performance art' in which, for example, she would pick a girl out of the crowd, stand her with her back to the audience, and carefully cut the dress off her. Or she might offer herself up for this ritual shearing. In the spring of 1967, Yoko persuaded 365 volunteers to have their posteriors recorded in full-screen close-up in a project entitled *Film No. 4*, described by its auteur as an 'aimless petition signed by people with their anuses.' One might say her interest in such things was bottomless, were the word not so inappropriate. Another of the more striking aspects of Yoko's art (particularly so in the context of the Sixties) was the pre-eminence given to women. Anyone reading her work was left in no doubt, as man after man was depicted as a fool or worse, that the world according to Yoko was electrified by the fervour of female intelligence. Not least hers. She and Cox had already come to the end of the road when, in August 1966, they casually accepted an invitation to a London symposium billed as 'The Auto-Destruction of Art'. Not long afterwards, Yoko dropped by both the Indica and an opening for the pop sculptor Claes Oldenburg, where she met McCartney, whom she thought might organise an exhibition for her. A day or two later Yoko turned up at Cavendish Avenue, talked her way inside, and asked Paul if he had any spare manuscripts of Beatles lyrics 'or other stuff' that she could present to her friend John Cage. He turned her down. Instead, McCartney suggested, she might like to try his old friend and partner out in Weybridge. Very progressive, was John.

Yoko, by at least one account, made quite an impression at Cavendish Avenue. According to this source, a man familiar with the day-to-day lives of the Beatles in 1966, the chemistry was very different than would be the case only a year or two later: 'People will tell you that they're incompatible . . . Not then they weren't.' McCartney, it's remembered, was particularly courteous towards his guest at the front door. 'They stood there up close, and she took his arm. He was hugging her.' Paul also reportedly showered enormous praise on Yoko's portfolio, which she lugged with her, of free-form perspex figurines all bundled together with a doctor's stethoscope – the future, as he supposed.

Yoko met John, and began the decade's most spectacular love affair. 'He warned me off her,' Paul would recall. 'Sort of said, "Look, no, no." 'Cause he knew I was a bit of a ladies' man – I liked the girls, no doubt about that.' Some three years later, during the making of *Abbey Road*, Lennon installed a twin bed in the studio so that Yoko, recuperating from a car crash, could survey proceedings and pass comment through a mike he had suspended over her. The other Beatles positioned themselves around the room as best they could. Yoko would later tell Paul that if, for any reason, he'd seemed to be standing too close to her, all hell would break loose when John got her home. Lennon, she said, was 'very paranoid' like that.

9 November 1966. When the 'Paul is Dead' rumours began in 1969, this was the date when he was supposed to have been decapitated in a fiery car crash.* The reality was more mundane: McCartney spent the day with his friend Tara Browne, tripping on pot and LSD, then managed to fall off a moped he insisted on demonstrating in Browne's garden. He cut his upper lip, sporting a moustache for a month or two to cover the scar. Browne himself died just five weeks later, smashing his Lotus Elan into the back of a parked lorry early one morning in West London. He was twenty-one.

If McCartney didn't die on 9 November, in some ways it was the beginning of the end. That happened to be the very night on which Lennon stumbled into the Indica gallery for a VIP showing of an exhibition called 'Unfinished Paintings & Objects by Yoko Ono'. The celebrated moment came when John climbed a stepladder towards a small canvas nailed to the ceiling, blank but for three tiny letters he read through a magnifying glass. They read 'Yes'. Yoko

---

* This heated Sixties debate, a few embers of which still smoulder today, owed its existence to various 'clues' found on LP covers and song lyrics, with the *White Album* providing a particularly rich fund. An actor, one William Campbell, was said to have stepped in to impersonate the late Beatle, though how he managed to write and sing in McCartney's exact voice for the next three years was never fully explained.

herself shunned a traditional introduction, instead silently handing John a card on which was printed the word 'Breathe'. He later claimed to have taken both these events as permission to leave the Beatles. Just an hour or two earlier on that same Wednesday evening, Epstein had formally announced that the band were finished with touring. Coincidentally, it was five years to the day since Eppy had first found his way downstairs to the Cavern and set the whole thing in motion.

Ten days later, McCartney, Jane Asher and Mal Evans boarded a BOAC jet in Nairobi bound for London. Paul used the time, typically, to map out a new twelve-month plan for the Beatles. The last US tour, added to the continuing death threats, had been enough to make him tear up the old one. By now, he conceded, even he 'really hate[d] that fuckin' four little moptops shit.' Sipping the first of several in-flight Scotch and Cokes, McCartney asked for a pen and paper, opened the tray table in front of him, took another sip, then wrote 'Big Brother Holding Nitty Gritty Quicksilver Fabs' on the sheet of blue airline stationery, drawing a circle round the last word. Just then lunch was served and Evans leant over to ask what Paul was doing.

'We need a freaky new name. Like those California bands. Any ideas?'

'Pass the pepper,' said Mal.

Once more Paul sipped his drink, then took up the pen again. Underneath 'Fabs' he wrote 'Pepper', drawing another circle round the word, which he attached to the first circle by a line. 'I can use that,' he said.

By the time the plane landed at Heathrow, McCartney had half the new album title and the basic concept, which he put to the others at a meeting in Abbey Road on 24 November. Their reaction was tepid, but eventually John warmed to the idea. He began to envision a life outside, yet still with the Beatles: a new bag, he nodded, very cool. By then, Paul had taken the trouble to bring in a whole series of storyboards and hand-drawn mock-ups of LP covers and publicity shots, making *Sgt. Pepper*, as he now called it, hard to resist. Whatever the daft bugger was trying to do, said John, he obviously didn't want to be talked out of it.

An innocent fan, catching a glimpse of McCartney at play, would have been hard pressed to relate to him as the fresh-faced singer of Yesterday. Instead, Paul was spending more and more of his time in the company of men like Keith Richards and Jimi Hendrix. He was developing a discreet coke habit. And he continued to support pop-art causes, everything from 'Groovy Bob' Fraser's Duke Street gallery to the situationist Bonzo Dog Doo-Dah Band. Over the course of a long evening, the latter – with their extended novelty songs and chaotic sketches – could try the patience of even the most earnest audience. McCartney, however, not only befriended the Bonzos. He produced their one hit single for them.

In mid-January 1967, McCartney met with the thirty-three-year-old playwright Joe Orton, award-winning author of *Loot*, to ask if he could develop a film script for the Beatles. This was something of a stretch for both parties. Orton's previous works had brought such topics as transvestism, matricide and the joys of incest to West End audiences. Paul was enthralled by the young firebrand, though quite candid about his aversion to following Jane Asher about in provincial rep. 'The only thing I get from the theatre,' he announced, 'is a sore arse.'

Two weeks later, Orton delivered the first draft of a script, *Up Against It*, which would have seen the Beatles, inter alia, dress up as women, commit murder, conspire to overthrow the government and then be sent to prison, where things would begin to get interesting. Epstein rejected it. McCartney did, however, take the opportunity to play Orton the tapes of 'two little things' the band had just cut. Both songs stated the boys' intentions with a vengeance. For weeks afterwards, Orton, not one to over-praise, could only conclude they were 'out of this world'. On 9 August 1967 he was battered to death by his lover, Kenneth Halliwell, who then committed suicide in the bedsit they shared.

The little things were Strawberry Fields Forever and Penny Lane. Both had been worked up, with only a quick break for the holidays, around Christmas 1966. Both ran with the basic idea of John's In My Life by offering an hallucinatory tour d'horizon and, more specifically, of Liverpool. Packed with overdubs and effects, exotic fills and kaleidoscopic lyrics, these were the bruised but marketable fruits of Lennon-McCartney's adolescence. The nurse in Penny Lane who 'feels as if she's in a play' . . . and 'is, anyway' remains Paul's most (drug) inspired image. Released as a double-A side on 17 February, the Beatles' masterpiece was kept off the top by Engelbert Humperdinck's melodramatic version of Release Me. The press immediately began protesting that the band was finished. *Revolver* was still up there in the chart, but to *Melody Maker*, for one, it seemed as if the dream would be over before you could say 'Bee Gees'.

In fact, Strawberry Fields/Penny Lane began a period of remarkable productivity. Between 4 January and 1 April 1967, the Beatles wrote and recorded most of the *Pepper* album as well as Carnival Of Light, single-handedly invented the concept of the rock video and still collaborated with everyone from Fats Domino to Donovan. Even John seemed reinvigorated by the idea of their *becoming* Sgt. Pepper's band. Meanwhile, by rising early and writing until one or two in the afternoon, Paul streaked along on the new songs, working out much of the raw material in the study at Cavendish Avenue. When he felt tired, he snorted himself awake again. A number of his handwritten lyrics to *Pepper*, left lying around the place, were stolen by overzealous fans and offered for auction, years later, in the hundreds of thousands of pounds.

If the songs came quickly, unprecedented amounts of time and money were being lavished on them in the recording. In total the

Beatles logged 700 hours' studio time, spread over twelve weeks, grinding *Pepper*. Once again George Martin was a key figure, serving as the band's producer, arranger, effects man and uncomplaining translator of requests such as Lennon's for Mr Kite!, 'I want to *smell* the sawdust.' Stress would reduce Martin's weight by a stone during the making of *Pepper*. Though moderate in his habits he began allowing himself a little brandy to help himself sleep, and was observed with a glass of champagne when the final session wrapped at six one Sunday morning.

Late on 19 January, the Beatles first turned to a song called A Day In The Life. It built through Martin's patient bricklaying over the next month, he and Paul eventually conducting a forty-piece symphony orchestra who, in a sign something unusual was happening, wore a variety of plastic stick-on nipples and red rubber noses for the occasion. McCartney's instruction to the musicians was to achieve a 'freakout' by climbing from their lowest to their highest note, steadily turning up the volume as they did so. For added atmosphere he had the studio filled with party balloons and flowers, with various Stones and Hollies sprawled around holding up joss sticks. Twelve days later, Paul, John, Ringo and Mal Evans simultaneously hit an orgasmic E-major chord on four pianos, a sound allowed to echo and fade away, the song's exquisite climax.

McCartney's 'freakout' approach was tempered by other *Sgt. Pepper* sessions typically more like a workshop than a circus. Micky Dolenz of the Monkees happened to be in town, and visited Abbey Road on 20 February:

Paul and I had had a drink the night before, and he invited me to the session. It was a weird scene. Christ, the *Beatles*, I thought. Better look the part. So before I got in the car to go over there I spent an hour dressing up in my best paisley flares and beads, with rings, bangles, and about half a dozen medallions. If I'd drowned somehow they would have had to send in a salvage crew for me. This is '67, and these are Paul and John, so I'm expecting peace, love and flowers at the studio. Instead, it's a factory: four guys sitting around on folding chairs, drinking tea. A minute or two later, George Martin comes downstairs in his suit and tie, says crisply, 'Right, lads, break's over', and everyone goes back to work. Very British. Very professional. Maybe *that's* why they succeeded and we didn't.

On the morning of 9 March, McCartney looked out his window at the pale, early-spring sunshine, turned to his companion and remarked, 'It's getting better.' 'All the time,' she agreed. At that Paul quickly got out of bed and went up to his den. By the time Lennon arrived at Cavendish Avenue an hour later, his host was ready for him with the title phrase and a basic chord structure, which he ran through on his guitar. 'Getting better all the time,' Paul sang, and John answered, 'Can't get no worse.' And that became the song. Simple – and stunning, just as pop should be.

Meanwhile, ignorant of these developments, more and more of the press were writing the Beatles off. The band, it was said, were 'hopelessly wrong' not to tour, 'badly advised', 'self-indulgent', 'kaput'. By now Epstein had brought in an impeccably smooth, Liverpool born, ex-*Daily Express* reporter named Derek Taylor to handle the media. Taylor spent much of his time firefighting, what with all the talk of a break-up, while teasing a few, hip titles into a state of arousal over *Sgt. Pepper*. Every week, he sent McCartney a large cuttings file he marked 'Stray Thoughts & Trivia from Fleet Street's Finest'.

And what an evil bunch of tossers they all were, Paul concluded, especially the ones who panned Strawberry Fields. Still, he did what he could to win back hearts and minds. Few of his interviewers, however jaded, were immune to McCartney's charm: the *Times* critic, for one, thought him 'a curious cocktail of earnest, decent, hopeful philosophy; a certain amount of rather spaced-out bunk, and a good deal of old-fashioned drive.'

This ambition grew legendary. McCartney was permanently in motion, whether leading John, George and Ringo through yet another take or bounding up the stairs, three at a time, to the control room to confer with George Martin. And he was doing it all stoned. Thirty-five years later, Paul remembered how he made *Pepper* on 'coke, and maybe some grass to level it out.' At the time, his chemical locker also included uppers, downers and copious draughts of Scotch. He's said he did heroin, just the once, with 'Groovy Bob' Fraser. Fraser took his stash down to Keith Richards' home one weekend that winter and got caught in the most famous drug bust of the decade. He served six months for possession.

On Sunday 18 June, McCartney's twenty-fifth birthday, the Beatles were splashed on the cover of *Life* magazine. Buried within was Paul's blithe announcement which caused such worldwide astonishment. He'd not only taken drugs, he said, but quite enjoyed them. '[LSD] opened my eyes,' he admitted breezily. 'We only use one-tenth of our brains. Just think what we'd accomplish if we could tap that hidden part.' Lest anyone miss the point, a day later McCartney confirmed to ITN News, 'I did drugs with a deliberate purpose in mind; to find the answer to what life is all about.'

There'd been hopes in Beatles circles that such a confession might 'clear the air' and 'let Paul move on': it didn't. The firestorm that followed was second only to the 'Bigger than Jesus' furore. McCartney was scolded in the *Daily Mail* as 'an irresponsible idiot'. Most public opinion was generally negative, at least as voiced in the letters pages of newspapers and magazines, which featured a large number of correspondents hailing from Tunbridge Wells. In this revised view, in which the word 'cute' was tempered by 'daft', several politicians and church leaders competed to denounce both drugs and McCartney. In Washington, the evangelist Billy Graham publicly fell to his knees and announced that he was praying for Paul's soul. 'He's reached the top of his profession and now he is searching for the true purpose of life. He won't find it through taking LSD.'

Back in Cavendish Avenue, McCartney was spending his time with Brian Jones and Keith Richards, tripping out in the glow of his new Takis sculpture, made from two flashing aircraft lights welded to tank aerials. It was Paul who now befriended the degenerate Stones. Sometime that year the idea occurred to him that both bands should combine to form their own record company, for which McCartney registered the name Mother Earth. Back to basics, he said. Cut out the middlemen. The moment passed, but Epstein had been put on notice. No way was he 'threaten[ing] anyone,' McCartney announced. Still, 'errors' had been made, millions of dollars blown. Eppy had at last renegotiated the Beatles' EMI contract, but to Paul it was still 'nothing great . . . We were used.' As well as this trifling disappointment, there were more practical problems: capital-gains taxes to be paid, loans coming due, houses to be furnished. Clearly, something had to give. Around the time of *Revolver*, Epstein had taken on a secretary named Joanne Newfield, who witnessed his decline at first hand. Once, she had to bring him round after Eppy took an overdose of sleeping pills. Newfield would remember that her boss had come to dread his business dealings with McCartney. 'Paul could get to Brian the way none of the other three could. Whenever I saw him put down the phone really upset, he'd always been talking to Paul.'

None of this was ever 'just about bread', because McCartney also went head-to-head with management on artistic matters – for instance, the cover for *Sgt. Pepper*. Here *was* a threat: a demand, on pain of scrapping the album, that EMI revise their normal policy of dummying up a quick pub shot at a cost of forty or fifty quid. McCartney was quite clear in his vision. He wanted a pop-art equivalent of a Northern floral-clock display, with something of Salvador Dali's hallucinatory high finish. For the first time in industry history, the song lyrics were to be printed on the back sleeve. Only the finest colour-separation processes and the heaviest paper stock would be acceptable for this *Mona Lisa* of LP covers. ('I got my thick cardboard,' Paul later noted.) Inside with the record would be a sheet of 'Sgt. Pepper' accessories, including a paper moustache. By now, what McCartney wanted to happen tended to happen, and what he didn't tended not to. The floral-clock display became a photomontage, designed by the artist Peter Blake, showing the band dressed in satin military garb, surrounded by their heroes. (Paul's wish list was headed by Brigitte Bardot.) Everything took weeks to assemble, there were frantic efforts to get permission from as many of the living celebrities as possible, and EMI were suitably horrified. The *Sgt. Pepper* jacket cost £1,500, and the record itself £25,030.

At dawn on Sunday 2 April, the Beatles left Abbey Road carrying a reel-to-reel tape, drove down to 'Mama' Cass Elliot's flat in Chelsea and, then and there, blasted out their new opus onto the King's Road. According to Derek Taylor, 'All the windows around us opened and people leaned out, wondering. Nobody complained. A lovely spring morning. People were smiling and giving us the thumbs up.'

Next day McCartney flew to San Francisco, where he stayed at a home on Oak Street, loosely hosted by members of the Jefferson Airplane and the Grateful Dead. Despite the unseasonable cold snap, everyone wandered outside after dinner, settled on the back porch overlooking the pool, kicked off their shoes and lit up. 'So, what's new with the Beatles?' somebody asked. Paul shrugged, fished around inside his kitbag and idly brought out the tape again. For the next half hour, the rich dense music echoed off the water and swirled in the air, right down to the final slamming note.

The other rock stars looked stunned. It was like music from Mars. The Airplane had come closest to it with *Surrealistic Pillow*, and that wasn't very close.

On 5 April McCartney flew to Denver to pay a surprise visit to Jane Asher, who was on tour with the Bristol Old Vic company. It happened to be her twenty-first birthday. Despite the romantic gesture, it occurred to insiders that what Paul most wanted was a stay-at-home girlfriend, a role Jane was totally unsuited for. She, in turn, wanted a boyfriend who was faithful, a role Paul was totally unsuited for. On their way across America, the party hopped a ride on Frank Sinatra's private jet (Mylar mirrors and bathtubs), so beginning a long and sometimes troubled relationship between the two superstars. Later that summer, Sinatra heard When I'm Sixty-Four, and declared himself 'knocked out' by this new, rooty-tooty music. He wasn't to know that McCartney had actually written the song back in 1959, when he was seventeen. A year or two later Sinatra put in a call to Abbey Road, asking Paul if he had any more like it. McCartney thought about it, and then came up with another Forthlin Road ditty, and a lyric that went:

> When she tries to run away
> And he calls her back, she comes . . .
> She'll limp along to his side
> Ah ha, I call it suicide . . .

Sinatra was unimpressed. 'The guy's out of his fucking mind,' he remarked to his handlers. 'I wouldn't sing that in my crapper.' The passage of twenty-five years did nothing to modify this bleak assessment, which, it should be stressed, was in no way reflective of the broader mutual respect. In 1993, the parties were reported to be 'keen' to collaborate on Sinatra's *Duets* album, though, in the end, both passed.

Back in California, the musical kibbutzing continued when McCartney made a flying visit to the Beach Boys' studio, where he found Brian Wilson working on a track he called Vega-Tables. Several sane critics have actually compared this moment to the meeting at Arles between Van Gogh and Gauguin. It was an arresting scene. To illustrate the song's lyric, the room was strewn with broccoli, carrots, celery, spinach, zucchini, onions and several kinds of dip. At Wilson's request, Paul, who needed little encouragement, contributed some percussive chewing sounds. He then sat down at the piano and gave the first public performance of She's Leaving Home from *Sgt. Pepper*. When it finished there was a moment of awed silence, then rapturous applause.

'Honey, take a picture,' Wilson told his wife. 'That's history.'

At six the next evening, McCartney and Mal Evans boarded the return flight to London. Once again, they put the time to good use. Paul began doodling on a napkin, writing the words 'Mystery Tour' and enthusing to Mal about this great idea for a film where everybody would get high and drive around England in a bus. While they were talking, he was sketching a pie chart with individual scenes: 'Roll up, roll up', 'Magician', 'Flying', and so on. There was little dialogue, less plot, and numerous production hassles to come. Eventually the BBC bought the whole thing for a bargain-basement £9,000. When it was aired on Boxing Day, *Magical Mystery Tour* led to renewed talk in the press that the Beatles were at best washed-up, and at worst seriously unhinged.

Lennon later complained that McCartney had made a power play, or grab, in that Summer of Love. 'He set up [*Mystery Tour*] and then he came and showed me what his idea was . . . He said, "Well, here's the segment, you write a little piece for that." And I thought, fuckin' Ada, I've never made a film, what's he mean, write a script?'

John was flinty and notoriously rude, but he'd remained impassioned, an idealist. By the time *Pepper* came around he'd already enjoyed the five years of fame he'd said was all he wanted. Within the band he was admired, envied, worried about, denounced and feared. That was the way he liked it. But now he was also tired. Lennon was looking for a way out. And here was our Paul, with his diagrams, 'rattl[ing] on about some Butlin's bullshit.' Not surprisingly, the sessions that began in Abbey Road on 25 April were a shade cool. John was ambivalent at best, one minute crowing that the Beatles were 'better than Beethoven', the next panning them as con artists. George, too, was growing weary of the game, complaining that Paul was a 'keenie', with – as if there could be anything worse – a tendency to rehearse. Ringo just played the drums.

Paul and John chose this of all moments to launch Apple, incorporated on 19 April 1967. The legendary Beatles folly (though thriving today) had its origins in a simple desire to avoid tax. By channelling their funds into subsidiary operations such as Apple Publishing and Apple Retail, the theory went, the band could rule over a Utopian empire – 'Western communism', McCartney called it – and save themselves a fortune in doing so. Under Apple's deeds of covenant, Paul, John, George and Ringo were to share everything equally for the next ten years. With the key exception of songwriting royalties, every penny went into the holding company, which would first pay its numerous managers and staff and then issue four identical cheques. Paul's smouldering discontent with this arrangement reached a peak in the summer of 1970, when his first solo album went platinum. As per the original contract, the profits were pooled and split evenly among Lennon, Harrison, Starr and himself, who by then were barely speaking to one another.

On 12 May 1967, the Beatles recorded a simple McCartney song called All Together Now, later to be a popular chant on Northern football terraces. Three days later he was in the Bag o'Nails in Kingly Street, Soho, relaxing to Procul Harum's A Whiter Shade Of Pale on the sound system, when a good-looking blonde in a short, fringed skirt walked by and gave him the eye. They got talking and she told him she was a New Yorker, in town to take photographs for a book called *Rock and Other Four Letter Words*. This seemed very urbane and progressive, that a chick with a German camera (so soon after the war) would be mingling on equal terms with pop stars. Her name was Linda Eastman.

Four days later, Linda was at Epstein's home in Belgravia for a *Sgt. Pepper* launch party. Her pictures from that night would acquire near-iconic status, particularly the one showing Paul and John laughing and shaking hands. Legend insists that McCartney invited her back to his place with the line, 'Come up and see my Magrittes.' (Happily for him, Jane Asher was still touring America.) Over the next few days, Paul and Linda seemed to be exactly what he called it: a match 'made in heaven'. Once or twice, Lennon had the opportunity to witness them together up close. Between her exaggerated sweetness and his courteousness, John noted, the effect was a bit like hanging out with a valentine's card. Towards the end of May, Linda flew back to New York, where she had a three-year-old daughter, Heather, waiting for her. A day later, Jane crossed the Atlantic in the opposite direction and returned to Cavendish Avenue.

A free spirit, Linda was the daughter of privilege. She was born on 24 September 1941, the second of four children to Lee Eastman, a high-powered entertainment lawyer and his wife Louise, whose people owned a chain of Midwest department stores. There was a family tradition of brilliant academic success, though Linda's Scarsdale High School yearbook describes her only as a 'strawberry blonde' with a 'yen for men'. By one of those strange Beatles coincidences, she went on to take design classes (though never formally enrolling) at Sarah Lawrence College, like Yoko before her. When Linda was nineteen her mother was killed in a plane crash and her father remarried. It was the Sixties, and Linda would recall 'experimenting with stuff' – she meant drugs – just as, in 1956, Paul had picked up the guitar following his own loss. And then the real rebellion began. Linda hitchhiked to Tucson, where she took Art at the University of Arizona and went through a shotgun wedding with a fellow student named Joseph 'Mel' See. By the time their daughter was born in December 1963, the marriage had failed. Announcing that he needed to tour central Africa to study geophysics, See asked that his wife keep in touch. When she did, it was to write to him saying that she wanted a divorce.

Linda took Heather and moved back to New York, where she studied photography and talked her way into a receptionist's job at *Town and Country* magazine. Music and musicians had always been a major part of her life. Old-time stars like Hoagy Carmichael and Frank Sinatra had visited the Eastmans' home in East Hampton and sometimes serenaded the children to sleep. Another of Lee's clients, the composer Jack Lawrence, had even written a ballad called Linda, which was later covered by the British crooner-turned-publisher Dick James – and, for that matter, by Jimmy Young. Now, two or three times a week, Linda called a babysitter and hotfooted it downtown to one of the newly opened rock clubs. In particular, she became a regular at Bill Graham's Fillmore East, where she was soon the unofficial house photographer. Over the next eighteen months, Linda was linked romantically with a variety of Graham's headline acts, including – the list isn't exhaustive – Jimi Hendrix, Stephen Stills, Steve Winwood, Jim Morrison, Eric Burdon, Tim Buckley, Paul Kantner and Sam Andrew, the bassist with Janis Joplin's band. (Joplin herself thought the fun-loving shutterbug, to whom she was by no means immune, 'sex on legs'.) In June 1966 Linda was the only photographer at a floating press conference on board the SS *Sea Panther* as it cruised around New York harbour with the Rolling Stones; her candid, frontal images of various band members slumped back in their seats, yawning, legs akimbo, put her on the rock 'n' roll map. According to Bill Wyman, she and Mick Jagger then spent the night together.

Two months later, Linda was backstage with her Leica at Shea Stadium and caught a glimpse of the Beatles as they were hustled to their car. 'It was John who interested me,' she recalled. 'He was my hero. But when I met him the fascination faded fast and I found it was Paul I liked.'

In May 1967, Linda was finished with *Town and Country* and working successfully as a freelance photographer. At twenty-five she was a veteran of both the Fillmore and Warhol's Factory, through which she knew 'everyone' in New York. She was smart, hip and thin as a cigarette. And, best of all, she was refreshingly relaxed about the Beatles, having thought nothing of coming home as a little girl to find Bing Crosby at the dinner table. She was some piece of work.

Revolver had been a masterpiece. *Sgt. Pepper's Lonely Hearts Club Band* was the big bang of rock music. The sheer sweep of it was impressive enough, from vaudeville to psychedelia. McCartney and Lennon's flair for seaming these different styles together gave tracks such as Lovely Rita and Mr Kite! an unmistakably British flavour, but what stood out more than the writing was the craftsmanship. The meticulous orchestrations, melodic subtleties and harmonic tang kept everything in character, perhaps the one lapse being Paul's ill-advised heavy riffing on the title track, where he seemed uneasily like a badminton champion who'd strayed inadvertently into the shot-putting cage. There's a cohesion to *Pepper* that its leaden imitators could only feebly approximate. Nearly forty years on, it remains a cause for both celebration and regret. The album's success eventually brought forth a torrent of 'concepts' and 'rock operas', usually involving the setting to music of some sci-fi romp packaged in a hideous gatefold. *Sgt. Pepper* went on to sell ten million copies in America alone, and thus helped make possible everything from the Stones' *Satanic Majesties* to contemporary horrors like Ayreon's *Into the Electric Castle*.

The critics outdid themselves. Kenneth Tynan declared *Sgt. Pepper* a pivotal moment in the history of Western civilisation. *Newsweek*'s cover story compared the Beatles to T.S. Eliot. Timothy Leary went one better, announcing that 'John Lennon, George Harrison, Paul McCartney and Ringo Starr are mutants . . . Evolutionary agents sent down, endowed with mysterious powers to create a new species.' When Lennon said to McCartney, 'How are we gonna top *that*?', Paul just smiled. Ironically, he may have been one of the few people to hear *Pepper* and keep his wits about him:

There was some stuff there that was a little second-hand. Certain repetitive tricks from *Revolver*. And George Martin got too much credit.

'It's a good wee record,' Paul later declared. 'But "God speaks"? You've got to be kidding.'

On 25 June 1967, an estimated 360 million television viewers in twenty-seven countries tuned in to a programme called *Our World*. This first ever global satellite hook-up, a sort of psychedelic Eurovision Song Contest, climaxed in a clip of the Beatles sitting on stools and surrounded by beaded friends like Mick Jagger and Eric Clapton, chanting Lennon's composition All You Need Is Love. Those were the first and second lines of the chorus. The third was 'All you need is love, love'. The fourth was 'Love is all you need'. Released as a single on 7 July, All You Need Is Love went straight to the top. Even so, cynics felt that the bauble was bestowed largely for John's title, which quickly became a catchphrase.

Four weeks later McCartney again outraged decent society by buying a full-page advertisement in *The Times*, headed 'The law against marijuana is immoral in principle and unworkable in practice.' He joined John, George and Ringo, theatrical types like Ken Tynan and Jonathan Miller, the author Graham Greene and Francis Crick, the Nobel-winning physicist, in demanding that 'the smoking of cannabis on private premises should no longer constitute an offence . . . All persons now imprisoned for possession of cannabis or for allowing cannabis to be smoked should have their sentences commuted.' Overnight, Paul McCartney, MBE (as he signed himself) was at the centre of another, or renewed storm. Several leader-writers, together with sundry MPs and bishops, denounced both him and the band as dope-peddling fiends. Over-caffeinated reporters took to phoning Britain's great and good to ask them, 'Do you agree with Paul McCartney that everyone should take drugs?' Next day, back at the office, Epstein (who'd loyally admitted to his own LSD use) was

greeted by demonstrators holding up signs calling his boys 'Shameful
. . . Sick . . . The Pervs.' He lost it and started to cry.

McCartney himself ducked the worst of it, being with the Beatles in
the process of buying their own Greek island. Lennon had first
conceived the notion of a sun-kissed commune, beyond the arm of
the Metropolitan drugs squad, in conjunction with his friend 'Magic
Alex' Mardas, a young day tripper and electronics whiz who, for only
a very modest fee, offered the Beatles a whole raft of wonderful ideas
and devices – an invisible 'sonic wall', for instance, that would
protect the band from their fans. Paul went along on the stoned
reconnaissance trip, but clearly thought it whimsical, at best, telling
Marianne Faithfull, 'They'll never get it together.' Just as he pre-
dicted, the hippy idyll came to nothing. The Beatles did, however,
prove to be quite astute capitalists. In mid-July, Paul and John had
authorised Alistair Taylor to transfer £90,000 into US funds in order
to buy their Aegean retreat. By the time they changed their minds the
exchange rate had swung in their favour, and they were able to show
an £11,000 profit for Apple.

The Summer of Love was now about halfway through, and how
everyone had changed. It wasn't just the Beatles and the Stones who
were swaggering around garlanded in flowers. Even in their shops
and offices, young adults were dressing up like slightly muted
versions of the *Sgt. Pepper* dandies. There were a few hold-outs, but
thanks to Paul, John and one or two other visionaries, most twenty-
somethings were running wilder and freer than any generation in
history. All You Need Is Love was released on a culture where 'doing
your thing' was ceasing to carry any hint of opprobrium, and where
the concept of delayed gratification seemed as dated as a chastity
belt. If you had any modern blood in your veins you laughed at the
Fifties, when men and women knew their place, everyone wore grey
and *South Pacific* was hip.

Ironically, McCartney himself stood at a remove from some of the
revolution he'd helped start. Self-discipline and civility were both
fine by him. By and large, he was polite not just to his friends, but to
everyone with whom he came into contact. He made no bones about
his love of 'old-fogey music', shown yet again when his father and
Aunty Jin spent the weekend at Cavendish Avenue, and Paul
knocked off a *Mystery Tour* tune – given a Busby Berkeley treatment
in the film – called Your Mother Should Know.

If a more fruity soul than some guessed, McCartney still worked
both sides of the street. He followed his MGM turn by, two weeks
later, joining in the swooping idiosyncrasy of Lennon's I Am The
Walrus. 'Compared to my family,' Paul allowed, 'I'm a freakout.'

On the Bank Holiday weekend of 26–27 August the Beatles sat at
the feet of the Maharishi Mahesh Yogi, who'd won them over at a
meeting two days earlier by comparing them to a rare flower, a
favourite allusion of his, needing but the 'loam of love' to make it
grow. The well-padded guru wore Central Casting's flowing white
robes and spoke in a near-squeak, like the sound produced by
rubbing the rim of a glass with a wet finger. He wanted each of his
devotees to pay him a week's wage. But John and George were
particularly drawn to his key spiritual message – 'Know yourself' –
urging Paul and Ringo to join them at an initiation seminar. This
took place in the mundane setting of a teacher training college in
Bangor, North Wales. It was the band's first real excursion without
their manager.

On the Saturday afternoon, the Maharishi and his famous
students agreed to hold a press conference. This consisted of the
Beatles being barraged with questions about drugs. 'They were just
something we went through,' McCartney said. 'Now it's over. We
don't need it any more. We're finding new ways of getting there.'

Later that night, Brian Epstein succeeded in killing himself.
Telling friends he was both appalled at the band's latest infatuation
and lonely without them, he'd apparently been planning some action

at his country home in East Sussex, but instead chose to drive back to Belgravia early on Saturday morning. Eppy awoke at five in the afternoon, ate breakfast, read the post and watched *Juke Box Jury* on television. For the first time, there were some mild satirical digs at the Beatles. 'I get by with a little help from de-pends.' Very droll. Could Brian care less? He downed some brandy and took another dose of six Carbrital, one of several drugs he'd been prescribed to help him sleep. The inquest, held on 8 September, found that this had amounted to an accidental suicide. When they broke down Brian's bedroom door that Sunday lunchtime they found him curled up in the foetal position, with a total of seventeen bottles of various pills strewn around on tables and in cupboards. The official verdict was that he had died from 'incautious self-overdoses'. Although the attending physician estimated Epstein had been in his mid-fifties, he was just thirty-two.

McCartney had been strolling around the grounds at Bangor when Jane Asher called him to the phone. They all saw the blood drain from his face and heard him shout 'Oh, Christ – *no!*' The Beatles then sequestered themselves with the Maharishi, who assured them that Brian's death was illusory and 'not important'. When the press bawled 'How do you feel?' questions at him later that evening, Paul replied, 'It's a drag' and 'I'm very upset.' None of the band attended Brian's funeral, held at the Jewish Cemetery in Liverpool, which nonetheless attracted several weeping fans; the *Post* conceded that this was 'only fitting'.

On 1 September, the Beatles met at Cavendish Avenue to discuss their future. The first order of business was whether or not to appoint a successor to Epstein. Allen Klein, the Stones' titanically aggressive business manager, had recently let it be known through his lawyer Marty Machat that he wanted the job. 'He thinks the Beatles can all be film stars,' Machat announced. 'The four of them together are much stronger than as individuals. Mr Klein thinks they could be the natural replacements to the Marx Brothers.'

McCartney declined both this offer, and one from Robert Stigwood, the genius behind the Bee Gees, on the band's behalf. The last five-and-a-half years had evidently cured them of the need for an old-fashioned, proprietary gaffer. Instead, it would be Paul himself who increasingly called the shots. From now on, he'd be the one turning out the memos about recording dates and shooting schedules, as well as redoubling his charm offensive with the press. 'I find it more of an effort *not* to make an effort,' he allowed. 'It's more false for me not to. So I might as well make the effort.'

One Fleet Street music journalist likes to tell the story of how she was introduced to McCartney on the set of *Magical Mystery Tour*. 'I'm always glad to help you lot,' Paul said. 'Just call me.' He then handed the woman his Apple business card, complete with half a dozen phone numbers, and continued to work the crowd. Five minutes later she was writing her notes when one of her colleagues dragged McCartney over to meet her, telling her she should fix up a date for a formal interview. She was just about to apologise for the mix-up when Paul took her hand and smiled warmly. 'I'm always glad to help you lot,' he said. 'Just call me.' He then obligingly peeled off another business card before vanishing back into the crowd.

Lennon and Harrison, meanwhile, continued to mutter about their 'keenie' colleague behind his back, and once or twice to his face. John was particularly narked. He and Yoko had begun if not an affair, then an arrangement: both parties remained married, but seem to have come to a tacit agreement with their spouses. John and Yoko had drawn closer still following the shock of Epstein's death, an event which hit Lennon ('We've fuckin' had it!' he'd spluttered) harder than most. And now they were expected to 'pretend it was *A Hard Day's Night* again', John carped, 'getting [up] each others' noses.' The very sight of Paul squiring his women around town was a daily affront. A new lover, a randy old mate: it was a one-two soap opera punch that would have given anyone pause for thought. Had they done it? The next six months or so of Lennon's life were a tailspin of fear, anguish, acid trips and marital disintegration. Some of these ingredients went into his masterpiece I Am The Walrus, recorded on 5–6 September, which turned out about equal parts Lewis Carroll and LSD.

On the 11th, principal photography for *Magical Mystery Tour* began in the West Country. The special psychedelic bus carrying the Beatles and their thirty-three guests arrived two hours late, and promptly got stuck on a narrow, stone bridge leading into the picturesque Devon village of Widecombe, Lennon leaning out of the window in his purple grannie glasses muttering 'Fook it.' Dartmoor had seen nothing like it. It was an inauspicious start to the whole misconceived project, which would then take twelve weeks, not the expected two, to cobble together in the editing room. McCartney began recording The Fool On The Hill back in London on 25 September, then turned to his blandly catchy Hello, Goodbye. On 17 October he and the band attended a memorial service for Epstein, held just around the corner from Abbey Road. One evening in the studio, where Paul was finishing The Fool, he called Mal Evans over to the corner. 'Does this song need a short?' he asked. 'No,' said Mal. 'Well, you're wrong, mate. Get us on the night flight to Nice, and we'll shoot something up on the cliffs there at dawn.' McCartney arrived at Heathrow without a passport or any money, but told Immigration, 'You know who I am, so why do you need to see a photograph of me?' Once on the Côte d'Azure, he, Mal and a cameraman took a taxi up into the hills and filmed Paul dancing around in the sunrise. Everyone was back in London before the other Beatles even realised they'd gone. The actual clip was terrific, all agreed.

One morning in October, McCartney's friend Allan Clarke found himself in Abbey Road listening to Paul doodle a melody on the piano. 'Nice one,' he told him. 'It'll be great when you finish the lyrics.'

McCartney's response to Clarke was that same challenging look of offended pride that was becoming familiar to the Beatles. 'They *are* finished,' he said. The song was Hello, Goodbye, which spent seven weeks at number one, making it the band's most successful single since She Loves You. Lennon was fuming. After a heated debate, I Am The Walrus had been relegated to the flip side. When John had protested further, things got personal. He didn't care for Paul's attitude, he said, or for his 'nursery-rhyme shit'. Alistair Taylor, Eppy's dapper assistant and the band's long-suffering Mr Fixit, was only slightly more impressed. He later claimed to have sat down with McCartney at the old, hand-carved harmonium in the dining room at Cavendish Avenue and co-written Hello, Goodbye 'in about five minutes'.

By then, rumours of a feud between Paul and John had found their way into print. The 'FABS FINISHED?' headlines had again been wheeled out following Eppy's death, along with anonymous complaints about a new, one-man 'dictatorship'. Lennon was often late and sometimes absent from the *Mystery Tour* sessions. When McCartney confronted him about it, John denied he was using drugs. Paul knew he was lying.

Later that autumn, Apple Corps moved into a four-storey red-brick house at 94 Baker Street, about a mile south of Cavendish Avenue. The lawyers and accountants occupied the upper floors, with the press office and other aides below. Ground zero was the Apple boutique. At a board meeting the previous August, Paul and John had formally moved to 'carry on the business of stockists, suppliers, shopkeepers and tradesmen', thus beginning the Beatles' short-lived career as high-street retailers. Simon Posthuma and Marijke Koger, two bell-bottomed young designers known collectively as The Fool, took £100,000 of the band's money and converted the stuffy, Edwardian rooms, hitherto occupied by a bank, into a bazaar of flowing oriental robes and Berber jewellery. One entire side of the building was given a swirling, psychedelic mural, later to be removed on the orders of Westminster Council. Numerous staff were hired: young girls in miniskirts as lures, and managers who wore caftans and beads, smoked dope and circulated memorial posters for Che Guevara. It's claimed the recruitment ads placed by Paul and John had specified 'no bread heads', and that 'previous experience in sales' was superfluous. It hardly mattered, since most customers preferred simply to walk in, scoop up some clothes, and walk out again. The official word from upstairs was that to prosecute shoplifters was 'uncool'.

Apple Boutique celebrated its grand opening on 4 December 1967. The dazzling laser show and 'sonic wall' promised for the occasion by Magic Alex both failed to appear. McCartney, too, stayed away. While the other Beatles wandered through the racks of tie-dyed dashkiris and spangled militaria, Paul and Jane were on the farm in Scotland. The couple spent the rest of the year secluded in their dank, unheated manse with the outdoor bath. On Christmas Eve, they phoned Jane's family to announce their engagement.

A storm of protest greeted *Magical Mystery Tour*, which was aired two nights later. Next morning, McCartney read the reviews aloud to a stunned crowd back at Apple: 'Blatant rubbish . . . Witless . . . The BBC should never have fallen for it.' There was guarded praise for the soundtrack, at least, though even here the critics noted certain 'way-out bits' and 'pseudo-Indian warbling'. Most of Fleet Street simply treated the whole thing as a joke. It was as if the Monkees, in their zany heyday, had decided to do *Hamlet*.

On 27 December, McCartney appeared on TV's *The Frost Programme* and neatly summarised the problem. 'The film was badly received because people were looking for a plot,' he said. 'There isn't one.' *Mystery Tour* was 'pretty good', Paul added, compared with the rest of the Christmas fare. 'Bruce Forsyth's show just wasn't funny, and you could hardly call the Queen's Speech a gasser.'

McCartney had been determined to realise his singular vision of *Mystery Tour*, and to retain primary authorship. As he'd ultimately insist, 'It was credited as directed by the Beatles. In actual fact, it was me that directed it.' Since he was also producer, performer, choreographer, writer-editor and chief barker, it's not surprising he took the reviews hard. By the same token, Paul revelled in the fact that *Mystery Tour* eventually turned a healthy profit. It was a particular hit on American university campuses, where it enjoyed the same midnight-cult status later conferred on *Monty Python*. A twenty-year-old student at California State College saw the film fourteen times, and would pay homage in 1978 by producing his own comedy feature about the Beatles. 'Paul McCartney opened a door in my mind,' he says. The feature was called *I Wanna Hold Your Hand*; the student was Steven Spielberg.

McCartney bounced back by writing a jazzy, barrelhouse tune he called Lady Madonna. Lennon thought this overrated. John was labouring on his own Big Statement, Across The Universe, which he claimed Paul 'sabotaged' in the studio. After some debate, McCartney's song became the Beatles' next single; Lennon's was eventually given to Spike Milligan, who sped it up, plastered it with bird noises and released it on a World Wildlife Fund charity album.

Back in the old days, even John had been forced to concede that McCartney, unlike him, could pull off brilliant impersonations of high-octane Fifties rock 'n' rollers. And Paul was still a chameleon, or liked to portray himself as one. The first thing he did each afternoon when he arrived in the studio was to warm up by hollering two or three Little Richard and Buddy Holly hits, then casually switch to Dean Martin mode. Once or twice, he succumbed to the charms of That's Amore. McCartney's vocal on Lady Madonna was a particularly rich, unpigeonholable mishmash – Memphis-cum-high Vegas, with funk and soul and boogie-woogie all showing up for the party. It was Elvis with a sense of irony.

On 19 February 1968 McCartney joined the other Beatles at the Maharishi's home ashram in Rishikesh, close to the Himalayan foothills. Although remote, this wasn't quite the spartan outpost sometimes portrayed; there were comfortable, English-style chalets, with TVs and radios, a nearly completed swimming pool and even a helicopter for the holy man and his guests' use. Over the next thirty-six days, Paul lived on a plentiful diet of soup, brown rice and spring water, augmented by wine and the potent local hash. The basic routine consisted of regular lectures and meditation, between which McCartney frequently strolled down to the banks of the heavily swollen Ganges with his guitar. He wrote 'about twenty' songs over the five weeks. George Harrison went so far as to complain that his fellow devotee was 'more into the next fuckin' album' than he was spiritual regeneration. Back In The USSR was the first in the bag, followed by Rocky Raccoon and Ob-La-Di, Ob-La-Da, the catch-phrase of a Nigerian musician called Jimmy Scott whom the Beatles had met hanging about the London club scene. John, George and Ringo all loathed the tune, it being a woeful lapse of taste, but Paul persevered; he eventually steered it through six sessions and three complete versions at Abbey Road, then wrote a generous cheque to Scott when the latter requested it. Grace under pressure, always.

Thursday 30 May: the Beatles regrouped in the studio, where they would remain for nearly five months. The word 'heavy' now entered their working vocabulary. In the meantime, Apple took a full-page ad in *New Musical Express*, showing Alistair Taylor performing as a one-man band over Paul's copy. 'This man has talent!' the caption ran. 'One day he sang his songs to a tape recorder . . . In his neatest hand-writing he wrote an explanatory note and, remembering to enclose a picture of himself, sent it to Apple Music. If you were thinking of doing the same thing yourself – do it now. This man now owns a Bentley!'

The result was a deluge of proposals – from, among others, the young David Bowie and a drifter named Charles Manson – that battered Baker Street like a particularly violent tornado. *I've been struggling to complete my album under the alias Buster Bloodvessel while*

*holding down two jobs to pay for mum's operation and the child care, and
just a fraction of the enormous sums you've so deservedly made would allow
me . . . A small cheque to one in need in the battle to fight the ignorant
corporate greedheads . . . You won't remember me but I sat behind you in
English at the Inny and I always knew that some day you . . . I enclose my
own privately funded LP, which consists of a mantra set to Indian . . .*
Many other applicants arrived in person at Apple high command,
whose reception area soon teemed with men and women bearing
everything from baroque architectural drawings to ventriloquist's
dummies. A number doggedly refused to leave the premises without
a friendly, artist-to-artist chat with Paul or John. 'It was a sweat,'
McCartney confirms.

Still, he was the one who tried hardest to be normal and accessible.
Paul walked the streets of London alone, often took the bus to Baker
Street and travelled on planes without bodyguards or the noisy
demands of celebrity. He was also responsible for signing Apple's
two most recognisable talents: the seventeen-year-old Mary (Those
Were The Days) Hopkin, and James Taylor.

Early that spring, McCartney and Jane Asher slipped off for a
weekend at his father and stepmother Angie's home in Cheshire.
Angie's own mother, Edie, happened to be staying. Although he wore
bell-bottoms and beads, and had just been voted 'Face of '68', Paul
had always identified with the older generation. He was enjoying a
nightcap with Edie, then, when she happened to mention that there
was a blackbird in the tree immediately outside, which had woken her
that morning. It was a bloody nuisance. Still, she rather liked its song.

So did Paul. At dawn, he was waiting with his new Brenell tape
recorder. Using the natural sound effects as inspiration, he
strummed up a lilting, folky number which evolved, over thirty-two
takes, into – the title came last – Blackbird. John Lennon listened in
silence when, a few nights later, McCartney once again tuned his E
strings down to D and picked out the haunting tune, with its lyrics
now 'a deep metaphor for the civil rights struggle' in America. On his

way home to Weybridge, John told his chauffeur that he thought Blackbird was really naff.

Paul and Jane were being besieged by fans – the so-called Apple Scruffs – back at Cavendish Avenue. She solved the problem by spending more and more time at the Bristol Old Vic. When pressed, neither party would ever give a date for the wedding.

On 11 May, Paul, John and their handlers had made a brief, chaotic, trip to New York to launch Apple USA. On the 14th there was a press conference at the Americana hotel, where John engaged in some blackout drinking and Linda Eastman left several messages. The following afternoon, she and Heather found themselves sitting between Messrs Lennon and McCartney in the limo taking them back to the airport. The two Beatles flew home alone, Paul to attend an Andy Williams concert, John, stoned, to meet Brigitte Bardot. Next morning a courier arrived at Cavendish Avenue bearing a package from New York – a wall-size blow-up of a photo showing Paul hugging Linda and her daughter. On the 18th, John called a board meeting at Apple to reveal formally that he was Jesus Christ. He wanted Derek Taylor in the press office to prepare a news release immediately to that effect.

According to the written notes, Paul stalled by 'ask[ing] for time to reflect on the announcement', but just days later he, George and Ringo were again left shaking their heads. Their co-director seemed to put it mildly, unpredictable.

On or around 20 May, John invited Yoko up to his home studio, obligingly equipped by Paul, recorded a sound collage they called *Unfinished Music No. 1: Two Virgins* (the front cover showing them full frontal; the back, their backsides), then, as dawn broke, fell into bed. Paul loathed both the photo and the album, but heroically kept his cool during a long meeting at EMI, in which Lennon announced he was 'splitting'.

'Do you hate me?' John asked him repeatedly. 'I'm crazy, you know.'

'No, I don't hate you.' McCartney spoke with his face partly averted from Lennon's rapt gaze.

'Aren't you pissed at me now, Paul? Not even a little bit?'

'I'm very proud of you.'

John eased off. 'Maybe I *won't* split.'

Two Virgins was released with a quote by Paul on the sleeve: 'When two saints meet, it's a humbling experience.' One afternoon that summer, an American employee of Apple was summoned to a meeting with Lennon and McCartney in the former's office. 'It was clear before I opened the door that John was making some small minatory remarks to Paul. The two words I distinctly heard shouted were *sabotage* and *album*. God knows why . . . McCartney was just sitting there; Lennon was behind his desk, pacing and rapping. I never even went in. I stayed in the doorway, which is where you're supposed to stand in an earthquake.'

On that note, everyone straggled back to the studio. The Beatles had had their ups and downs, but nothing could compare to that long summer, framed, on a wider canvas, by the second Kennedy assassination and the Vietnam protests in London. McCartney found the few creative exchanges frustrating. From time to time, he and John took to recording their contributions in a different room, sometimes in a different building. There was post-psychedelic dissolution of reason, images twisted with lurid expressionism to represent moral decay – and then there was the utter dross of What's The New Mary Jane, a track John apparently wrote with Yoko and Magic Alex. On 11 June, while Lennon was in Studio 3 compiling the tape-loops for Revolution 9, McCartney was in Studio 2 singing Blackbird. When everyone did meet, it was as a quintet. John insisted that Yoko now accompany him everywhere, and that she critique each and every track. Her list of suggestions was long – very long. That McCartney fall in with Lennon's wishes was the least of it. Paul later told Barry Miles, 'When Yoko referred to the Beatles, she called them "Beatles": "Beatles will do this. Beatles will do that." We said,

"*The* Beatles, actually, love." "Beatles will do this. Beatles will do that." She even took our personal pronoun [sic] off us, you know?'

Later in June, a pert twenty-four-year-old New Yorker named Francie Schwartz read of the wonderful new opportunities at Apple and beat a path to Baker Street, where she actually met McCartney and told him she wanted to 'make a movie'. Twenty-four hours later a motorcycle messenger arrived at her King's Road flat bearing a letter on company stationery; 'Come, call, do something constructive.' It was signed, 'With love, Paul.' She could forget about the film, McCartney promptly announced. But he could definitely use a friend at Cavendish Avenue while Jane was out of town. Schwartz was in residence there, on and off, throughout the summer, also attending several sessions at Abbey Road. It did seem, to some, that there was an 'atmosphere' at both places, and that it might have been better if Harrison, among others, didn't continually refer to Yoko as 'it'. Schwartz had taken some Creative Writing, and later described Paul as 'petulant, outrageous, adolescent, a little Medici prince, pampered and laid on a satin pillow at a very early age.'

On the evening of 20 June, McCartney flew to Los Angeles to attend the Capitol Records sales convention. According to Apple's Ron Kass, who accompanied him, he was bedding down on an industrial scale, enjoying 'his own black and white minstrel show' – a Swedish supermodel and the African-American actress Winona Williams, who stepped out a few years later with David Bowie. Despite the formidable competition, Linda Eastman flew in, at her own expense, to join him. The next morning Paul and Linda were strolling through the lobby of the Beverly Hills hotel when Williams appeared and, as she recalls, 'went into a pout. Paul said, "Come on, love, don't be like that." I asked, looking at Linda, "What's the deal here?" He said: "I've just been informed that I'm going to have a baby."'

In fact, it would be fourteen months before Linda gave birth to their first child. But then, back in London, Mal Evans noticed a subtle change in McCartney. 'He suddenly went from "Jane this, Jane that" to "our Linda" and her "lovely little kid."' When Asher came home Paul bought her five dozen roses, exhilarated once again at having not been caught.

On 30 June, McCartney was driving back from Bradford after producing two songs for the Black Dyke Mills Band, a pet project of his, when he stopped off for a pint at the Oakley Arms in Harrold. Within a few minutes he was laying out Little Richard tunes on the old pub piano. Beaming with pleasure, he told one of the locals, Alan Hazen, 'Now *that's* entertainment.' But Paul was even more thrilled at showing Linda off to his audience. 'He had this photograph he handed round,' recalls Hazen. 'Like a kid who's got a hot date – the one who brings the best-looking girl to the dance.'

Two days later, surrounded by their respective armies of highly paid lawyers and PAs, Paul and Sir Joe Lockwood, chairman of EMI, met with Lord Poole of Lazard's, one of the City's oldest merchant banks, to seek his advice about the growing rot (or 'fiscal imbalance' as Lazard's put it) at Apple. The parties eventually declined to enter into a contract. McCartney and Lockwood then approached Dr Richard Beeching, the man who, at a stroke, reorganised British Railways by axing a third of its network, with the loss of 67,000 jobs. Beeching looked over Apple's books and admitted defeat. His parting advice to Paul was, 'Get back to making music.'

On 17 July McCartney turned up, alone, to join John and Yoko at the London premiere of the *Yellow Submarine* animated feature. On the evening of the 18th he first howled the lyrics to Helter Skelter, the Beatles' emulation, or parody, of the Who. In the early hours of the 19th, Jane Asher came home unexpectedly from Bristol and finally 'confront[ed] Paul about various issues.' These apparently included his being in bed with Francie Schwartz. Later that morning, Margaret Asher appeared at Cavendish Avenue and swiftly removed all her daughter's clothes and personal effects. That

Saturday Paul tuned into BBC TV's *Dee Time* and declared himself 'well surprised' to hear Jane, appearing as one of the show's guests, reveal that her engagement was off. 'I haven't done it,' she announced. 'But it's over, finished.'

'I don't remember the break-up as being traumatic, really,' McCartney later told Barry Miles. Mal Evans and Alistair Taylor (who would call himself a 'grief counsellor' in the weeks ahead) took a very different view. 'When Jane left, Paul and the house both fell apart,' Evans remarked. McCartney obviously enjoyed being looked after in the routine sense – of having the toothpaste squeezed onto the brush for him, or having his boots polished and a new shirt laid out whenever he wanted it – and the business of actually fending for himself was so tedious and time-consuming that he never made much more than a few brief stabs at it. He was a dab hand at brewing tea, but that was his one and only feat in the kitchen. Without either Jane or the Kellys around, there was a tendency for unwashed dishes to pile up in the sink and for discarded tapes and clothes to be strewn across the floor. Paul had always enjoyed his Scotch and Coke, sometimes to excess. Now, accompanied by Mal (whose own drinking recognised no limit but unconsciousness), he began to 'royally overdo it . . . sink[ing] a bottle a night' chased by the best Peruvian flake.

Compounding the problem was the crisis at Apple, whose Electronics, Film and Publishing units were all haemorrhaging money. The group's business advisers had finally ordered an audit of Apple Retail, which was now being managed by a young man known only as Caleb, who went directly from Baker Street to a lunatic asylum. The boutique closed its doors for the last time on 30 July, having lost some £240,000 in its seven-and-a-half months of trading. Several policemen fought to control the riots as the remaining stock was simply given away to the public. The Beatles, Paul announced to the press, were 'tired of being shopkeepers'.

In the midst of this, McCartney was able to spare a thought for

Cynthia and Julian Lennon, the family John had abandoned for Yoko. 'I felt it was a bit much for them suddenly to be personae non gratae,' he said. So, very creditably, 'I decided to pay them a visit.' One summer's morning, the Aston Martin headed onto the familiar road to Weybridge, and as the mock-Tudor villas washed by in the sun, Paul began to sing. He had a tune: portly, anthemic, even if nothing to yet get audiences swaying and clapping along all around the world. On the return journey he hummed and whistled some more. The gentle swell of the music was soon matched by the lyrics, which were intended to console not only the Lennons but Paul himself. Hey Jules, he called it, before changing it to 'something a bit more *Oklahoma!*', an 'up' song. Back at Cavendish Avenue, McCartney sat down and played all seven minutes' worth for the Beatles. John Lennon unhesitatingly called it the best thing he'd ever heard, a classic. George had a heated debate with Paul about how the guitar part should go, but conceded it was a 'cool melody'. Ringo joined the consensus.

Hey Jude was released on 30 August 1968 and went to number one in Britain, America and fourteen other countries. It was the Beatles' most successful single.

As Mal Evans recalled it, McCartney 'sometimes came on a bit heavy' in the studio, perching on a high stool, 'working [the Beatles] hard when he wasn't upstairs on the intercom.' Once or twice, a musician came back from a break to find him playing their instrument. Even Ringo snapped when 'Sir Paul' publicly chided him during the rehearsal of Back In The USSR, actually quitting the group for a week. McCartney himself capably played the drums in his absence. When Ringo returned to Abbey Road he found that Paul had decked out his kit with bouquets of roses, and a banner saying 'WELCOME BACK'.

The album was now about halfway finished, and it had become almost a parlour game to try and guess what John saw in Yoko, or, rather, why he kept bringing her to the studio. McCartney showed real restraint, allowing only that 'Yoko's a very strong woman' and that 'she opened a lot of avenues for him. The trouble [was] that it encroached on the framework that we'd had going for us.' He, John and Yoko were actually the co-sponsors of a new, budget-price label for experimental and spoken-word albums, to be called Zapple. Paul wanted this to include the work of everyone from Ken Kesey to Fidel Castro, the idea being to take 'situationist stuff . . . electronics, speeches, poetry' to the masses.

On 9 September George Martin suddenly announced that he felt tired of the Beatles, felt they were wasting time, and said he was going on holiday. His worst fears would have been confirmed at that night's session, where Lennon played the sax, Mal Evans the trumpet, and McCartney vainly tried to keep order. At about the same time, Francie Schwartz left London and returned to New York. On the 18th, Paul walked into the studio humming a riff which became the catalytic blast of loud, electric rock he called Birthday*. The next week, Linda Eastman flew in to spend a month at Cavendish Avenue. She was shocked to find hordes of young girls outside, and only a lump of cheese and a bottle of sour milk within. The Apple Scruffs had tolerated, even liked Jane, but would never quite warm to the pushy New York divorcee with the young child back home. A night or two later, graffiti appeared, not for the last time, on the black metal gates to No. 7: GET LOST LINDA YOU SLUT. By mid-morning the last two words had been erased by an unknown fan, who still agreed with the main thesis. 'All very sad,' said Paul. 'People preferred Jane Asher. She fitted. Linda didn't fit.'

Alone of the Beatles, McCartney attended several marketing meetings at EMI that autumn. After a while, he started to notice how many of the top brass now looked like over-dandified relatives of the band: men in their forties and fifties who sported lime-green safari suits and wore frizzy hair with bristling moustaches. 'About the

* Frankie Avalon, whose 'pinched nose' vocal style McCartney admired, turned twenty-nine that day.

album cover,' they told him. 'We'd like to get your slant on some mock-ups we're working on. We're just mad about what this new designer has done, she's *just* out of St Martin's, but that folk-art-cum-abstract wave pattern with the 3-D finish, and the multi-coloured embossing—'

'Fabulous,' McCartney agreed.

But instead, he found a Royal Academy graduate named Richard Hamilton, and gave him a rather different commission. Paul wanted a plain white sleeve, he announced, with a stark, blind-stamped name: *The Beatles*.

The band took new premises that autumn, a listed Queen Anne mansion costing them £460,000 at 3 Savile Row. McCartney was consumed with the refurbishment and decoration of this 'keen pad', once the London residence of Nelson and Lady Hamilton. It became his latest obsession once the 'white album' sessions were finally brought to a close. Paul arranged for the numerous chandeliers and fireplaces to be cleaned, and the vintage, green carpets relaid, once reportedly turning up in a pair of overalls to lend a hand. Despite telling Apple's board that he wanted 'the very best' fixtures and fittings, McCartney kept a close eye on the bottom line. 'What a rip-off!' he said of a £90 bill for luxury wallpaper.

Paul also took Linda to Scotland for the first time, then made a flying visit with her to New York. He managed to see more of America in those few days than he had during three entire Beatles tours. By pulling on an old coat and a hat he was able to wander about Manhattan, 'just ambling up and down, going into bars, exploring.' The sight of Paul McCartney calmly walking around hand-in-hand with a blonde for once failed to cause a riot. Four-year-old Heather Eastman was apparently content with the arrangement. Linda's father had a similar soft spot for their house guest – possibly because, like Paul, he'd pulled himself up from an obscure lower-middle, if not working-class background, the kind despised by so many of his neighbours in East Hampton.

At the end of 1968, Linda again told Paul that she was pregnant. Happily, there was no mistake. Late on the night of 11 December, the Beatles' biographer Hunter Davies was woken up in his Algarve holiday home by someone throwing pebbles at the window. It was McCartney and his girlfriend asking if they could stay, and, having no cash on them, if Davies minded paying off their taxi? The driver went straight from there to the local radio station; so many reporters arrived in town the next day that Paul had to hold a press conference on the beach. Sometime later that week, he asked Linda to marry him.

The 'white album' had appeared on 22 November, five years to the day since the Fab Four – looming out from the cover with their fringes and black polo necks – released *With The Beatles*. Now sporting shoulder-length hair and shabby chic gear that might have come from Oxfam, Paul and the boys looked at least a decade older. Some days they were communicating with each other through their lawyers, and some days they didn't even bother.

All double albums should be made on cheap four-track recorders in St John's Wood, with creative differences being not so much aired as bawled out and everyone breaking up with their long-term partners. That way they might sound half as good as *The Beatles*, which played the pop-rock field – from the neck-snapping beat of Birthday to the lullaby of Good Night. Running in-between were the clipped, metallic riffs and acoustic singalongs that had begun life in the ashram. McCartney's Ob-La-Di, Ob-La-Da was probably the most commercial, crossing a ska beat with a cheerfully silly chorus. The reviews were not favourable, as was to be expected when a number starts off with Lennon pounding a Goon Show-style piano and ends in a sound distressingly like that of a chipmunk. Thirty-five years later, an online poll would rank this the 'worst song of all time.' Even so, Paul had the last laugh. At least fifteen other groups covered the tune, two of them hitting gold, helping it to an Ivor Novello award as the most performed hit of 1969 on British radio.

The album itself was a Christmas number one and spent six months on the chart. *Sgt. Pepper* may have been more organic, but this was a flawed, sprawling masterpiece, the last great extreme work the Beatles did.

As Paul and Linda settled down together, John and Yoko were busy outraging the public. There was the *Two Virgins* cover, followed by the news that Yoko was pregnant, then the morning they were busted for drugs. It was McCartney's well-intentioned idea that the couple should live at Cavendish Avenue, under the care of Mal Evans, while awaiting their baby. Complications arose and Yoko was rushed to Queen Charlotte hospital, where she lost her unborn child. Five days later, John pleaded guilty to possession of hash and was told by the magistrate, 'I am going to fine you according to your means.' (£150, with twenty guineas costs.) Lennon, understandably, was becoming a touch paranoid about life. But Paul, who could be 'uptight . . . a right Chairman Mao' when things were going well, had a rare gift for friendship when they weren't. He sought out the best lawyers for Lennon's case, and continued to make his own London home available whenever John and Yoko needed it.

From 10–12 December, the Rolling Stones rented the old *Ready Steady Go!* studios in Wembley to host a Christmas revue they called *The Rock 'n' Roll Circus*. There were cowboys on horseback, trapeze artists and clowns. The Stones and the Who both performed. As a sideshow attraction, Lennon joined Keith Richards, Eric Clapton and Mitch Mitchell in a hastily assembled supergroup to play John's Yer Blues.

Three months earlier, Mick Jagger had been hopelessly miscast as a sex-crazed rock star in the film *Performance*. His leading lady was Anita Pallenberg, Keith Richards' live-in girlfriend. Such was the zeal of Jagger and Pallenberg's lovemaking in the movie that a ten-minute snippet was entered in a Dutch porn festival, where it won the Golden Dong.

Tom Keylock, the Stones' long-time friend and tour manager, would apparently witness a curious scene backstage at Wembley. Lennon and Keith Richards were enjoying a smoke in the dressing room, where the 'white album' was blasting from someone's stereo. *Why don't we do it, do it in the road?* sang McCartney. Between drags, Keith was muttering about *Performance* and how Mick, his mate, had so taken to his role with Anita. '. . . cat told me it's in the script,' Keith could be heard saying, half narked, half amused. 'Can you believe that? "In the script," he says.'

'Of course I can believe it,' Lennon snapped. 'Listen to that!' And he pointed to the record player.

One day that winter, each of the Beatles received a five-page registered letter from Stephen Maltz, a partner in Apple's accountants Bryce Hanmer. He had some news that shocked them. Apple had been floated with a £1 million kitty, but had run through that, and a further £400,000, and now needed a fresh infusion of cash. Meanwhile, all four band members had heavily overdrawn their corporate accounts, McCartney by some £67,000.

'As far as you were aware,' wrote Maltz, 'you only had to sign a bill and payment was made . . . You were never concerned where the money came from or how it was being spent, and were long under the idea that you had millions at your disposal . . . Your personal finances are in a mess. Apple is in a mess.'

Looking back a few months later, Paul shook his head as if he still couldn't quite believe it. Thanks to heavy overheads and tax bills, 'we needed to earn £20,000 for every £1,000 we spent.' Maltz had urged them to 'cut Apple to the core', but there seemed little chance of any such outbreak of sanity. As well as their Mayfair headquarters, the group owned at least three other buildings with luxurious suites for press and PR officers, film-makers, conceptual artists and various friends, including a daily visitor who claimed he was Hitler. Two full-time chefs were on hand to supply the Beatles and their staff with cordon bleu meals. John and Yoko, during their frequent forays on Piccadilly or Bond Street, thought nothing of blowing £1,000 of Apple cash on clothes and shoes. Thousands more were being lavished on limos, private jets, hotels and pet projects notable only for their start-up costs. The laid-back management style had been forged early on, when an Apple director, in the course of moving files to Savile Row, had left the Beatles' personal financial records in the back of a taxi. They were never recovered.

Like so many potential 'friendly chats' at Apple, the interview that McCartney arranged with Dick James didn't go quite as smoothly as planned. Making his way to the oak-panelled boardroom, the Beatles' long-time publisher was surprised to be met by a professional cameraman and a sound recordist. 'I hope you don't mind this being filmed,' Paul said, adding that it was 'standard practice'.

Before James could respond, McCartney began his pitch: it was high time that he and John got a bit more in royalties. The original deal was a slave contract. James had come a long way from yodelling *Robin Hood* to his being the biggest and richest name in the business. And he owed it all to Lennon-McCartney. 'We appreciate what you've done for us,' Paul added suavely. 'We really do. But this isn't 1963 and we're not kids any more. It's an insult to our intelligence, asking us to accept forty per cent!'

If, for a fleeting moment, McCartney had ever imagined he could talk James around, he soon knew better. 'I'll take it under advice; I don't negotiate on camera, Paul,' he announced, not having bothered to open his briefcase. That concluded the meeting. At midnight on 31 December 1968, as the champagne corks popped, James made two resolutions for the new year: he'd lose the weight he'd begun to put on as a middle-aged man in the late Fifties, and Lennon-McCartney could go screw themselves.

CHAPTER FIVE

The End

At ten o'clock on the morning of 3 January 1969, a heavily bearded McCartney was sitting in the canteen at Twickenham film studios, where he'd arrived by bus, having his usual breakfast of baked beans on toast, smothered in brown sauce, with a cigarette chaser. His tea mug, an extension of his arm, was refilled about every five minutes. He had a friendly word for the various technicians, all of whom, however lowly, he knew by name, hustling by onto the set. Paul was 'extremely chuffed' to be back on the scene of *A Hard Day's Night*, where the band would be filmed rehearsing for a live concert – to be performed in either the Cavern or a Tunisian amphitheatre, according to mood – and/or a TV special. Although the project had formally gotten underway the day before, this was the first full working session. As the roadies arrived, banging drums and tuning guitars, an air of excitement prevailed. The Beatles were back: official.

All the good vibes vanished when John, George and Ringo walked in two hours later. None of them had appreciated McCartney's efforts to jockey them through the first day, which had yielded little usable material for the enterprise known as *Get Back*. As Lennon would say of the whole ordeal, 'It was set up by Paul, for Paul . . . I pretty damn well know we got fed up with being sidemen for Paul. After Epstein died, that's what began to happen to us.'

Just four days later, the cameras caught McCartney in conference with his colleagues:

I don't see why any of you, if you're not interested, got yourselves into this. What's it for? It can't be for the money. Why are you here? I'm here because I want to do a show, but I don't see an awful lot of support. [Long pause for response; none forthcoming.] There's only two choices: We're going to do it, or we're not going to do it. And I want a decision – because I'm not interested in spending my fucking days farting around here while everyone makes up their mind whether they want to do it or not. If everyone wants to do it, great. But I don't have to be here.

Three days after that, George Harrison quit the band in disgust. His departure was followed by a session of primal screaming witnessed by the film director Michael Lindsay-Hogg. 'When George left, the others went back down into the studio and started to play this really demonic riff . . . And then Yoko sat on George's blue pillow, and she sang her kind of crazy caterwauling singing, and they played for like half an hour; I mean, just *desperate* music. Desperate, desperate. They had this outburst of anger – anger at him leaving, anger at their needing him, anger at where they'd gotten to.'

George came back on 15 January, telling Paul in no uncertain terms that he could stuff the live gig and the TV special. He would, however, consent to an album. This would be produced not by George Martin, but by the Stones' own mixologist Glyn Johns. On the 22nd, everyone assembled in the half-finished basement studio at Savile Row, where they proved notably productive: John's Don't Let Me Down and Paul's Get Back (supposedly a dig at everyone from Yoko to Asian refugees), Two Of Us (for Linda), Let It Be (about his mother) and The Long And Winding Road (a ballad hawked to Tom Jones) all followed within four days. The sessions looked both forward and back: the Beatles rehearsed some of the material that surfaced on *Abbey Road*, and, on 28 January, took the opportunity to re-record the hit which started it all, Love Me Do. John got out of bed early and drove himself in from the country just to play with the band that morning, but could barely be heard as Paul stripped the original down and sang it in a low, bluesy growl.

The week before the roof fell in, everything seemed to be going well for McCartney. A *Yellow Submarine* soundtrack was following the 'white album' up the charts, the new tunes kept coming, and he no longer bothered pretending that he and Linda were 'just good friends'. Sometime towards the end of January, he took his fiancée to Cheshire to meet his father and stepmother. Jim liked his future daughter-in-law, although Angie had her doubts – 'I remember her looking around Rembrandt, which Paul legally owned, with a beady eye. Sure enough, next month a team came up from London to rip up all the carpets and paint the walls in loo-roll tones of lilac and pink.' The visit proved particularly happy for Paul, who happened to sit down next to ten-year-old Ruth at the piano, where she was learning Thomas Dekker's seventeenth-century lullaby Golden Slumbers. Ruth recalls her stepbrother liking the tune precisely because it was 'basic – not too many squiggly lines', and had the added advantage of being 'well out of copyright.' Golden Slumbers appeared on *Abbey Road*.

When Paul married Linda, he made it abundantly clear that he expected her to share his work. She took up the offer with gusto, and would frequently lock antlers with John and Yoko on the group's commercial and financial affairs. Although Linda had her engagingly hippyish side, she was also a shrewd businesswoman. While Paul and John were growing steadily apart by their late twenties for a variety of reasons, it's arguable that their choice of spouses hastened the process. Linda certainly came none too soon to Cavendish Avenue, which had been deteriorating badly since Jane Asher's departure. Like Rembrandt, McCartney's London pad was now also done up. Alistair Taylor supervised the month-long project, then presented the bill to Paul, who cheerfully signed it. At that point Linda looked at Taylor and said, 'And how much are you skimming off the top?'

Both Paul and Linda voiced their concerns about the permanent party now going on at Apple, which was awash in drink and drugs. The already heady mix of sex, scandal, art and fabled excess was spiked with a growing dose of politics, generally involving McCartney and partner attempting to impose some sort of order. One of Derek Taylor's numerous assistants in the press office recalls 'everyone hav[ing] a hard time squaring the old Linda of New York-groupie fame with the woman who prowled through [Savile Row] like an efficiency expert, with a notebook and a calculator.' When Taylor himself gamely asked for any cost-cutting suggestions, Linda took a deep breath and told him, 'I have *plenty* of them. People are fleecing Paul left and right here, with all the booze and coke and ordering in shit from Fortnum and Mason. Then there's that state-of-the-art studio. Don't make me laugh! Half the stuff's still in its packing cases and the Beatles can't even hear themselves properly through those crappy speakers. I've seen better control panels in an old Buick. And the other thing is publishing. Paul made a very reasonable offer to whatsisname [Dick James], who's made an effing *fortune* off him and John, and the guy, can you believe it, just split. Can we make him somehow see sense? Can we please do that? And another thing is tax. I want *someone* in charge here to sit down and tell me why Paul had to write out a personal cheque for sixteen grand to the Revenue. No one believes that he did, but I saw him do it, and I want you to get someone responsible in here and explain it to me. Today.'

An anonymous source would tell the author Geoffrey Giuliano that John Lennon physically menaced Linda during a particularly intense meeting at Apple in 1969. 'We couldn't hear what she actually said that upset him so. But whatever it was must have been brutal. John leapt to his feet like a madman, waving his clenched fists over his head like an angry gorilla . . . Paul threw himself in the middle of the fracas in the nick of time.'

Between the in-house strife and the non-stop siege at the door, Savile Row brought new meaning to the words 'hostile working environment'. Paul started to appear there less and less, leaving the place to John and Yoko and their guests.

'We haven't half the money people think we have,' Lennon confirmed to the press during the *Get Back* sessions. 'We're losing £50,000 a week . . . If it carries on like this we'll be broke in six months.' It was the moment thirty-seven-year-old Allen Klein had been waiting for all his life. The pop stars' accountant, famous for nosing out unpaid dues, sometimes in the hundreds of thousands, on behalf of his clients, was on the next flight to London. Klein was incredible. Squat, beady-eyed and built like a bag of spanners – habitually dressed in ill-fitting jeans and greasy sweaters – his greatest coup had come in July 1965, when he shouted at the elderly chairman of Decca Records, 'You've been fucking us over!' and in quick order netted a million-pound advance for the Rolling Stones. (A robust negotiator, in other words.) Both the industry and the press had long since treated him with awed respect, 'THE TOUGHEST WHEELER-DEALER IN THE POP JUNGLE' being one frequent headline. Klein was currently the subject of ten US tax-violation charges, would cross swords with the Securities and Exchange Commission, which briefly suspended trading in his Cameo-Parkway Inc, and enjoyed a virtual season ticket to the Manhattan court system. Not that the various writs and complaints were one-sided. Klein himself was lightning-quick to sue. He would even, as a snake when aroused will supposedly bite itself, sue his own lawyer, if he felt a suit had been inadequately prosecuted.

John and Yoko fell heavily for Klein, who charmed them by serving a meal of macrobiotic rice and quoting the right song lyrics.

The man 'did his homework', they reported. Lennon happened to be in a particularly fragile state, and may have recognised a kindred spirit in the 'hard-knocks guy' who, like him, had barely known his parents. At the end of their getting-acquainted session, Klein leant forward and asked the couple a simple question. 'Listen,' he said, before lapsing into one of his catchphrases. 'Whaddaya want?'

'We want bread, and we want a one-woman show for Yoko in New York.'

'You got it,' said Klein.

McCartney, however, betrayed minimal enthusiasm, even while reportedly acknowledging that 'Apple [was] rotten.' Klein's various tax plans didn't add up, and his slangy verbal gymnastics, which would be well suited to a neighbourhood bar in Newark, always seemed to confuse rather than clarify. On 12 February, Paul took the trouble to incorporate Adagrose Ltd, his own company outside the Beatles. He was also lobbying for a rival management appointee, his prospective father-in-law Lee Eastman. According to several witnesses, McCartney had to be hosed down when Lennon referred to Eastman as a 'country-club cunt', in contrast to the Jewish, working-class Klein. It was left to Linda to point out that her father was a self-made man whose own parents had arrived in America as penniless Russian immigrants. Once in the new world, it was learnt, the family had changed its name from Epstein.

John and Yoko had met Klein in his hotel suite on the night of 27 January. On the 28th and 29th the Beatles elected to record some of their old Cavern club ravers for the first time in seven years. On the 30th they were still talking vaguely about playing a show for the cameras, maybe in a Tuscan colosseum or somewhere in the Sahara, when Paul shrugged, decided oh, well, what the fuck, and ushered everyone up to the Savile Row rooftop. A full revolution had led the band back in a circle, hustling out some R&B chestnuts to a smattering of friends and admirers. The final concert lasted exactly forty-two minutes, until the woollens merchant next door, one

Stanley Davis, called the law. 'I want this bloody noise stopped,' he announced. The band were playing their third version of Get Back when a middle-aged PC in a raincoat picked his way through the chimney pots, tapped Ringo on the shoulder and drew his finger across his throat in the international sign for 'Gettoff'. Paul managed an ad-libbed 'You been playing on the roof again, You know your Momma don't like it, She's gonna have you arrested', before bowing to the tiny audience.

John then leaned into the mike and cracked a joke. 'I'd like to say thank you on behalf of the group,' he said. 'And I hope we passed the audition.'

Paul made his move early in February, asking Lee Eastman to come to London post-haste and inspect Apple's books. Instead Eastman sent his son John, fresh out of law school, a tactical blunder that miffed the other Beatles. Lennon later said that he would have probably signed with Eastman had he bothered to fly over in person. A meeting of all parties at Claridge's Hotel quickly degenerated into a slanging match. Klein claimed that his fellow New Yorker took the occasion to 'launch an attack on my personal integrity', and that McCartney and the firm of Eastman & Eastman were denying him access to vital records at Savile Row. Among these were the various files on NEMS, Brian Epstein's original management company which continued to bank the Beatles' royalties, deduct twenty-five per cent, and then post a cheque to Apple. Alarmed by the Klein-Eastman hostilities, Eppy's younger brother Clive now took the opportunity to sell the firm, for a million pounds in cash and stock, to a concern calling itself Triumph Investment Trust. Klein promptly called another summit, in which he vowed to extricate the Beatles from Triumph (or 'Tit' as he dubbed it) and its shyster quarter-share in their earnings. McCartney boycotted this particular conclave, instead sending his solicitor, a Charles Corman. John Lennon leant over the boardroom table and asked Corman if he could play bass guitar.

On 12 March 1969, Paul married Linda at Marylebone Register Office, having found their way in past the dustbins at the back door. This was followed by a brief church blessing ceremony. Although several hundred fans enlivened the occasion, there were only a few invited guests. Paul's father stayed home and his brother Mike, the best man, arrived an hour late after his train had broken down. John and Ringo both sent regrets; George was busted that same day for drug possession, and so unable to attend. When Paul and Linda drove back to Cavendish Avenue they found that more graffiti had been daubed on the wall, and crude petrol bombs thrown at the front door. After that, a policeman stood on guard outside the house until 17 March, when the couple flew to New York to spend a month with Paul's new in-laws.

Eight days after the McCartneys' wedding, Lennon and Yoko Ono went through a civil ceremony in Gibraltar. They held a riotous press conference later that evening in Paris, before staging the first of their famous bed-ins at the Amsterdam Hilton. On 21 March every British newspaper ran front-page pictures of the couple, prominently featuring Yoko and her dramatic white miniskirt. 'We're so much in love,' remarked John. 'It's a sacred thing . . . We would have liked to have been married by the Archbishop of Canterbury, but they don't take divorced people.' A few churlish observers felt the Lennons' chief motivation may have been neither romantic nor spiritual. Rather, it was competitive.

On 28 March, Dick James sold his shares in Northern Songs to Associated TeleVision (ATV), the network run by the cigar-chewing mogul Lew Grade. That the £3 million deal went through behind Paul and John's backs only added to their displeasure. McCartney apparently learned of the sale when a journalist managed to phone him in New York, seeking a comment. Paul replied in words of one syllable, requesting that the press leave him alone. McCartney himself then called Neil Aspinall at Apple, who confirmed the worst. At a stroke ATV had acquired thirty-five per cent of Northern, with its 160 Lennon-McCartney copyrights, and soon offered £9.5 million for the remainder of the company. When pressed, Dick James would admit, 'It was unfortunate . . . I could have telephoned Paul and John, but it would have been difficult. The call would have gone through a number of people and there was a need to keep it quiet.' McCartney theorised that 'our Dick' was off his rocker, though that told only half the story. James confirmed to his friend Ray Coleman that he'd resented 'hav[ing] a camera stuck in my mush' when invited to the Apple boardroom and, further, he wanted nothing to do with Klein. He was too old and too rich, James added, to 'put up with that sort of shit.'

Ironically, James' act of revenge brought Paul and John closer together than at any time since *Sgt. Pepper*. Once back in London, after mutually denouncing their ex-partner, they instructed Klein to put together a cash counter-bid. This was complicated by the arrival of a third party, a consortium of City brokers and investment fund managers, on the scene. When the consortium withdrew, selling out its own interest to ATV, Lew Grade summoned the *Financial Times* and announced 'the Beatles are mine'. At that stage, Paul and John sold their remaining shares in Northern, netting about £2.7 million between them. Any slight pleasure they may have taken in their windfall was rather spoilt when Lennon discovered that McCartney owned 107,000 more shares in the company (worth some £150,000) than he did. Paul, it emerged, had been quietly buying Northern stock at strategic moments ever since its flotation in February 1965. John was to claim intemperately that this was a 'shafting', and that he and McCartney had had a verbal deal to keep their ownership on a fifty-fifty basis.

In the midst of this, the Beatles released their nineteenth single, Get Back. Paul's fitfully inspired rocker, sporting lyrics about transsexuals and pot smoking, made do with two chords. It topped the charts in Britain, America and around the world, selling four million copies.

'Surreal' was the word most insiders used to describe the atmosphere that spring at Apple, where Klein and the Eastmans somehow
coexisted as, respectively, the band's acting business manager and
lawyers, though they might as well have exchanged their business
attire for the helmet and chain mail of the medieval jouster. This pact
had been reached after Lennon again objected to the Eastmans'
outright appointment. Or, as John later expressed his reservations to
Rolling Stone, 'They're *fuckin' bastards*. Eastman's a WASP Jew, man!
[And] that's the worst kind of Jew on earth!'

To anyone who knew Klein, what happened next was entirely
predictable. The Terror that spread through Savile Row was as
palpable as if a guillotine had been erected in the marbled lobby. Ron
Kass and Jane's brother Peter Asher, despite having helped to sell
some twenty million records for Apple, were both terminated.
Dennis O'Dell, head of Apple Films, went; so did the cordon bleu
cooks, the liveried doorman and the in-house translator to whom
Yoko liked to chat in Japanese. Apple was wound up as abruptly as
if Klein had physically pulled a plug on it. Apple Retail, Apple
Electronics, Apple Publishing – all liquidated. In a tale of three
Taylors, Alistair was unceremoniously axed; James asked for his
release, citing an aversion to 'politics'; Derek, albeit with one
assistant instead of five, survived. There was even talk of sacking
McCartney's friend Neil Aspinall, the man who used to drive the
Silver Beatles around in his old Commer van. Attempting to win
Paul's approval, Klein had called an emergency board meeting,
which kicked off aggressively. 'This is no place for sentiment,' he
announced. 'You've got to have brass balls!' Then, as soon as he was
challenged by his calm and determined opponent, Klein relented.

The stand-off at Savile Row lasted until early May. On the 8th,
Klein agreed terms with John, George and Ringo which formally
appointed him their manager in exchange for twenty per cent of the
action. In material terms, he thus became the 'fifth Beatle'. Paul was
willing to let Klein act for him, at least in a cost-cutting capacity, but

only for fifteen per cent. He was outvoted. Klein then attended a recording session on 9 May, where he allegedly waved the contract in McCartney's face, urging him, 'Sign here! Twenty per cent! My board won't accept any less!' From this point on, things began to deteriorate badly. 'You've got to be fucking kidding!' Paul replied. 'That's the dumbest thing I've ever heard in my life. What board? Don't make me laugh!'

Later that night McCartney joined in a session for the American guitarist Steve Miller, flailing the drums on a track called My Dark Hour.

It wasn't long, however, before Glyn Johns excitedly arrived at Savile Row bearing an acetate of the *Get Back* album. It was well named, he insisted. Here was the Beatles as nature intended, playing live, with no studio hocus-pocus or even that many overdubs. Where a *Sgt. Pepper* had mesmerised, *Get Back* mustered its force into a brass-knuckled punch. 'It's really *raw*,' Johns enthused, the cri de coeur of the back-to-basics rock 'n' roller.

Too bad the record stank. Paul and John both vetoed it, though they did collaborate on Lennon's account of his wedding and its aftermath, an engaging toe-tapper called The Ballad Of John And Yoko. It, too, went to number one.

A hardy reporter made it up to the McCartneys' Scottish farm one day that summer. He wanted to know if Paul was indeed dead, as rumour insisted. All he got was an earful from Linda. But the investigative journalism (muckraking, as it was called back then) didn't end there. After another bawled exchange, McCartney himself appeared, haranguing his visitor from behind a bottle of wine, confirming that he was very much alive, even if, as he made clear, unavailable for comment. 'I was switched on for ten years and now I'm switched off,' he's said to have shouted as the man retreated down the dirt road to Machrihanish Bay. A rather bitter story was subsequently filed, then spiked, complaining that Paul was living in a 'straggly collection of tin shacks' with a 'ferocious, and heavily pregnant gatekeeper.' There was a grain of truth to it: Linda would later refer to herself as the 'Berlin Wall' between her husband and the world, loyally screening him from fans, press and, most notably, management. By now even the McCartneys were reconciled to the new arrangements at Apple. The outlaw, as Paul wryly noted, had screwed over the in-law. To convey his disdain for the whole business, McCartney now rarely if ever appeared at Savile Row, preferring to send his Mr Corman to represent him in meetings with the other Beatles.

Later that summer Paul and Linda spent a month in sun-drenched Benitses, a then tiny and undiscovered fishing village in Corfu. No Beatle holiday could ever be entirely tranquil, even so, and before long the couple were again dodging 'Are you dead?' and 'How's Yoko?' questions from the media. McCartney was convinced that if only the band could get back to playing live, perhaps under an alias like Ricky and the Redstreaks, everything would still be all right. He even drew up a typically detailed plan for a tour of clubs and cinemas – only to read on the day he returned to London that George Harrison was refusing to set foot on stage again.

A day or two later, Paul invited Ringo (to whom he'd sent a postcard enthusing, 'You're the greatest drummer in the world. REALLY!') to have dinner with Linda and him at Cavendish Avenue. Unhappily, the talk soon turned to the goings-on at Apple. Ringo would later remark, 'It seemed as soon as I started saying, "Well, maybe Klein isn't so bad and we should give him a chance," Linda would start crying. In a few minutes, I'd be saying the same – "He isn't *so* bad" – and Linda would start crying again. "Oh, they've got you, *too*," she kept saying.'

After that, McCartney turned his attention to George Martin, asking him to produce a new Beatles album 'the way we used to do it'. Martin was surprised to learn that Paul had somehow convinced John, George and Ringo to convene, once again, at Abbey Road. As it was, the sessions got off to a notably shaky start. McCartney was the only Beatle present on day one; George and Ringo drifted in the next evening, John (after being involved in a car crash while on holiday in Scotland) a week later. Yoko would also be on hand, surveying proceedings from her bed installed in the middle of Studio 2.

On 9 July, everyone was together in the same room to record McCartney's incongruously chirpy tale of serial murder, Maxwell's Silver Hammer. Some of the critics would later call this a gutsy departure, showcasing Paul's metaphorical lyrics and subtle use of a Moog synthesiser to broaden the scope of even the simplest tune.

John Lennon called it bullshit.

'By the time we made *Abbey Road*,' McCartney noted, 'John and I were openly critical of each other's music. He wasn't much interested in performing anything he hadn't written himself.' Paul would say of Lennon's Come Together, recorded in late July, 'I would have liked to sing harmony on it [and] I think John would have, too. But I was too embarrassed to ask him, and I don't work to the best of my abilities in that situation.'

On 8 August, the Beatles strolled over the zebra crossing just outside the studio gates to provide the famous photograph for the album cover. The next night, in Los Angeles, Sharon Tate and four of her friends were butchered by the Manson clan; Manson claimed to have found his inspiration in Paul's song Helter Skelter, which its author intended as 'symbolic of life's ups and downs.' On 15 August, half-a-million concertgoers assembled at Max Yasgur's farm in Bethel, New York, for the start of a three-day festival known to history as Woodstock. The Sixties were swinging faster now. On the 18th, Paul settled at a piano for the last full session and sang the lines to The End custom-fitted for the occasion. 'The love you take,' he concluded, 'is equal to the love you make.' In the early hours of 21 August, everyone sat upstairs in the Abbey Road booth and listened to a playback of the completed album. The final touch was twenty seconds of silence followed by McCartney's acoustic fragment Her

Majesty. It would be the last time all four Beatles were in the studio together.

A week later, Linda gave birth to the McCartneys' first child, Mary Alice. Ringo, alone of the band, sent his compliments. Of course, no joyful emotion remained untinged by another, rather less happy one, for very long. A few nights later, McCartney happened to pass the Lennons in the corridor at Abbey Road, where he was helping record the Apple protégés Badfinger. Paul and John sat down for a moment and somehow got talking about money. It's unlikely that a self-made millionaire of John's stature could be found who knew less about personal finance than he did. He had no idea how to balance a cheque book, nor that loans were generally repaid at interest. When he signed for two new cars, a Maxi and a Mini, he thought that 'the firm' would simply foot the bill. Because it was impossible to listen to Lennon for very long without wanting to impart advice, McCartney said something responsible about how he and Yoko might want to draw up a budget. John went loco, and told Paul to fuck off.

Late in the afternoon of 19 September 1969, after flying back from the debut performance of the Plastic Ono Band in Toronto, Lennon assembled everyone upstairs in Savile Row and announced that he was no longer a Beatle.

'You don't mean it,' said Paul.

John brought his fist down on the boardroom table. 'Don't you get it?' he shouted. 'It's *over*. I want a divorce, just like my divorce from Cynthia.' Paul started to remonstrate, but found that, for once, he was talking to himself. John was already running down the stairs with Yoko.

Basically a set of solo turns, *Abbey Road*, out that week, hangs together remarkably well. In particular, the flip side, or Long Medley, stands as a testament to McCartney and Martin's skills at the mixing desk, a host of synthesised fills, orchestral washes and slick segues disguising the paucity of the actual tunes. Right up until the last moment, Lennon had wanted his material on one side of the album and McCartney's on the other, with an announcement to that effect stamped on the sleeve.

This is one of those official classic rock records, like *Bridge Over Troubled Water*, whose reputation ought to be sealed up in an eternal amber of chart and sales statistics. (*Abbey Road* sailed to the top before Christmas.) Yet side one, at least, combined a still vivid, fallible talent with proper songs. McCartney's masterful production job contained both gems (John's Come Together, George's Something) and clunkers (Octopus's Garden – a poor man's Yellow Submarine). The whole thing ended with Ringo's first and last ever drum solo, Paul, John and George's duelling guitars and McCartney's immortal rhyming couplet. His piano accompaniment here was slightly flat, the one technical blot on the album. Almost forty years later, *Abbey Road* still holds up, and the lyrics still serve as a send-off to that innocent, idealistic decade. The lines about Paul never getting his money are almost unbearably poignant. It became a document: not only expertly put together, but, to some, actually epitomising the Sixties. Seeing off the likes of Cream and Jethro Tull, it spent four months at number one. Right in the midst of their break-up, the Beatles hit their commercial peak.

Acting as both the band's creative director and cheerleader, McCartney would go to any lengths to polish the end-product until it gleamed. Lennon couldn't tolerate repetition. Indeed, he didn't much care for the protracted hassle of making a record. Often friction broke out when Paul's sensitivities clashed with John's impatience, as happened during one of the final days' work on *Abbey Road*, when Lennon arrived to find that McCartney, piqued by something said in the studio the night before, had decided to stay home with Linda.

According to one of the Apple Scruffs still keeping vigil, around ten that morning an indignant Lennon appeared in Cavendish Avenue and began hammering on Paul's gate. As soon as someone answered the intercom, John let rip with a whole series of complaints, shouting, 'You fucker! We've all shown up and you're sulking! Get your arse out here!' A moment later, the machine spoke back: 'Don't be silly. I'll be there in half an hour.'

While McCartney coped with the ups and downs of the Beatles, he was also enjoying mixed reports from Apple. Allen Klein had, at first, signally failed to renegotiate the ten-year deal which Epstein had signed with EMI in February 1967. (With brutal simplicity, Klein then informed the label that, unless they agreed to his terms, no further Beatles product would be forthcoming – sufficient to ensure a 'marginal hike'.) Nor had he prevailed over ATV. By late 1969, Lew Grade's network controlled more than ninety-nine per cent of Northern Songs, including the golden copyright to Yesterday. Klein had, however, convinced Triumph, with some encouragement from the High Court, to part with its quarter-share of Beatles income in return for a £1,125,000 cash settlement.

By far Klein's greatest coup came that September, when he persuaded the Beatles' American label, Capitol, to raise the band's royalty from forty to fifty-seven cents an album, or twenty-five per cent of wholesale, jumping to seventy-two cents after three years. These were unprecedented figures in the record business. What's more, Klein had swung the deal at the very moment Lennon had announced he was quitting. No one at Capitol had any idea of the stormy goings-on at Savile Row. All they asked was that the band fulfil their commitment to two albums and three singles a year, inclusive of re-releases, and that they show up occasionally for a photo-op in the Capitol boardroom.

According to testimony Klein later provided the High Court, he 'more than doubled the Beatles' income in the first nine months after I took over as manager in May 1969 . . . As a result of my efforts, their partnership monies increased from £850,667 for the year ended

March 31 1969 to £1,708,651 in the nine months ended December 31 1969.' Klein added, 'I deny that the Beatles have been prejudiced by having me as their manager. On the contrary, they have greatly benefited. Mr McCartney has made attacks on my commercial integrity in general, and my dealings with him in particular. I am concerned to answer these attacks, [to] rebut McCartney's allegation.'

According to Klein, the Beatles and their remaining employees had much to thank him for. 'Paul McCartney never accepted me as his manager, but he accepted the benefits which I have negotiated in that capacity . . . For the first time, the Beatles partnership is solvent.' A dark mood, even so, prevailed at Savile Row. Although Klein held court in the formal dining room most lunchtimes, his table was never crowded. He'd alienated too many people, and there was the residual shock of all the sackings. Sure, he'd taken some tough decisions, Klein allowed, and maybe some of those guys were sore losers. There was Alistair Taylor, for one, who'd faithfully served both NEMS and Apple for over a decade. It was Taylor's signature that witnessed the first Beatles contract, after which, as he puts it, he'd 'arranged flights, deflected paternity suits, lent money and often a shoulder to cry on, becom[ing] a grief counsellor for Paul McCartney when Jane Asher dumped him.' When Taylor was summarily fired he spent two days trying to phone Klein, Paul and John to discuss the matter. None of them would take his call.

Late in October, McCartney retreated to Scotland with Linda, Heather and the newborn Mary, writing some of the songs that appeared on his first solo album. It was the only time that friends would remember seeing him so depressed. Many of the same friends credited Linda with steering him through that winter into his fabulously successful second career. Like Paul, she was meticulous to the point of perfectionism. Bit by bit, she educated herself on every aspect of his craft – all his foreign sales and royalties, the copyrights held by ATV, Klein's dealings with Capitol, and that mysterious American entity, Maclen. She went to the stationer's in

Campbeltown to buy Paul's preferred brand of felt-tips and made sure that he had a fresh supply of his favourite paper. When he wanted company she was there, sunny and attentive; when he wanted silence, she disappeared. Once inspiration struck, she sang harmonies with him into a Studer tape deck, working up the tracks that he released commercially six months later. No wonder the first title McCartney wrote down in his notebook was The Lovely Linda.

Ten years earlier, Paul had rung in the Sixties as one of the Nerk Twins, crooning country and western hits in a suburban pub. Now he drove back to his St John's Wood mansion with all the Magrittes. That he'd caught and changed the spirit of the decade, making music that was wildly popular and still out there, was beyond debate. But, for him, money and power were balanced by the realisation that it was 'fucking heavy' being Beatle Paul.

On New Year's Eve, both he and George were guests of honour at Ringo's pad in Highgate. McCartney had used the opportunity to write Lennon a long, conciliatory letter. He noted that Klein had delivered the goods with Capitol, which, Paul admitted, was pretty rich stuff. He added that making *Abbey Road* had been a pleasure, and that he still wished they could release *Get Back*. He concluded that a lot had gone down since Epstein's death, and that he sincerely hoped they could all meet over a smoke, at Ringo's, for a discussion of those issues which lay between them.

John declined the offer.

One night early in the Seventies, McCartney sat down in Cavendish Avenue and listened to a newly edited version of *Get Back*. After working on it for six months, Glyn Johns had managed to pare a hundred tracks of opiated sloppiness to a dozen that were merely rough and ready. Paul would recall thinking, 'This is brave . . . It was the Beatles stripped back, nothing but four guys in a room with [keyboards player] Billy Preston. It was almost scary . . . I remember being in this empty white room, and getting a thrill. It was very minimalist and I was impressed.'

Allen Klein, however, was after something very different. Concerned that *Get Back* was insufficiently commercial (or, as Klein allegedly expressed it, 'a crock of shit') he arranged with Lennon to bring in the wall-of-sound producer Phil Spector, who happened to be working with John on his single Instant Karma. McCartney knew all about Spector, but not about the full extent of his brief. The 'tycoon of teen', in something of a career slump since February 1964, would take the opportunity to spatter *Get Back*, and in particular The Long And Winding Road, with a rich variety of strings, horns and heavenly choirs. This radical surgery took place at Abbey Road between 23 March and 2 April, an event Klein considered of such little consequence that he didn't even mention it to the song's composer. The first Paul heard of it was when he received a test pressing of the album, along with a curt note giving him its release date. He went nuts.

McCartney: 'I wasn't involved and I wasn't consulted. At least in the past if you were going to put strings on it, someone would run the arrangement past me . . . The [final] straw was not being asked, then putting what I thought was crap on it. It was the worst time of my life.'

Meanwhile, McCartney had continued his boycott of Apple, preferring to spend his time with Linda and recording his own album. From 12 February to 16 March he was at Morgan studios, just west of Abbey Road, working night-shifts under the alias Billy Martin. How much he'd invested in the whole project became clear when Klein and the other three Beatles casually vetoed its release date. They wanted to put out the *Let It Be* album (as *Get Back* was now known) that same month. Paul nearly came to blows with Ringo on the matter, but eventually persuaded George and him, as co-directors of Apple, to let his record appear three weeks before the group's. Klein's secretary conveyed the news to John, who had a distinct response.

'That *cunt*,' he said.

By 6 March the Beatles had put out their twenty-second and final single, the title track of *Let It Be*. Lennon hated it. 'Are we supposed to giggle during the solo?' he'd unkindly asked McCartney. The public, too, bought the song (today an anthem) in only moderate quantities; there's something hapless about a tune kept off the top of the chart by Lee Marvin's Wanderin' Star. Later that month, John and George sent Ringo to Cavendish Avenue to discuss scheduling arrangements with Paul. The drummer would later give the High Court a lugubrious account of their meeting. 'McCartney went completely out of control,' he said. 'He shouted at me, prodding his fingers towards my face, and said: "I'll finish you now!" and "You'll pay!" He told me to put on my coat and get out.'

On 23 March, McCartney put the finishing touches to his solo album, designed and proofed the cover, and collaborated with Apple's Peter Brown on a press kit. This took the form of a bland self-interview about the songs and their recording, until Paul reached question twenty-four:

Q: Is it true that neither Allen Klein nor ABKCO Industries have been or will be in any way involved with the production, manufacturing, distribution or promotion of the record?

A: Not if I can help it.

Q: What is your relationship with Klein?

A: It isn't. I am not in contact with him and he doesn't represent me in any way.

Paul then asked himself whether he was planning a new album or single with the Beatles; whether he could foresee Lennon-McCartney becoming an active firm again; and whether he missed working with John, George and Ringo. The one-word answer, repeated three times, was 'No'.

For six months, Lennon had laid off on his demands for a 'divorce' so as not to jeopardise Klein's various deals on the band's behalf. And now, John noted tetchily, Paul was 'go[ing] public . . . There's something wrong in your personality where you constantly need the press for your own self-benefit.' Some felt that Lennon objected more to McCartney's tactics than to his actual decision. After all, they basically wanted the same thing. 'I'm doing what you and Yoko are doing,' Paul had told Lennon one night on the phone. 'I'm putting out an album and leaving the group, too.'

'Good,' John replied. 'That makes two of us who have accepted it mentally.'

On the night of 1 April, Spector grafted eighteen violins, seventeen other musicians and a fourteen-piece choir onto The Long And Winding Road. Five days later, McCartney heard the full horror of *Let It Be* for the first time. What had started out as a plan to make a record of the Beatles live had turned into a much overdubbed patch-up job. Paul fired off a letter to Klein which began, 'Dear Sir: In future no one will be allowed to add to or subtract from a recording of one of my songs without my permission', and went on from there to get crisp. Klein didn't bother to reply. McCartney then authorised Peter Brown to release his promotional questionnaire. On 10 April 1970, the world's press would run endlessly varied stories under the single headline: 'PAUL IS LEAVING THE BEATLES'.

It had to happen eventually. McCartney put out a record that wasn't perfect from start to finish. His homespun solo debut was essentially Paul amusing himself as much as his fans, the last of his albums to be locked down before the excesses of Seventies rock-stardom with Wings gripped him for a decade. Though lumbered with lazy throw-aways – elemental jams that the Beatles wouldn't have considered worthy of release – there was also a charm and warmth that turned serviceable songs into hits-in-waiting. After repeated listens, even a track like Junk would roll over and reveal its charms. Every Night and Maybe I'm Amazed, in particular, exuded a happy mix of blues, soul and classic pop balladry that never strayed into schmaltz. It was a testament to McCartney's self-confidence that he could stick Top Twenty fare like this next to a sound collage of Linda and him rubbing the rims of their wine glasses. For good measure, he even threw in a snatch of Suicide, the tune spurned by Frank Sinatra.

McCartney was released on 17 April; eight years later, the critics Roy Carr and Tony Tyler would write that 'it was hastily made, [and] the very unpretentious qualities which McCartney tried to emphasise were badly misconstrued. Hindsight displays its class.' The album sold over two million copies.

Ironically, *McCartney*'s success coincided with its author's first real money worries in seven years. The royalties were still flowing, but only after Lew Grade and ATV deducted both their partnership and management fees. Maclen Music, the company that actually banked the funds, was aggressively pursuing ATV for 'lost dues' from past public performances of the songs, an action that would drag on (with the freezing of most Maclen assets) until 1983. Paul had signed away the earnings from everything else he did to Apple, which divided the profit, if any, equally between the four Beatles. Klein administered this at a remuneration of twenty per cent of the gross receipts. Thanks to the various court actions and management commissions, McCartney's actual post-tax income in 1970 was between £120,000 and £125,000. After paying repair bills and salaries at High Park Farm and Cavendish Avenue (where, at Linda's insistence, he again employed a full-time housekeeper) he had between £75,000 and £80,000 cash in hand, for a year that would require at least £100,000. While *McCartney* was going multi-platinum, McCartney was sitting down with his accountant, worrying about gas, phones and electricity.

Early that spring, Paul sent a Mr Abbott to Cheshire to go through his father and stepmother's books. As a result of this audit, the McCartneys' joint bank account was closed down. Instead, Jim was given an allowance of £7,000 p.a., to be paid in a lump sum each April. Even in 1970, it was a relatively modest income for a family with heavy medical bills and an eleven-year-old child in school.

'The long and short of it,' says Angie McCartney, 'is that we were suddenly short of money. Overnight, we had a real headache.'

As Jim's health worsened, the family moved out of Rembrandt and into a two-bedroomed bungalow nearby. Paul himself helped make the arrangements and often visited with Linda while on their way to Scotland. It remained a close father-son relationship, which, even so, was sometimes difficult. Several of Jim's relatives wanted him placed in a nursing home, and came to regard Angie – who cared for him night and day – as a gold-digger. 'The McCartneys had their ups and downs and disagreements,' she notes. 'But at the end of the day they were very loyal and very protective of one another . . . If someone seemed to attack one of them, they mobilized.'

Out that May, the *Let It Be* album and film. The former came in a glossy boxed set, sheathed in black, giving it the feel of a marble tombstone. The latter proved something of a shock, particularly after the non-stop advertising blitz promising 'The Beatles Live!' and 'Classic Concert Performances!' Anyone who went to see it on that basis would have felt sorely cheated: much of the action consisted of a glassy-eyed Paul muttering at an oddly subdued John, George and Ringo. None of the band would bother to attend the premiere. Reviews were generally poor, the *New York Times* calling it 'sad and none too artfully made . . . The most intriguing figure of the film is Yoko Ono, [who] remains at her husband's side, expressionless and silent, her eyes never leaving him.'

Amongst the album's little, honking guitar songs, Spector's Radio 2 strings and massed choir were judged, by the same critic, 'mildly over-done'. To the more hard-boiled reviewer at *Village Voice*, the orchestrations stood out 'like a turd in a teacup'.

McCartney needed no further encouragement. On 15 June, he

had Lee Eastman write to Klein to insist that the Apple partnership be formally dissolved. Once again, Klein didn't reply.

As things reached their nadir, McCartney contacted Lennon direct, suggesting a clean, four-way split, and enclosing a twelve-page draft petition. John replied with a postcard which read: 'Get well soon. Get the other signatures and I'll think about it.' Paul would later note that this was the moment when he first feared he might have to sue the Beatles.

He would reach this decision only after six months of soul-searching and consultation. In his typically meticulous, unhurried manner, McCartney sat down with the Eastmans and his British lawyers, notching up some fourteen meetings between 3 July and 29 August, to weigh his options. On the one hand, there was the cast-iron agreement of April 1967 which bound everyone together for ten years. On the other hand, there was the fact that Paul and George weren't speaking, Ringo apparently wanted to become a film star, and John – now in primal scream therapy in California – was busy recording the song God, which featured the lyric 'I don't believe in Beatles.'

The fault line had been there at the outset, of course. If McCartney had thought he was the one true pioneer of the group, Lennon, it emerged, had long thought of himself as saddled with a 'pop-type guy', while he and George, by contrast, he told the court, 'preferred what's now called "underground".' The cracks had really begun to appear only around the time of *Sgt. Pepper*. Things had gone so well up until then that the band had actually turned out three chart-busting albums – including songs like Yesterday – without a contract.

With his career seemingly crashing around him, McCartney retreated back to the farm in Scotland. The place had the advantages of both rugged beauty and almost total inaccessibility. To reach the house, a visitor had to climb a turnstile to pass down a tiny, potholed lane and would be met, even then, by a flimsy, three-roomed shack, where the living-room sofa consisted of a potato crate with a mattress thrown on top of it – hardly the typical rock star Taj Mahal. Paul and his family spent much of the summer there. He later remembered it as a low time, accusing Klein, among others, of waging a vendetta against him. Lee Eastman flew up for yet more meetings. It attests to the strength of their relationship that McCartney still hesitated to sue Lennon, whom, he thought, might yet have a change of heart. 'It's happened before,' he noted quite factually. But as Linda, her father and a guest sat around the kitchen table with Paul one August night, it soon became clear that something was dreadfully wrong. As the others chatted, McCartney remained focused on a bottle of Scotch. The hours passed and he barely spoke, instead knocking it back as fast as his body would allow. With each swig, a deepening anger seemed to set in. When the bottle was finished, Paul simply tossed it aside, staggered to the cupboard, and picked out another one.

In time, the man who was famous for his self-control was as wrecked as anyone could ever remember seeing him. Paul started mumbling, in a voice so low that they had to strain to hear it from three feet away. The same broken phrases were repeated over and over again.

'Fucking carve-up!'

'Fucked me up!'

'Fuckers!'

The ravings continued, until Linda stood up and gently steered her husband from the room.

Speaking to *Time* six years later, McCartney would painfully recall that long summer. 'It was murderous . . . I was having dreams, amazing dreams about Klein, running around after me with some hypodermic needle, like a crazy dentist.'

When the producer Mickie Most went to Scotland to offer Paul a part in a film called *The Second Coming of Suzanne*, about Christ returning to earth as a woman, he found his host hollow-eyed, bloated and unshaven, looking 'a bit like Jim Morrison after a bender.' But apparently more astute: Most's picture was eventually shot in 1974, with Richard Dreyfuss in the role McCartney rejected. Over time it would come to grace most of the 'Worst Movies in History' lists.

On 15 August, *Melody Maker* ran an interview with Apple's Peter Brown. Brown declined to say whether Paul, John, George and Ringo would ever work as a group again. Two weeks later, the paper published a letter from McCartney himself. 'In order to put out of its misery the limping dog of a news story which has been dragging itself across your pages, my answer to the question, "Will the Beatles get together again?" . . . is no.'

On 9 October, Lennon turned thirty. There was a party in, of all happy places, Abbey Road, where he was recording his *John Lennon/Plastic Ono Band* album. In a *This Is Your Life* moment, George and Ringo both arrived unexpectedly and sang a number specially composed for the occasion. Paul, who was in Cavendish Avenue, had to run through some details with Lee Eastman that afternoon, so was unable to attend.

On 21 October, the McCartneys took ship for New York, telling the press that they were 'getting away from it all'. John and Yoko would follow the same route, just six days later. In the eight weeks that they were living across town from one another, the two couples never met. Paul would tell his friend Barry Miles, 'I [was still] having a bad time, almost a nervous breakdown. I remember lying awake at nights shaking . . . One night I'd been asleep and awoke and I couldn't lift my head off the pillow. My head was down in the pillow; I thought, Jesus, if I don't do this I'll suffocate.'

By now John, George, Ringo and Allen Klein had apparently begun to feel that breaking up wasn't a good idea, after all. At least none of them wanted to formally terminate the four-way partnership, and thus deprive themselves of a percentage of McCartney's solo career. Klein was back in residence at the London Hilton that

November, a conspicuous presence in his elastic-waist 'weekender' pants and loud shirt, issuing memos about what very considerable losses (their American royalties, for example) the Beatles could suffer by a dissolution. McCartney knew now that it would have to end in court. He also knew that Apple (now overseen by Neil Aspinall) would have to be wound up, at the very least reordered. Paul's share-and-share-alike dream, or 'Western communism', was over. The psychological mix of it all was toxic, and he reacted by hitting the bottle even harder. A New York woman named Libby Fields came across a figure, early one autumn morning, slumped on a bench in Harlem's Marcus Garvey park. Fields, who was a Beatles fan, didn't know whether to laugh or cry when she realised who it was. Nothing about the jaded-looking man, dressed in army surplus fatigues, particularly invited company. But this, along with Bobby Darin, was her 'major childhood hero'. When Fields finally got up the nerve to approach McCartney she asked him if he could wait there, for five more minutes, while she ran home to 125th Street for her camera. 'Why not?' Paul shrugged. 'I'm not going anywhere.'

A week later, McCartney met George Harrison by arrangement in a midtown hotel. Paul told George he just wanted to get off the label, meaning Apple, and would come to any reasonable accommodation with the other Beatles.

George told Paul, 'You'll stay on the sodding label. Hare Krishna!'

How did it all go so fucking bad?

Fans like Libby Fields would repeatedly ask themselves that question over the next year, as a band once synonymous with love and peace bickered about matters both personal and professional, before taking the whole sorry business to court. McCartney himself, he stressed, would do everything possible to avoid a bitter and embarrassingly public feud. Just before leaving England, he'd made a final appeal to Ringo (the only one who admitted he actually missed the Beatles), telling him that 'This isn't about us. It's about

Klein.' Ringo had replied that it was about Lee and John Eastman, too. At that Linda had burst into tears.

Meanwhile, Lennon's attitude to McCartney would come to reach the level of a pure and honest personal hatred rarely seen outside marriage. John at last wrote a letter to Paul and Linda late that autumn. 'I hope you realise what shit you and the rest of my kind and unselfish friends laid on Yoko and me since we've been together', he opened. John went on to call Linda 'cranky' and 'middle-aged', adding that he didn't expect the McCartneys' marriage to last. 'Of course the money angle is important, especially after all the shit that came from your insane family . . . Petty fuckers . . . Twats . . . God help you and Paul. See you in two years – I reckon you'll be out by then.'

Lennon (whose mood wasn't improved when the Plaza violinist greeted him, not for the last time, by breaking into Yesterday) would call McCartney just twice while in New York. On both occasions, he challenged him to disown the 'evil shit' John still saw being levelled at Yoko. Paul believed that he had done so repeatedly. Neither conversation finished with a promise to stay in touch.

On Monday 16 November, McCartney's solicitors announced that they would be suing John, George and Ringo to dissolve 'the partnership business carried on . . . under the name of the Beatles and Co.' By now it had become fairly clear that the band had problems, but the eventual High Court proceedings were still something of a shock. Between 19 January and 12 March 1971, the bench would hear a sorry tale of financial mismanagement, breach of trust, professional jealousy, artistic sabotage and collective malice towards Yoko. That was for starters. There was also the whole decline and fall of Apple – once again, rampant with firings as it had been with waste – which showed cash on hand of £738,000, with an outstanding tax bill of £680,000. As *The Times* reporter was left to ask, 'When the spokesmen for the peace and love generation loathe each other, what's the generation supposed to think?'

Lennon, meanwhile, had released his new album, including his disavowal of such Sixties gurus as Kennedy, Dylan, and the Beatles. McCartney admitted that he quite liked the record, but scoffed at John's decision to name one of the tracks Working Class Hero. He'd 'grow[n] up in a fucking palace' compared to Paul's digs in Speke. Later that same week, Lennon sat down for a long, freewheeling interview with *Rolling Stone*. He portrayed the Beatles as the 'biggest bastards on earth' and McCartney as a self-promoting hustler who only announced the break-up of the band to 'sell an album'. The recantation over, John and Yoko then returned to their current New York projects. These included the films *Up Your Legs Forever*, eighty-two minutes of continuous panning shots of human limbs, and *Fly*, which recorded the activities, in extreme close-up, of a winged insect exploring the crotch of a naked woman by the name of Virginia Lust.

McCartney wasn't present at *Fly*'s Manhattan premiere, so he didn't hear the mingled retchings and applause. Just before Christmas, he and his family had flown back to Scotland. Surrounded now by their respective teams of high-powered surrogates, their every thought channelled through a PR agent, Paul and John didn't speak anymore. McCartney had struggled to the bitter end to reach an accommodation with the band, and had repeatedly told Lee Eastman his beef was with Klein, whom he characterised as 'a thug'. No argument there, Eastman had replied. Even so, it was John, George and Ringo's signatures that appeared on the partnership agreement. To them, an amicable divorce simply wasn't an option. At nine in the morning of 31 December 1970, Paul's writ, number 6315, was lodged with the Chancery Division of the High Court. 'I want out,' he confirmed to the press. 'The group is finished. We've split and everything that we've ever earned should be split . . . That's all I want.'

Early in the new year, a film-maker named Bruce Perret went up to the farm at Paul and Linda's request to shoot some 'wild' footage of them riding horses, paddling in the sea and strumming guitars.

With their pot-fuelled campfire singalongs, the McCartneys reminded Perret of 'stoned Everly Brothers', if not quite as tuneful. On 4 January, the family headed back to New York to begin recruiting a band to play on a new album. Two days later David Spinozza, a hot young guitar-for-hire, fresh from having rocked up Perry Como's latest single, took a call from the woman he now knows as the 'queen of the groupies'.

'This is Mrs McCartney,' the voice announced crisply. Spinozza thought the whole thing might be some sort of joke, and asked the caller her business. 'Capitol Records gave my husband your name,' she replied. 'He wants to get together with you and check you out. We're making an album.'

'Do I know your husband?'

At that, Linda exploded with exasperation. 'Paul McCartney, for fuck's sake! The Beatles! Does *that* ring a bell?'

After some more in this vein, Spinozza was persuaded to appear at a 'filthy loft on 45th Street', where he auditioned to Paul's satisfaction. Formal sessions for what became *Ram* began on 10 January at the nearby A&R Studios. Spinozza later gave a somewhat mixed account of the experience. 'Here I am meeting Paul McCartney,' he recalled, 'and he played these basic rock 'n' roll things – ching, ching, ching. It was embarrassing . . . He didn't even know what the chord was called.' There was 'no challenge', and Spinozza's own ideas weren't sought. He merely played what he was told to play. It was as though McCartney was finished with all this 'democracy bullshit'. Everything was 'very businesslike,' Spinozza added. There was 'no smoking pot, no drinks or carrying on, nothing. [It was] all straight ahead.'

On 19 January, the Beatles dissolution case got under way in McCartney's absence. Paul's counsel, David Hirst, QC, revealed that the band's finances were in a 'grave state'. There was only 'just enough in the pot' to meet their individual tax demands. McCartney's petition asked for a full set of audited accounts to be made, and a Receiver appointed. The judge agreed that it was 'obviously an urgent matter' and set 19 February as the date for a full hearing. Lee Eastman told Paul that he should fly back, put on a coat and tie, and be there every day in court. 'It's all or nothing,' he advised his son-in-law. 'You could end up a free man, or working the rest of your life for Allen Klein. Everything you've ever done is at stake.'

McCartney thought that this was a fair appraisal, 'no shit, simply the facts', which in the end were harsh enough: that, after eight years as one of the most successful entertainers on earth, he was nearly broke.

The twelve-day hearing saw McCartney and his barrister mount a spirited attack, then, on Klein, who happened to have been convicted on ten tax offences by a jury in New York just three weeks earlier. Although John, George and Ringo all stayed away, it was an authentic Beatles 'event', with TV crews and fans jostling each other on the courtroom steps. Each day, ten minutes before the start, Paul arrived, a pale, heavily bearded figure moving through the spectators like Moses parting the sea. A hushed silence came over the hallway as he made his way towards the courtroom's swing doors, wearing the same black Tommy Nutter suit he'd sported on the cover of *Abbey Road*. He was accompanied by Linda, David Hirst, his junior and a bodyguard. They took seats in the front row, immediately in front of Klein and his lawyers.

On 26 February, McCartney went into the box to rebut Klein's affidavit claiming the group's assets were enormous, and that the film of *Let It Be* was even then 'mak[ing] an absolute fortune for all four of them.' Paul countered that it might have been even more lucrative had the rights not been transferred, without his approval, from Apple to United Artists. He then recalled a phone conversation 'in which Mr Klein had told me, "You know why John is angry with you? It's because you came off better than he did in *Let It Be*." Mr Klein also said to me, "The real trouble is Yoko. She's the one with ambition." I often wonder what John would have said if he heard the remark.'

In his summing up, David Hirst was able to produce a smoking gun. Out of a waist-high pile of documents, he flourished a cancelled cheque from Capitol Records to Klein in the amount of £852,000. McCartney and his counsel argued that this represented a twenty per cent cut of the Beatles' total US royalty, rather than, as agreed, twenty per cent of the recent increase – an overpayment of some £500,000. Klein's defence was a letter dated January 1970, signed by John, George and Ringo, which seemed to him to endorse the commission. Paul replied that not even the three Beatles had the right to alter management's terms and conditions without his consent. Mr Justice Stamp seemed to agree, dismissing Klein's testimony as 'the prattling of a second-class salesman'. On 12 March, he granted McCartney's application for a Receiver to manage the group's interests, 'pending a permanent fix'. The judge concluded, 'The controversy in this action has centred around the personality and the activities of Mr Klein . . . However successful Klein may have been in generating income, I am satisfied that the Beatles' financial situation is confused, uncertain and confusing. A third party is needed not merely to secure the assets, but so that there may be a firm hand to manage the business fairly and produce order.' So ended the partnership.

There was a small celebration later that evening, which happened to be the McCartneys' second wedding anniversary. According to published reports, Paul and Linda were relaxing in Cavendish Avenue when John, George and Ringo drew up outside in Lennon's white Mercedes. The three men were seen to rummage around in the boot, where they found an unusual gift for their old colleague. Laughing maniacally, John stepped towards the gate and threw a brick through the McCartneys' front window. George and Ringo hugged him.

★

Ironically, it was Paul himself who, back in the States four days later, collected the 'best original score' Grammy for *Let It Be*. Attired for the black-tie event in jeans, a red floral shirt and tennis shoes, he accepted the gong from John Wayne, saying only 'Thank you!' for the TV cameras. Once back in the press tent, however, he made a gracious speech paying tribute to the Beatles, and saying he owed everything to Linda and to the selfless devotion of others too numerous to name. Not to mention the truly wonderful crew at Apple. There'd been a few hang-ups, but the album had been a gas to work on. Thank you. You're great people. Really great. The crowd gave him a thunderous ovation, after which a reporter managed to bawl out a question about what McCartney was doing these days. 'I have a knife and fork and I'm here to cut a record,' he replied smoothly.

Sources close to the principals, ATV, EMI and Capitol – all with a vested interest in it – agree that he also needed a hit. On 31 March, Paul submitted the first year-end accounts for his new company, McCartney Productions Limited. They showed income of just £3,017, with expenses of £5,417. This was disappointing enough, but nothing compared to the larger crisis. As a result of the High Court ruling, both the Apple kitty and most of the *Let It Be* film receipts were frozen, and likely to remain so for years. The Beatles were each receiving an allowance of £5,000 a month.

Back in the studio, McCartney polished the catchy melodies and radio-friendly arrangements before turning over *Ram*'s master tape to EMI. His first solo single, Another Day, had already promptly gone gold. Paul then made a no-hard-feelings call to Richard Hewson, the man who actually scored the strings on *Let It Be*, and told him he wanted to make a 'freakout' version of the new album, replacing all the pop instruments with an 'avant-orchestra'. This went out under the alias of Thrillington – evidence not only that McCartney liked to wax outside of his famous brand name, but that he could let his hair down in the studio. 'In the back office with a bottle of Scotch' is one of the snatches of dialogue heard between tracks, pleasantly anachronistic amidst all the 'prog' and 'chill-out'. A well-known jazz musician who worked on the project would recall a 'constantly stoned' Paul and the band 'hav[ing] made a cult classic without fully knowing what we were doing.'

On 12 May, Mick and Bianca Jagger went down the aisle at the small, whitewashed chapel of St Anne on a hill overlooking St Tropez. Keith Richards graced the reception dressed as a Nazi. Paul and Ringo were both in attendance, but didn't speak; the lawyers had told them not to acknowledge one another pending the 'permanent fix' to the Beatles' case. John and Yoko happened to be just thirty miles up the coast at Cannes, where, on 14 May, *Fly* was screened at the annual film festival. Coincidentally, George and his wife Pattie were relaxing on a yacht moored in the local harbour. Still no contact.

Ram. John (*Plastic Ono Band*) and George (*All Things Must Pass*) may have hit their strides first, but this was the album, full of potential or actual hits with cheery tunes and punchy but understated musicianship, that came closest to the spirit of the Beatles. It managed a miracle, sounding both mainstream and experimental. The arty squawks were balanced by a cleverly sequenced mix of gauzy, intimate ballads and knees-ups like Smile Away. The latter packed as much guitar wallop as Status Quo. And for the cryptically minded, there were *Ram*'s carefully scattered clues as to McCartney's true feelings for his ex-bandmates. Accusing Lennon of cant, the opening track, Too Many People (with its gnomic intro, 'Piss off, cake') would start the exchange that enlivened the charts over the next year or two. Paul's more sardonic epitaph on the old firm was *Ram*'s back cover photo, which showed two beetles screwing. Lest anyone miss the point that he'd moved on, the album sleeve also included the message 'LILY', or Linda, I love you.

This all-things-to-all-people confection was a major worldwide smash, hitting number one in seventeen countries. 'Censure [being] the tax a man pays for being eminent', as Swift tells us, most of the critics hated it. To them *Ram* was the first step on an easy-listening continuum that compared badly with Lennon's angry, purgative songs. (John himself called the album 'grannie music'). After *Ram*, a reaction set in which portrayed McCartney as a smug popsmith and Lennon as the edgy one with street-cred. This simplification seemed to gain momentum when, ten years later, Paul summed up his post-Beatles career as 'Ballads and babies. That's what happened to me.'

One of the uglier consequences of *Ram*'s success was a bitter dispute between McCartney and Lew Grade of ATV. The latter found it hard to accept that Linda (not a party to the Northern Songs deal) should be credited as Paul's co-writer on six of the twelve tracks, thus depriving ATV of hundreds of thousands in publishing fees. The case eventually went to court, where Linda was able to demonstrate her compositional talents. On 10 June 1972, the parties announced 'Settlement of all outstanding difficulties.' McCartney agreed to a seven-year extension of his 'exclusive rights agreement' with ATV, for whom he also made an hour-long television special. Linda got to keep her royalties.

Ram grossed £4.2 million in its first four weeks: at some point during that month, McCartney decided to put a band together. A competent American drummer named Denny Seiwell returned from the album sessions. Linda would say she then 'spent about a week' waiting for David Spinozza to call her back. In the end, he never did. At that stage McCartney suddenly remembered a guitarist named Brian Hines, known professionally as Denny Laine, whose band the Moody Blues had played on the under-card to the Beatles. It was 400 miles from Laine's unpretentious digs in London to the McCartneys' farm, the last twelve of which were the worst. Paul met Laine at the airfield in a battered transit van with no passenger seat, and took off with him bouncing up and down amongst some sacks of spuds in the rear. They made the run in ten minutes.

On 3 August 1971, McCartney formally announced a line-up consisting of himself, a now heavily pregnant Linda, Laine and Seiwell. For some compelling reason, he was toying with the name Turpentine.

By the late summer, the band and their families were living together at High Park Farm. Laine's future wife would describe conditions there as spartan. 'The place they expected us to stay in was more like a barn than anything resembling a home . . . The walls, floors, everything, was all cement. We used to call it "the bunker". There was no carpeting, only a couple of chairs and some ragged pee-stained mattresses.' In one remote outhouse, a shrine seemed operative: beads, tinsel, burned-out candles and photos of Elvis furnishing the band room, or so-called 'Rude Studios'. McCartney had taken a break from rehearsals there one Saturday night to watch the Lennons appear on the chat show *Parkinson*, an interview partly conducted, at their request, from inside a black bag. Like John, Paul had then declined to join George and Ringo onstage in New York at the star-studded Concert for Bangladesh, allegedly because the cause was 'a downer'. Speaking to *Melody Maker* a few weeks later, McCartney firmly corrected the record:

> I was asked to play and I didn't. Klein called a press conference and told everyone I had refused to do so for the Pakistani refugees – that's what he called them. It wasn't so. I said to George the reason I couldn't do it was because it would mean that all the world's press would scream that the Beatles had got back together again, and I know that it would have made Klein very happy. It would have been an historical event and he would have taken the credit. If it wasn't for Klein I might have [done] it.

As well as Scotland and Cavendish Avenue the McCartneys also set up house on Long Island, where they would spend several weeks a year in a cottage on the Eastmans' estate, attended by 'this impossibly sexy French maid', notes one of their neighbours. The ceiling apparently featured a fresco of a beatific God looking passably like Paul himself, floating in an aquamarine sky among cream-coloured clouds. By now it had become fairly clear that Linda had strongly developed tastes, which were generally described as 'rich hippie' and ran to Op-art and fluorescents. She was also responsible for a lifestyle decision she recalled in an interview twenty years later:

> Paul and I were on our farm in Scotland, where we'd been raising sheep. One day we were sitting down to Sunday lunch, about to eat roast lamb. We were also looking through our windows at the baby lambs gambolling in the field. We suddenly looked down at our plates and made the connection: leg of lamb on the plate; lambs gambolling outside. We were horrified. We said to each other, 'What are we doing?' We put down our knives and couldn't continue eating. And from that moment on, we never ate meat again.

On 13 September, Linda gave birth to the couple's second daughter and her own third, Stella. The familiar traits of civility and squeamishness emerged in the McCartney who was seen signing autographs while pacing the hospital corridor during the caesarean delivery. So did whimsy. Later that night Paul told Linda that he'd had 'a vision' while praying, and that their band would be called Wings.

From the very start, it was a, or *the* consummate Seventies act, with a regular Thursday night spot on *Top of the Pops* and a taste for hip-hugging tartan flares. To Wings' many fans, the band was a continuation of the Beatles by other means; to critics, one of those curious phenomena of the time, like spandex and the success of Max Boyce. The launch party, a fancy-dress affair held in London's Empire Ballroom on 8 November, touched all the bases. There was a mirrorball on the ceiling, beaming a psychedelic light-show of velvet- and lace-clad writhing figures that included the likes of Cliff, Elton and sundry Faces.

'Why here, on a wet Monday night?' Paul was asked.

'Why not?' he replied. Then, perhaps thinking this a bit lame, he added, 'EMI are paying for it.'

Another journalist then asked McCartney if he were putting the band together purely for the money. Paul assured her that nothing could be further from his mind. 'It's for love, darlin',' he chortled. 'For *love*.'

That same week, Lennon's album *Imagine* hit number one in Britain and nine other markets. The title track got all the airplay, but the one that stuck it to Paul was How Do You Sleep? In this tune John's perspective on the Sixties was revealed to moving effect. The freaks had been right when they said that McCartney was dead. All the latter had ever done was 'yesterday'. (The punchline 'And you probably pinched that bitch anyway!' was deleted on legal advice.) John concluded by saying that the sound Paul now made was muzak to his ears.

These rebukes must have hurt, but McCartney was heroically restrained in his critique of *Imagine*, an album he insisted he liked. Of How Do You Sleep? he said merely, 'It's silly. So what if I live with straights? I like straights. I have straight babies . . . He says the only thing I did was Yesterday and he knows that's wrong.' When prodded further about the song title, McCartney had the pat answer: 'I sleep fine, thanks.'

On 9 October, Allen Klein had fulfilled his promise to arrange a one-woman show for Yoko's found art. This took place at the imposing I.M. Pei-designed Everson Museum in Syracuse, New York, which more typically specialised in hosting career retrospectives involving hundreds of works viewed by crowds in their tens of thousands. Yoko herself had only a few pieces, and paying attendance, as opposed to popular interest, was unexceptional. Still, it was an arresting scene. There were hydraulics, platforms that went up and down, stark white lighting effects. An entire gallery was devoted to John and Yoko's minuscule 'part paintings' of 'cloud, glacier, moon, Ku Klux Klan, smog, albino.' One much-noted exhibit featured a milk bottle alongside a green plastic bin bag. The museum allocated $107,000 to stage Yoko's show, which she named *This Is Not Here*. Cost overruns forced Apple to contribute a further $75–80,000, meaning that Paul himself paid out some $15,000.

A month later, *Melody Maker* splashed McCartney's mild remarks on *Imagine* under the headline 'Why Lennon is Uncool'. John went nuts, firing off a letter which he insisted the paper publish on the grounds of 'equal time'. The lawyers removed nine lines for fear of libel, but what remained was plain enough. Lennon's seven-part attack opened with the startling assertion that Paul's 'politics are very similar to Mary Whitehouse's.' Most of the rest was a partial account of the couple's falling-out over Apple and Maclen. Pelting McCartney with mere business differences, however, wasn't enough. Lennon would go on to compare Paul to Engelbert Humperdinck (thus infuriating Engelbert). He put the boot in to Wings and, more pertinently, their keyboard player. John's distaste for Linda and her family was such that once, when invited to a meeting with the ex-Beatles and their lawyers, he said he'd go only if he received a letter stating that none of the 'WASP Jews' would be present in the room.

It was a street brawl McCartney had no desire to join in. 'I was there and I [know] what happened,' he said. 'That's enough. I'd never say the things he did.'

John eventually relented. Three years later, he would get up on stage and sing I Saw Her Standing There, for old times' sake. But the old times were gone.

The first fruit of Wings' Scottish retreat, *Wild Life*, was universally judged a failure – one of those 'honourable' failures, however, that rather endear a superstar to his critics, who noted that the album had been cut, on a tight budget, over just three days. McCartney himself would later admit that *Wild Life* might just have been over-hurried, and that the band itself could have used a few more shifts in the rehearsal factory. Songs like Mumbo, Bip Bop and I Am Your Singer – all unfortunate, although the impact was softened by Love Is Strange, the first decent reggae track ever recorded by caucasians. The whole brisk business (thirty-five minutes in all) ended with Dear Friend, a conciliatory open letter to Lennon.

John hated this one too.

'It's true. I never dug that flowery pop, and the whole cute Paulie bit. We were too busy pouring buckets of shit over each other.'

Sales of *Wild Life* probably weren't hurt by the continuing feud, which was a staple of the music press over the next two years. The album eventually went gold, though not before the letters pages of *Melody Maker* and the rest had roundly panned McCartney's 'prop band' and 'drone of a piano player'. The more successful Wings got, the more flak they took.

Paul never got the criticisms of Linda out of his system. Understandably, he bristled at particularly snide reviews like the one alleging there were 'just three things wrong with Mrs McCartney: she can't write, can't play and can't sing.' What deepened his chagrin was the fact that Linda herself shared some of the same misgivings. 'I really tried to persuade Paul that I didn't want to be part of it . . . The first time I hit the stage I was so nervous that I cried. I didn't know what I was doing there.' Late in her life, Linda would recall that her becoming a musician had 'killed my career as a working photographer.'

The Beatles' civil war provoked widespread gossip and opinion, some of which wasn't so much aired as shouted out and nearly all of which deplored McCartney's lawsuit. Newly radicalised rock 'zines like *Crawdaddy* depicted Paul and Linda as bloated pigs, and wished Wings a 'crash landing'. Most insiders took a more practical view.

McCartney's unabashed love of a 'proper tune' was what most obviously galled Lennon. 'It's not just two billionaires engaged in a cat fight,' said Lee Eastman, a man who knew something of song-writing as well as high finance. 'The real question – of whether an artist should please himself or his public – is probably the great musical-theatrical debate of the twentieth century.' (This was to modestly downplay Eastman and Klein's own roles in the band's demise.)

On 6 December 1971, the High Court appointed a Receiver for Maclen Ltd, the company which banked the songwriting dues from ATV. This meant that the recording, publishing and licensing divisions of the Apple empire were all now under judicial control. Just a week later, McCartney paid a call on Lennon at the latter's Greenwich Village apartment. Paul, according to most versions, was irked by John's response, which was to promptly refer to Eastman as 'a yid'. The mutual wrangling then became noticeably bitter. There was some hard talk about *Wild Life*. Paul was further distressed, say the same sources, when the Lennons were then unavailable to take his phone calls. They were too busy, a flunkey allegedly told Linda, organising both a benefit concert for victims of the Attica jail riot and a street march on behalf of the IRA. On that note, Paul and Linda flew back to Scotland for Christmas.

On 27 December, *A Hard Day's Night* got its usual festive airing on British television. As a goodwill gesture, the BBC sent each of the ex-Beatles a newly restored print of the film. For most of 1971, McCartney seemed to have been on an emotional roller coaster that paused only for him to alight at court hearings. But even he must have been struck by how the year ended: sitting in a dank home projection room, reliving the vanished, golden days when, the blurb went, 'everything seemed possible'. The BBC would run several such trailers during the week, insisting that John, Paul, George and Ringo had been 'the world's best-loved entertainers' and 'the greatest force for change' in history.

It was almost as if the Corporation was talking not simply about the band but *to* them – begging them to get back together, or, at the very least, to acknowledge publicly that they still cared, both about the fans and one another. But it didn't happen.

CHAPTER SIX

Pizza and Fairy Tales

'Looking at it purely bluntly', McCartney would reflect of the early Seventies, 'there was sort of a dip for me and my writing. There were a couple of years when I had sort of an illness.'

Although Paul had a low opinion of his own creative powers at the time, and focused more on performing, Wings would turn out three hit singles in 1972. He wasn't surprised when all three created a national outrage. The first, Give Ireland Back To The Irish, was recorded on the morning of 1 February, less than forty-eight hours after the events of Bloody Sunday, when thirteen Catholic protesters were shot dead in the course of a riot in Londonderry. McCartney followed it by releasing his full-length version of Mary Had A Little Lamb. Finally, just before Christmas came a bouncy pop-rock carol called Hi, Hi, Hi. This consisted mainly of the lyric 'We're gonna get hi, hi, hi' set to a shrill, three-note melody. The first and last of these songs were promptly banned by the BBC. Although Paul's nursery rhyme somehow escaped, over the years it began to acquire cult status as 'one of the most unintentionally hilarious tune[s] of all time . . . So bad it's actually enjoyable . . . Uniquely appalling.' When Lennon (then promoting his own new single, Woman Is The Nigger Of The World) was asked to comment, he replied: 'Why should I?

What could I possibly add? The fact that he put it out is comment enough.'

McCartney would later rue the fact that 'no one in the Wings family' had dared to confront him. 'None of them would say, "No, Paul, that's a mistake."' On the other hand, McCartney made no bones about the fact that 'I love singing songs for kids. There's no bullshit there.'

This might be just the start of a long second act in showbusiness, he hinted; plans were already afoot to put Rupert Bear, among other childhood favourites, on the chart. As Lennon noted, 'Paul is hoping to live forever.'

McCartney was equally preoccupied, in that winter of 1972, with getting his new band on the road. Here, one of his main concerns was damping down press and public expectations. 'In the Beatles, we'd always known we'd be a hard act to follow,' he allowed, glumly. 'I soon found out just *how* hard.' Excessive marital fidelity rarely seems to be a problem for rock stars, but McCartney was loyal truly to a fault. Sources close to the Wings brains trust note that managers at both EMI and ATV argued that his hiring Linda might, just conceivably, be an error. 'The suits,' says one associate, 'all felt that it wasn't fair on her because she wasn't a professional.' The debate was settled when Paul blithely announced that he would only go out on tour if his wife accompanied him. Over the years, one or two of Linda's colleagues in Wings would look back on that decision and blame uxoriousness – morbid attachment to one's spouse – for some of the band's problems. Perhaps to balance the generally 'warm, family vibe' of the group, Paul would soon enrol a heavy rocking Irish guitarist named Henry McCullough. The latter had no quarrel with Linda, 'a homemaker who, whatever people say, soon learned the piano as an alternative' and 'put a unique stamp' on Wings' accomplished mix of pop, rock, reggae and soul. McCullough was, however, startled to find himself promptly dressed up like a shepherd, miming Mary Had A Little Lamb on early-evening television. 'It's not exactly Muddy Waters, is it?'

On 9 February 1972, McCartney and Wings began a short, unannounced bus tour of northern colleges and town halls. This was the low-key return to the road he'd urged, unsuccessfully, on the Beatles. 'Playing, that's what I missed,' Paul told *Life*. 'Being a good musician requires this contact with people all the time – the human thing.' McCartney walking onto a stage was a bit like Steve McQueen walking into a garage, or Oliver Reed into a pub; he was glad to do it, and they were more than happy to see him there. These latest concerts were arranged by the simple expedient of pulling in to the nearest student union building and asking, 'Fancy a show tonight?' It was defiantly informal. When Wings appeared for the first gig, at Nottingham University, all five members were wearing Rupert Bear checked trousers and a variety of cuddly sweaters. Their legend was nailed.

The second night's performance, held in the dining room of York's Goodridge University, was, it has to be said, a disaster. There was loud audience participation throughout, much of it ill-mannered and sexist. Admittedly, Linda's long, lank hair was not good; it combined with her pronounced jaw muscles to make her look, in one review, 'like an overgrown Pekinese.' The real problem, though, was that she gave a mediocre performance. She seemed to not so much fluff as simply forget the piano intro to Wild Life, which Paul had to demonstrate. Then there were the other, obviously hasty arrangements. Both the PA and the stage lights kept cutting in and out, the band stabbed haphazardly with green, mauve, red. The sound failed completely during a rave-up encore of Lucille, causing Paul's orgasmic howl to end in a drone. 'Oh dear. My mike's not working,' he announced. This was the cue for some heartless soul to yell, 'Give it to Linda, then,' and there were soon dull thuds and groans heard from that general direction of the hall.

Meanwhile, McCartney had put a lot of mileage between himself and his former band. There were no Beatles songs in the new stage act. At least once every performance, a cry of 'Love Me Do!' or 'Yesterday!' would surge up from the stalls. When pressed, Paul would at least speak fondly of John in interviews, whose headlines stole towards variants of 'HE LOVES YOU' and 'GET BACK'. John said that to the extent he considered Paul at all, it was as a sell-out. To him, Wings were self-styled 'crowd pleasers . . . about [as] underground as my granny.' Throughout the Seventies, both men would continue to obsess about one another's marriages, keep abreast of one another's careers and snap up one another's records, and then fussily deconstruct them. Of his own *Sometime in New York City* (a critical and commercial bomb), Lennon would say poignantly, 'I'd like to hear what Paul thinks of the songs. He knows me, and he might like them.'

In fact, McCartney was a consistently good and often generous friend to his peers. Everyone from Dylan to Des O'Connor would remember him having noted their latest releases, often, when he got the critical itch, with witty, detailed reviews. One of David Bowie's band recalls 'Herself, Elton and McCartney sitting on a sofa in the studio talking about each other's albums: this brotherhood of musicians. Try to imagine, you know, Kid Rock and Eminem sitting around, helping each other. It's mind-boggling.'

Later that spring, the young David Essex would find himself singing The Long And Winding Road to a sparse audience at London's Revolution club. At the end of the song, Essex noticed that McCartney himself was applauding warmly from the second row. From then on, he appears to have taken to the star of *Godspell* in a way few other critics did. Every twenty minutes or so, whether in private or at press conferences, Paul promised somebody or other that Essex was going to be 'huge'. It was a typical gesture by a man who supported and encouraged scores of those in no position to return the favour.

Henry McCullough: 'If you were a musician and you wanted to

discuss a problem with Paul, he'd always sit down and really discuss it with you. He'd have a serious, deep talk and try to help you.'

After banking the tour swag (an estimated £3,000 gross) at Coutt's, Wings flew to Hollywood to begin recording tracks for the album *Red Rose Speedway*. Second in the bag was Paul's ballad My Love. Lush, cocktail-bar strings ushered in McCullough's take-one guitar solo, then cleared a space around McCartney's voice, which went places most rock stars – for whom a case could be made for subtitles – can only dream of. The renowned lyrical sensibility infused even the most banal romantic tripe with real eloquence, charm and emotional depth. Few men, before or since, have sounded so consumed by what they were singing. The *Red Rose Speedway* tapes got an Abbey Road makeover and were eventually released in May 1973. Most critics hated this album too, straining for abusive puns apparently prompted by the title. Words like 'wreck' and 'pile-up' went round like drunks in a revolving door. One wag wrote that 'the whole thing [was] more like a demolition derby, a berserk collection of Macca's worst back-slapping, c'mon-boogie-down tunes.' *Red Rose Speedway* went straight to number one.

On 31 March, McCartney Productions Ltd declared income of £4,234 for its second year of trading, with expenses of £13,446. Most of the Beatles' assets remained frozen. There was, however, both a settlement (freeing Linda's royalties) and a new long-term contract with ATV. As he approached thirty, Paul would allow himself certain rich man's playthings, including a production model Lamborghini and some major jewellery. Courtesy of Linda, he also acquired his signature mullet haircut, at once hideous and perfect. McCartney's flares- and-tank-top-heavy wardrobe was like a period rock-star detail in itself. As *Time* noted presciently, he was fast 'becom[ing] the complete Seventies icon.'

McCartney celebrated his birthday at home in London, with just Linda, the children and several dozen of his best friends. The BBC chose that same evening to air part six of *The Beatles Story*, an instalment called 'The World Surrenders'.

Three weeks later, Wings began a full-blown European tour at the Centre Culturel, Toulon. Everyone travelled in an open-top London bus, which was adorned for the occasion with blue and red psychedelic swirls. 'Very 1967,' notes Henry McCullough. Still, the McCartneys were able to enjoy one or two extracurricular perks, such as flying soft-class to New York to party with the Rolling Stones and fellow guests like Zsa Zsa Gabor in the elegant environs of the St Regis hotel. Alerted by a thoughtful Stones publicist, the press and paparazzi had staked out the Arrivals hall at Kennedy airport, which was also crowded with scores of fans lost in earnest disquisitions on the merits, say, of *Revolver* versus *Ram*. The couple were bombarded immediately they showed: *Are the Beatles getting back together, Paul? What will you be saying to John, Paul? Why did you break up the band, Paul?* Linda, who adored the attention, eagerly waded up to the cameras, flashing a peace sign, and firmly stayed on message as if no harsh questions had been asked: 'We're here for a private event . . . Have you heard Mary Had A Little Lamb yet? It's fabulous.' Paul himself had nothing to say to the media, either then or later in the week.

On 10 August, following a performance at the Scandinavium Hall, Göteborg, McCartney walked offstage to be met by fourteen Swedish police officers. They were curious about a package containing seven ounces of Peruvian flake that had been sent from London to the hotel where the band were staying. Paul did not interact well with law enforcement, and a tense scene ensued as he, Linda, Denny Seiwell and a secretary named Rebecca Hines were taken away for questioning. McCartney was later charged with possession, fined the equivalent of $1,000 and effectively kicked out of the country.

'We smoke it and we like it,' Paul told the press. 'At the end of the day most people go home and have a drink . . . Well, we play a gig and we're exhausted, and Linda and I prefer to put our kids to bed, sit down together and smoke a joint. We've never gone further than grass.'

The failure of *Sometime in New York City* was a hard blow to Lennon, selling as it did only half the total of *Wild Life*. Compounding the problem, John and Yoko were beginning to have their doubts about Allen Klein. At the same time as the 'Wings over Europe' tour was drawing to a close in Berlin, the Lennons were hosting New York's 'One to One' benefit gala for mentally handicapped children, an event which apparently confirmed Klein's long-held belief that it was John, not Yoko, whom the fans wanted to see. There was also growing frustration at the glacial pace at which the Beatles lawsuit seemed to progress. Six months later, Lennon would tell a British television audience, 'There are many reasons why we finally gave [Klein] the push . . . I haven't been particularly happy for quite a long time with the situation. Let's say possibly Paul's suspicions were right.'

Four years of further litigation ensued, Klein insisting that John, George and Ringo owed him $1 million in personal loans and more than $5 million in back salary and commissions, which he 'would pursue to the ends of the earth.' It was a typically robust prosecution. The war that came to occupy the business and trade press between 1973–7 made Klein's original dispute with McCartney look like a trivial misunderstanding. So anxious were the ex-Beatles to get out from under their manager's thumb that they collectively paid him $5,009,200. John signed his release papers at the Plaza hotel, where, for once, the violinist failed to serenade him with Yesterday. He played Eleanor Rigby instead.

On 8 September 1972, a Scottish police constable named Norman McPhee completed a drugs identification course held at the central training college in Glasgow. Eleven days later, McPhee decided to apply his new-found expertise by paying a visit to High Park Farm. He would not leave empty-handed. The next morning, McCartney was charged on three counts of growing and possessing marijuana, allegedly found 'completely clogging' his large greenhouse. Through his lawyer, he claimed that 'some seeds' had been sent to him by a kindly fan, and that he, Paul, had had no idea what they were when he planted them. On 8 March, he pleaded guilty to a single, reduced charge of cultivation. Fined £100.

During the period between the front-page reports of McCartney's bust and his committal hearing, Wings released their third single. It didn't go unnoticed that it was entitled Hi, Hi, Hi. 'Inappropriate lyrical content' was the BBC's 'cardinal' objection, it was stated, although musical considerations might have made a bid for second place. Many fans actually preferred the B-side – a cross-marketing opportunity (pop, with a tropical lilt of reggae) called C Moon.

Above all, McCartney's band were attuned to what their management called the zeitgeist factor. Since around the time of the Beatles' break-up, rock music had become increasingly big business, contributing tens of millions of dollars to the bottom lines of those like the Kinney Group, a sinister parking lot- and mortuary-based concern that enjoyed a controlling interest in the likes of Led Zeppelin and the Stones. Although the 'underground' bands survived, finding a permanent clubhouse in longhaired bedsits, the 'gig guide' pages of Sounds and the fulsome copy of various right-on critics, the dominant trend of the Seventies was towards inoffensive, crossover fare – the so-called 'great average'.

Here, again, McCartney was obviously in tune with his times. As he noted, he wasn't interested in turning Wings into a mere cult, or one of those glitter-laden Top of the Pops bands whose fifteen minutes of fame seemed to expire before your eyes. Rather, he wanted the 'biggest possible market . . . [to] reach mum, dad, nan, the kids', and presumably anyone else with a disposable income. His fame and bank balance both took another giant leap in early 1973, when United Artists needed a title song for the latest James Bond blockbuster, *Live and Let Die*. No problem, said McCartney. Wings quickly recorded a track, which, while not much of a tune (a few notes and some syncopation) benefited hugely from George Martin's baton. Here was one 'symphonic-rock' fusion that didn't need to be smashed against a wall. Quite the opposite: Live And Let Die was a collage of freewheeling, playful ideas wedged into three minutes. The mood swings came on fast: Paul's spare piano dissolved into an orchestral power chord that deserved its own STD code. Strings, flutes, rumbling drums, a slash of reedy guitar. Some cello. Linda's perky reggae break – gotta give the other fella *hell!* – and that big brassy push to the finish. This was not a song that made the mistake of keeping it simple.

After the session, George Martin left bearing a tape and took the night flight to Ocho Rios, where he sat down in a beachfront villa with the film's producer, Harry Saltzman. Saltzman was fifty-seven; his idea of a hip vocalist was Shirley Bassey, or, at a pinch, Thelma Houston. When the recording ended he lit another cigar, sighed and muttered, 'Not bad, for a demo. Who's gonna sing it?'

Martin cleared his throat softly. 'I think you've misunderstood. That's the finished track.'

'What's the guy's name, again?'

The will to live left Martin. He seemed to have passed into a parallel universe, he reflected, where the Sixties hadn't happened. 'McCartney – the *Beatles*,' he said in exasperation. 'The world's biggest recording star, and he's singing over your opening credits. I don't think it's ever been done.'

'It's been done hundreds of times,' said Saltzman, apparently accommodating himself to the idea. 'They all come running eventually. Tell McCarthy we'll take it.'

And Martin, vowing he would never understand the film business, least of all the Bond franchise, flew back to give the news to Paul.

A month later, McCartney himself was in Jamaica, where he took the opportunity to visit Steve McQueen and Dustin Hoffman on the set of *Papillon*. Evidently there was some confusion with the arrangements, because McQueen threw a fit, demanding that 'members of the public' be removed from his presence. (Hoffman would generously chalk this up to 'Steve's artistic temperament', and later call their relationship one of 'friendly rivalry.' McQueen wouldn't bother to call it anything at all, and after *Papillon* the two actors never spoke to one another again.) Three days later, Hoffman and his wife Annie invited the McCartneys to their cottage for dinner. 'He was asking me how I write songs,' Paul recalled. 'I explained that I just make 'em up . . . He wanted to know if I could do it at will. I [said] I could.' At that Hoffman pulled out the current issue of *Time*, which featured a story entitled 'Pablo Picasso's Last Days and Final Journey'. McCartney went out to the car for his guitar. When he came back, he settled in a chair and strummed the track that became Picasso's Last Words. Hoffman leapt out of his own seat and yelled, 'Annie! Annie! The most incredible thing! He's doing it! It's coming out!' The actor was later to comment, 'It's right under childbirth in terms of great events in my life.'

My Love hit the top of the chart later that same week. The prevailing view among critics was that this was among the greatest pop ballads ever, rivalling even Yesterday. A notable exception was Lennon, who thought it 'crap'. 'If only everything was as simple as McCartney's new single,' he remarked, 'then maybe Dean Martin and Jerry Lewis would reunite with the Marx Brothers.'

An unnamed member of Klein's staff obligingly sent a copy of this review to Paul.

In *Red Rose Speedway*, McCartney retained his ability to give the public exactly what it wanted. My Love aside, there may have been no obvious take-home tunes, but it still contrived to be one of the few albums to sound good thirty years later, brimming with sunny, semi-psychedelic songs and lyrics, which ran into a critical barrage – 'The most tedious LP of recent memory' – in the likes of *Crawdaddy*. This was classic pop storytelling, with a great gatefold sleeve.

On 11 May 1973, Wings began their first major British tour. There was a kick-off press conference at the Randolph hotel, Oxford. Linda used the occasion to announce herself 'pig sick' of animal cruelty, thus coining a phrase, and to hold forth on a variety of other subjects from Greenpeace to nuclear disarmament. Onstage, too, her maturing voice was now pushed up in the mix among the loose drums, the rollicking bass and the spare piano and guitar. The funky Maybe I'm Amazed was again the band's calling card, but there were also red-hot versions of the last two albums and a runaway-train climax of Little Richard hits. Once or twice, the capacity audiences seemed to flag a little in mid-set. One minute they'd be hollering along as Paul tooled up the riff of Hi, Hi, Hi. Next minute they'd be talking amongst themselves, their minds wandering, and an entire song, possibly Linda's solo turn Seaside Woman, would go by almost unnoticed.

With magnificent self-restraint, Paul kept each show down to eighty minutes. Despite raucous appeals, there were still no Beatles songs.

You could be a working journalist and have all the badges and passes that one's heart could desire, but you still couldn't hope to interview McCartney and Wings. Not, that is, unless you signed the five-page agreement provided by the band's management which stipulated that 'If anyone alludes to the Beatles, Apple Corps or ABKCO Industries in any context, that person will be immediately removed from the premises, whatever his status.' One journalist who made the cut, a displaced New Yorker named Max Paley, recalls 'Paul com[ing] into the room where the first-night party was – Linda hanging onto his arm for dear life – to schmooze down by the cash bar and the ice sculpture. He had a hand-rolled fag in his hand, of course. The day you turned up to interview McCartney and discovered that he didn't have a fag in his hand was the day you'd turned up at the wrong place. When he saw someone he knew he'd speed up, puffing smoke like a small steam train and giving the thumbs-up. I must say I liked the guy . . . I mean, Paul McCartney looking you in the eye and asking you, "What was good and what was bad about the gig?", as if he valued your opinion. It's very flattering.'

To new-found fans like Paley, it hardly seemed possible that this was the same McCartney who was still embroiled in the bitter fallout from the Beatles. Paul would remember this as a time when 'I'd ring John [and] he'd say, "Yeah, what d'you want?" "I just thought we might meet?" "Yeah, what the fuck d'you want, man?"' Lennon concluded one such conversation by remarking, 'You're all pizza and fairy tales.' (McCartney thought this a good album title.) After being treated to some choice New York slang, Paul brought another exchange to a close by snarling, 'Fuck off, Kojak' and slamming the receiver down.

When the time came for the Lennons to move from their cramped apartment into New York's venerable Dakota Building, it took McCartney 'three or four weeks' to track down the new number. Even then, a caller was apt to receive one of three responses, according to John's mood.

The first, with Lennon pretending to be his secretary: 'Sorry, he isn't here right now.'

The second: 'The Lennons are out of the country. Goodbye.'

The third, with John dropping the act: 'Whaddaya want?'

McCartney caught him on a bad day. John answered in his own voice and promptly launched into another lengthy harangue about how Yoko had been treated as 'some Jap freak with big tits' rather than a serious artist, before throwing in some venomous remarks about Linda. Shaking with rage, McCartney hung up and then rang Lee Eastman to recount the conversation. 'You'll never guess what that arsehole Lennon just said,' he blurted out. A familiar nasal voice replied, 'This *is* that arsehole Lennon.' In his haste, McCartney had redialled John's number.

For Lennon, it was a painful period. The 'One to One' gala benefit had been poorly received, even though a film of the event would be given a Hollywood respray and successfully released twelve years later. To John, it was unthinkable that his and Yoko's music could be virtually ignored while McCartney was being fêted all over Europe. 'That was the worst experience I ever had,' he said later. 'I felt like crap.' When his old band was discussed it was remembered as a 'shower of shit' or the 'biggest bunch [of] bastards on earth'. A year earlier, Paul, John, George and Ringo had all met in New York and apparently agreed that, whatever their current differences, the Beatles legacy was worth preserving. (About the same time, Brown Meggs – the same Capitol manager who'd listened to I Want To Hold Your Hand and said 'We'll do our best' – was announcing plans to release two lavishly promoted, double compilation albums celebrating 'the greatest band in history'.) That decision went the way of the wild, however, when John had told a reporter from *Look* that he would 'rather open a vein than [collaborate] with McCartney.' The Sixties, he confirmed, were 'finally over'. Early in 1973, it was reported that the Cavern club had closed its doors and was threatened with demolition. The *Sunday Post* revealed that, when approached, all four ex-Beatles were allegedly 'completely uninterested' in the building's fate. Various rescue schemes were proposed, all of them floundering for lack of capital. Eventually Liverpool Corporation tore down the premises to make way for an underground waste duct, 'not see[ing] sufficient incentive to preserve the site.'

And then the real fun began. Klein sued Lennon for $508,000 in unpaid loans and began his protracted legal campaign against Apple. After McCartney's original action it seemed that the Beatles break-up couldn't get any worse, and yet it did. On 2 November 1973, John, George and Ringo counter-sued Klein for alleged mis-representation. Klein counter-counter-sued, demanding $19 million in back fees and damages. A separate attempt to pursue McCartney individually for $34 million was thrown out of court. During the early days of the Klein litigation, which came to occupy some forty attorneys, the Lennons split up. For most of the next sixteen months, John lived with Yoko's young assistant May Pang. After a par-ticularly heavy session with the lawyers (he was also fighting deportation) Lennon would flop into his music room, pick up a guitar and tear into a primal-scream version of Yesterday. Sometimes he tried a little writing of his own. Usually he just sank further into the one Beatles song he never quite got over. Friends would find him sitting in the dark, lost in Paul's ballad.

On the evening of 5 July, McCartney picked up the other members of Wings in his Rolls and drove them to the London opening of *Live and Let Die*. At the party afterwards Peter Cook did a revue that turned 'fuck' into the longest one-syllable drawl in history, and then went on from there to get dirty. McCartney was on good form throughout; over the next year, his theme song would be heard by some sixty million Bond fans worldwide. People who never bought a rock album would now know the name Wings.

On the hot summer night of the film's premiere, the mood was very up. Amid all the beautiful people, Paul's appearance was uniquely striking. He wore an immaculate dinner jacket and black tie, but no shirt. In its place, someone appeared to have drawn a nude woman on his chest.

Late in July, Wings went back to Scotland to begin five weeks of rehearsals for their next album. Paul had elected to record this at the EMI studio in Lagos. By now the group, while wildly successful, seemed to suffer from a problem of what their advertising agency called brand contamination. The songs themselves might be individually ace, but the band somehow contrived to be critically hated. There was strife in the ranks, too, notably between the McCartneys and Denny Laine's exotic (and heavily pregnant) girlfriend, JoJo. Laine would have to explain gently to the future mother of his children that 'Linda reckons you're a groupie, and you're after Paul.' But the real aggro began when both Denny Seiwell and Henry McCullough decided to leave. This had 'virtually nothing' to do with Linda, notes McCullough. 'The truth is, we were on call 24 hours a day. Everyone got a retainer [£30 a week, in some reports]. Paul kept promising us various things financially, but they never came about. I'd ask him, and he'd change the subject . . . We were up on the farm, grinding away day and night, and I couldn't take it anymore.' Shortly thereafter, Seiwell made a similarly abrupt departure. It happened to be exactly forty-eight hours before Wings were due to begin recording. Overnight, the 'jolly, extended family', as the EMI publicist called them, were reduced to a squabbling trio on a flight to Nigeria. Now McCartney was ready for his masterpiece.

When asked why he chose Africa to record in, Paul would reply blithely, 'Well, the sun shines out there.' In fact, Wings' arrival on 30 August happened to coincide with the rainy season. It poured in Lagos for four straight weeks. During the month, there were problems with snakes, spiders, cholera, drinking water, bribes and student riots. The EMI complex was little more than a tin shack which made 'Magic' Alex's druggy prank at Savile Row look efficient by comparison. Despite McCartney's advance requests, no vocal isolation booths were there – nor booths of any description. The sole recording device was a malfunctioning eight-track of the kind that went out of fashion around the time of *Get Back*. Nor had it occurred to the house engineer to plug in any of the microphones. Instead, he'd induced a more homely note: there was a seedy red plush sofa, some old Sinatra photos pinned to the walls, a spittoon and a malodorous spirit stove, on which a brass pan of coffee simmered perpetually. The building itself had only three complete walls. The fourth was dilapidated and part-exposed to a wilderness of plants and vines. In a stone-floor room immediately behind the main studio several Nigerian employees were engaged in working a vast, 1940s-vintage record pressing machine that clanked and thumped and whirred throughout the day. Outside was a swamp, and just beyond that a raw green mountain plunged straight from the heights down into the valley where the ocean began. The building manager – and apparently McCartney's primary interface with the local community – was a machete-wielding former Igbo guerrilla who had been shot in the course of Nigeria's military coup seven years earlier. The bullet had missed his brain by a fraction of an inch and was still lodged behind his right eye, despite a surgeon's gougings, giving him a ferocious stare. He had never previously heard of Wings.

One relatively dry evening, Paul and Linda decided to walk the two miles from the local swimming club to their villa. After only a few minutes, an ancient Chevrolet jeep pulled up alongside them. McCartney at first thought that the passers-by might simply want his autograph. He was already amiably strolling towards them when half a dozen young men jumped down, brandishing guns and knives. It suddenly occurred to Paul that perhaps they weren't fans, after all, and, more to the point, that the weapons weren't for show. Even as the men were vaulting the jeep's doors, they let off a ragged volley of welcome.

At that point, Linda drew her husband back and began screaming, 'Don't kill us! He Beatle Paul! *Sgt. Pepper*!' There were no psychedelic-pop fans among the gang. The middle-aged figure wearing a Hawaiian shirt and carrying a camera meant nothing to them except as an easy mark. Relieving the McCartneys of their cash and valuables, the men left as quickly as they'd come, pausing only to toss a cassette they found in Linda's handbag into a nearby drainage ditch.

The tape contained all the demos of the songs for the new album.

Luckily, McCartney could remember most of them. When he and Linda got back home half an hour later, they found themselves in the midst of a power cut that affected most of southern Nigeria. Darkness fell on a subdued household.

Some time later, McCartney 'began to feel a bit odd and then fainted. Linda thought I'd died. She had a point – when I came round even I was convinced I was going to die. I felt like I had a lung collapse. We got a cab to the hospital, where the doctor said I'd been smoking too much and suffered a bronchial spasm.'

The following day, a Lagos entrepreneur and musician named Fela Ransome-Kuti appeared at the studio, apparently concerned that Wings were out to 'steal the local rhythms'. He also had his doubts, it's said, about the technical proficiency of the visiting rock star. McCartney was able to reassure him on both points, going so far as to demonstrate several rolls and fills on the drums which, in Seiwell's absence, he was playing himself. Presently Ransome-Kuti said, 'One of the things which brought me here this morning was to see if you understood percussion. You know, you seem to me a good chap. Why not come to my place tonight for dinner and a little concert?'

By concert, he meant his various wives dancing topless in grass skirts to a tattoo-like massed beat. The large audience was in mixed attire: some in uniforms of a kind, tunics frogged with gold braid hinting at Nigeria's colonial past; some in native costume of striped silk. As Paul and Linda stepped from their car an irregular platoon lounging in front of the stage greeted them by snapping to attention and raising their machetes in salute. Towards the end of each number, the detail would turn towards the crowd to actively encourage their prolonged applause.

Eventually, Wings were able to get down to recording *Son of Always* or, as they hastily renamed it, *Band on the Run*. The three musicians left Lagos on 23 September (their flight on the 22nd having been cancelled due to engine failure), and spent a week mixing the tapes at Abbey Road. A month later, McCartney agreed to put out Helen Wheels, a fast-moving single that attempted to do for the M6 what Bobby Troup had done for Route 66, about which he seems to have had mixed feelings. The title referred to Paul's Land Rover, and the song told the story of a trip from Scotland to London.

With their fluffy sweaters and 'jolly, extended family' values, winsome lyrics that invited warm boy-girl romance and the folky sweetness of their singing, Wings echoed pop of a time so innocent it was as if the Beatles hadn't happened. But their success was absolutely of the moment. *Band on the Run* was full of euphorically silly titles and danceable songs with enough hooks to hang your entire wardrobe on. The McCartneys' vocals (often achieving a breezy polyphony) and the bouncy, Ringo-style drums propelled the whole thing to a commercial triumph at last matched by a few appreciative nods in the press. Had Wings sold a billion fewer units, they might have enjoyed their critical vogue sooner. *Band on the Run*, perversely upbeat for all its hassles, showed that they'd earned it.

It was already ten years since *With The Beatles* first crackled over the wireless, but, at its best, *Band* recaptured some of the old glory. The title track wasn't quite All My Loving, but it still fairly swaggered from the speakers. Jet married yet another ode to one of McCartney's dogs with a classic, amps-at-eleven chorus. Let Me Roll It set a raw guitar against an oddly familiar, reedy vocal. Such pastiches were, of course, nothing new for Paul, who'd been regularly exploiting his gift for mimicry since the day he first heard Hound Dog. What was different was that instead of imitating Elvis or Little Richard, here McCartney was 'doing' Lennon.

Band on the Run was a typically warm, well-crafted affair. What made it an international smash was a combination of musicianship and salesmanship. Step one was devising a marketing strategy as unusual as McCartney's choice of studio. Among the eyebrow raisers was the decision by Capitol's West Coast promotions man Al Coury to pull three singles from an album which Paul himself had thought hit-free, one of which, Jet, was released with two different B-sides. Many diehard McCartney fans bought both versions. But the most creative aspect of the plan was to join forces with Apple and EMI to coordinate a truly global launch – specifically including the Soviet Union, where, Paul was assured, 'We'll be the biggest thing since Sputnik.' Just as Coury promised, *Band on the Run* would top both the British and American charts (no less than three times), in the process becoming the first fully certified platinum album. He also delivered on his boast: it flew off the shelves in Moscow.

Even for McCartney, the first week of 1974 was something special.

On Wednesday, the 2nd, he began a player-manager job on his brother Mike's LP *McGear*. Overnight, news came in that Helen Wheels, the song he once barely thought worth releasing, had gone gold in America. Paul and Linda were also being Oscar-nominated for Live and Let Die. The next evening, there was a getting-acquainted session for McGear's band. A roadie went out to buy beer, among other things, and stopped off at the corner shop for the trade press, which contained rave reviews of *Band on the Run*. By the time he got back some of the group couldn't read – Paul himself was off in a side room, giving an interview – but it was a great party. *Band* sold over a million copies in America that week, and would do better business than *Abbey Road*.

All this was but a prelude to that Friday afternoon, when Al Coury rang from Los Angeles to reveal that *The Early Beatles* album was now poised immediately behind Wings themselves in the *Billboard* Hot One Hundred. Two separate greatest-hits collections were similarly jockeying for ascendancy in the British chart. In his most conciliatory interview since the break-up, Lennon would tell *Melody Maker*, 'There's always a chance [of] a reunion. As far as I can gather from talking to them all, nobody would mind doing some work together again. There's no law that says we're not going to do something, and no law that says we are . . . We're closer now than we have been.'

A reporter from the same paper then asked McCartney for his thoughts on the subject. 'I wouldn't mind us working on a loose basis,' he commented.

'BEATLES GET TOGETHER!' ran the next week's headline. Paul corrected the record by telling ABC Television, 'We might do bits together again . . . I don't think we'll re-form as a band. I just don't think it'll work. It wouldn't be as good. I saw Jerry Lewis talking the other day about Dean Martin; it's a little like that.'

Even these remarks were slugged 'GET BACK!' and 'YEAH YEAH YEAH!' in the New York tabloids. Two widely reported legal actions seemed only to fan the reunion flames. In late February, the High Court approved a new plan for administering the Beatles' affairs. 'As soon as things are sorted out we can all get together again and do something,' McCartney noted optimistically. A judge in New York then heard depositions in the case of Klein v Apple, during which a high-powered attorney pleaded ignorance of key Beatles partnership documents, called the band's break-up amicable, and quibbled over such words in inter-group memos as 'breadhead', 'bastard' and 'ugly tart'. (After initially insisting that the last was a term of 'myriad meanings', the lawyer eventually conceded that it was usually not nice.) He even quibbled over the definition of 'Beatles'.

McCartney would say that, about this same time, Yoko once again appeared at his door, 'looking like a widow, a little diminutive sad figure in black' and asked for his help in getting her back together with her husband. She proceeded to give Paul and Linda an elaborate list of instructions – John would have to court her, he'd have to send flowers – for them to pass on. When Yoko was asked if she wouldn't prefer to speak to John direct, she seemed almost puzzled. 'No, why should I?' she enquired.

Very generously, McCartney would act as a go-between at various key moments during the next twelve months, taking some credit for the eventual outcome. Yoko would later insist that his role in the affair had been negligible.

Repairing to South London, Paul and Linda became part of the all-star cast guesting on Ron Wood's first, and, as critical diction has it, 'gloriously sloppy' solo LP, *I've Got My Own Album to Do*. (The title was a dig at Rod Stewart, who was busy just then cutting *Smiler* instead of touring with the Faces.) The sessions took place in Wood's Georgian mansion, craning out over Richmond Hill like a pop Berghof, and were notable, he said with some pride, for 'hav[ing] put 20 points on Smirnoff stock.' Nor was any band with Keith Richards in it likely to be a stranger to drugs. McCartney seems to have primarily used the occasion to try and recruit Woody and the drummer Andy Newmark into Wings. Both turned him down. A few weeks later, Paul hired the guitarist Jimmy McCulloch (part of the *McGear* troupe) and a karate black belt named Geoff Britton on mallets. Keen-eyed observers didn't miss the point that this meant the band had now had four Macs and two Dennys in its ranks, while Britton would in turn be replaced by one Joe English, who was American.

On 2 March, George Martin collected a best-arrangement Grammy for Live And Let Die. It lost out in the category of best-vocal to Gladys Knight and the Pips. A month later, the Oscar went to Marvin Hamlisch's theme song for *The Way We Were*.

On Thursday 28 March, the McCartneys, on a working holiday in California, took a cab from their Beverly Hills hotel to the Burbank studios where Harry Nilsson was recording his album *Pussy Cats* – a project that made Ron Wood's seem like a temperance meeting. For Nilsson and his band intoxication was the rule, and prolonged consciousness the exception. Among those involved in the sessions were Jesse Ed Davis, Klaus Voorman, Keith Moon, Ringo Starr; and John Lennon, there with his companion May Pang. They were just sitting down to listen to the first night's playbacks when Paul strolled in with Linda, looked around and said, 'Fuck me! Anyone left alive?'

The next few moments were exciting. One or two of the band rubbed their eyes and Lennon, who didn't like bad language ever in front of women, reddened visibly, as though keeping his temper in check. A kind of scowl had crossed his face when he saw who it was. Apart from this brief, scarcely perceptible contraction of nose and lips he expressed no further welcome. However, he stepped down from the control room.

Paul then crossed to the middle of the floor to greet his old friend. It was noticed that he didn't hug John, but he did give him his number-one handshake, pumping up and down for several seconds and saying warmly, 'Wotcher, cock.'

'Valiant Paul McCartney, I presume?'

'Sir Jasper Lennon, I presume?'

A promising start. These were the old *Beatles Christmas Show* handles. One or two of Nilsson's waxworks began to revive again.

May Pang: 'McCartney then wanted to play. John told him they were finished for the night, but even so I could see him and the band adjusting to the idea. Within a minute or two everyone plugged back in and ripped through Midnight Special. Ringo and Moonie were off somewhere, so Paul played drums. It sounded great, they were all tooting away, and even John was grinning. You could see these jaded musicians standing there in shock, staring at the two Beatles. People were coming in from other rooms just to check. I remember a door opened, and suddenly there was Stevie Wonder.'

Three days later, Lennon invited the McCartneys to his rented home on Pacific Coast Highway – the very house in which Jack and Bobby Kennedy once entertained Marilyn Monroe – where they jammed on another seven or eight numbers. Among these were tub-thumpers like Never Trust A Bugger With Your Mother, Let's Stomp and Paul's helium-voiced take on Lucille. After several poolside refreshments, McCartney then managed to get Lennon alone in the back room, where he told him about his visit from Yoko. Fuelled as he was by brandy and hog tranquillizers, John had already rebuffed two previous emissaries, telling one he 'didn't give a fart' about his wife, or any reconciliation. This time, though, the mood was different. When Paul finished his pitch, Lennon slowly removed his glasses, rubbed his eyes and quietly admitted that he'd been a fool to leave.

One way or another, there was more goodwill that evening than at any time since the Summer of Love. After the McCartneys left, John turned to May Pang and said, 'You know, I sometimes worry about George and Ringo. Never about Paul. The guy's just so together.'

That was the beginning of a relatively civil year for the ex-Beatles. 'Everyone was sweet,' says May Pang, then unaware that Paul was jockeying John away from her, 'and everything was cool again.'

On 4 April the McCartneys decided to pay a visit on Brian Wilson, the great songwriter now known for his Zen-like solitude, at his Bel Air mansion. Nobody answered the door. Wilson was believed to have been home, since they could hear somebody inside gently crying to himself. The couple had marginally better luck next day, when they called on Stephen Stills, an old flame of Linda's. Stills (for some reason, wearing several daisies in his hair) was in a small room, apparently decorated by a voodoo fetishist, rehearsing with Crosby and Nash, breaking off from one of their soaring, superbly layered harmonies to announce he had some career advice for their guest. Paul was flattered. But he felt he was in a madhouse.

'It's very simple,' Stills said. 'We gotta toss the bass, man. I'll take you shopping. That fucking Hofner . . .'

As a rule, McCartney saw no profit in disagreement. This time, though, he drew the line. They could kiss his arse. He wasn't tossing anything, and no Yank with flowers on his bonce was getting anywhere near him. That concluded the McCartneys' tour of California.

Once home, Paul and Linda bought a two-bedroomed cottage,

named Waterfalls, just off the medieval streets of Rye, East Sussex, a marginally easier commute than Scotland. (Several American authors would insist that the McCartneys made the move primarily to shield ten-year-old Heather from the temptations of drink and drugs, but this merely confirms their ignorance of English rural life.) The house was round, and abounded in comfy furniture with delightfully mismatched chintz, stained glass and engraved 'Guinness' mirrors salvaged from the local pub. Chunky oak beams and an arched fireplace featured in the living room, from where a panelled door led back to the garden – soon home to a stable of horses, ponies, sheep, ducks and hens – with dense, or as Linda said, 'enchanted' woods beyond. Armed with the first royalty cheque from *Band on the Run*, McCartney paid £40,000 for the property, where he retreated with his family and animals. From now on, even time spent in London would be time away from home.

On 18 June, McCartney allowed himself a birthday gift in the form of a month's recording in Nashville, where he and Linda stayed on a sprawling ranch belonging to the songwriter Curly (The Green Green Grass Of Home) Putnam. Out of the sessions came Junior's Farm, a second-division hit later that autumn, and the hitherto obscure Jim McCartney number Walking In The Park With Eloise. The critics would greet both with restraint. Money, though, continued to rain down on McCartney Productions: *Band on the Run* had already spent six months of its continuous two-and-a-half years on the chart. Though the family now had plenty of cash, they worried about it anyway. Evidently Paul's childhood poverty still haunted him, as did his fear that 'the dosh [could] go as fast as it came'. It was left to Linda to splash out on occasional treats for her husband. One day in Nashville, Paul happened to mention how much he'd always loved Heartbreak Hotel, one of the great growth rings of rock 'n' roll, and of his own obsession. A day or two later, Linda went out and bought him the original double bass used on the song.

Largely thanks to McCartney, Apple's profits the first half of 1974 were up seventy-five per cent, and sales had doubled since 1970. Not coincidentally, Lennon was at his most affable by far that year. On 16 July he and May Pang took up residence in a penthouse on New York's East 52nd Street – about a mile and a half from Yoko in the Dakota – from where, for the first time in years, John began to correspond with his Liverpool family, occasionally even entertaining his eleven-year-old son for the weekend. Among Lennon's regular visitors were the McCartneys. According to John, the two couples would enjoy a number of 'Beaujolais evenings, reminisc[ing] and singing along' while Beatles bootlegs (already a cottage industry) played on the stereo. May Pang actively encouraged the jamborees, even as Paul took the opportunity to repeat quietly to John how much Yoko missed him. John always replied that, much as he loved his wife, he was fast warming to his smart, sexy, and above all loyal companion. Everyone agreed May was devoted to her man, whom she saw then as 'basically sweet, [more] compassionate than strictly kind, but sensitive . . . Really, it was the happiest time.'

In his euphoria Lennon told people he'd broken through to a higher plane, but it proved to be a trampoline, his manic highs followed by suicidal lows.

A prominent record business executive, who calls John 'one of the few exceptional men I've met in my life', recalls lying in bed one night watching Lennon on a Hollywood chat show promoting his new album *Walls and Bridges*. When John calmly described his relationship with Paul as one of equals, the television viewer began laughing so violently his wife asked him what was wrong. It was, he told her, the notion of Lennon's letting anyone be his equal; nothing could be funnier. John soon let his feelings be known when *Walls and Bridges* stalled at number six on the chart topped by *Band on the Run*. 'Little Paulie' had pulled off something he, Lennon, had tried and failed to do since *Imagine*.

★

The crush of fans and the media scrum that surrounded John's every public activity was compared to the frenzy of Beatlemania. But very little of the interest expressed was in *Walls and Bridges*. Instead, the 'WILL THEY OR WON'T THEY?' headlines scrolled across a world anaesthetised by the likes of John Denver, the Carpenters and Donny & Marie – the other main pop idols that autumn. Even the *New York Times* found it necessary to ask on its front page, '"FAB FOUR" TO REUNITE?' Behind the scenes, John would tell a few insiders, like May Pang, that he was now 'seriously considering' a 'small, unpublicized gig' involving the Beatles and Harry Nilsson. Perhaps in some out-of-the-way town like Buffalo. In the event, the nearest Lennon came was on Thanksgiving Day, 28 November, when he joined Elton John onstage in a packed Madison Square Garden. A few *Pepper* uniforms in the audience, which had been tipped off in advance, female shrieks, followed by a sprinkling of bras and knickers. As John announced 'One by an old estranged fiancé of mine called Paul', there was bedlam in the hall. With the chugging opening notes of I Saw Her Standing There, Lennon began to morph into something larger than the bag of nerves who'd spent the previous two hours getting high on coke and throwing up backstage. Elton's band quickly got a groove going, and the transformation was complete – it was *just like the Beatles!* And the crowd went crazy.

George Harrison happened to be touring America at the same time, and answered the stock question by showering praise on John and Ringo, before concluding 'I'd join a band with Lennon any day, but I couldn't join a band with McCartney. That's not personal, but from a musical point of view.' Paul and Linda, even so, attended George's own Madison Square Garden concert on 19 December. They sat in the second row, both sporting Afro wigs and droopy moustaches. George neglected to introduce them, but did take the opportunity to promote his current single Ding Dong, Ding Dong/I Don't Care Anymore.

Harrison's next order of business was the 202-page Beatles dissolution document, scheduled to be ceremonially signed later that same night. After nearly four years, the lawyers had finally arrived at a compromise agreement whereby the band's royalties would be unfrozen, and each of the four members be party to a complex series of payments, loans and trade-offs. McCartney was to receive an instant £300,000 in cash and, more importantly, the exclusive rights to any and all future solo earnings. (Apple would continue to act as a clearing-house for the Beatles' group income.) It would be hard to overestimate his relief as, pausing only to doff his wig, he made his way uptown to the Plaza hotel. The momentous encounter, a rock version of Gerald Ford, that first impeachment summer, declaring that 'our long national nightmare is over', was due to take place at midnight, in a lavishly appointed suite adjacent to the one the Beatles occupied on their first night in America. Paul arrived early, with his own TV cameraman in tow to record the event for posterity. George came in good time, and Ringo (fearful of a writ from Klein) remained at the other end of an open phone line from London. Then, as twelve o'clock came and went, a disturbing rumour began to spread through the room. Lennon had apparently not attended the concert, and was now home in 52nd Street, less than a dozen blocks away, with the phone off the hook. When one of the lawyers finally managed to reach him, John blithely announced that he'd meditated all evening, and that he wasn't signing anything. The 'stars weren't right' for it.

Or, that's one version. Essentially, says May Pang, Lennon's concern was neither spiritual nor astrological. It was fiscal. Under the terms of the dissolution, John was to receive some £1.5 million of impounded Beatles royalties, as well as various EMI stock and other assets. A number of loans would be written off. Nobody could say with any certainty how the Internal Revenue Service might react to this windfall. Lennon's own attorney had warned him that, in a worst-case scenario, he faced a 'potentially ruinous' audit, perhaps touching on the enigmatic relationship, say, between Northern Songs and Maclen. (Some put Lennon's worldwide tax exposure at $2 million.) At the time, John's primary income remained his monthly allowance from Apple, most of which he was paying direct to Yoko in the Dakota.

May Pang: 'The McCartneys showed up at the door the morning after the aborted signing . . . Paul, I have to say, was great – very supportive and concerned about John. The upshot was that everyone went over to Lee Eastman's office, of all places. Paul was sort of the head boy, Lee the headmaster. John laid out the problem, and from that point on things were worked out. The McCartneys flew back to London, and John and I took Julian to spend the holidays at Disneyworld. Lawyers were calling us there the whole time. As soon as we got back, John signed the papers.'

On 31 December 1974, the Chancery Division of the High Court announced that it would formally wind up the partnership and void the action brought by McCartney exactly four years earlier, thus dissolving the Beatles.

A more secure man might not have marketed his next single as 'WRITTEN AND PRODUCED BY PAUL MCCARTNEY/Recorded by Wings.' But it was hard to be humble when everyone from Cliff to Johnny Cash was knocking on the door panting to have Paul play with them, and three major labels were proffering million-dollar deals to lure him away. McCartney might have taken one of the offers – or so he said – had EMI/Capitol not put up an improved, long-term contract, reportedly worth $8 million. Repairing to Allan Touissant's Sea-Saint studios in New Orleans, Paul and the band began to rehearse for a new album that would attempt the most difficult trick in showbusiness – the follow-up.

It was eighty-two degrees when Wings pulled up at the white stucco building located at 3809 Clematis Street on the afternoon of 16 January 1975. The temperature within the band was appreciably higher. After eight months, the judo-suited drummer Geoff Britton was already mutinous, later telling the press that McCartney had promised him royalties in 'telephone numbers', but that all he saw was a scale wage and the occasional bonus*. Britton (soon to leave the band by mutual agreement) was even less taken by his fellow musicians. When a journalist apparently misquoted him on the subject, the drummer angrily called *Melody Maker* to set the record straight.

'They say I hate Jimmy McCulloch's guts,' he noted. 'What I really said is that he's a nasty little cunt.'

McCulloch was just twenty-one, and smoked and drank as if he had no wish to see twenty-two. Once or twice he collapsed on the studio floor, or plunged through a plate-glass window in his hotel, which didn't endear him to the boss. McCulloch, too, harboured doubts both about Linda's musicianship and his own terms of engagement, once giving voice to his frustration by shouting 'Fuck you, you bastard! I'm getting off your fuckin' shithole farm!' in his employer's face. Even Denny Laine, the one constant factor, had begun to fret about money. After Laine threatened to leave, McCartney upped his salary to around £70,000 a year. It was good pay, but it wasn't quite enough. In 1981, Laine sold McCartney Productions his publishing rights to the smash hit Mull Of Kintyre, among other songs, for a one-off purse of £130,000. Legal and tax bills soon accounted for even this relative fortune. Just five years later, Laine was declared bankrupt with debts of £76,035 and no assets.

Between recording duties in New Orleans, Paul and Linda were to pay another visit on Lennon and May Pang in East 52nd Street. John thought it would be fun for everyone to cab over to the Hotel Pierre and see David Bowie, who hero-worshipped him. Bowie, then

---

* Britton, who made a reported £7,000 during his time with Wings, may not have known that Paul's first phone number – which he never tired of quoting – was Garston 6922.

concave from drugs, ushered in his guests to his penthouse suite and entertained them with a test pressing of his new album, *Young Americans*, released to some acclaim that spring. After that he began an impassioned, track by track review of the record, describing in detail how he'd achieved his breakthrough 'plastic soul' sound with the help of Luther Vandross at a 'funky-butt joint' in Philadelphia. When he finally concluded his remarks, Bowie flipped on the album again. Before he could play it a third time, McCartney asked, 'Could we hear something else?'

Bowie put on *Young Americans* again.

After three or four further plays, the two ex-Beatles and their partners stood up. Bowie told McCartney that he really wanted his opinion on some new tracks he was laying down later that week. Paul told Bowie they should do lunch one day. In the lobby, as the two couples made their brisk way to the street, they couldn't help but notice a framed poster for the number-one box office film, *The Towering Inferno*. The ad line above it read, HELL ON THE TOP FLOOR . . . NO WAY DOWN . . . NO WAY OUT.

'That went well,' said McCartney.

May Pang says Lennon then planned to drop in on the Wings sessions in New Orleans, only for Yoko to call on the Friday in question and insist that John instead visit a hypnotist who was to help him, once and for all, quit smoking. That was the last Pang saw of Lennon for three days. When she happened to run into him in a dentist's waiting room the following Monday, John 'looked at me vaguely and seemed dazed. His eyes were dilated and his manner [was] weird.' May knew as soon as she saw him what was coming.

'I guess I should tell you,' Lennon said, once back in 52nd Street. 'Yoko has allowed me to come home.' At that he started to pack a bag.

John then made love to May, smoked a cigarette, and took a car back to the Dakota. With this move went the last real prospect of a Lennon-McCartney collaboration, if not a Beatles reunion.

★

From New Orleans, McCartney moved shop to Wally Heider studios in Los Angeles. He enjoyed life in southern California, and even took to strolling around between takes on Hollywood Boulevard, just a block to the north. The only drawback was that, sooner or later, some tourist would give him that 'Beatle Paul!' look he both loved and hated, and a mob would gather. McCartney told his friend, the producer Jeff Griffin, that he 'walk[ed] fast, wore a hat and kept his head down.' If all else failed, Paul just smiled and scrawled an autograph, often styling himself 'Ian Iachimoe', or, for a lark, Ringo.

On 1 March, McCartney scored two Grammy awards for *Band on the Run*. One of the show's presenters (though not for that particular segment) was John Lennon.

Two nights later, Paul was driving Linda and the three girls in a rented Lincoln Continental from the studio in Hollywood to their temporary base in Malibu. After apparently running a red light, they were stopped on Santa Monica Boulevard by a highway patrolman who later said he smelt a 'strange odor' and saw 'enormous clouds of smoke' pouring out of the window, which gave him his due cause.

After asking everyone their name and business, the officer shone a torch over the inside of the car, where he found a smouldering joint under the front passenger seat. A search of Linda's purse turned up a plastic bag containing eighteen grams of Colombian gold. The cops then took everyone downtown, where Linda was booked on possession – though not, as initially feared, child endangerment – and released on $500 bail.

A month later, a Los Angeles County judge dismissed the charge after Linda agreed to attend a 'court-approved workshop on the evils of narcotic abuse in expiation.' At her lawyer's request, this class took place in London.

On 24 March, McCartney threw a wrap party for his new record on board the *Queen Mary*. Proving the breadth of his appeal, the guest list included everyone from Rudy Vallee and Dean Martin through to the members of Led Zeppelin. Paul would describe the album itself, *Venus and Mars*, as 'kind of about an imaginary bloke who's got a girlfriend who's into astrology . . . [And] someone sitting in a cathedral waiting for their transport from space' – evidence, perhaps, that Linda wasn't alone in enjoying a toot. There was whimsy aplenty on *Venus*, which featured titles like Magneto And Titanium Man and ended with Paul's version (surely the definitive treatment) of Crossroads – not the Robert Johnson blues, but the theme to the TV soap opera of the same name. There was also an abundance of the finely honed melodic stuff, goosed here by one or two Cajun rhythms, that would attract not only critics but real people as well. A single called Listen To What The Man Said brought Wings' tenth consecutive top-twenty hit. The album itself went platinum.

A month later, Paul and Linda had dinner with the newly reconciled Lennons at their home in New York. There were some shared laughs, not least about Allan Williams' book *The Man Who Gave The Beatles Away*, though John would later complain that he'd had to sit through his guests 'brag[ging] about how wonderfully they were doing.'

The McCartneys, in turn, listened at length to Yoko discussing her 'numbers'; how, for instance, she and John would only ever fly in a westerly direction, seated in a specific row, and on certain precise dates determined by a psychic reading. Paul told various friends that, whatever one thought of Yoko, she was very clever. Look at the way she'd let John go out and sow his oats, giving May Pang her blessing, then carefully effected his return. Another thing apparently struck Paul: the moment Yoko got what she wanted, she had no more use for him.

The previous January, McCartney had paused before boarding a New York-bound plane at Heathrow to talk to reporters. 'I'm relieved the legal links between the Beatles have been separated,' he announced, referring to the High Court ruling. 'I'm a very tomorrow kind of guy . . . That [part] of my life is over.'

Except, of course, it wasn't. In some ways it was just beginning; the lawyers would be kept busy for years to come, not least in regard to Northern Songs, which contentiously changed hands once again in 1985. Some two-and-a-half years later, McCartney would decline to join George, Ringo and Yoko for the Beatles' induction into the Rock and Roll Hall of Fame, citing 'still-existing business differences' and concluding, 'It would have been hypocritical to appear on stage with them, waving and smiling.' As well as the continuing legal fallout, there was also the worldwide fascination, if not clinical obsession, with Paul's former band. Even as Wings began a thirteen-month tour of Britain and nine other countries, the first question at press conferences was always the same: What about a reunion?

Wings' opening night, 9 September 1975, was a triumph. For their £2.50 admission money the fans got a twenty-nine song set, McCartney relaxing his ban on pre-1970 material with stirring renditions of The Long And Winding Road, Lady Madonna and Yesterday. A new single taken from *Venus and Mars*, Letting Go, fared less well. That Christmas, three songs would compete in the annual trade press readers' polls as 'worst 45 of the year'. Two were by the Bay City Rollers. The third was Wings'.

When it came time to play Australia, in late October, Paul and Linda overslept and kept their otherwise fully-laden Qantas 747 waiting on the ground at Heathrow for nearly an hour. The airline fined them £80 a minute for the delay. (They could afford it: McCartney Productions showed profits of £466,867 for the year, exclusive of Beatles royalties.) Once down under, the comedian Norman Gunston leapt up at a packed press conference to ask Linda whether 'the only reason [she was] in the band was because she slept with the lead singer?' After the laughter had died down, Paul was left to admit that that seemed to be the general perception. Even Linda, however, was a conservatory-trained virtuoso compared to Wings' youngest recruit. When Jimmy McCulloch, whose aptitude for searing guitar was limited by his inability to pluck the strings, lobbied McCartney to include his own, autobiographical song on the next album, he called the tune Wino Junko. To make matters more poignant, there were moments when McCulloch seemed to both recover his touch (this was the man who'd played on a number-one record at sixteen), and resolve to kick his habit. It became a routine. While on tour, McCulloch would call his dealer and, in a novel twist, offer to pay him to stay away. The dealer, after taking his money, agreed. A pattern evolved. McCulloch would pay the dealer to leave him alone, then he'd call for drugs. The dealer, ever solicitous, would show up in minutes with a pile of heroin.

Wings wound up their Australian tour at Melbourne on 14 November 1975. Long-awaited concerts in Japan were cancelled when the Ministry of Justice branded McCartney a 'cultural pollutant', apparently a reference to his Scottish drug conviction. Instead, everyone headed to New York. On Saturday night, 13 December, the Lennons, identically clad in kimonos, their hair tied in ponytails, were relaxing at home with their newborn son Sean and a journalist friend when they heard carol singers outside the door. Impulsively breaking his recent vow of seclusion from the public, John opened up. Standing before him were Paul and Linda, bearing Christmas gifts. By all accounts, the chemistry that evening was still somewhat off. While Lennon and McCartney strolled back to the kitchen to fix drinks, their wives 'sat among the Egyptian antiquities, on which squatted gangs of cats', both women gazing up at the ceiling and unable, apparently, to find common conversational ground.

Aristocratic idleness was abhorrent to Paul, who toiled away the rest of the winter on Wings' fifth album. He also elected to tour North America, his first concerts there in exactly a decade. There was a tragic reminder of those days when, on 4 January 1976, the Beatles' long-suffering friend and roadie Mal Evans, sometimes credited with the original *Sgt. Pepper* concept, was shot dead by Los Angeles police. It was a shocking, but not totally surprising story.

To all outward appearances, the thickset, bespectacled Mal had changed little since the day in August 1963 when he first signed on with Brian Epstein. However, like most of the band's entourage, he never quite recovered from the break-up. Shortly after separating from his wife, Mal had done what many an English rock veteran does when London ignores his services. He drifted on to California, where he scratched a living as a gofer and would-be producer while working with a ghostwriter called John Hoernie on his tell-all memoir, *Living the Beatles Legend*. Just a week before the book's due-date, Evans' girlfriend Fran Hughes asked Hoernie to come urgently to their duplex, warning him that Mal had 'flipped out' from taking pills. A struggle ensued when Hoernie arrived, in the course of which Evans picked up a .30 calibre rifle he kept under his bed. Hughes called the law. At the official inquest, it was stated that Evans had ignored repeated police requests that he lay down his weapon, which he instead 'pointed deliberately' at them. Other eyewitness accounts seem to at least partially rebut that thesis. According to them, following the initial scuffle Evans had locked himself in his bedroom, where he could be heard sobbing uncontrollably and threatening to shoot himself. To avert this, the cops had broken down the door and fired six rounds at Mal's head and chest, killing him instantly. An autopsy showed a 'therapeutic level of Valium' and the equivalent of one pint of beer in his bloodstream. His rifle had not been loaded.

The sad and most plausible version of events is that Evans had succumbed to a fit of self-destructive despair and, like three to four hundred other predominantly white, middle-aged men each year in America, committed 'suicide by cop'. Quite coincidentally, Mal had recently been in touch with both McCartney and Lennon to discuss whether he might be due various back wages. Even while finishing his book, he'd trumpeted it around town that he confidently expected a 'five-figure cheque [from] the office.' On the afternoon of his death,

Evans had rung his friend Ken Mansfield, the former US manager of Apple Records, who recalls his sense of unease at the conversation:

> I asked him how he was, and [Mal] started rambling on how well everything was going. Something seemed funny even though he was professing optimism, and in the middle of his good news I asked him what was wrong. 'Nothing's wrong,' he said. 'Paul and I just worked out some problems, and he's going to give me credit for some of the things I wrote with him—'. I interrupted again, asking him what was wrong.

McCartney was later to call Evans 'a big lovable bear', and to rue the events of that Sunday night in Hollywood. 'Had I been there I would have been able to say, "Mal, don't be silly." In fact, any of his friends could have talked him out of it; he wasn't a nutter.' Evans' body was cremated in Los Angeles three days after his death, which was ruled a justifiable homicide. Possibly because Harry Nilsson made the arrangements, the urn carrying the ashes was somehow lost in the post on the way back to England. *Living the Beatles Legend* has never been published.

McCartney was in high spirits as he headed for European shows starting on 20 March, prior to crossing the Atlantic. On the 18th his stepmother Angie rang to say that Jim, whose health had deteriorated in recent months, had died peacefully at their home on the Wirral, aged seventy-three. His final words were, 'I'll be with Mary soon.' John Lennon was one of the first people to call the family with his condolences. (By another of those Beatles coincidences, John's own, estranged father died just a fortnight later.) He was more solicitous in this regard than many of Jim's immediate clan. Angie reports that, with the exception of Paul and his brother Mike, 'they treated me like a leper from that day onward. While one of them removed everything from the house that wasn't nailed to the floor, another let it be known I was nothing but a gold-digger – a "married-in" as they called it –

who, after twelve years, was still unwelcome.' In the weeks ahead, the McCartneys expunged all physical traces of both Angie and her daughter, including removing their names from the announcements of Jim's death and snipping them out of family pictures. 'They not only froze us out,' says Ruth, 'it was as if we'd never existed.'

Jim's funeral took place in Liverpool on 22 March. Paul was travelling between gigs in Germany at the time, and thus unable to attend. He didn't even mention the matter until a French television reporter happened to enquire about his parents in the course of an interview. 'They're both dead,' McCartney said. Denny Laine reports that he 'nearly fell off [his] chair' at this revelation. Paul stopped his father and stepmother's annual allowance as soon as he got back to England on the 29th. When a distressed Angie rang McCartney Productions to enquire about her cheque, she was told, 'Sorry, love; no one here knows anything about it.' Twenty-four hours later, the office changed their phone number. Mother and daughter then had £3,000 in cash and other assets, and an overdraft roughly four times as great. They were also faced with paying off Jim's final medical bills. After moving out of their bungalow, various circumstances would lead to their sleeping rough on the floor of a vacant building and applying to the labour exchange ('where they saw the name McCartney and assumed we were millionaires') for the dole. Four years after Jim's death, his widow again appealed to Paul for help. 'Stay at home and bottle fruit', he reportedly advised her. 'It's more character building for you to go it alone.' In 1983 Angie sold her last remaining box of Beatles memorabilia, which contained a copy of her stepson's birth certificate, for which an American collector paid $1,500. McCartney would fume about this treachery in the press before ringing Angie to complain. Ruth happened to pick the phone up and, after listening to Paul's heated opening remarks, put it down again. Neither mother nor daughter has contacted him since.

Out the week of Jim's service, *Wings at the Speed of Sound*.

McCartney's image as a smart but essentially lightweight pop sentimentalist took another leap forward with the inclusion of the singles Let 'Em In (which name-checked most of his family) and the number-one smash in which he announced his intention to 'fill the world with silly love songs' and asked 'What's wrong with that, I'd like to know?' This latter tune was, on the face of it, just a sub-Soul Train romp, but the extra-crunchy bass and clever build-up to the finish would make it an almost guiltily enjoyable listen. Silly Love Songs topped the US charts an unprecedented three times over the summer of 1976. Other than these two, critics were pushed to name a favourite track on *Speed of Sound*, because, despite McCartney sharing the vocals, they all sounded exactly the same. Fortunately, they all sounded rather good: the sort of simple, tender lyrics and good-rockin' riffs that never go out of style.

More was in the immediate offing. To capitalise on McCartney's American tour, EMI reissued no fewer than five old Beatles songs, including Yesterday, thus putting Paul in the position of competing with himself on *Top of the Pops*. Capitol Records took the opportunity to release an upbeat anthology, *Rock 'n' Roll Music*, on which, in the face of a recession, they chose to spend a million dollars on PR alone – the largest campaign in the company's history. Reunion rumours enjoyed much the same mixture of tenacity and optimism. Typically, John or Ringo would teasingly fan the brush fires, only for George to stamp them out. Or an unnamed band spokesman would suggest that all four were 'keen on the idea', provided 'difficulties' could be resolved. Tactlessly asked to comment only minutes after a sold-out Wings concert in Detroit, Paul would snap, 'Look, mate; it's 1976 and I don't think most of the people here care about what happened ten years ago. All they're interested in is what I'm doing now. The past is gone and it won't come back.' The reporter gave it a second, and then asked his follow-up question: 'Will John be onstage with you in New York next week?' That concluded the interview.

★

Yet amid the fun-house of hype, there was one man who was deadly serious about a Beatles reunion. That March, the Hollywood-based promoter Bill Sargent offered Paul, John, George and Ringo $50 million to perform one, twenty-minute concert. He agreed that perhaps this was a bit high, but remained confident of selling the show on pay-per-view TV to some seven million fans worldwide. One of Sargent's female associates allegedly then found herself backstage at a Wings show in Chicago, and offered to seal the deal by taking McCartney to bed. Paul demurred, but assured her that she'd find other members of his band more accommodating. In the end, the nearest the promoter came to realising his dream was when Ringo climbed up on stage in Los Angeles to present Paul with a bunch of flowers. 'We're just a couple of mates,' McCartney told the press afterwards. 'No big deal.'

'If it isn't important,' a reporter asked, 'then why's someone offering you $50 million to work together?'

'No big deal,' Paul again replied.

On Saturday 24 April, just before starting their tour, the McCartneys had called on the Lennons at the Dakota Building. They started off by chatting about Klein, who was still suing for millions in unclaimed commissions. Paul commiserated about this and various other legal hassles, as well as about the death of John's father. John told Paul what he thought of Silly Love Songs. Then a lull. The McCartneys asked if they could pick up baby Sean and give him a hug. Yoko asked them not to. At that stage, John lit everyone a cigarette. Later in the evening, the two couples sat down to watch *Saturday Night Live*, in which the producer Lorne Michaels famously parodied Bill Sargent by offering the Beatles $3,000 to perform on his show. According to John, 'Paul and I thought it would be funny if we went down there, just as a gag. We nearly got into a cab, but we were actually too tired.' Around one in the morning, the McCartneys left their hosts sitting in front of the 1960 sci-fi film *The Time Machine*.

Encouraged by the generally good vibes, Paul told Linda he planned to drop in on John once again the following afternoon. He returned to a noticeably cooler reception.

'Please call before you come over,' Lennon told him. 'It's not 1956. You can't just turn up at the door any more.' Paul and John, who would win his coveted 'green card' three months later, giving an air of greater permanence to his American exile, never met again.

Wings' first and only tour of America was launched with a *Time* cover story and the sight of whole families moving onto the street, sleeping in doorways for nights on end, all on the mere rumour of tickets. When showtime came, in Fort Worth, the audience rose to its feet before the first note of the first song and applauded for three minutes. As he surveyed the 14,000-strong crowd, McCartney's gaze would have rested on a happily diverse group. From small children to grannies – with one middle-aged man in the front row literally screaming 'Paul!', as if the former Beatle were treading on his corns – this was a far cry from the pubescent mobs of old.

The music, too, proves a richer and more satisfying blend than in the past. To say nothing of the stagecraft: 'Y'all ready to rock?' Paul hollers at length, thumbs aloft. The band punch up the grainy chords of Venus and Mars/Rockshow. Intercut with this is a bank of flashing lights, rippling like the facade of a Vegas casino, and a rhythmic chanting of 'WINGS, WINGS, WINGS'. The set is a hi-tech marvel that resembles something out of the climactic scene of *Moonraker*. There are strobes, lasers, flame-spewing pipes and clouds of dry ice, as well as that key mega-tour accessory, a giant video screen. Everything is amped up to the pain threshold. The band themselves are quickly off to the races: Linda bops from foot to foot as Laine scampers about before coming to a skidding halt in front of the trumpet player, who waves his horn around like a fly-swat. About the only composed figure is Paul, who neither levitates nor explodes. Midway through the performance, he sits down by himself and sings Yesterday. *Then* the place goes nuts.

'The ex-Beatle was bubbling with enthusiasm and obviously happy,' wrote the *Times* critic. 'He was also the calm center throughout the two-hour show, compelling by his very presence. He said he was relaxed and he looked it.'

On 9 May, McCartney's old flame Dot Rhone was picked up by limo and taken to Wings' show in Toronto. Both George and Ringo were also present, though unannounced among the 18,000-strong audience. In Atlanta later that week, Paul agreed to put his hands into the 'Pavement of Stars' walkway outside the downtown branch of Peaches Records. Any lingering doubts about his pulling power in 1976 were dispelled when 4,000 fans lined up around the block to ogle him. Fearing a riot, the authorities insisted that the ceremony instead take place in private. While a work crew jackhammered up the pavement, a second unit conveyed a tray of wet cement to the band's nearby hotel. Once McCartney had left his mark this was returned under police escort and carefully lowered, under the supervision of the mayor and city engineer, into its new home outside the record store.

In McCartney's authorised account of the American tour, there would be no tantrums, no coke buys, no death threats and no near-disaster when a drunken roadie seized the controls of the private jet. There were only sunny afternoons with Linda and a well-drilled band that was 'pretty normal'. No outing with Jimmy McCulloch could be that mellow, even so – earlier in the year, the guitarist had broken his hand while exchanging views with a reporter, so postponing dozens of concerts – and, after a coolly received gig in Boston, he apparently had words with Linda and then refused to join the others for an encore. When McCartney realised he was a man short, he ran back down to the dressing room and promptly offered

McCulloch a choice. 'Do you want to tear up your contract, and piss off' he was asked, 'or fucking perform?'

Fucking perform.

There were altogether warmer scenes in Tucson, where McCartney celebrated his thirty-fourth birthday. The record company paid the up-and-coming John Belushi $6,000 to perform his popular Joe Cocker impersonation at the party. (Belushi would always remember this commission. At the time, he was typically earning between $500–700 a week.) The *National Enquirer* stringer talked his way past security and impertinently asked Paul whether he wasn't too old to rock. Paul pursed his lips and promised to be 'real blunt' in his reply, which turned out to be no. There were record-breaking crowds up and down the West Coast. 'McCartney's demeanor was entirely Beatlesque,' wrote the *Seattle Times*. 'He was quick with a joke or wry comment, friendly, gregarious . . . [A] spectacular night . . . Spellbinding . . . Electric . . . One of the great excitements of the evening was the deafening roar of 67,000 people at the end and the sight of thousands of matches lighting the darkened hall before the encore.'

By the time he reached Los Angeles, McCartney had played to just over a million American fans. A short continental tour, including a UNESCO-arranged benefit in Venice, officially made Wings the top box office draw of the year. Taped inside the jet, Paul had a Sambo's Let's-Clean-Up-America map, printed for that summer's Bicentennial, in which he stuck different coloured pins as a review of each performance along the way: a red pin – hot stuff; a black pin – only fair. The verdict was 19–2 in Wings' favour.

After that there was little for the critics to write about except the McCartneys' decision to take their three daughters, aged twelve, six and four, out on the road with them. 'The media asked what we were doing, dragging our children around the world,' Paul would note. 'Let's just hope they brought up their kids better. I doubt it.'

While McCartney's detractors continued to fault his parenting plan, others wondered aloud about drugs. Recalling the tour twenty-five years later, Paul would assure these same critics, 'When we had parties, we made sure the kids were in bed first . . . We played it pretty straight with them and they had as near to a normal life as possible.' There may have been what he called 'herbal jazzed cigs' around, but the 'heavy shit' was the sole preserve of the band and their entourage. Denny Laine's fiancée would recall scalping some tickets one night and buying a sack of cocaine large enough for six or seven people with the proceeds. Jimmy McCulloch snorted the lot.

When Wings started out, curious university students would pay 50p each to watch them, and Paul split the take evenly among the band. Between the five of them they grossed some £3,000 for the fourteen-day tour. Four years later, McCartney Productions would net $3.8 million for thirty performances, exclusive of a line of 'top accessories' – everything from satin bomber jackets to ladies' knickers. Paul could afford to charter his own transport and rent houses, rather than hotel rooms, for his family. The fine print in the American tour programme listed a fifty-strong crew, including several muscular ex-FBI agents, two nannies and a 'smoothie girl' engaged to whip up high-energy drinks. There were also no fewer than four travelling accountants. By his thirty-fourth birthday McCartney was valued at £10 million, more or less. At times his net worth slopped around by a few hundred thousand pounds a day, like water going back and forth in a bathtub. Some said he was already the wealthiest man in showbusiness, richer than Sinatra.

The press would make much of McCartney's sunny, exuberant side. Friends would also see his occasional stubbornness, and a frugality defined by a fridge containing nothing but old takeaway cartons and a bottle of milk. He showed various other signs of thrift. 'Paul', as an acquaintance notes, 'could always sit down to dinner and remember three hours later who had the soup and who had the papadoms.' But, particularly after 1976, McCartney also gave willingly of his time and money when the mood took him. Everyone from Dusty

Springfield to the Liverpool boxer Johnny Owen would be a beneficiary, as were a raft of environmental and animal rights groups later in the Eighties. The gifts weren't only generous, but almost always anonymous.

McCartney Productions (now relaunched as MPL Communications) would soon move to a five-storey Edwardian house in London's Soho Square. Paul installed bullet-proof windows and a full-scale model of Abbey Road's Studio 2 in the basement. Works by Magritte, Rauschenberg and de Kooning, and various gold discs lined the walls. Shortly after banking his American tour receipts, McCartney's company bought out the music publisher Edwin H. Morris, which included most of the Buddy Holly catalogue. That September, Paul threw a seven-day festival celebrating what would have been the great rock 'n' roller's fortieth birthday. Holly's manager gave him the cheap cufflinks his client had been wearing at the time of his fatal plane crash, and Paul kept these as if they were more valuable than any Grammy.

Regular readers of the London *Evening Standard* between 1976 and 1978 would have noticed a series of increasingly way-out classified ads. 'Percy Thrillington has been persuaded to prolong his stay in Paris as he finds the springtime atmosphere most conducive to creativity,' ran the first. And, 'Mr T, despite excesses on both social and business time, hopes to lend his support to today's daffodil ball' . . . 'While unmarried, Thrillington extends his compliments to feminine subscribers of all ages' . . . 'Will attend tonight's production of *Don Giovanni* and awaits with eager anticipation a scintillating performance from Miss Hayashi.' (Alas, he never did.) An entry from March 1977 noted that the elusive Thrillington would be 'taking an extended holiday in South America following the rigours of launching his first record album.' From there he apparently travelled to Newmarket, where, a day or two later, his 'condition [was] causing grave concern following injuries sustained [beneath] the thundering hooves of runners in the 3.30. No grapes, by request.'

The saga went on for so long that it developed a cult readership, and was credited with adding several thousand to the *Standard*'s circulation. People began writing in demanding to know who Thrillington was. The paper even put its star reporter Stephen Clackson to work, looking for clues as to the perpetrator's identity.

Neither Clackson nor anyone else on the *Standard* ever got their man, allowing that he'd 'pulled off [an] obscure prank.' But eventually it emerged that it was the world's most popular recording artist, who indeed liked a day out at the races. The prankster was McCartney.

After a biblical-seeming period encompassing seven years of artistic struggle, coupled with a legal saga involving everything from corporate break-ups to drug busts, McCartney was once again on a major career roll. By the end of 1976 you tended to either love Wings or hate them. What few people did was to ignore them.

The debate was particularly vibrant because McCartney, his wife and friends were a sitting target for the likes of the Sex Pistols and those coming up behind them fast. Now was the time of punk rock – of low-slung guitars scrubbed furiously by Messrs Thunders or Vicious, frequently in an atmosphere akin to Brueghel's depiction of hell. It would be hard to exaggerate the sheer loathing Paul, with his sweaters and his bouncy duets with Linda, some of which, admittedly, made Mike and Sally Oldfield sound like the Clash, attracted from such quarters. To one wag, he was the 'doe-eyed ham who sang Let 'Em In, also Junior's Farm and Big Barn Red and Mary Had A Little Lamb, unless my mind's playing tricks and all four lines come from the same tune.' (Mild compared to the critic who called Yesterday 'the worst song of the last fifty years.') Certainly nobody demonstrated better than McCartney how rock 'n' roll had come to accommodate the 'great average'. Later in the Seventies, the Muzak Corporation would report that, between his two bands, Paul ran neck and neck with Elvis as the preferred listening in American elevators, supermarkets and doctors' waiting rooms.

None of which greatly concerned Wings' millions of fans. To them, McCartney's Seventies songs had all the multiple layers, musical and lyrical, that informed the Beatles' greatest works. Among these virtues was a sense of breezy unorthodoxy. There were peerless tunes on *Speed of Sound* and the rest, but there was also some quite radical twiddling. In the same week he was being voted 'Old Fart of the Year' in *Sounds*, Paul was also the first customer in line for one of Lol Creme's 'Gizmos' (a device for making a guitar sound like a slightly deranged violin), which made its debut on his next-but-one-album. Such touches were, of course, nothing new for McCartney, who'd been regularly slipping in a little of the avant-garde since mid-1963. This ability to be both comfortably safe and exhilaratingly strange was at play even in the rhodium-selling Silly Love Songs. The tape-loop of chugging industrial noise that ushered in the core *Dance Fever* beat was pure McCartney. It's interesting to listen to David Bowie's piston-hissing experiments six months later on *Low* in the context of this work, and to compare critical reaction. Even one or two of the heavyweights, like *Rolling Stone*, wondered aloud if the former Fab wasn't getting to be a bit of a drag.

The official tour souvenir, *Wings Over America*, proved another spectacular success. Selling over six million copies, it was the definitive triple-album mix of gatefold art, chant-along choruses and intros mired in endless takes on 'How you doin', Texas?' For their £6.80, punters got thirty songs in all, five by the Beatles. Paul had the credits for these printed as 'McCartney-Lennon', moving John to mark his displeasure by dropping his presentation copy of the album out of a seventh-floor window.

On the same day as *Wings Over America* hit number one, Neil Aspinall and Apple's remaining employees moved out of the Queen Anne house at 3 Savile Row. It remained vacant for some time. A few months later, the building's caretaker would tell the *London Evening*

News that he was convinced the place was haunted. Sitting alone there at night he would hear music, followed in turn by raised voices and the noise of a slammed door from the general direction of the basement studio.

CHAPTER SEVEN

Coming Up

On 10 January 1977, eight years after the Lennons had walked into Allen Klein's hotel room and told him they 'want[ed] bread, and a one-woman show for Yoko', Apple was finally able to disengage from its former business manager. The settlement cost the company $5,009,200, or approximately £2.8 million. As the bulk of his income prior to *Band on the Run* had gone directly into the partnership, McCartney had good cause to feel aggrieved. (Apple Corps reported a net profit of £1,389,841 for the year 1976–7, prior to its paying Klein.) Meanwhile, the promoter Bill Sargent improved his offer to bring about a Beatles reunion. Whatever they wanted, he told them in strangely familiar terms, was theirs – once the deal was signed. Sargent reiterated that John, Paul, George and Ringo could perform at any location of their choice and that they could also play individually, provided they appear together for a minimum of twenty minutes. The fee: $60 million.

Let me talk to my people, said Lennon.

A new level of activity began. Sargent's offer led to renewed interest by Sid Bernstein (promoter of the Beatles' first New York concerts), who had a charity show in mind. The Secretary General of the United Nations then proposed that the group 'do something for world peace', assigning a senior member of his staff, one Mal Hipple, to liaise with Apple. Hipple brought with him two deputy-assistant secretaries, a lawyer and a publicist. It somehow seemed only fitting that the negotiations proceed in an atmosphere reminiscent of a medieval court. Nowadays, for each ex-Beatle there were scores of personal aides and an etiquette of finely tuned call and response: George's manager would communicate with Ringo's agent, and John's assistants had assistants, who in turn arranged for the palmist or the *katu-tugai* man (whose job was to advise the Lennons on which days it was prudent to travel, and which to stay home) to drop by. It was to McCartney's credit that he shunned the elaborate protocol system favoured by the others and, for the most part, kept his own counsel. After several weeks' futile debate on the matter, Paul formally announced that there would be no Beatles reunion in 1977. He wanted to spend more time with Wings; and Linda was pregnant again.

There's probably a law that defines the rate at which an album gets worse as its budget increases. Wings' seventh, *London Town*, began life promisingly, and logically enough, at Abbey Road. First in the can there was Denny Laine's big statement Feel The Love, which Paul retitled Deliver Your Children. A few days later, everyone then moved to the SS *Fair Carol*, moored off the American Virgin Islands, where, so the press release said, they would record such gems as 'Morse Moose And The Grey Goose – a funky rocker with hot and nasty guitar lines and intense lead vocals by Paul as he tells a mystical sea story, appropriate to the offshore setting.' (The tax break didn't hurt, either.) The reality of what ensued was some half a dozen interchangeable belters and two or three tuneless grey ballads. Linda apparently didn't enjoy her confinement, and the US Coast Guard twice saw fit to scour the floating studio for drugs. Even when the tapes were rolling, the *London Town* sessions were marked by a disastrous series of bad 'vibes' and mysterious accidents. Paul's associate Alan Crowder flew in and immediately fell off a ladder on the *Fair Carol*, breaking his ankle. The engineer Geoff Emerick put a plug in the wrong socket and blew the shoes off his feet. Laine went down with sunstroke. Jimmy McCulloch drank a bottle of dynamite-strength local spirit and promptly went blind for a day. Trying to light a flaming torch on deck one evening, a roadie managed to set fire to his shorts instead, and had to jump into the sea to extinguish himself. McCartney then got it into his head to have the band strike up while the ship was put in gear, and dutifully joined in the subsequent search party for scraps of Joe English's drum kit. Linda did a bit of singing but otherwise kept below, leaving Paul to direct proceedings. Denny Laine was having child custody problems back home and wanted to call one of the tracks Daddy And Heidi. (Other versions insist it was Denny And Heidi.) Too sentimental, McCartney told him.

Nor was Jimmy McCulloch feeling the love he'd enjoyed when Paul first hired him. Back in Scotland that summer, the guitarist apparently had a creative difference with his boss, resulting, later that night, in his pointing a loaded gun through the McCartneys' bedroom window as they lay asleep. What happened next, from one biographer's point of view: 'McCulloch's arm outstretched through the window . . . his hand began to shake, at first almost imperceptibly, and then fully, violently, until even holding onto the tiny revolver seemed impossible . . . Jimmy began slowly pulling the trigger. Watching the shiny hammer tediously pulling itself back, gathering up the momentum to launch the explosive charge that would free him once and for all from the oppressive McCartneys, [he] suddenly changed his mind at the last microsecond and caught it with his thumb.'

Not too long after that, McCulloch would decide to leave Wings. 'I enjoyed playing with them and I learned a lot from Paul,' he told the press. In September 1979, McCulloch's older brother Jack broke down the door of Jimmy's flat after he had failed to show up for a rehearsal. Amid the piles of tapes, scattered record sleeves and empty bottles, the young guitarist was slumped in an armchair with a burnt-out joint still clamped between his fingers. It was estimated that he had been dead for up to thirty-six hours. The inquest would officially record an open verdict. Although the autopsy found collectively fatal traces of drugs and alcohol in McCulloch's body, the coroner would note that there were 'some odd circumstances': no money was found in the flat, and a security chain had been broken by someone other than Jack McCulloch. All this would lead to persistent rumours of foul play – that McCulloch was 'done', as one source puts it, for reasons buried somewhere among the frenzy of his ten years as a rock star.

Joe English also decided to leave the band at the end of 1977. He too loyally insisted that 'I enjoyed playing with Paul and I learned a lot . . . I just wanted to come home and see if I could make it on my own.' (Years later, English would tell *Beatlefan* magazine that he'd been 'continually promised a share of the royalties, [but] didn't get any'; McCartney would dryly note that his drummer had still somehow managed to buy a Porsche.) Paul's next venture with a clipped Wings turned out to be the greatest success of his career.

On 12 September 1977 Linda gave birth to the couple's first son, James Louis McCartney, at the Avenue Clinic in London. 'I'm over the moon,' Paul confirmed to the evening press. 'When I knew the baby was a boy I really flipped.' Later that night, McCartney heard something he had never thought he would live to hear.

That Yoko Ono would call from Japan with her 'love' and 'con-gratulations' was startling enough. But there was more, allegedly, to follow. John himself was meditating, Yoko announced, and thus unable to come to the phone. The fabled 'reunion' amounted to a static-ridden exchange of niceties with a surrogate.

The late Seventies saw a lot of veteran artists take early retirement – at least until the Nineties, when CD reissues and the advent of 'classic rock' radio moved fans to reconsider some of the old-timers they'd long since consigned to the nostalgia circuit. McCartney himself avoided this fate. He never enjoyed an artistic renaissance, for the simple reason that he never disappeared in the first place. *Wings Over America* marked his band's sixth consecutive hit album, five of which had gone multi-platinum. Some of his critics had since become more tetchy, making it a point of honour to show their independence by carping. To *NME*, for one, he was 'a bit Vegas, a bit Liberace'. But such gripes as there were were too late, and often too obscurely argued. Strange as it seems today, there was a period around 1977–8 when Billy Joel, hot off his album *The Stranger*, enjoyed a season as the so-called 'lost Beatle'. This 'elegant master of songcraft', intoned *Sounds*, 'ha[d] more snap, crackle and pop at [his] disposal than any surviving member of the 60s elite.' Yet, as a simple track-by-track comparison proves, it would still take ten bowls of Billy Joel to equal one bowl of McCartney.

By late 1977, Paul and the Beatles were trapped in a kind of limbo, having apparently declined to regroup but still not having permanently ruled it out. In the meantime, various satellite projects were launched on a hungry public. The musical *Beatlemania* began its run at the Winter Gardens in New York, where the actor playing Paul, one Mitch Weissman, was regularly mobbed by ecstatic fans at the stage door. Legendary mogul Robert Stigwood was preparing his big-screen version of *Sgt. Pepper*, starring Peter Frampton and the Bee Gees, which would be released, to critical derision, in 1978. An organisation called Lingasong Ltd took the trouble to fight off a legal challenge by Apple in order to release a double album entitled *The Beatles Live! At the Star Club in Hamburg, Germany*. This had been recorded by a lone microphone propped up on a table one night in 1962 and sounded, not surprisingly, a trifle rough. It hit number 111 on the chart. The official concert album, taken from the band's Hollywood Bowl performances, and remixed by George Martin, enjoyed rather more of both production and marketing budgets. The ex-Beatles would spend much of their time that year plugging the record on anything with a tube. There were four solid weeks of TV, radio and print advertising; huge colour posters adorned the window of every high-street outlet. According to *The Times*, 'this [was] one of the most full-blooded campaigns ever undertaken to sell an LP.' *The Beatles at the Hollywood Bowl* was fortunate enough to reach number one. Six months later, another after-the-fact collection, called *Love Songs*, brought off the same trick. Among the various TV specials, spin-offs and docudramas doing the rounds, there was Eric Idle's Beatles-spoof *All You Need is Cash*, which first aired in March 1978. Fans would particularly note the Allen Klein character, whom John Belushi played as a human tank who ploughed through walls, terrorised his clients and beat up his own bodyguards. The actual Klein was being indicted just then on US tax charges that dated back to 1970–1, and would eventually serve two months in jail.

Ironically, about the only exception to this renewed outbreak of global Beatlemania was to be found on Merseyside. On 19 October, by a vote of nine to one, Liverpool City Council rejected a plan to erect a monument to the Fab Four. The boys were certainly once great, it was officially minuted, but had 'reached a place [where] they hadn't been doing their best work in years.'

McCartney's bagpipe-stoked ballad, Mull Of Kintyre, was released on 11 November 1977, the same week in which *Never Mind the Bollocks Here's the Sex Pistols* topped the album chart. As Paul himself wryly acknowledged, 'At the time I thought, we *are* kidding, aren't we? Releasing a Scottish waltz in the face of all this furious spitting and gobbing . . . [But] we turned out to be bigger than any of the punk records.'

There was no real tune involved, just the old Rocky Raccoon riff and some timely intervention by the Campbeltown Pipe Band. (One or two of whom would later complain of being underpaid for their labours.) McCartney's 'singalong, glass of ale in your hand'

Christmas anthem was, however, strangely affecting. Backed by the hard-rocking Girls' School, Mull Of Kintyre would top the UK charts for nine weeks, becoming the biggest selling British single since She Loves You. (It tanked in America.) There was also a memorably silly video by Michael Lindsay-Hogg and Wings' legendary appearance on *The Mike Yarwood Show*, with Paul, Linda and Denny Laine miming away while Yarwood, dressed as 'Chunky Punky, the new-wave Chancellor', bellowed his approval like a branded bullock. Mull Of Kintyre eventually sold 2.7 million copies in the home market, and nine million worldwide. It would remain the UK's most successful 45 until Band Aid's Do They Know It's Christmas? overtook it seven years later. As McCartney appeared on that record, too, he'd then graced all three of the best-selling hits in British history.

Early in 1978, the McCartneys spent £120,000 on East Gate Farm, a secluded, five-bedroomed property close to their existing cottage in East Sussex. The 160-acre estate, tucked somewhere between the A259 and the river Brede near Peasmarsh, would come to feature a swimming pool, stables and a paddock for the family's reindeer, as well as a nearby windmill converted into a studio. There was also a six-foot fence and an imposing watchtower, leading journalists to dub the place Stalag Luft III, or 'Paulditz'. Some of the exterior was painted the 'loo-roll tones' Linda had once selected for Rembrandt, with one or two more rustic touches: the interior was a vast shambles. Piles of newspapers, jumbles of coats, a very old piano, and in Paul's small study some rickety card tables and a collapsed sofa. There were shaggy dogs dozing on the floor and a small child hiding behind every chair. Although the property would soon be worth more than a million pounds, there was no equity in the furniture.

According to the *Daily Express*, the McCartneys enjoyed a home life 'straight out of *Emmerdale Farm*', if not quite as racy. But there were still one or two rock-star accessories on hand, even in their rural idyll.

Take, for instance, drugs. Denny Laine, for one, would marvel at the McCartneys' ingenuity when it came to carrying their stash around. Preferred hiding places, he claimed, included the hood of six-year-old Stella's coat, and inside baby James' nappy. Despite Linda's completion of a court-imposed course on 'the evils of narcotic abuse', it seems fair to hazard the guess that both she and Paul continued to indulge for some years. A regular visitor to East Gate Farm in 1978–9 recalls McCartney sitting downstairs one night, 'reading a fairy story while squashed up on the sofa with two or three small kids and a stuffed Rupert Bear.' Several hours later the children were in bed, which didn't stop Paul from continuing to hug the bear with one hand, while smoking a joint with the other.

Such grafting of the naughty onto the nice would remain the hallmark of McCartney's home life for the next twenty years. Something similar went on at work, where the studio became not only a hit factory but also a lab for Paul's edgy interactions with the world of Gizmos, cut-ups and random poetry readings. From the off-the-wall Rockestra Theme to the loopy guitar distortions of To You, Wings' final album would be a perfect example of a record that managed to be technically 'finished' and yet open to chance procedures borrowed from the avant-garde. This swirl of extremism horrified the suits at EMI, but made total sense to McCartney. 'If you're a man you've got to push,' he apparently reasoned. 'You must grow . . . Art must be useful.'

First, however, *London Town*.

Fourteen years earlier, in May 1964, McCartney had written the darkly beautiful Things We Said Today while cruising on a yacht in the Caribbean. His new album shared the same humble roots but instead offered a line in slick, mainstream pop. *London Town* never got beyond an icy professionalism. It was flawless, facile and com-pletely forgettable.

Legend insists that a certain record company publicist, an old mate of McCartney, and like him from Speke, was invited to Soho

Square (which was being redecorated, and thus littered with workmen's tools) for the first playback of *London Town*. Relaxing into a G-plan chair with a herbal cig, the flak listened closely, from the first line of the title track – 'Walkin' down the sidewalk on a purple afternoon/I was accosted by a barker playing a simple tune' – through to the closer Morse Moose And The Grey Goose. When it was over, Paul asked him what he thought.

'Well,' said the PR, 'I'd like to hear the finished version first.'

'That *is* the finished version,' said McCartney.

'Well, I'm not sure people are going to like it.'

McCartney reportedly went ballistic. 'Fuck off!' he shouted, jabbing his finger at the man's face. 'I fucking brought you here from Liverpool! Some fucking thanks!' After his guest left, there was a noise from Paul's office almost as though somebody there was servicing his hi-fi with a hammer.

The message and the messenger were one. As far as McCartney was concerned, that was the end of the friendship.

In time, *London Town* would go gold, giving the likes of Boney M a run for their money. The album's first single, With A Little Luck (updating the We Can Work It Out theme), again nailed down the *Top of the Pops* formula. It also became Wings' seventh number one in America. The follow-up, I've Had Enough, was perhaps too cleverly titled for its own good, stalling at number forty-two. London Town itself won some favourable reviews but avoided any sales.

Not long after that, the guitarist Laurence Juber and drummer Steve Holly became members of Wings (the line-up known as Mach VI), cutting their teeth on a song called Same Time Next Year and several Rupert Bear-themed tunes.

McCartney wanted to get his 'new, improved brand', as he called Wings, out on the road. But he also kept an eye firmly on his old label. The extension of Paul's original whim from a groundbreaking album into a cottage industry continued in 1978, with the release of the big-budget *Sgt. Pepper* film. This wasn't just a bomb, it was a critical holocaust. Robert Stigwood didn't yet know what McCartney thought of his project ('a crock of shit', he found out later), but the general consensus was voiced by Janet Maslin in the *New York Times*. 'This isn't a movie,' she concluded, 'it's a business deal set to music.'

McCartney and Lennon didn't speak to one another again that year. They stewed and they brooded, and, while they did so, the record company put out Sgt. Pepper/With A Little Help From My Friends as a single, earning everyone a mint. According to one biographer, John had become the Howard Hughes of rock 'n' roll, wasted down to 130 pounds and spending much of his time holed up in his bedroom, crammed with heroin. He admitted to one visitor that, whenever he heard Paul's name, he thought not of music but of all the 'business crap'. Although they didn't meet, we're told 'Lennon's obsession with McCartney went off the chart . . . Whatever Paul was doing, John had to know.' Meanwhile, George had taken a pasting for his latest release, *Thirty Three and a Third* and, not coincidentally, was now more into producing films, among them Monty Python's *Life of Brian*. Ringo hadn't had a hit album in five years.

In September 1978 Wings set up shop in Lympne Castle, a fourteenth-century pile in Hythe, Kent, to cut most of what became their swansong. The roadies threaded dozens of cables into the front hall, and everyone plugged in against a backdrop of musty chandeliers and baronial suits of armour. McCartney's amp was set up at the foot of a medieval staircase. Laurence Juber, the new guitar player, was pleasantly surprised by 'just how hip Paul was', with his use of radio collages and his locker of unreleased 'techno stuff' he liked to relax to, with titles like Fishy Matters Underwater.

There was also a Thrillington-like diversion to the proceedings. After further approaches from the UN, Paul had decided not to reunite the Beatles but to recruit a 'rockestra' to join him on two numbers that would later form the basis of 'The Concerts for the

People of Kampuchea'. On 6 September Paul and Linda hosted their third annual Buddy Holly party, where they took the opportunity to invite Keith Moon to join the likes of Pete Townshend, Dave Gilmour and Hank Marvin in their massed band. Moon agreed, but died later that night. Rockestra Theme and So Glad To See You Here were recorded, by means of Paul synching up no fewer than twenty-two musicians, some three weeks later in Abbey Road. As well as helping the people of Kampuchea, both songs were ground-breaking in their use of forty-eight-track technology to beef up largely improvised, random compositions – as even Frank Zappa remarked, a dazzling aural 'trip'. 'Freak out!' *Daze* splashed in a diagonal banner across a picture of Paul conducting the troupe.

On 5 November, Denny Laine and his long-time girlfriend JoJo were married on a party boat docked in Boston harbour. Paul and Linda couldn't make it. According to the bride, a roadie eventually dropped off the 'official' wedding gift – a set of bed linen still in the original shopping bag. 'My wife didn't get on well with [the McCartneys]', Laine notes, 'and didn't get to spend enough time around us. That's not good for a family relationship.'

Later that month, McCartney felt confident enough to put out *Wings Greatest*, which featured an '$8,000 cover photograph of a mystical she-god' that managed to look like a cheap statuette, and which, for reasons of space, omitted eleven Top Forty hits, any one of which would have made a lesser man's reputation. Released into the teeth of a recession, it became the only Wings album not to crack the US top ten. Shortly after that McCartney decided to leave EMI/Capitol after fifteen years, and sign with the highest bidder. CBS Records won out with a strikingly handsome offer of a $2 million advance against a twenty-two per cent royalty, as well as various buyouts and perks that included the gift of Frank Music, the CBS publishing arm that owned *Guys and Dolls*. Total value: an estimated $15 million.

As McCartney himself noted, it was the 'sweetest deal in rock music history.' For his part, CBS president Walter Yetnikoff (the man who introduced Michael Jackson's *Thriller* to posterity) apparently saw it as a trophy signing. As one of his colleagues later put it, 'It was too much money, [but] how can you argue with buying a Beatle? You should have been in [CBS headquarters] Black Rock the day Paul came in to press the flesh. It was like royalty. I've never seen anything like it. Everybody in the building came out of their offices and were just shaking.'

'I just drive in, make music all day, drive back, go to sleep, get up, drive in, make music all day.' That's the way McCartney described his life in 1979. Despite the unresolved conflicts of the Sixties, they were palmy days for Paul and his 'new, improved brand'. One early spring Friday afternoon, he felt sufficiently emboldened to make the other members of Wings an offer: if they could come up with a good enough song, he'd put it on the B-side of the next single. At a conservative estimate, such a gesture would have earned the lucky composer an instant £25–30,000, and a tidy annuity for life. 'It's easy,' said Paul. 'I want everyone to split for the weekend and come up with something that's three minutes long and sounds shit-hot on the radio. We'll record the winner.' If Linda had been there, she might have asked to compete, but she wasn't and therefore didn't.

The three seasoned musicians disappeared for two days and came back admitting defeat. After doodling a few perfunctory notes on the piano, McCartney knocked off the tune himself.

The winning entry was a bouncy paean to Linda that Paul had first hummed at Lympne Castle, called Daytime Nighttime Suffering. It became the flip side of Goodnight Tonight, which went gold in March 1979.

Before long, McCartney even felt able to offer his professional advice to any of the surviving punk bands willing to take it. 'It would be very easy,' he allowed. 'I'd know exactly what to tell them, having come through it. I really understand people like that.' In the end,

Paul's services as a mentor weren't to be required, although he remained a popular motivational speaker at organisations like CBS. 'The Beatles never apologised for being successful and neither do I,' he reportedly noted at one glittering reception hosted by the president and board. 'Making profits is not incompatible with making a real difference in our society.' Yetnikoff would drink to that.

By the end of the evening, label and artist were of one mind. Together they could sell even more records, if humanly possible, than the 200 million or so albums and singles that Paul had managed up until then. And they'd make the world a better place.

To most people who actually got to know him, McCartney was a genuinely nice, down-to-earth fellow. On 20 May 1979, he joined George and Ringo, and most of the other British rock elite, at Eric Clapton's place in the Surrey countryside. They were there to toast Clapton's wedding to Pattie Boyd, who happened to be George's ex-wife. Late that evening, it was Paul who called his 'two old flames' up on stage for the jam session, thus achieving for love more than Bill Sargent had managed for $60 million.

Up north, meanwhile, Allan Clarke had left the Hollies and was 'drifting around, covering a few Springsteen tunes' when, out of the blue, McCartney invited him to sing on Wings' new album. 'The whole thing was great . . . About three months later, a black stretch limo pulled up outside my door. A guy in uniform marched up and, without a word, presented me with a brown paper bag. Inside was a solid gold bracelet, and a note from Paul. I thought it was a cool thing for him to do, something he didn't have to do, to say thanks.'

Another old trouper, 10CC's Eric Stewart, was nearly killed in a car crash that summer. He would spend several weeks in hospital. 'I was messed up so badly,' he says, 'I was drifting in and out of a coma. The very first thing I remember after coming round was a nurse leaning over me saying, "Mr Stewart? Can you speak? Paul McCartney's on the phone." To this day, I've no idea how he found me . . . We chatted, and [McCartney] asked if I fancied getting together, working with him, and right then – I'll never forget – I knew I was going to recover. And *that* was Paul.'

McCartney confounded his critics on Wings' ninth album, *Back to the Egg*, by venturing outside of his normal security blanket of singalong pop. A hint that something more exotic might be in mind came at the press launch. On 11 June, Paul, Linda and a design team managed to turn Abbey Road's Studio 2 into a giant frying pan. There was a specially installed black lacquered floor, tables painted yellow and white, and sizzling effects courtesy of the EMI tape library. After everyone had taken a tomato-shaped seat, a valet handed round glasses of vintage champagne said to have been in the studio's cellar 'since Elgar's day'. The same improbable mix of the trad and the avant-garde distinguished the album, a departure in both senses of the word.

Wings' last five releases had, like Russian dolls, become diminishing versions of the same good idea. This one had a few twists. Paul's epic melding of the Sex Pistols, Talking Heads and *Low*-era Bowie inevitably coloured the music with shades at the murkier end of the spectrum – indeed, if the LP had a failing, it was that it could leave you longing for something to hum. McCartney's disco smash, Goodnight Tonight, didn't even make the cut. In its absence, Arrow Through Me was the sort of thing Stevie Wonder might have aspired to, Getting Closer an unrepentant plunge into the muddy waters of punk. There was also a supple little rocker called Old Siam, Sir. *Back to the Egg* may have hatched no real hits, but it remains one of the success stories of 1979: the spacier touches, like The Broadcast, appealed to lovers of chilly electronica – then all the rage – while the melodic sensibility and generally sunny lyrics attracted those more staid souls not quite ready for Kraftwerk. It spent four months on the chart.

The album also enjoyed a promotional blitz robust even for McCartney. For the most part, Paul's interviewers came away talking about not only his music but about other gifts he possessed – skills he'd been using all his life, and that he now used again, vividly, in a dozen cover stories.

One was an ability to put on a show, a front – not to change his nature, but to conceal it – an ability that had always been one of McCartney's key assets, as had a strength of will that had enabled him to bring it off.

In June 1979, Allen Klein's good fortune finally ran out when a US District Court judge gave him a two-year sentence, all but two months of it suspended.* McCartney could apparently barely contain himself, telling a friendly musician who worked with him in Scotland, 'That shit! He tried to bury me!' (At that moment, his friend realised something about McCartney vis à vis Klein that he hadn't grasped before: that 'there was a sort of dementia there.') Asked to comment in *Rolling Stone*, however, Paul was altogether more conciliatory.

'I feel sorry for Allen now,' he said. 'I was caught in his net once, and that panicked me . . . But it all turned out OK.'

McCartney's charm offensive wasn't just confined to the press. His treatment of potential or actual customers who were similarly impressionable – waiters and shopgirls, doormen and cab drivers – was the same. After one typically frank exchange of views at an Apple board meeting in New York, McCartney is said to have slammed the door with a loud 'Fuck!' on his way out. A company flak, who had been assigned to drive him to his hotel, was dreading the ordeal. ('I was warned to just sit there and keep my mouth shut.') A few minutes later, the man watched in awe as Paul breezed into the lobby, where he greeted 'a conga-line of fans' by posing, thumbs up, for photos. He then happily signed an autograph for the

* Due to appeals, it would be 1980 before Klein actually served time.

porter who carried his luggage to his room. After the porter had put down the bags, the Apple man started to give him a tip. 'It's my pleasure,' Paul told the bellhop with a wink. He handed him a twenty-dollar bill.

The shouting matches across the boardroom table were, for the next year, to be succeeded by day after day of the more familiar corporate scene, with teams of imported London lawyers (overseas duty reportedly bringing a ten per cent supplement, or 'refresher', to their already impressive rates of up to £400 an hour) poring over contracts. After a series of such high-octane meetings and transatlantic phone calls, the four ex-Beatles finally came together not to make music but to sue their old record companies. According to claims filed in the High Court, EMI had allegedly stiffed the group by £1.2 million over a period of thirteen years. A separate action then requested $42.5 million from Capitol. McCartney and the others also sued the producers of the *Beatlemania* revue, which was playing to full houses on Broadway and elsewhere. Some of these suits would continue until 1989, by one account making Apple the most 'implacably litigious' name in even the entertainment business. 'Paul and John enjoy a godlike reputation,' noted one New York journalist. 'Both men come across as thoughtful and sensitive . . . They also surround themselves with people who are as feared as they're respected . . . Speaking from experience, some of their mob are just this side of an oil slick.'

It seemed crazy in a way, Lennon and McCartney fretting about what had happened in the Sixties, a view John sometimes endorsed by repeating a line he'd coined in Savile Row. 'It's like playing Monopoly,' he said, 'but with real money.' In his darker moments, he reflected that he'd most likely be dead and gone before it was all settled. Nor was he filled with a sense he could do something about it. It had stopped meaning anything.

By now, it had been more than three years since McCartney and Lennon last met. While in New York, Paul and Linda often stayed at the Stanhope, a short stroll across Central Park from the Dakota Building, which they could actually see from their penthouse. Somehow, it was never mutually convenient for the Lennons to receive them. At least in one sense, however, John was still alive to his past. His latest therapeutic exercise was to tape an oral history of his life, from his earliest memories of being expelled from kindergarten through to his current opinion of Paul, whom he portrayed as a 'company man'. And where had it gotten him? Old Siam, *shit*. While John was at work on his memoir, Yoko was buying up an impressive variety of real estate, including a fourteen-bedroomed retreat on Long Island, a beachfront villa in Florida, two dairy farms in Virginia and several additional rooms and apartments in the Dakota.

On 24 October, in London, McCartney was honoured by the *Guinness Book of Records* as the best-selling composer of all time. It was exactly a decade since the BBC had solemnly enquired, on *The World This Weekend*, whether 'Paul really [was] dead.' The years 1974–7 had been 'pretty good', he allowed, with four platinum discs and half a dozen chart-topping singles. Mull Of Kintyre had done better business than anything by the Beatles, and was still ticking over two years later. After reading the 'Fort Knox figures' quoted in the press, George Harrison had felt moved to ring McCartney and ask, a trifle brusquely, '*How* much money are you making?' When the United Nations again came calling, Paul told them that they could forget about a reunion, but that he'd do something for the people of South-East Asia on his own. This veto didn't stop the *Washington Post* from running yet another 'YEAH YEAH YEAH!' headline. Their front-page story read, 'The Beatles are close to reuniting, for the first time in ten years, to give a concert in aid of the Vietnamese boat people,' an event, it was said, 'many will find more relevant, in both personal and political terms, than recent strategic talks in Vienna . . .' It really did seem as historic as the Carter-Brezhnev handshake.

★

On 23 November, in Liverpool, Wings began a short British tour. They were received warmly. In particular, some of the fans were beginning to think that they might have been too hard on Linda. Admittedly her keyboard work remained rudimentary. Nor could it be concluded, from her recently re-released single Seaside Woman, that her songwriting skills had exactly flourished. She and Paul did blend, however, on some transcendently sweet harmonies. Seven years on the road had done wonders for both her voice and her stage fright. Waving a variety of scarves and flags, Linda was a non-stop cheerleader who conducted the audience through most numbers. Perhaps she was a tad overfond of rock-concert clichés, such as shouting 'Hello, Wembley!' at the top of her lungs, but you could forgive that because of the obvious pride she took in her work.

On 27 November, there was a nostalgic outing on the *Royal Iris*, the Mersey ferry on which the Beatles had played eighteen years earlier. Then, McCartney was hailed as 'a great favourite with the "teen-agers", all of whom describe [him] as FABULOUS!' Now, while still packing them in, he was getting mixed reviews. It seemed to some that, for once, his heart wasn't fully in it. 'Everything about this performance,' *Rolling Stone* wrote of a gig at London's Rainbow theatre, 'was designed to take the spotlight off Paul McCartney and spread it among the rest of Wings . . . the impression was of a band on stage for the hell of it.' In Brighton, the drummer Steve Holly passed by the McCartneys' dressing room in order to mention how well the show seemed to have gone that night. 'It stank,' said Paul succinctly.

Walter Yetnikoff and his board at CBS wanted Wings to keep on going, and, as their memo put it, 'allow North American cities the magic essence of a live superstar.' To that end, everyone sat down with the promoter Bill Graham, who projected gross box-office receipts of $30 million. As a sweetener, the label would throw in their corporate jet for the McCartneys' use. Meanwhile, Paul ordered up a short but personally gratifying tour of the Far East. After months of patient negotiations, the Japanese government had finally relented and issued the so-called 'cultural pollutant' a work visa.

Often, when McCartney's phone rang the caller wasn't a lawyer or promoter but a supplicant hoping to take advantage of his good nature. He had himself to blame for these intrusions: although he'd once announced, 'Starvation in India doesn't worry me one bit, not one iota' he'd become increasingly public-spirited down the years, lending his name to a number of high-profile causes: the *New York Times* food bank, for instance, to which he donated $10,000 every Christmas. After yet another summit with Kurt Waldheim at the UN, Paul and his 'rockestra' collective threw four London benefit concerts which raised some £160,000 for victims of the Khmer Rouge and related horrors. Although the year ended in a blaze of activity, a few intimates confided that McCartney was reviewing his options. Like the Beatles before them, Wings would prove to be a one-decade band. Laine and the rest weren't even credited on Paul's holiday single (a British number six), Wonderful Christmastime. Twenty years later, he'd reflect that 'by the time we got Steve Holly and Laurence Juber in Wings I was a bit fed up . . . It was all a bit boring, to tell the truth – another dollar, another day, kind of thing. Even though they were good players, the whole Wings thing was becoming a bore for me.'

The armchair psychological theory of what followed a month later, in Japan, goes like this: McCartney was getting that solo feeling again and acted out a subconscious need to sabotage the tour. According to this reading, imprisonment was a means by which he meant to set himself free. Perverse as it sounds, the death-wish version of events has at least one significant supporter – Paul himself, who later noted, 'It was the maddest thing in my life, to go into Japan [with] a bloody great bag of pot right on the top of my suitcase . . . Another strange thing is, we hadn't really rehearsed enough. For the previous Wings tours we rehearsed a lot. It was almost as if I *wanted* to get busted.'

McCartney rang out the Seventies by buying Linda a ranch in Tucson that she'd fallen in love with while attending the University of Arizona. The property, which cost $40,000, would feature prominently in news reports eighteen years later. He also took the opportunity to phone Lennon: a 'perfectly good chat,' Paul insisted. 'He was cooking . . . I happened to ask him about music and he said, no, at the moment he doesn't particularly feel like doing that any more.' That Christmas saw a glut of Beatles films on both British and American TV, as well as the release of an album called *Rarities*, which, despite an astronomical £55,000-a-week ad budget, limped to only number seventy.

The whole grim business began when the McCartneys' regular New York drug connection made his way up to their suite at the Stanhope hotel around lunchtime on 14 January 1980. After their habitual post-prandial joint that night, Paul and Linda wrapped the remaining half-pound stash in a clear plastic bag which they packed in her hand luggage. Everyone was still on a high – 'Real cool, real excited,' Paul assured the press at Kennedy airport – when they left for Tokyo the following afternoon.

But then McCartney's past allegedly came back to haunt him: according to Lennon's biographer Albert Goldman, Yoko Ono had a quiet talk with a cousin who worked in Japanese Customs. 'One call from [her] and Paul was finished.' While not totally implausible, Goldman's account does seem curiously at odds with Yoko's role in helping to get Wings a work visa in the first place. Foreign passengers' luggage at Narita airport has always been opened as a matter of routine. No one would have needed to call anyone else in order to 'finish' McCartney. To Denny Laine, who'd witnessed similar events in the past, his employers had only themselves to blame. 'I think that [Paul] and Linda thought that if they managed to smuggle grass into Japan it would be one up to them – "Everyone thinks you can't do it so we'll show them we can" . . . Paul and Linda are the couple who have everything. That can get boring. What they crave is excitement. They did it for the thrill.'

Just over ten years earlier, McCartney had driven Lennon and several others half mad by leading them through twenty-one consecutive takes of *Abbey Road*'s Maxwell's Silver Hammer. Paul later called the song title 'my analogy for when something goes wrong out of the blue, as it so often does, as I was beginning to find out at that time in my life.' The events of 16–25 January 1980 would seem to richly merit the phrase. McCartney's arrival and swift arrest came together in an ordeal that stretched from the airport's Drug Supervision Centre to a downtown Tokyo jail cell. The clang of the door behind him – which a guard then locked, banging him up with the murderers and rapists confined there – was followed by the confiscation of his wedding ring and other personal effects. Soon Paul found himself singing not to tens of thousands of fans but a more select audience of guards and inmates, who demanded only Al Jolson show tunes and certain Beatles standards.

After several spirited renditions of Baby Face, McCartney politely enquired when he might see his lawyer.

'You have no lawyer.'

'Well, my wife can call one.'

'You must wait. Our ministry will contact your consul.'

'How long will that take?'

'A day . . . two days . . .'

McCartney had finished Toot, Toot, Tootsie, Goo'bye and was nearing the end of Hey Jude when the consul came.

'You could get seven years,' he told Paul.

'My wife will call her family. They're attorneys.'

'Oh, I wouldn't advise it. The Japanese won't look favourably on an outside lawyer – it's one of their customs.'

Later that night McCartney met his public defender, Tasuko Matsuo, who cheerfully advised him that two local men had recently been sentenced to three years hard labour for attempting to smuggle marijuana through the airport. They'd been arrested with less than half the quantity he had.

'The first night I didn't sleep; the third night I had a blinding headache,' McCartney would recall. 'After a while, though, your natural resilience brings you back. You think, "Come on, I'm not going down the Black Hole of Calcutta" . . . You start looking forward to visits, clean shirts, stuff like that.' Clearly, he wasn't a man to succumb to adversity. Even in the dark days of 1969–70, Paul had managed to retain a shrugging, on-with-the-show personality that had both impressed and infuriated the other Beatles. After a week in a four-by-eight-foot cell, however, even the 'most positive guy in the world', as he'd once called himself, could have been forgiven his pangs of doubt. Quite apart from the criminal charge, that half-pound bag of pot was fast proving very expensive. The abrupt cancellation of the tour cost McCartney some $300,000 in lost fees and compensation to the Japanese promoters, with the members of Wings each forgoing an estimated $80,000 bonus. No wonder Lee Eastman, before flying to Tokyo, described his son-in-law's situation as 'a hell of a mess'.

A combination of Eastman, the local lawyer, consular pressure and a show of contrition by the accused – a key factor in Japanese justice – finally sprang McCartney after nine days. An official statement would note that 'charges were not brought against Mr McArty because he had brought in the marijuana solely for his own use and that already he has been punished enough.' Once back at the airport, the irrepressible showman grabbed a guitar and strummed a few bars of Yesterday for the assembled media, before being hustled onto a London-bound flight. His final words as he disappeared down the jetway were, 'Japanese fans are great. I want to come back if I'm allowed.' (Lee Eastman was heard to remark that this was unlikely.) Once safely aloft, reunited with his wife and small children, Paul tearfully told a reporter from the *Daily Express*, 'This is the longest

I've ever been away from my family in ten years. I don't want a separation like it again.' He and Linda would duly spend every night together, some 7,000 in all, until April 1998.

Five days later, a large crowd was on hand to greet the McCartneys as they drew up outside the MPL offices in Soho Square. Linda, in a stylish yellow coat, leaned over to whisper in her husband's ear several times. He nodded and smiled. When he paused on the step to wave, looking once again tanned and fit and sporting a slim red tie of the kind Little Richard once wore, her eyes followed him approvingly. 'I feel great!' Paul announced. While he signed autographs Linda's arm, almost absently, snaked around her husband's back. As fast as a turnstile, his free hand shot up and circled her waist.

The strange year, that began and ended so dismally, was also one of real achievement. On 26 February, McCartney was named 'Outstanding Music Personality of 1979' as voted by listeners of Radio 1. The next day, his Rockestra Theme won him his tenth Grammy. Two months later there was a Novello award in the same week as Oscar Grillo's film *Seaside Woman*, based on Linda's song, took the Palme d'Or at Cannes. Between times, McCartney scored another number one with an eerie novelty – a funky little tune with a kazoo riff called Coming Up. It was his twenty-first hit inside a decade. Even he needed a break from fronting the most commercially successful band in the world, and, when Paul wasn't busy recording thumpingly good pop songs with Wings, he retreated to Scotland to record thumpingly good pop songs on his own, presumably as a form of relaxation. The result was *McCartney II*, released in mid-May.

Meanwhile, the projected $30 million tour of America was quietly cancelled. McCartney spent some of the time he might otherwise have been enjoying the CBS corporate jet in the same way he'd spent his hours of enforced idleness in jail. He performed.

From Scotland, Paul returned in late March to London to work with the director Keith McMillan on a short for Coming Up. This genuinely inspired film brazenly defied the convention demanding that an artist need only glower furiously while miming his latest hit. Instead, through the wonders of modern technology, the McCartneys appeared on screen as no fewer than twelve characters, from a convincingly goggle-eyed Buddy Holly to Beatle Paul. This, too, won a clutch of awards. There was then an ITV special that veered erratically from dark to singalong mode, under the curious title *Meet Paul McCartney*. As the year went on, the promotional pace quickened. No matter how early he arrived at Soho Square, the day was never long enough for all the exclusive, in-depth interviews, for all the calls that had to be made or returned. Every time Alan Crowder appeared in the doorway of the inner office, more pages of the yellow legal pad he held in his hand would be filled with urgent requests for a moment of the boss' time. McCartney was also engaged helping out old friends like Ringo and Zoot Money on their comeback albums. (There was a 'gleam' the ex-Beatles had when they were together, Linda would note; the two of them had 'a thing' that was so 'natural' it was 'beautiful to see'.) When not in the studio, Paul found time to grace everything from *This Is Your Life* to *News at Ten*, with a special cameo appearance on *Tiswas*.

The build-up to *McCartney II*, his first fully solo release in a decade, was reverential. About the only exceptions to the general effusion were his fellow members of Wings. Here, some discrepancy exists between McCartney's public assurances ('There's nothing against the band in this; we'll pick it all up again') and one musician's terse summation ('We were dumped'). Another of Paul's colleagues allegedly came to hear of his album only by reading about it in the press. After a long session in the pub, he then phoned his employer at Soho Square for a full and frank exchange of views. A 'gutful of plonk' loosened former impediments to conversation. McCartney's bandmate enquired what the fuck he'd been thinking of to walk through Japanese Customs with a half-pound of weed; Paul replied that he honestly didn't know what had possessed him.

McCartney's second solo album was, like his first, a homegrown, small-scale affair on which he composed all the songs and played all the instruments himself. The only other party involved was Linda, who donated a harmony vocal when she happened to wander in with sandwiches and tea. Paul picked his own pocket once or twice, resulting in an unfortunate, Wings-lite slab of synthpop called Frozen Jap. There were other lapses: dreary melodies, like that for Waterfalls, whose only purpose was to be described as 'haunting'; vocals smothered in reverb; a general fondness for laid-back tunes punctuated by enormous, operatic crescendos; and an almost crazed use of varispeeding – either revving up or slowing down specific instruments on a track, the end result sounding like a stock-car race.

Happily, the various eccentricities were kept in check with euphoric moments such as Temporary Secretary, McCartney's accomplished bastard mix of rock, funk and electro, and the similarly dance-friendly Coming Up. This clubland hybrid was Paul's most successful single since Mull Of Kintyre; the album went straight to number one.

And then, as *Variety* put it, 'Wings Flapped, Folded.'

McCartney spent most of that summer and autumn working with George Martin in London's AIR Studios, a soundproofed oasis located immediately above Oxford Circus. Some of the sessions were for a projected *Rupert and the Frog Song* animated film. Denny Laine drifted in and did overdubs. Then Paul hired a thirty-eight-piece orchestra and a boys choir to record We All Stand Together – good, singalong stuff, with some spirited handclaps. The flip side was a humming version of the same tune, credited to McCartney and the Finchley Frogettes.

'The guy has that Disney side to him,' says Henry McCullough. 'It's deep in the mix.' Other friends of Paul's echo this particular complaint.

Meanwhile, Lennon had returned to the studio in New York to

record *Double Fantasy*, his first new album in five years. Most of the LP was completed by 9 October, when John and his son Sean celebrated their mutual birthday. Yoko hired a skywriter to mark the event. McCartney rang about seven that evening, a conversation he recalled as 'very nice. I remember he said, "Do they play me against you like they play you against me?" Because there were always people in the background pitting us against each other. And I said, "Yeah, they do . . ."'

It was the last time McCartney and Lennon ever spoke. Late the next night, after reading John's remarks in *Newsweek* about having wanted to 'get out of the band from the day I filmed *How I Won The War*' – September 1966 – Mark Chapman and his young wife Gloria returned to their room, where he lit several candles and switched on his specially high-pitched tape of Beatles songs. Gloria watched uneasily as, adopting the lotus position, her husband then began chanting, '*I'll kill you . . . I'll kill you, you phony bastard!*'

Two weeks later, after quitting his job, Chapman walked into the J&S shop in Honolulu, where an obliging clerk named Ono sold him a gun.

Over the course of ten years, the 'Beatles reunion' saga had shown unusual resilience, joining the likes of Elvis, cancer cures and Soviet psychic phenomena as a tabloid staple. Once or twice, when a Bill Sargent or Kurt Waldheim intervened, the press had had a real story to work with. They covered it with flair, infusing it with drama, noting, for instance, 'Literally thousands of refugees in Kampuchea and around the world could be saved' by the proceeds of a single concert, or that, 'While their music has been routinely recycled, a new Beatles album would be greeted like Moses returning from the mountain with tablets of stone.' The band themselves had sometimes quietly stoked the rumours. Even in 1980, McCartney confided that he 'still dream[t] of doing something' with Lennon, if only on a modest scale.

That dream ended with an early morning phone call on Tuesday 9

December. Yoko had contacted the MPL office and spoken to the new managing director, Steven Shrimpton. Shrimpton rang the McCartneys' farm in Sussex and broke the news to Paul. At that stage much of the story was still garbled, but all of it was terrible. After standing in wait outside the gates of the Dakota Building, Chapman had fatally shot John as he returned home from a recording session.

A few minutes later, Linda came back from taking the children to school and found Paul sitting at the piano, shaking violently.

Early death is often seen as a sort of martyrdom. John Lennon's brutal murder at the age of forty would be widely portrayed that way, and his many fans proved adept in peddling the 'holy man' myth that John himself sometimes liked and sometimes didn't. On 14 December 1980, crowds collected in cities throughout the world to observe a ten-minute vigil, followed by many emotional renderings of Give Peace A Chance. In Liverpool, some 30,000 mourners paid tribute outside St George's Hall. Lennon's life and death led all that night's news broadcasts, ahead of the story of Iraq invading Iran. In New York, where normal protocol was suspended for much of the week, an estimated 120,000 braved a freezing wind and snow flurries to gather in Central Park. For many there, the sense of loss was deepened by Lennon's recent re-emergence as both an artist and a local figure. In a statement, Yoko concluded, 'Bless you for your tears and prayers. I saw John smiling in the sky. I saw sorrow changing into clarity. I saw all of us becoming one mind.'

McCartney went to work as usual on the morning of 9 December. George Martin had to call the police to secure AIR studios from the boisterous crowd of press and photographers, one of whom sought to crawl in from the fire escape. The track Paul happened to be working on that day was called Rainclouds. Around seven in the evening, after phoning Yoko and members of John's family in Liverpool, he made his way out of a side door to his car. When a reporter bellowed 'How do you feel?' McCartney turned around and said, 'It's a drag.'

Later, sensing that the remark might appear glib, Paul went on to tell his friend Ray Coleman, 'Of course when I got home that night I wept like a baby, calling Chapman the jerk of all jerks. If [that] had come out in the press, I would have looked better. I'm actually very bad at showing my true emotions at times like that.'

People debated just how McCartney really did feel, and whether, as he claimed, 'in the end – it's one of the great blessings of my life, seeing as he got shot – John and I made it up. Thank God for that. I would be so fucked up now, if I'd still been arguing with him and that had happened.'

Few people disagreed, however, that McCartney always cared deeply about Lennon's opinion of him. He was still insecure enough on this point to invite Andy Peebles, the Radio 1 DJ who interviewed John the weekend before his death, to join him early on the morning of 10 December. Peebles went to AIR, where he found Paul both 'deeply shocked [and] obsessed about what John and Yoko had said about him.' An irony not lost on Peebles, among others, was that Lennon himself had repeatedly tried to find out what Paul had thought of *Double Fantasy*. 'For public consumption,' says another of his final interviewers, 'John claimed not to care. The fact that he mentioned McCartney's name on average ten times an hour suggests otherwise . . . The strong feeling was that Paul and Yoko were the only two people in the world whose approval he gave a toss for.'

As Lennon's posthumous legend grew, so did Paul's ambivalence on the subject. 'Despite it all,' he announced in 1986, 'there was a time when *I* was the avant-garde one in the band – around the time of *Sgt. Pepper*. That was largely my influence.' Nine years later, the *Anthology* executive Bob Smeaton would explain why that project succeeded where the likes of Bill Sargent and the United Nations had failed. 'It's become very much "John Lennon and the Beatles",' Smeaton said. 'And I think Paul desperately wanted to put his side of the story across.'

Friends also noted that McCartney sometimes spoke very differently about Lennon in private than he did in public. Recalling the whole Beatles break-up, he at least once used the phrase 'manoeuvring swine'. A mutual colleague adds that 'after *Imagine* appeared, you used to hear Paul talk about John and his vendetta. I don't think it was blind love at all.' 'It [wasn't] pleasant,' McCartney himself told *Rolling Stone*. 'A lot of the accusations John made were slightly wild . . . I bent over backward trying to see his point of view. I still bend over backward trying not to malign him.' But all sides agree that though the 'love' wasn't 'blind', love it was. Simultaneously promoting the *1* album and marking the twentieth anniversary of Lennon's death in 2000, McCartney revealed that he was spending the day in Abbey Road 'because it's what we enjoyed doing best together . . . If John were alive, I'd be chuffed to let him know that his album has gone to number one in 28 countries. He'd be tickled by that. I'll be thinking of all the great times that we had together, and I'll be remembering him with all the love in my heart.' In the hundredth edition of *Mojo* magazine two years later, McCartney nominated Lennon as his 'ultimate hero'.

Time passed. Paul locked the door of his home studio in Sussex and played (Just Like) Starting Over, the first single from *Double Fantasy*. Top volume. For days. Christmas came, with its inevitable reruns of Beatles films and other tributes. A fan brandishing a knife tried to break into the McCartneys' estate. Paul put up more barbed wire and floodlights. A month later, in February 1981, he went back to work.

His first project was to reunite with George Martin on an album called *Tug of War*. Denny Laine, Steve Holly and Laurence Juber were all under the impression that they would be involved on this. Laine even attended a few sessions at Martin's studio on Montserrat, but then discovered that his wife, JoJo, wasn't included in the arrangements. McCartney 'certainly tried to get rid of her,' Laine said, 'and probably thought he was doing me a favour. Paul and Linda's refusal to allow JoJo on Montserrat went a long way to destroying my marriage.' Holly and Juber then each got a phone call suggesting that their company, too, would be more sparingly required. Martin had apparently decided that *Tug of War* 'wasn't suited to the group format.'

A few more calls, and various old friends started flying out to help. McCartney's pickup band included Carl Perkins, bass player Stanley Clarke (from Return to Forever) and a fit-again Eric Stewart. Ringo was drumming. On 27 February, Stevie Wonder arrived to sing on Ebony And Ivory, Paul's exquisite, if metaphorically flawed, plea for racial harmony. After this uplifting duet, the two superstars started jamming on a number they called What's That You're Doing? Linda was the only other participant. After McCartney fluffed his drum fill, Wonder stopped playing, stood up, banged the lid of his piano, and motioned for his impressively well-built bodyguard to walk him to the door. As he did so, the minder somehow collided with a heavy speaker cabinet, which fell onto several sets of cymbals. They went over with a molten crash.

'They're playing our song,' Wonder told Paul, not missing a beat.

On 27 April, the McCartneys were among the guests at Marylebone Register Office for Ringo's wedding to the actress Barbara Bach. Paul was also bankrolling a short called *The Cooler* to help promote his old drummer's latest, and woeful album. 'That whole film was a treat,' says Lol Creme, who co-directed it. 'Non-stop professionalism. You could tell Paul really cared about Ringo.'

At thirty-nine, McCartney was entering his late period, but still kept the pace of a man half his age. Colleagues like Eric Stewart were struck by a work ethic that seemed to belong to another time, more specifically the Brill Building of the early Sixties. Paul wrote fast, to belabour being to risk the raw exuberance and spontaneity of his best work. 'He wasn't one of those guys who sweat over a handful of tunes a year,' Stewart notes. McCartney kept it moving, not only turning out his own singles and albums but collaborating with everyone from Carl Perkins to Michael Jackson. This speed and productivity didn't enhance his reputation among certain critics, but other artists were as quickly won over as the 'ordinary fans', who couldn't get enough of him.

Early in 1981, Tim Rice was producing an album for Elaine Paige, star of the original stage production of Rice and Lloyd Webber's *Evita*. It was Paige's first outing under a new contract, and hopes were high. 'We were scrounging songs from successful writers,' Rice says. 'People like the Bee Gees. Gilbert O'Sullivan was actually involved . . . At some stage I rang McCartney and asked if we could do Hot As Sun, from his first solo album. I wanted to put a lyric to it. Paul's prompt response was, "Write everything down and bring it to Sussex." A couple of days later he ran through the tune, singing the words I handed him, nodded and said, "OK, mate, it's a deal." A pleasure to do business with.'

Less agreeable was the Friday night, later that spring, the McCartneys found themselves sharing a town car with Denny Laine. Their destination was George Harrison's pad in Henley-on-Thames, where the four collaborated on All Those Years Ago, George's peppy tribute to John Lennon. A *Get Back* mood quickly prevailed, with Paul, it was noted, seeming to take on the role of a schoolmaster and George his under-achieving pupil. 'Everyone was uptight,' Laine would recall. 'When Paul and Linda left, the atmosphere suddenly changed and became more relaxed. Everybody seemed to physically go "phew" and start enjoying themselves.' Laine formally left the McCartneys' employment shortly afterwards. All Those Years Ago made it to number thirteen on the chart.

One old hand who describes McCartney as 'my best friend but worst enemy', says that when he dared to criticise George's single as lightweight, 'Paul literally went red . . . He told me I didn't know a fucking thing about Lennon . . . For about a year Paul didn't talk to me.'

★

In the Wings break-up, also made public that spring, there wouldn't be as much as a gesture of reconciliation until 2001, when McCartney released a two-CD retrospective accompanied by a TV documentary and a book. MPL took the opportunity to send each of the former band members a cheque in appreciation. 'I got enough to buy a used car,' says Henry McCullough.

McCartney's 1981 reminiscences, *Composer/Artist*, were a publishing coup but only a modest success. His few written remarks garnered less attention than the line drawings with which he illustrated forty-eight of his best-known songs. Many of these were dashed off in the studio, where McCartney liked to doodle, bass in lap, while smoking a joint. 'You can't see Monet doing that,' he observed. For the most part, Paul's cartoons were simple, direct and often very funny, in the tradition of James Thurber. A year or two later he started working on canvas, the first step on a continuum that would result in thousands of sketches, hundreds of paintings, a roaring trade in signed lithographs and much, much more.

There was also the happy dividend from McCartney's past, with the *Beatles Ballads* compilation enjoying five months on the charts. By 1982 Apple was turning over some £6 million annually, with retained profits of over £8 million. Everything and everyone involved with the firm continued to earn vast sums, without ever being, as Paul said, 'anally attentive' to detail. Nor, however, were they inattentive. One former manager notes that, as a director, McCartney 'authoris[ed] expenditure as if it were his own money', which, indeed, much of it was. Yet another Beatles anthology, meanwhile, this one called *20 Greatest Hits*, sold over three million copies that winter.

In November 1981, it was reported that Lew Grade, having lost $30 million on the film *Raise the Titanic*, was seeking a buyer for ATV Music, which included Northern Songs. McCartney made straight to Grade's office and offered to do a deal. The two men sat down at the tycoon's 'battleship-sized' desk and revisited the issue that had driven Paul to distraction some twelve years earlier: the ownership of his 'babies', as he called his back catalogue. Both parties agreed that McCartney would be the ideal proprietor. But a problem, they soon realised, was Paul's lack of interest in ATV per se, which controlled not only the Lennon-McCartney copyrights but a musical empire including both RCA and Pye Records, five or six studios and even a chain of classical-instrument shops. Rather generously, Grade agreed to give Paul the first refusal on Northern should it ever be hived off from the parent company. Following the meeting, which ended with warm handshakes, the seventy-four-year-old mogul and one-time chorus boy hitched up his trousers and did a soft-shoe number for his guest. 'He was a lovely guy and I got to like him,' says McCartney.

Back in Liverpool, the Council, perhaps only now realising what they were dealing with, had entered into a partnership with Wimpey Homes to open an estate with the street names Paul McCartney Way, John Lennon Drive, George Harrison Close and Ringo Starr Mews. At one stage there was reportedly to have been a gala opening ceremony, with assorted flower-strewn floats, brass bands and a yellow submarine. Unfortunately, the authorities planned such a lavish affair that, after several ratepayers complained about the cost, they had to cancel it.

CHAPTER EIGHT

Vegetable Matter

McCartney had been working with his pickup band for a year, on and off, when he assembled them one spring afternoon in Abbey Road. They could all take a week off, he said, they'd earned it; he and Linda would be away in the States, 'seeing an old mate and helping out on an album.' The mate was Yoko, the album was *Thriller*.

On 9 April, Paul, Linda and the Eastmans met John's widow for lunch at Le Cirque in New York, where they discussed Northern's prospects. Meanwhile, on the West Coast, there was announced 'a mammoth recording session by Columbia signing Michael Jackson, who will be joined in the studio by a galaxy of International Talent.' The mammoth session took place in Los Angeles between 14–16 April, during which Columbia's two star assets duetted on The Girl Is Mine, the first of seven smash singles to be culled from *Thriller*. McCartney resisted Jacko's pleas for repeated takes of the song, preferring to nail his vocal and then affably sign autographs for the crew. Some of the teenage entourage reportedly expressed surprise that the ex-Beatle, seemingly out of a Jurassic social order, looked so young. Paradoxically, Paul's presence there harked back to pop's golden age, when hits were made for kids by clever adults.

McCartney's own new opus, *Tug of War*, followed on 1 May 1982.

A year to the day after formally disbanding Wings, he had a solo hit. Rising to number one in June, it remained on the chart for seven months, straight through to Christmas.

Critical consensus names *Band on the Run* as McCartney's finest post-Beatles hour, but *Tug of War* would make a strong bid for runner-up. It stands in stark contrast to much of today's pop. No banshee guitars. Nothing steeped in the heritage of the blues. Instead, you get eleven well-heeled tunes with some seriously lush vocals. The most striking effort is the single Take It Away, where the McCartneys and their friend Eric Stewart combine on the sort of lit-from-within harmonies Stewart trademarked on I'm Not In Love. Even the John Lennon tribute, Here Today, positively luxuriates in its melancholy. Of George Martin's production, *Time*, donning its beads, would note, 'It recalls the groovy, insidious lilt of *Pet Sounds*, if not quite *Sgt. Pepper*.'

Unfortunately, while McCartney is on peak form melodically, he's still stunted when it comes to lyrics – witness Ebony And Ivory, which brings to mind a politically correct Hallmark card. (Nor, as the *New York Times* wrote, was it quite right to use the keyboard as an image of racial harmony: 'The simple, acoustically pure intervals one hears in much of the world's folk music have been compressed or stretched to fit into an arbitrary subdivision of twelve notes to the octave. The piano is a better image of race relations as they actually are than of the Utopia Mr McCartney envisions.') All you need really *is* love, *Tug of War* tirelessly avers. Somebody Who Cares assures us that 'I know how you feel/But somebody cares'; Be What You See imparts the information that 'The one you wanted to be/Is the one you see'; and so on. Gush like that raises two contradictory questions. The first is: how could a self-styled 'yobbo from Speke' write so poignantly, as he did in Eleanor Rigby, of middle-class despair – the face that Eleanor 'keeps in a jar by the door' displaying, in the view of A.S. Byatt, 'the minimalist perfection of a Beckett story'? The second is: having done so, how could he then relapse into bilge like this?

Paul and Linda spent much of the spring promoting the album on American television. It didn't go unnoticed that it was also the twentieth anniversary of Love Me Do. At the NBC studios in Rockefeller Center, Bryant Gumbel introduced McCartney to the *Today* audience as 'Mr Sixties'. Paul hated it. The audience loved it. Paul loved it.

As for Britain, McCartney mixed everything from *Desert Island Discs* to *i-D* with yet more studio work. On 18 June he was at Elstree, shooting a video for Take It Away, when a young woman named Susie Silvey enlivened proceedings by strolling on the set dressed in high heels and a basque, which she then shed. It was Paul's birthday tribute from the crew. Everyone agreed that he looked in fine fettle. The only hint of age were the few flecks of grey in the moptop that flopped over his unfurrowed, forty-year-old brow. McCartney still drove himself to his relatively modest farmhouse every night, and still drove in to London every morning. He carried his guitar with him wherever he went, thought nothing of spending twelve hours in the studio (if a lot of the songs weren't improvised, he worked hard at pretending they were), rarely went on holiday, and had to be forced to relax even then. Old habits.

Six months passed. Then one autumn day the phone rang and it was Lew Grade, calling back, just as he'd promised. Against the advice of his own board, he was considering selling Northern Songs as a separate entity and wanted to offer Paul first refusal. The asking price was £20 million.

'I gulped, thinking, "Oh my God, I wrote them for nothing,"' McCartney told Ray Coleman. 'My own children are going to be sold back to me for a price . . . [But] I said, "Let me get back to you. It's very nice of you to ring and let me know. How long have I got on this?" He said, "Well, I'll give you a week or so." He was really nice about it. He didn't need to ring me at all. He could have just gone, like everybody else, behind our backs.'

McCartney consulted the Eastmans, then phoned Yoko Ono with

an offer: the two of them should each chip in £10 million, and thus return the songs to their rightful owners. Failing that, Paul's lifeblood could, and likely would, go to the highest bidder.

Yoko eventually passed on this arrangement.

Shortly afterwards, the Australian cattle and media baron Robert Holmes à Court won control of ATV Music. He promptly disposed of ATV's stake in Britain's Central Television (acquired by Carlton) as well as a few dozen cinemas and clubs, at which point McCartney phoned to ask what the position might be regarding his babies. Holmes à Court's response showed him a worthy successor to Allen Klein. The price was £30 million, Paul was told, and as part of any deal he'd be expected to go to Perth and appear at both a gala to raise funds for a children's hospital, and at other, less obviously charitable events of his host's choice.

This time, it was McCartney's turn to pass.

He did make a smaller, but significant investment when, in late 1982, Linda exhibited her photographs at select galleries in London and Paris. According to published reports, Paul himself paid some £15,000 for the forty works that remained unsold, managing to keep the deal quiet from his wife.

At around the same time, McCartney decided to make a feature film of a script based on an idea – about a musician losing a tape – he'd been kicking around since 1980. The title was *Give My Regards to Broad Street*, and there was little in it that required the Method approach. The first scene would show Paul, playing a very rich rock star, driving to London. Later on, he would sing some songs, attend a board meeting, and perform in various studios. 'It was the old emperor's clothes bit,' says Eric Stewart, who helped on the soundtrack. 'Nobody involved would tell McCartney the truth. Somewhere in that two-hour movie there was a great video signalling to get out.'

Just before *Broad Street* was commercially released in 1984, McCartney showed a cut of the film to several friends, including the producer David Puttnam. At the time, Puttnam enjoyed a growing reputation both as a talent scout and a hard-headed businessman. Eighteen months later, he would be appointed chairman and chief executive officer of Columbia Pictures.

'Brilliant!' said McCartney's guests after the screening – and Paul shyly concurred. So he was most surprised when, at a quiet moment, Puttnam took him aside and told him *Broad Street* wasn't very good. 'It's basically a home movie,' he confided, a view the critics sadly shared.

On the morning of 2 February 1983, a twitchy figure dressed in black military garb with a variety of sashes and medals, and wearing a surgical mask, passed through Immigration at Heathrow and was driven, along with his eight-man guard, to the McCartneys' home in Sussex. Michael Jackson would occupy the small spare room there for the next fortnight, occasionally venturing in to Abbey Road with his host. Eric Stewart recalls that 'every so often, Paul would tell the band not to come in the next day. Jacko would only work with Himself.' On 12 February, a Saturday, Paul and Linda took their house guest for lunch at the home of the hiccup-voiced Sixties singer, Adam Faith. After the meal, Faith recalled that McCartney and Jackson 'spent about thirty minutes gabbing together in the corner.' It was a half-hour with fateful consequences for Paul and his songs. Essentially, Jackson asked for advice on how to invest his booty from *Thriller*, and McCartney told him to make sure he worked with someone he could trust and to consider getting into the music publishing field. Jackson flew home to California, fired his manager and started looking for some copyrights to buy.

Early that April, the twenty-year-old Bettina Heubers went to court in Hamburg in a failed bid to establish that McCartney was her father, and requesting an annual grant of £4,500 to supplement her earnings as a factory worker and topless model. Although the case was dismissed without a stain on Paul's name, it came in the same month that Denny Laine's estranged wife JoJo went into print deploring the McCartneys' alleged meanness and lack of appreciation for her talents. In all, Paul had to take several weeks of tabloid flak. Perhaps nothing stung as much as when the *Sunday Mirror* seemed to question the state of the McCartneys' marriage. One or two American supermarket titles went so far as to make outrageous claims that, over the years, Paul might not have been completely faithful.

The slurs – especially compared with the adoring press of the Sixties – raised the question of how a man who seemed so nice could apparently have irked so many people, particularly when, as he said, he only wanted to fill the world with love songs.

One clue to the answer was that, for all his self-effacing charm, McCartney had a healthy ego. No one who heard him talk in private, forcefully, emotionally, about all the cutting-edge shit he was doing, about how right he was and how wrong his critics were, could miss the point. A few years later, *Rolling Stone* would ask Paul where he put himself in rock 'n' roll's pecking order. 'At the top,' he said. 'I'm a competitor, man.' Nor could anyone miss the large number of fronts on which McCartney felt he had to fight. By 1983, he was engaged in various feuds both with his two former record labels and the distributors of an album entitled *John, Paul, George & Ringo*, as well as with the ex-Beatles themselves, who had instigated lawsuits against McCartney, MPL and Lee Eastman for a larger share of the action. He was even suing his old agent Allan Williams over the disputed ownership of a pair of leather trousers Paul had worn in 1961.

When Angie and Ruth McCartney decided to sell their one box of Beatles memorabilia in 1983, they 'made every effort [to] contact MPL.' Receiving no reply, they eventually turned to an American collector, with whom they completed the transaction in a Burbank motel. Paul 'wasn't happy; in fact, he went spare.'

The other side of the coin was McCartney's generosity and

stubborn loyalty to old friends. Fifteen years after going on trial with Mick Jagger and Keith Richards, Paul's art- and drug-dealing connection from the Sixties, Robert Fraser, had been reduced to sending out begging letters. While many of those rock stars who normally flock to a cause were suddenly remembering pressing appointments elsewhere, Paul and Linda went out of their way to help. They not only bought their Magrittes through Fraser's gallery, but often invited him to the Sussex farm. When he fell seriously ill they continued to write and call, 'the only two real mates,' he once said, he felt he had. Robert Fraser died of an Aids-related disease early in 1986.

Actually, it had been Linda he 'adored', remarking that she was both 'ballsy' but with a 'wonderful Earth Mother tenderness' about her. Stella McCartney would add a bit more of the flavour when she wrote, twenty years later, 'My mum had her individual style . . . She cut her own hair, didn't wear make-up, didn't shave her legs and wore vintage gear when nobody else was doing it.' As Paul often asked, who could want more? In 1984–5, Magritte's widow Georgette held a series of studio sales, at one of which Linda bought a job lot of easels, brushes and other items that she presented to her husband as a Christmas gift. He was thrilled. Several of McCartney's own canvases would eventually be offered for sale. For the most part, this was 'dark, semi-figurative stuff' – red-brown acrylic splotches and abstract tree trunks that at least initially failed to excite the public. Paul's later pictures based on Old English images were rightly seen as a turning point in the cult status of Celtic folklore: the mythologist as pop god. These solid works polarised the critics and became the second act to his career.

Early in the morning of 16 July 1983, passers-by outside London's Leicester Square station might have noticed a middle-aged busker, none too polished, dressed in torn jeans and a T-shirt, lustily playing a honky-tonk version of Yesterday. It was McCartney. His rendition was filmed from inside a darkened van parked nearby, and would be included in *Give My Regards to Broad Street*. Much to his obvious delight, Paul collected a total of £2.40 from sympathetic pedestrians, one of whom enquired if he needed a hot meal. There was also 'the old Scottish drunk [who] unloaded all his change at my feet, put his arm around me and said, "Awright, son, yer doing greet!"' After paying off the song's copyright owners, who requested a £1 fee for his performance, McCartney donated his earnings to the Seamen's Mission.

Nine days later, now wearing a well-cut suit, hair perfectly coiffed, McCartney slipped in to the bar of Kensington's Gore hotel. He was there to meet Harrison and Starr. The result was as anyone but a Beatle might have foreseen. There was a near riot to collect autographs, and rowdy whoops of 'Paul! George! Ringo!' that continued even after their hurried adjournment to a private room. For the rest of the evening, as fans and photographers jostled on the pavement, policemen were busy arranging barricades and assuring tourists everything was under control. One *Times* reporter would sniff that, whatever one thought of their music, 'common sense and organisation' weren't the band's strong suit.

The talks between the three weren't an outstanding success either, mainly because Paul was reportedly keen to commission a documentary about the band and George (who told the *Sunday Times*, 'People aren't interested in me, they're only interested in the Beatles – what guitar I played on *Sgt. Pepper* and all that crap') hated the idea. Ringo, as ever, proved the voice of reason. He was able to point out that, whatever their artistic merits, *20 Greatest Hits* and the rest had made for a bumper harvest at Apple: £9 million in retained profits that tax year.

In late October, as an obvious companion piece to *Tug of War*, McCartney released *Pipes of Peace*. This weak tea bag of an album, with its sleeve note insisting 'In love all of life's contradictions dissolve and disappear', got a mauling, perhaps because people knew he could do so much better. The title track did provide Paul with a number one Christmas hit. There was also the Michael Jackson duet Say Say Say, backed by Ode To A Koala Bear.

Then came Barbados. On Sunday, 15 January 1984 the temperature on the southern side of the island reached ninety-nine degrees, with a cooling sea breeze. Taking little pleasure in the gorgeous weather, however, were those in a sombre parade at Bridgetown police station, which included the McCartneys, four drug-enforcement agents and several hastily summoned lawyers. Paul and Linda had opened the door of their rented beachfront villa to a knock from the law around two that afternoon. It was another Maxwell's Silver Hammer moment. The officers' search swiftly turned up just over ten grams of pot on Paul and a further seven on Linda. Appearing the following morning before Judge Haynes Blackman, the couple were formally charged and pleaded guilty to possession. Their local barrister, David Simmons, informed the bench that 'The male accused is a very talented and innovative soul. People who have this talent sometimes need inspiration. I'm instructed that Mr McCartney and his wife obtained the vegetable matter from a party on Holetown beach. They're not pushers.'

The Crown prosecutor then made a rambling speech in which he argued that McCartney had been caught with quite a lot of drugs, and had written some songs which mentioned the stuff. He couldn't immediately remember which ones. Nonetheless, he was sure he had. An Inspector Allan Long from the narcotics squad was called to the box to testify that Paul and Linda were setting a poor example to 'impressionable young people, who hero-worship them.' The judge had to gavel down the laughter. At the conclusion of the proceedings he fined the defendants $200, or roughly £70.

The McCartneys and their children were on the first London-bound jet later that afternoon. 'I've got absolutely no grudges and no complaints,' Paul announced to reporters. 'It was a fair cop.' But the ordeal wasn't quite over yet. A search of the family's luggage on arrival at Heathrow turned up five grams of ganga in a film canister belonging to Linda. While the press watched, she was once again led away to be charged and bailed. A week later, her solicitor assured Uxbridge magistrates that 'Mrs McCartney is genuinely sorry, and wishes to make a genuine apology . . . I urge you not to make an example of her just because she is famous. My client is a thoughtful, likable woman who has done far more for other people than those who sneer at her.' In truth, it was about as mild a drug case as can ever have been brought before the courts. Linda was fined £75.

Her critics remained unsatisfied. In the days ahead, one or two cynics would argue that it took self-destructive skills of a high order to be busted twice, for the same offence, within forty-eight hours. Sharp-eyed reporters didn't miss the fact that Paul's trial in Barbados came four years to the day after his arrest in Japan, and subsequent pledge 'never [to] do pot again.' Then there was Denny Laine's series of ghosted articles in the *Sun*, which confirmed that the McCartneys enjoyed a smoke and, at one stage, were spending some £1,200 a week on the stuff.

Later that year, McCartney and his Frog Chorus' single, We All Stand Together, proved another gift to those, like *NME*, who thought him 'slushy . . . vapid . . . wince-inducing.' The accompanying video – 'rather twee' even to the *Express* – provided an indelible image of a once-great career apparently in free fall. Though Paul claimed not to read his own press ('I either think I'm too great or I get paranoid'), he was well aware of John Lennon's posthumous reputation, carefully curated by Yoko, which would soar with the re-release of Give Peace A Chance, as well as several rapturous biographies. In critical circles, it was fashionable to assume that Paul's stock would continue to plummet the longer he went on, while John was now immortal.

Only the public, it seemed, could hold in its head simultaneously the ideas that McCartney was, indeed, an innovative soul; that his ballad style sometimes went over the top; and that, like Lennon, he needed a good editor. While Paul's post-Beatles canon was by no means universally loved, he had fans of all ages and persuasions. Frank Sinatra famously told a London audience that McCartney was still 'the only pop star worth a shit'. Meanwhile, in rural Washington state, a troubled high-school senior called Kurt Cobain spent much of the winter of 1984–5 listening to the soundtrack of *Give My Regards to Broad Street*, on which he wrote a 2,000-word essay. 'I loved Paul McCartney,' Cobain would say. 'He meant more to me than my own parents.'

In early October, the owners of Northern Songs agreed to pay McCartney and Lennon's estate £2 million over apparent royalty discrepancies. A week later, strolling through the lobby of New York's Carlyle hotel, Paul met John's son Julian for the first time in ten years. Finally, on 28 November, Liverpool Council bowed to pressure and awarded the Beatles the Freedom of the City, which McCartney collected on the band's behalf. A lunchtime crowd of 3,000 waited in the rain outside Picton Library, where the mayor handed over the key, and a gilt-edged scroll. At four, there was a press conference, in which someone asked McCartney how long he intended to keep working. 'Until I drop,' he replied. At seven, everyone repaired to the Odeon for the UK premiere of *Give My Regards to Broad Street*. Around midnight, the MPL office started faxing Paul and Linda the reviews.

The film, which cost $9 million and nearly two years' work, would go on to join the likes of *Popeye* and *My Bare Lady* in the 'Worst Musicals in History' lists. About the only criticism of the accompanying album – a worldwide number one – was McCartney's policy of releasing the single, No More Lonely Nights, in '7″ ballad', '7″ dance', '12″ extended', '12″ picture disc' and '12″ extended ballad' formats. There was even a pressing of around 100,000 copies with the misprint 'Lonley' on the label, making six different versions in all.

That same week, McCartney recorded two more songs that tried too hard, both would-be theme tunes for Relate, called Lindiana and We Got Married. Although unable to make the session, he then lent a spoken message to the Band Aid charity single Do They Know It's Christmas?/Feed The World. The holidays brought another such gesture, Paul's donation of music to an *Horizon* documentary about Ivan Vaughan, the Liverpool friend who introduced him to John Lennon. Vaughan, who was suffering from Parkinson's disease, spent several weeks staying with the McCartneys that new year. His death in 1994, aged fifty-two, was the starting point for Paul's first volume of poetry, *Blackbird Singing*.

The Beatles story took another sorry turn in February 1985, when George, Ringo and Yoko filed a further lawsuit against McCartney for breach of contract. Papers were served on him in the same week *Give My Regards to Broad Street* went to video. The gist of the complaint was that Paul was enjoying a preferential royalty rate from 'historic recordings [as] a material incentive for him to re-sign with Capitol as a solo artist.' Rather than deny it, his lawyer simply pointed out that 'Nobody [was] decreasing payments to John, George and Ringo.'

It was this mess the seventy-five-year-old Lee Eastman was trying to resolve before 'everyone can move on,' he said, this tangle between managers, agents and half a dozen New York law firms, all revolving around three middle-aged men and their mate's widow who could never decide if they loved one another or rued the day they met.

Late in March, Michael Jackson came back to stay with Paul and Linda, now without the mask but dressed in a gold lamé astronaut's suit, striking here in East Sussex. By then Jackson was seriously in the money, with *Thriller* still a fixture on the chart after more than two years. Taking McCartney's advice, he was busy investing in both stock and publishing catalogues. There'd been occasional murmurs about Jackson's long-term intentions, and a McCartney eyebrow or two had arched when, in late 1984, Eastman rang to report that someone appeared to be researching Northern Songs.

That, though, was the limit of the warnings. Jackson again proved a model guest, taking time to help Linda with the cooking and cleaning, as well as to look after the kids. One or two of their young friends even called him 'Mr Mum', and told of the time Jacko had read out the Winnie-the-Pooh stories and cried at the part where Christopher Robin went off to school.

On 13 July McCartney broke off from recording with his band, telling them he had 'this little gig to do' in London. A roadie drove Linda and him into town, depositing their blue Mercedes in a public car park. The three then appeared anonymously at the employees' entrance of Wembley stadium, and enquired politely if they might be let in.

The little gig was, of course, Live Aid. These vast communitarian shows, held in London and Philadelphia, would raise $100 million for the starving of Ethiopia, and be aired to 1.5 billion people around the world. Standing at the side of the stage, the home event's MC, Andy Peebles, looked up to see Paul and Linda strolling towards him, 'arms wrapped around each other, cuddling like a couple of kids.' 'I *am* going to enjoy this,' McCartney enquired. 'Aren't I?' He then gave his well practised thumbs-up to a number of friends who called his name, and muttered the word 'vibes' several times. There was a generous minimum 'vibe' quota at Wembley that evening, but, even so, Paul seemed to be aiming for a world record, inserting it into the most banal sentence to the point where, for the first time, the word seemed to have reached the end of its usefulness: 'How you vibin'?' he asked David Bowie's sax player. McCartney then chatted affably with well-wishers while his roadie slipped on stage with his personal radio mike, which he clamped to the piano.

Around ten on the now balmy summer night, Peebles made his announcement. McCartney ducked through a flap in the canvas backdrop, grinned, waved, and settled at the keyboard. His show-closing performance of Let It Be was only half audible, owing to the radio mike not being tuned to the house PA. Even so, Paul's bluff congeniality lifted everyone's spirits. At the end of the song many at Wembley were smiling through their tears, and even some in the press box broke into wild applause. In that instant, the star of *Give My Regards to Broad Street* became relevant again.

Two days later, the BBC's Jeff Griffin went to Soho Square, where McCartney meticulously recorded overdubs to his Live Aid vocals.

Shortly afterwards, Michael Jackson purchased the ATV Music catalogue for $53 million. The first McCartney heard of the sale was from a journalist asking for a quote. Paul in turn rang Lee Eastman, who confirmed the news that Jackson had outbid stiff competition from CBS, Warners and the Coca-Cola Corporation to win control of Northern Songs. Although McCartney would continue to earn royalties from his babies, he had no say in how they were licensed or marketed. Even that iniquity, though, paled by comparison to the sense of betrayal. To him, Jackson's investment was an act of bad faith not seen since the days of Dick James. After Paul calmed down he went on to note, with commendable understatement, 'That's where our friendship suffered a bit of a blow . . . I've hardly spoken to Michael Jackson since then, except to [ask], Will you give me a deal? I'm under a slave agreement. Talk about stonewalling! He's worse than all of them. At least James said: "I'm sorry, lads, I can't do anything."'

More frustration lay in store. Six years later, McCartney was able to make an appointment with his one-time house guest, who was in Los Angeles shooting a clip for *Dangerous*. Jackson was 'friendly enough', Paul recalled, but in no mood to accommodate him. 'He said: "You know, I've cried so much about this, Paul." I'm going: Well yeah, OK, Michael, but please, will you see your people? Give me a promise that you'll talk to your people about this. He said: "I've cried. I have told them . . ."'

More wounding to McCartney than the slave agreement was the fact that Jackson had, by then, turned three of the best known Beatles songs into TV commercials. After hearing Revolution used to promote Nike, Paul sent Northern's new owner a long, handwritten letter complaining that his good name was being blown on rubber soles, and urging his old friend to respect his wishes by not exploiting the works further.

Jackson declined the request.

On 29 October 1985, McCartney left CBS and re-signed with Capitol Records. Paul was in the studio in Scotland and so missed the splendid welcome-back bash. When it came time for Capitol's chairman Bhaskar Menon to speak, he was interrupted by a reporter asking about McCartney's 'disappointing' sales over recent years. 'Whether those albums were successful or not, I really don't know,' Menon replied smoothly. 'But we're talking about the world's most distinguished musical genius. We have every reason to believe he has a boffo career and audience before him.'

Two weeks later, Capitol released McCartney's Spies Like Us, the theme song to the Cold War-spoof film of the same name. On 18 November, it became his hundredth single to enter the *Billboard* chart.

MPL soon grew so powerful it branched into areas never penetrated by traditional rock superstars. The parent group controlled seventeen separate publishing companies, administering half a dozen hit musicals and more than a thousand other songs, only two of them by the Beatles. There were subsidiaries responsible for press and merchandising, and a two-man unit that did nothing but read scripts that might interest McCartney. He was in his mid-forties now, an age at which a singer grows tired of being jerked around by some cigar-chewing manager. Over the years Paul had sized up the moguls who ran pop music and judged himself smarter, tougher, harder working. Now he joined their club.

His first move, after rejoining Capitol, was to cut an album that would put him up there with Jackson and Madonna. McCartney wanted something, like *Thriller*, that wasn't strictly speaking an LP at all, but what the labels like to call a multimedia event: a hard kernel of music wrapped in hype. He called in Eric Stewart and Hugh

Padgham (the genius behind Phil Collins) and asked them to co-produce. Paul told them that he wanted a slick end product to sound great on CD – 'it should leap out of the speakers.' He even had a helpful title: *Press to Play*.

It was a fateful step, because all three men differed about what constituted the world's most distinguished musical genius in the mid-1980s. Six weeks into recording, Eric Stewart got a phone call from MPL. 'They told me there was a contractual problem,' he recalls. 'Padgham's management had evidently decreed that he be the sole producer. I was paid off.' The resulting album (Stewart: 'possibly overdone'), packed with drop-in friends like Collins, show-cased several thin but urgent tunes performed by bouffant-haired men on synthesisers and a guitarist who liked to roll up the sleeves of his jacket.

Shortly afterwards, MPL's long-serving MD Steven Shrimpton left the company. His replacement, Bob Mercer, lasted just a month.

McCartney had nothing public to say that February, when Dick James leant over a poker table one Saturday night to collect his winnings and was smitten by a fatal heart attack. He was sixty-four. Nor, a month later, did Paul manage to see Yoko during the British leg of her first solo world tour. This enjoyed some critical acclaim but a disappointing box office. Not long after that, a High Court judge ordered that EMI pay Paul, George, Ringo and Yoko £3 million in back royalties.

The folk memory of the Beatles is of the caustic and politically active Lennon growing steadily more weary of the 'cute' McCartney. It's an enduring caricature. In fact, several acquaintances, like William Burroughs, considered John's occasional philanthropy to be com-pounded more of personal pride than good nature, and noted the speed at which he tended to move on. Despite the fact that nobody has ever been able to say conclusively which, if any, of the Beatles was more right-on, this hasn't stopped people taking sides and facing off with all the fury of Lilliput and Blefuscu fighting over whether to break eggs at the big end or small end. McCartney himself seems to have moved more to the left the older and richer he got. He made no secret of his quarrel with Margaret Thatcher when it came to the nurses' and miners' strikes, or of his views on race relations.

'Britain's attitude toward apartheid [is] crazy,' McCartney announced. 'I mean, *still*, after all those years of Martin Luther King and everything, they're *still* buggering around with black and white. It's so *insane*. Couldn't they just wise up? But there's Maggie saying, "We don't need to do sanctions", while everybody else [is] saying, "But you *do*".'

How real was McCartney? Well, Thatcher herself let it be known that she was 'shaken' by the tone of a telegram he sent her. Another decade would have to pass before his name resurfaced on the honours list. Meanwhile, some on the left, like the firebrand reporter Paul Foot, admitted they now 'quite took' to the millionaire entrepreneur. They came to positively admire Paul's wife, or at least her authenticity, fervour and willingness to back a cause. One glowing magazine profile referred to Linda as 'beautiful, intelligent, modern, friendly, confident, vigorous, earnest, successful, optimistic – a "can-do" American dynamo in our midst.' That 13 June, she went on *Woman's Hour* to launch her campaign against the Treasury's proposal to turn Fairlight Down, near the McCartneys' farm in Sussex, into an onshore oil field. Linda was also at work promoting vegetarianism and animal welfare. 'I want to convert people from demanding flesh on their plates,' she said. 'Eating meat,' she went on, 'takes a real perversity . . . They must be aware of the alternatives . . . My kitchen is the sexiest, most creative room in the whole house – apart from my bedroom.'

The McCartneys courted controversy of another kind with the release of their eight-year-old Oriental Nightfish cartoon as part of the *Rupert and the Frog Song* short. *Today*'s review found the clip, co-directed by Linda, to be 'hippy tripe about an extraterrestrial'.

Though it 'might appeal [to] small children,' the paper doubted whether their mums would appreciate 'the animated nude woman who wiggles across the screen.' Ilford Council duly responded to complaints and sued the distributors over 'inappropriate content'. By the time the *Frog Song* aired on the Disney Channel six months later, the offending image had been removed.

On 20 June, McCartney closed the Prince's Trust Tenth Birthday Party Concert by performing Get Back with a pickup group including Eric Clapton, Elton John, Mark Knopfler and Tina Turner. Shortly afterwards, Paul told Kurt Loder of MTV that he was thinking of going back on the road. 'The Beatles used to say "We won't be rock and rollin' when we're forty,"' he noted. 'But I still love it. It feel[s] really great. I could do it every night.'

McCartney then flew to New York to suppress excitement for *Press to Play*, which followed in August. This collection of otherwise turgid stomps contained two standouts, songs that struck a compelling balance between Paul's yen for experimentation and his gift for articulate schmaltz. 'Hillmen come down from the lava' droned the synth-based Pretty Little Head, a track that sounded like an acid-fuelled outtake from *Sgt. Pepper*. However Absurd was even odder, being a stream-of-consciousness trip through the works of W.H. Auden, as orchestrated by Art of Noise's Anne Dudley. Both tunes had an air of inspired recklessness, evidence of a left-field sensibility beneath all the hairspray. The rest was fusion – genetically modified disco, featuring Padgham's brashly upbeat arrangements.

Eric Stewart, who co-wrote six of the tracks on *Press to Play*, thought it 'basically a good album that got lost in translation.' (McCartney himself would concede, 'I wasn't that keen on it.') It proved a modest hit: number twenty-nine or thirty on the American chart, depending on which paper you read. In either case, it wasn't the 'boffo' result Capitol had hoped for.

McCartney was philosophical. 'You can't get it right all the time . . . Looking back on some of [my] stuff now, I think, "You didn't

Wings just before
their first ever tour,
which grossed them
a total of £3,000.

Circa 1973, Paul poses
with his wife Linda and
their daughters, left to
right, Stella, Mary and
Heather, at Heathrow
airport, at the time of
Band on the Run.

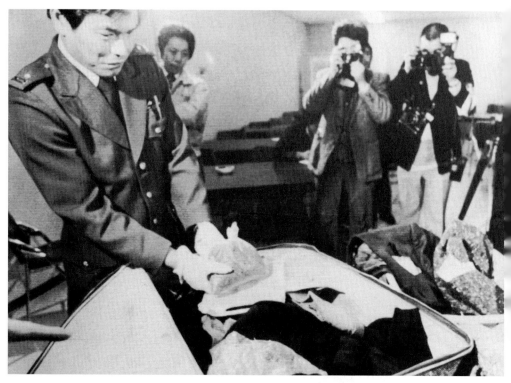

When McCartney landed at Narita airport, Tokyo in 1980, there were no CBS Records reps there to greet him – but plenty of Japanese Customs officers and the world's press.

Paul was all smiles on his release from jail in Tokyo. However, more trials were ahead.

Ringo Starr's wedding to Barbara Bach in 1981 brought the three surviving ex-Beatles together for the first time since John Lennon's murder four months earlier.

Paul and Linda pick up a British Video Award for his classic amphibian anthem Rupert and the Frog Song.

McCartney's triumphant comeback tour Get Back played to audiences in thirteen countries.

McCartney's show-closing performance at Live Aid in 1985 was only half-audible, owing to technical problems. Even so, his rendition of Let It Be moved many to tears. In that instant, the star of *Give My Regards to Broad Street* became relevant again.

McCartney was to venture into both poetry and painting in the '90s. Few of the reviews seemed prophetic of a glorious second career.

June 2001, Paul and Heather Mills hosted an Adopt-a-Minefield gala in Los Angeles. Just over a month later, they announced their engagement.

McCartney, organizer and headliner at the Concert for New York City, held to raise funds for survivors of the 9/11 tragedy.

Stella McCartney's design labels were widely admired in fashion circles, even if high street sales were initially disappointing. She's seen here after receiving an honorary degree from the University of Dundee in 2003.

McCartney's first concert in Moscow took on all the trappings of a state visit, including a warm Kremlin welcome from President Vladimir Putin.

Super Bowl XXXIX -- the year after Janet Jackson's 'wardrobe malfunction', McCartney performed four ecstatically received oldies to a live TV audience of 145 million.

finish the bloody thing" . . . So, yeah, I might have been a bit soft . . . Sometimes a critic will say, "That's really lousy" – and I'll tend to agree with him.' In November, he headlined yet another Royal Command performance, serenading the Queen Mum with Only Love Remains from *Press to Play*.

Two days later, the new album disappeared from the *Billboard* Hot One Hundred. McCartney told his account handler at Capitol to find him a touring band.

Early in the new year, *Woman's Own* ran a poll to honour the most 'popular and respected' Britons abroad. McCartney placed narrowly behind Princess Diana. 'This [was] unheard-of prestige for a mere pop star,' noted *Today*. Paul was not only 'tremendously famous' but 'also a significant earner [who] has never so much as considered tax exile.' In all, 'his worldwide success and his apparent modesty [both] make him unique among today's entertainers.' He was 'a rare example of core British values in the rock and roll age.'

He wasn't only rich and famous, he was a national asset. Even Thatcher admitted she 'quite liked' McCartney's oldies, before paying him the ultimate compliment: 'What an export.'

There was more.

As luck would have it, the next twelve months saw hundreds of thousands of fans trade up from their original vinyl recordings to CD. The first four Beatles albums were rolled out in February, the rest, along with assorted compilations and anthologies, following at roughly quarterly intervals. McCartney also took the opportunity to re-release his solo LPs in the new format. By now internal memos at EMI referred to him as simply 'The Generator'. It was their verbal-shorthand way of acknowledging the seven or eight million units he sold annually.

Less welcome was Michael Jackson's decision, that spring, to turn not only Revolution, but All You Need Is Love and Good Day Sunshine into advertising jingles. (Hello, Goodbye narrowly missed the same fate, when a haulage firm bid for it.) Unlike the Stones –

who seem to have never written a tune that hasn't been in a commercial – or Dylan, Bowie, Sting and others who've rented their music to Madison Avenue, the Beatles had always fiercely protected their songs' integrity. While Yoko was said to be 'fine' with the arrangement, McCartney wasn't happy. Nor was it Jacko alone who'd 'shafted' him: after twenty-four years, Paul still laboured under the terms of his original 1963 contract. He was on a 'shit deal', he fumed. 'I signed away my babies,' McCartney told one close friend. 'It's the single worst move of my career.'

One of the best was his 1987 recording of *Choba B CCCP*, an album of rock 'n' roll covers aimed at the Soviet market. After obtaining clearance for the once-subversive material from the Ministry of Culture, Melodiya had originally thought that they might dispose of between 40–50,000 copies. But the label's estimate soon proved far too modest. The sensational figure of 620,000 confirmed sales (and as many again on the black market) was eventually reported back to MPL. The pictures of young Muscovites queuing up outside music shops achieved global circulation in the winter of 1988–9. West Berlin's *Morgenpost* described the scene as 'a defining moment' in the infiltration of 'free goods and values' behind the Iron Curtain. According to this reading, McCartney was as responsible as anyone else for the slow but irresistible rise of Russian consumerism, and ultimately for the collapse of the old regime.

Back home, McCartney's career was rekindled by the coming of Elvis Costello. Although he didn't say so directly, there was something familiar about his latest sarky Liverpudlian collaborator. Of recording their very first duet, Paul would recall, 'I'm saying, "I've loved her so long", and he's saying, "I know you did, you stupid git!"' When they heard the results, one or two critics openly speculated that McCartney was trying to relive his glory days. 'Costello liked Paul,' says the same close friend. 'But in the way that Lennon liked him. You wouldn't give them the Nobel Prize for chemistry. I used to hear things like "Cut the crap", "Pull yer finger out", "Just put a fucking beat to it".'

On 19 October – Black Monday – the Dow-Jones industrial average fell 508 points, nearly a quarter of its total value. As shares dropped vertically with no one buying, even some of the best managed investors, including a number of rock stars, lost millions.

Forty-eight hours later, Harrison and Starr came to visit McCartney (whom they were still suing) at Cavendish Avenue. All three men, it appeared, were now keen to commission a documentary about the band. Conventional wisdom holds that George, in particular, could no longer afford to turn it down. He later allowed to a few regrets, noting that he'd been 'warped back to 1969' – not his best year. Another wounding reminder was the film's working title, *The Long and Winding Road*, which Harrison thought 'too McCartney'. Eventually, they settled on the more neutral *Anthology*.

Two weeks after this summit, Paul put out his own greatest hits CD, *All The Best*. It spent six months on the chart.

Almost as soon as McCartney's new manager, Richard Ogden, arrived, he, too, was steering his client back on the road. 'I wanted to know that Paul wanted a full-time career, including playing concerts, which are very important in the overall picture,' Ogden revealed. 'I was convinced that he did.' Over seven successive Friday nights that winter, Paul and Linda sat either in a rented studio or downstairs at Soho Square and auditioned would-be bandmates. McCartney gave each of the sixty applicants a warm handshake, a cup of tea and the chance to play Live And Let Die. Eventually the group came to include guitarists Hamish Stuart (Average White Band) and Robbie McIntosh (Pretenders), and one Paul 'Wix' Wickens on keyboards. A long-running rumour in *Today* insisted that 'a certain old mate' would occupy the drum stool.

Ringo never actually materialised, but in spirit he did, throughout early 1988, as the Rock and Roll Hall of Fame inducted the Beatles. A blue-riband committee of journalists and label executives had voted to include the group which (possibly thanks to the Hall's inscrutable rules) two previous inductions had somehow missed. A second panel then toiled over the exact details for six months, while the band themselves brooded in their tents. One staffer recalls that there were 'daily faxes going in and out of McCartney's office . . . First he was boycotting us, then coming, then sulking again.' The whole saga came to a climax on 20 January, at a glittering ceremony in New York's Waldorf-Astoria hotel. Mick Jagger did the honours, which were graciously accepted on the Beatles' behalf by George, Ringo and Yoko. McCartney didn't show. 'He despises Harrison and blames Yoko for supporting Michael Jackson,' an unnamed friend told the press. No one mentioned the breach-of-contract suit the others were still pursuing against Paul in New York's supreme court. The plaintiffs' claim: $8.6 million.

'We want the Beatles!' the audience at the Waldorf-Astoria had begun chanting, as Jagger made the introductions. What they got was a short rap from George:

'I don't have much to say 'cos I'm the quiet one. It's unfortunate Paul's not here as he's the one with the speech in his pocket . . . We all know why John can't be here; I'm sure he would be. It's hard, really, to stand here supposedly representing the Beatles . . . We're all that's left. But we all loved him so much, and y'know we all love Paul.'

Five days later, Harrison released his single and video When We Was Fab, both mines of Beatles references. (One well known music journalist devoted no less than three closely-spaced columns to deconstructing the film – was it actually Paul dressed up in the walrus suit, or a ringer holding his bass upside down in order to seem to be playing left-handed? – yet still kept his job.) George then put out a book full of his song lyrics, which he sold for £235 a pop. Later in the spring, he was asked about McCartney's recent remark that the two of them might even write together.

'It's pretty funny,' Harrison replied. 'I mean, I've only been there about thirty years in Paul's life and now he wants to work with me. Maybe it would be quite interesting . . . But that's the thing with Paul. One minute he says one thing and he's really charming, and the next he's all uptight. You've got to find the centre.'

On 26 February, George picked up a video award at the San Remo music festival. McCartney contrived to debut his band on the same stage twenty-four hours later. In interviews, Paul insisted that the reason he'd stayed off the road for so long was that 'I couldn't be bothered . . . And nobody asked me. Nobody asked me personally, anyway. It never seemed that vital to me; I was already enjoying myself.'

While it's clear, from the fact that he spent every night with them, that McCartney preferred his family over making millions on tour, it often seemed even clearer that his wife wanted it that way. Linda had taken a critical pounding in the Seventies, and was in no rush for 'all that shit [to] fly again.' By and large, she disliked rock society and, particularly, 'kiss[ing] some journalist's ass,' preferring to stay home on the farm. Sometimes it did indeed seem, as Linda said, 'the animals [were] a lot nicer than the reviewers.' By now she was justly famous for her vegetarian cooking, and would soon put her name to a book on the subject that sold half-a-million copies. The McCartneys also had three school-age children. A questionnaire submitted to Linda by the Hall of Fame was filled out by an aide who gave her favourite hobbies as 'family' and 'photography'; but he couldn't say 'which of today's bands', if any, she admired.

On 12 July, in Brighton – at an event covered by film crews from around the world – McCartney received an honorary doctorate from the University of Sussex. Shortly afterwards, he found himself shooting a video at his old school, the Liverpool Institute, which had closed its doors in 1985. Paul looked around and decided that the stately Victorian pile could be refurbished into a performing-arts academy. (The Kids from *Fame* had been very big in Britain a year or two earlier.) Over the next five years, he set about raising £13

million towards the project. Everyone from the Prince of Wales to
Lou Reed made a donation. McCartney himself subscribed a million
pounds. The shiny new facility would open in January 1996, offering
its 200 full-time students a degree course in 'the realities of working
in the entertainment industry'.

Five months later, the Inny's most famous old boy came back to
visit with the Queen and several reporters. 'She was friendly, but
she didn't play the game as McCartney did' says one of the press
pool, AP's Tony Gill. 'He asked the right questions, took an
interest in your affairs . . . I lapped up Paul, who knew how to make
people feel good.'

McCartney's sentimental journey was but one of several
indications of his feelings about Liverpool – more specifically,
about Lennon. In August 1988, John was effectively assassinated a
second time in a sensational biography by Albert Goldman. Paul
told fans and friends to boycott the book, which went on to be a
runaway best-seller. The journalist Paul du Noyer would later note
that 'you almost had to coax McCartney off the subject of Lennon',
and how the two had been 'so close' at the end.

The once-guarded McCartney was now effusive. 'It was cool that
I'd started ringing John,' he said. 'We'd had a bread strike over here
and I rang and was saying, "What are you doing?" He says, "I'm
baking some bread." Oh! Me too! Imagine John and Paul talking
about baking bread . . . It was really warm to be able to talk to him
that ordinarily. It was like we'd got[ten] back.'

There they were, in other words, exactly as they'd been before the
fur flew. But Paul wasn't necessarily as conciliatory towards John's
family. A member of Klein's staff, seconded to Savile Row in 1969,
muses that Yoko's role there left McCartney redundant, 'a spare dick
at a wedding, as he put it . . . I think he clearly felt betrayed.' Twenty
years later, Paul 'still had [his] issues' with Lennon's widow. He
particularly rued the fact that she'd apparently blown their chance to

buy back Northern Songs, something she denies. Yoko, in turn, firmly rejected the idea that McCartney had in some way been responsible for saving her marriage in 1974–5. 'Let him say what he wants to say,' she scoffed. 'I feel sad he needs to do it, but if he wants to get credit for it, why not? That's fine . . . I know [John] didn't come back because Paul said a few words, or something like that. He's put in the position of being a Salieri to a Mozart.'

Meanwhile, in December 1988, Michael Jackson's film *Moonwalker* was released to an eager public. The script for this collage of MTV videos and fantasy sequences had been sent to Yoko, who allowed her twelve-year-old son to appear as one of the 'lost boys' saved by Jacko, who then closed proceedings with a moving rendition of the Beatles' Come Together. That was the end of McCartney's Christmas cards to the Dakota Building.

Stadium rock was already suffering a slump in 1989. It had grubbed to the very bottom of its bag of tricks. Bands were working half naked on revolving stages that exploded during the encore. Sets had been built to resemble the Nuremburg rally, or a particularly tacky Vegas casino, with hundreds of white neon tubes that flashed on and off while the singer performed what looked like a fertility rite dance. Yet attendance figures had been falling steadily since Live Aid; the average A-list ticket price had doubled in just three years, and even some of Jackson's well-oiled shows failed to sell out. A year later, after employing every known PR ruse, including billing the event as 'Mick Jagger's birthday – the party of a lifetime', the Stones would play a gig in front of 3,000 punters scattered around Rome's cavernous Flaminio stadium; they fared marginally better in London. While there was still a market out there for McCartney, there was also real pressure on him to succeed.

As Paul saw it, ten years off the road was 'no big deal . . . you pick[ed] it up again like riding a bike.' To others, the comeback remained one of the hardest tricks in showbusiness. The ex-Beatle was 'locked in a kind of pre-iconic limbo,' said *RPM*, 'not hav[ing] died young enough for a romantic flameout.' Of course, their correspondent allowed, 'most songs have a shelf life. His are timeless.'

On 26 January 1989, McCartney went on the World Service and spoke to an estimated twenty-one million listeners behind the Iron Curtain. Of the fourteen phone calls he took on the air, thirteen asked him about his tour plans. By then, Paul had had nearly a year to bond with his new band. His own market research had projected a gratifying $20 million profit for playing thirty-five to forty dates in North America. Double that, if he threw in Europe and Japan.

The day after his phone-in, McCartney finally gave word he was ready. At forty-seven, he'd go back out there and sell more tickets than anyone else in pop music history. Again.

On 4 April, McCartney received an Outstanding Services award at the Ivor Novellos in London. He enlivened proceedings by dropping to one knee to deliver an impromptu 'Novello rap'. On a more sombre occasion a fortnight later, he furnished vocals for a charity version of Ferry 'Cross The Mersey in aid of the Hillsborough Disaster Fund. At the end of the month he called in the band and put them to work on a thirty-song repertoire. McIntosh, Stuart and Wickens were joined by Linda and the drummer Chris Whitten. Paul would take not only star but also solo billing. The key word, he impressed on them in rehearsal, was 'focus'. They were to follow his lead and stick closely to the spirit of the original recordings. As Robbie McIntosh noted, 'It was never my place to start changing guitar parts. I was only ever more than delighted to keep people happy and reproduce the [songs] as faithfully as possible.'

Three weeks later, Paul and Linda were scheduled to appear together on the *Wogan* chat show. Early-evening viewers would see an obviously close-knit couple, twenty years on, who still somehow managed to combine work and play. (Along with the band, they would ham their way through two numbers.) It was part of their appeal: whatever you thought of their music, the McCartneys' family values were in stark contrast to the vulgar abandon and quick turnover of most rock-star unions.*

As he left MPL for the *Wogan* studio that afternoon, McCartney was accosted by an attractive, well-dressed blonde in her mid-twenties who rushed at him out of a crowd, screaming, 'Why don't you acknowledge me? Why don't you acknowledge me?' Security guards quickly hustled the woman in one direction and Paul, visibly shaken, in the other. A few moments later, his car set off towards Oxford Street; the McCartneys' friend Jackie Stewart might not have been disappointed by the speed with which they took the corner. The whole distressing episode was over as suddenly as it had started. The woman was never identified.

6 June. D-Day for McCartney's collaborative album with Elvis Costello, *Flowers in the Dirt*. The thirteen songs were written or co-written, arranged and produced by Paul, who presumably, had he found the time, would have played every instrument as well. In the event, he was forced to make do with musicians, and it was a pretty strong team: apart from Costello there was Dave Gilmour, Trevor Horn and veteran Stones sideman Nicky Hopkins on piano. *Flowers* would often sound like a bumper compendium of popular music, ranging from vaudeville and doo-wop to reggae and hard rock, all fused with a snappy beat that managed to stir something primal within – the urge to dance, mainly. Did it work? As usual, Costello notwithstanding, McCartney could have done with a good editor – some of the weaker fare, like Motor Of Love, barely scaled the ladder to songhood – and critical trendspotters would find nothing grungy or alternative about the palatable suburban riffs. Even so, this was his best outing since *Band on the Run*.

The album yielded four singles, most notably the sprightly

---

* Bill Wyman and Mandy Smith went down the aisle a few days later.

transatlantic hit My Brave Face. Its three successors were reasonably toothsome disco fodder, but tanked. McCartney eventually released eight different versions of the track Ou Est le Soleil?, making No More Lonely Nights seem hopelessly backward by comparison, and arousing cries of consumer exploitation. *Flowers in the Dirt* sold four million, and actually toppled Guns N' Roses from number one.

For the next year, McCartney plugged himself back in like a neon sign. As ever, the trimmings around his 'Get Back' tour – opening 28 September in Sweden, the first of 102 dates in thirteen countries – were just right for the times: Paul lacing the shows with Golden Greats (fifteen Beatles tunes, and an *Abbey Road* encore), thrashing his mane around in the ravers and wielding a left-handed Hofner bass, just as he had in the Sixties. The basic production was heavy on *Sgt. Pepper*-era kitsch, with psychedelic lighting effects and lava lamps bubbling on the amps. To the *Herald Tribune*, 'it [was] as if Paul had finally recognized his own strengths and returned to the decade that had made him.' Nostalgia ruled. Dick Lester emerged from semi-retirement to shoot the concert film, and the band, recognising that such moments are sacred, stuck to note-by-note covers of the classics. This was perhaps the first stadium tour in history where the music managed to overshadow the visual ancilliaries.

Though McCartney set attendance records wherever he went, the press was patchy in the extreme. One churlish critic described Paul as 'more and more resembl[ing] a chipmunk' and the tour as 'the unedifying sound of a millionaire's pension plan being topped up.' As usual, each and every one of Linda's extracurricular activities was trotted out to mask the essential truth about the woman: not some tawdry secret from her Fillmore East past, not drug busts or cookbooks, but rather the curious fact that Mrs McCartney was a competent musician who had, over the years, become a rather endearing figure – Jerry Hall with a singing voice.

The band, it should be noted, never had any doubts about Linda. Working with her was 'great', 'a lot of fun'. Not only that, she was 'very professional'. Looking back on the tour, one of Linda's publicists would remember having to read her 'some of the bitchiest reviews of all time', including the ones as good as – if not actually – calling her a useless slag. 'She had a wonderful sense of humour about it. A lot of people would have been crushed, or at least gone screaming for a lawyer. Not her. She just took it very easy.'

There have been some turnarounds in the history of pop, but none more dramatic than the change in McCartney's fortunes over the winter of 1989–90. *Flowers in the Dirt* actually enjoyed a few broadsheet raves, as well as spending five months on the chart. He was back in the trade press, and My Brave Face seemed never to be off MTV.

Audiences in North America, where McCartney arrived on 23 November, were warmed up by an eleven-minute film of Beatles and Wings performances juxtaposed with archive news footage. It set the mood nicely for what followed. 'Mr McCartney emerges briskly,' the *New York Times* noted, 'and he's the same old Paul – tuneful, amiable, still boyish . . . For most of the concert, the emphasis would be not on rock spontaneity but on proficiency. Even in tepid versions, the songs are brilliantly made.' It wasn't all hot flushes and wet seats, of course: Let It Be was received with something like religious awe, and during Yesterday fans were busy swooning in the glow of several thousand cigarette lighters. Paul's ad-libbed remarks were smoothly done, as was the moment in Band On The Run when he appeared to referee a mock duel between his two guitarists. The finale to Hey Jude pressed everyone's emotional buttons, even if the singalong itself was like that for a hymn, politely half-hearted. In fact, about the worst anyone could ever say of the shows was that they somehow failed to spark the sort of communal frenzy the Stones (then also touring America) could create. The one act presented a neatly mown lawn, the other a jungle.

That November, the Beatles' claim on EMI/Capitol and the separate, but related matter of *Harrison, Starr, Ono v McCartney* were settled out of court. After exactly twenty years of fussing and fighting, and more than a decade's litigation everyone had only the 'greatest friendship and respect' for one another, or so the news release said. The long-overdue reunion was soon back in the headlines, when Paul again suggested that he and George might write together for the first time since mid-1958. (He didn't mention anything about collaborating with Ringo or Yoko.) Twenty-four hours later, Harrison gave his answer in the form of a statement issued by his business manager: 'As far as I'm concerned, there won't be a Beatles reunion as long as John Lennon remains dead.'

The familiar traits of class and grace surfaced in McCartney who, in turn, noted, 'I loved the guy; John and me were *mates*.' So did competitiveness. Paul devoted a chapter of the slick, hundred-page tour programme (given away free) to a detailed account of just who it was, all those years ago, who'd tuned in first. 'I'm not trying to say it was all me,' he wrote. 'But I do think John's avant-garde period later, was really to give himself a go at what he'd seen me having a go at.'

In years ahead, complaints about Paul's not having 'grown' or that he was 'a hoofer' became code words for Yoko's contrary view that there was only one visionary in the Beatles. 'I know Paul thinks he was leading, or something like that,' Yoko told a BBC children's show. 'The way John led the band was very high level, on some kind of magical level. Not a daily level like Paul say[ing], "Oh, but I was the one who told them all to come and do it. I made the phone calls." John did not make the phone calls. He wasn't on that level,' Yoko said. 'He was on the level of a spiritual leader, a seer, and that's why the Beatles happened.'

On 15 December 1989, McCartney stepped off stage after a triumphant date at Madison Square Garden. It seemed as if all New York graced the post-gig party at Sardi's restaurant. After donating a cheque for $100,000 to Friends of the Earth, the McCartneys took the next Concorde home, where they had a fortnight off before the tour resumed.

In the public eye, Paul had spent his entire life avoiding controversy and unseemly spats. But clearly, he also still had something to prove. Over the next fourteen days he locked himself up in his home studio and wrote a series of inspirationally odd tracks, mixing tape-loops with an out-of-tune guitar, various 'aleatory' or random effects and a climactic noise like that of a dog being violently ill. This foray into sonic chance would form the soundtrack to Geoff Dunbar's award-winning short *Daumier's Law*, which premiered at the Cannes festival in 1992.

As the film's music was submitted anonymously, none of the distinguished panel who hailed it as 'obscure . . . extreme . . . a subversive masterpiece' could have known that its author was the world's most commercially successful pop star, with his own multi-national company, and an income of some £2 million a week.

CHAPTER NINE

'Him and the Queen Mum'

Twenty-four hours after handing in his 'freakout theme' to *Daumier's Law*, McCartney kicked off the new decade by playing the first of seventeen sold-out arena dates in the UK. They were warmly received. Paul was clearly happy to be on home turf. He grinned and waved and bobbed and bowed, and flashed the V-sign more often than Churchill did in the whole war. According to published reports, McCartney would gross some £3 million for the short tour, which also put *Flowers* back on the chart and revived his entire back catalogue. All in all, not bad for a man whose career obituary was being written just a couple of years earlier.

But not everyone was enthralled by McCartney's comeback. Paul's friend Denny Laine had fallen on hard times since their split, declaring bankruptcy in late 1986. Along the way, there'd been an undignified tiff about songwriting royalties, touched upon in several colourful tabloid stories, though, as both parties said, these may have been exaggerated. Some of Laine's reported remarks had been so out there that he perhaps thought it a hoax when, one evening in February 1990, a friend announced that McCartney had been on the line and would ring back. 'He wouldn't even remember me,' said Laine. A bit later, he picked up the phone. Paul not only remembered him. He wanted Laine to come to a concert and hang with him, 'just like old times', afterwards.

McCartney's chauffeur John Hammel duly made the arrangements. A 'very optimistic' Laine watched the show, which included five Wings numbers, and was then taken down a long, roped-off hallway leading to Paul's private dressing room. Twenty or twenty-five other people were standing in line outside, apparently awaiting their turn to try and impress him.

Laine spent the next half hour leaning against a backstage wall, clinging to the last vestiges of his optimism. After a while, a drinks trolley rolled past him into the inner sanctum, closely stalked by a celebrated, superbly cool rock journalist, who failed to recognise him. Hammel or another aide would trot out from time to time to announce that 'Paul's just finished an interview, and he's in the shower – I'll be right back' . . . 'Paul's still in the shower, but Linda's free now, and says she's looking forward to seeing you' . . . 'Paul's out of the shower now, it shouldn't be long.' After half a dozen more such bulletins, Laine gave up and left, none the wiser as to what, if anything, McCartney had wanted to say to him.

Paul was then back stateside, bringing the Beatles oeuvre, something which not long ago had been held to be as rare and fragile as a Ming vase, to the Midwest. There were box office records along the way – a million dollars' gross in Cincinnati alone. As a sweetener he would do a quick side deal with Visa, who ponied up $8.5 million to print their name on the concert tickets. McCartney claimed to have vetted the credit card company as thoroughly as possible, and denied having any ethical problem with them. 'It may be true that they're a gigantic money corporation,' he allowed. 'But I can't see what's wrong with that, unless you can prove any South African links.'

The inevitable comparisons to the Stones (then taking Volkswagen's money) were becoming more flattering, if no less tedious. One long-haired young man jumped up at a press conference and asked McCartney where he got off charging people $30 a ticket. 'I'm cheaper than Mick,' Paul shot back. '*And* I keep me trousers on.' He gave the same smooth reply later in the tour, substituting 'Tina' for 'Mick'.

On 21 February, McCartney picked up a lifetime-achievement Grammy, presented to him by Meryl Streep. A week later, he was in Tokyo for the first time since being unceremoniously driven to the airport and deported ten years earlier. By coincidence, the Stones were also in town, playing the last of ten sold-out *Steel Wheels* shows. McCartney would be seen out and about with Keith Richards. By now, the self-styled codgers were interested less in scoring drugs than in finding a satellite decoder to pick up the Test cricket from the West Indies. Next morning, Keith flew off and Paul dutifully did the rounds of the press and local charities. His attitude, the *Asahi Shimbun* theorised, seemed to be: I'm here to help. Whatever it takes. The same ferocious discipline would be brought to his stagecraft, where Paul disliked nothing more than to be thought of as wildly spontaneous.

McCartney did six three-hour shows, starting at five-thirty every afternoon. He 'appeared punctually', said the *Shimbun*. 'There was utter professionalism, [though] many abandoned their seats to *sing and dance*,' the paper added reprovingly. Paul, generally treated with Shinto-like awe, was given the Freedom of the City of Tokyo.

Japan was a turning point. From now on, there would be no more 'no-go' areas. Paul was everywhere, most immediately back in the States. The McCartneys got so-so reviews in Seattle, where, sniffed the *Times*, Linda played 'not very noticeable keyboards [and] sang backup, sometimes hitting flat notes. She seemed to be there mostly for moral support.' For a lark, Paul introduced his wife to the crowd as 'Gertrude Higgins – master musician'.

Some boorish audience members jeered the last bit. Paul requested, in words of one syllable, that they cease.

An hour later, the McCartneys were in their suite at the Olympic

Four Seasons hotel. Paul was apparently upset when the management sent up only one masseuse instead of the two he requested. 'Pack up', he's said to have yelled. 'We're getting the hell out of this dump . . . It's a rip-off! . . . They're ripping me off again! . . . Rip-off! . . . I hate being ripped off! . . . Fucking rip-off! . . . Send Ogden in here!' McCartney's manager was able to swiftly defuse the situation, reporting that his client had just played a 'killer gig' and was, not unreasonably, tired. There was more: the next morning, Paul put on a thank-you show for the staff, hoking it up with a ukulele to an audience of maids and bellboys.

McCartney's next two concerts in Berkeley, California, grossed $3,550,560, the best American box office of the year.

He did even better at the Maracana stadium in Rio, where he packed in a world record paying audience of 184,368. There were no apologies this time, no between-song patter asking the kids to bear with him while he went 'back through the mists of time, to a trip known as the Sixties.' This was the Beatles-by-proxy, with half a dozen Wings and solo hits thrown in. A lot of hardcore fans had never heard Yesterday played live, let alone all the stuff from *Sgt. Pepper*. Even the London papers spoke of a 'once in a lifetime extravaganza'. McCartney was back in England that summer, playing for charity at the Knebworth festival. It was 'fucking cool,' he told the BBC's Bob Harris; he was hip again now. But, then again, there was Linda. Towards the end of the show, someone saw fit to illicitly record the band playing Hey Jude. This party then wiped all the instruments and vocals from the track except Linda's and sent the tape to various radio stations, where it was a source of raucous on-air mirth for years to come. An internal McCartney investigation into the affair would turn up the name of a recently hired roadie, though nothing was ever proven. Linda herself was stoic, but told her publicist that her 'heart [was] broken' by the humiliation.

★

On 29 July, Paul and Linda put on happy faces to perform the tour's final rites in Chicago. The live album followed three months later. Proceeds from this, combined with *Flowers* and continuing royalties from the back catalogue gave Paul a warm feeling of solvency. He was now said to be worth £400 million. Twenty-five years after their last formal gig, the Beatles were still on the *Forbes* list of the world's highest-paid entertainers, with earnings of £30–35 million a year. That October, they sued the computer company Apple for an unspecified sum, reported as 'more than 100 [actually 250] million dollars' for trademark infringement. The word 'apple' had seemed like 'a bit of a lark' to McCartney in 1967, a vague homage to his hero Magritte. Now it was big business; the Beatles' affidavit modestly called them a 'well known and active concern, be[ing] producers, licensers, licensees, performers, agents, artists, distributors, contractors, publishers and dealers.'

No wonder that the headline of the *Shimbun* article was 'McCartney: The Man Who Has It All'.

On 25 January 1991, Paul and his band performed for an audience of 175 at Limehouse Studios in East London, a set released as *Unplugged – The Official Bootleg*. The drummer Chris Whitten had departed after just one tour. MPL said he had not been fired – presumably he felt so comfortable with his legacy that he was ready to leave at any moment, or just fancied a change; a Blair Cunningham replaced him. For someone capable of spending a year on an album, McCartney was almost casual about this one. 'It was a gas,' he would say of his latest platinum record. 'I figured that as *Unplugged* would be screened around the world, there was every chance some bright spark would tape the show and turn it into a bootleg. So I decided to, myself . . . We heard the tapes in the car driving back. By the time we got home, we'd decided to do it.'

Later that spring, McCartney announced that he'd embarked on a full-scale symphonic work, the *Liverpool Oratorio*. The reaction was interesting. Most of the press were amused, and even some friends thought it a joke. It was as if Sir Adrian Boult, in the twilight of his long career, had chosen to record a disco album. Although there was ample precedent for the pop-classical crossover, most of the results had turned out to be turgid and pretentious. As the critic Stephen Pettitt says, 'Therapy for the creator, maybe, but dull for any reasonably intelligent listener.' In order to realise his own piece for orchestra, Paul would sign up the fifty-four-year-old American-born composer Carl Davis. 'If it moves,' the latter once said, 'I can score it.'

Davis went down to the farm in Sussex and agreed on a division of labour. McCartney would write the 'primitive' music and a familiar-sounding libretto: Liverpool boy undergoes various trials of teenage confusion and solitude, then comes to experience love, fame and even religion. ('God is good without an "o"' would be one deathless avowal of faith.) Davis would apply the classical wash. The two men worked separately and together for the next six months, some 900 man-hours in all. When he was asked about how writing with Davis differed from writing with John Lennon, Paul replied, 'I bossed Carl around more than I bossed John.'

There were, Davis discovered, certain advantages to collaborating with a man of McCartney's stature and wealth. Everyone went first class; even the rough tapes were taken to and fro by limo. What McCartney wanted to happen tended to happen, regardless of cost. 'One day Paul said, "I'd like to hear what we've written",' Davis recalls. 'So he booked Liverpool Cathedral, the city orchestra and choir, the cathedral choir, four soloists and a recording unit, just so he could hear it all properly.'

The finished piece would celebrate the 150th year of the Liverpool Philharmonic, and was part of Paul's recent entente with his home town. In just the last few months, this had seen him donate to the performing arts academy, make several appearances at area hospitals and star in a promotional video on behalf of the council. Various local authorities, in turn, had taken the opportunity to plaster McCartney's name, sometimes without him even knowing it, on everything from a nursery to a garage and, the capstone of this phase of his career, a mobile fish and chip shop. Even his childhood home would be turned into a museum. There were also Beatles plaques, clubs, theme pubs, walks and bus tours. The city elders perhaps forgot that they'd largely ignored the group throughout their career and the ten years that followed.

On 28 June 1990, McCartney and his band had appeared at Liverpool's King's Dock and debuted a 'Lennon medley', among other material, before attending a gala civic reception. Even in this august company, he was bothered by autograph hunters every few minutes. 'I'd find it very tiresome,' a councillor remarked. 'It's just part of the package,' said Paul, who went on to give a short speech to the assembled guests about how much roots and tradition meant to him. So when the city came to decide on its favourite son for the *Oratorio* project there weren't many contenders, and the verdict was quickly reached. Brian Pidgeon, the general manager of the Liverpool Philharmonic, wrote to MPL; Paul soon accepted the commission, which would come to involve live performances in Britain, America and twenty other countries, as well as a CD and two singles, numerous TV screenings, a theatrical release and a video – quite a lot for what he'd called a 'municipal gig'.

McCartney balanced his highbrow fare with a series of six *Unplugged*-style concerts, heavy on Fifties covers, around Western Europe. As he rightly commented, it proved he could handle any format. After a Maracana stadium, Southend's 1,600-seat Cliffs Pavilion must have seemed like someone's living room. For Paul, hustling out the sort of R&B chestnuts the Beatles had loved reminded him of his early days slogging around the club circuit. 'It made me feel good,' he noted. 'It made me feel sort of complete, working both ends of the scale.'

On Friday 28 June, a year to the day after his gala homecoming,

McCartney's *Oratorio* was premiered to a full house of 2,500 in Liverpool's Anglican cathedral, where he'd failed an audition thirty-eight years earlier. The piece enjoyed a standing ovation, with Paul and Carl Davis shaking their fists aloft in triumph, but only mixed reviews. The Liverpool *Post* noted the work's 'memorable passages', though these were 'interspersed [with] periods of near tedium.' To *The Times*, 'the churchy choral parts and laboured orchestral interludes [made] Brahms' *Requiem* seem like a hotbed of syncopation.' The *Guardian* complained that the *Oratorio* was 'afraid of anything approaching a fast tempo', and specifically that 'the sugary libretto needs an editor with even a fraction of John Lennon's cynicism.' McCartney told the *Guardian* they were full of crap. This particular debate would be the biggest thing in British classical music that year.

In America, where the *Oratorio* was first performed five months later, the press brought out the ninety-six-point headline font that had greeted the Beatles in 1964. Some of that same hysteria was present on the night of 18 November, when McCartney took his seat in a first-tier box at Manhattan's Carnegie Hall. 'The audience erupted in excitement,' the *New York Times* said in its review of the opening. 'Fans on the second and third tiers leaned perilously over the rails . . . Their ovation when the performance ended seemed partly in celebration, partly in relief that the seriousness always claimed for Mr McCartney had at last been confirmed on seriousness' home turf.'

Other critics weren't quite as convinced. *Newsday* called the evening a 'sprawling, mawkish, excruciating, embarrassing ninety minutes of ego.'

A few days later, back in England, a reporter asked McCartney what he thought of it all. 'Well, the press were OK, but it's the ordinary folk I listen to. Neil Kinnock told me it was bloody fantastic.'

On 1 December 1991, George Harrison began a tour of Japan supported by his friend Eric Clapton and his band. After seventeen years off the road, George was reportedly surprised and pleased at how it went down, particularly the nine Beatles tunes. Wild, sustained applause, some knicker-throwing. Meanwhile, McCartney had tried to solicit interest in the *Anthology* project by sending form letters to the likes of Steven Spielberg, Martin Scorcese and Ridley Scott, allegedly asking each director to state in 500 words why he was the right man for the job. Harrison, who knew something of the film industry, told McCartney he was out of his mind, you didn't treat Talent like that, and to leave it to him, George – he was back on board now. Paul was chastened. 'It was a mistake,' he told *Rolling Stone*.

There it was left until the day, three months later, when McCartney, Harrison and Starr met up at a small, nondescript studio in Wendell Road, West London, to begin filming *Anthology*. The director was Geoff Wonfor, formerly of Channel Four's *The Tube*.

He earned his fee. Although there were hordes of fans who'd kept track of their heroes' every move for the last thirty years, the Beatles themselves all suffered from selective memory loss. George, in particular, seemed unable to keep his focus on the main story and found himself wandering off in areas that were at best tangential to the script. Typically he would begin a riff, ramble on for several minutes, and then recognise that he was creating a sideshow, a diversion, rather than advancing the plot. This was a new problem for Wonfor, something that almost never happened during his *Tube* days. Ringo, for his part, was affable, but would privately concede that years of heavy drinking (he'd taken the cure in October 1988) had likewise done for some of the fine detail. Even Paul had no choice but to call in the Beatles' scholar-squirrels to remind him of exactly what had happened.

McCartney was back in the trip known as the Sixties when, later that spring, he and George Martin starred in the *South Bank Show* special *The Making of Sgt. Pepper*. This went out across the ITV network on 14 June. The Disney Channel version in America was significantly shorter, owing to its deletion of all references to the part played in the creative process by drugs.

Around the same time, Harrison rang McCartney with the 'dead serious' proposal that the three Beatles stand in the British general election on behalf of the Natural Law party. This was the political rump of the Maharishi's sect, whose manifesto favoured a daily regime of meditation and yogic flying. The party put many of the UK's problems just then down to the fact that the prime minister lived in a house with a south door, and that the newly built Channel Tunnel provided a south access. Such things went against the principles of Natural Law.

'I'd have thought people would say thank you,' George would recall of his approach to certain prospective voters and candidates, 'instead of what they did say, which was "Fuck you".'

A familiar tremor, part joy, part revivalist frenzy, spread across the Atlantic in May when Apple confirmed that Paul, George and Ringo would be working together for the first time in twenty-three years. To call the reaction ecstatic would be an understatement. Apart from what Harrison termed 'the legitimately, clinically insane fans . . . the ones writing *those* letters, the messiah ones' there was an immediate, round-the-clock media siege of both Apple and MPL. McCartney's own press was being handled by one Geoff Baker, thirty-six, a freelance who'd progressed from selling showbiz tidbits to the likes of the *Sun* to representing the world's most beloved entertainer. The result would be a true and time-tested partnership, at least until the bizarre events of September 2004.

On 18 June 1992, Paul McCartney turned fifty. There was a party in Sussex, attended by Linda, the kids and some 200 of their best friends. Harrison and Starr couldn't come. 'Despite all the hits,' Paul said, 'I just want to write one really good song. People say to me,

"What's left for you to do?" But I still have a little bee in my bonnet telling me, "Hang on, the best could be yet to come, you could write something incredible" . . . That keeps me going. Looking at things now, I don't seem to be over the hill.'

As if on cue, McCartney went into the studio that October with noted dance producer Martin Glover, aka Youth, on one of his oddest jobs ever. Over the course of several late nights the pair created the seventy-seven-minute CD *Strawberries Oceans Ships Forest* that Paul credited, in honour of his father's wartime work, to the Fireman. The lead-off track, Transpiritual Stomp, in which a banjo loop built to a sustained crescendo while a voice like Barry White's growled, 'I sense the situation' gave due warning that this was something other than *Wings Greatest*. Subsequent cuts on *Strawberries* included Trans Lunar Rising, Transcrystaline and nine minutes of throbbing bass and heavily treated chanting entitled Pure Trance.

After listening to the final tapes, Youth ventured the opinion that it was a bit far out, and suggested they edit the whole thing down into one 12″ single. McCartney told him it was the best thing he'd ever done, and that he was keeping it as a full-scale album. *Strawberries Oceans Ships Forest* was released, with only the Fireman's name on the cover, in November 1993; it got rave reviews and didn't trouble the chart.

Twenty-four hours after parting from Youth, McCartney was in Lille for the gala French premiere of the *Oratorio*. Princess Di was present, and reportedly not amused when Paul kept her waiting backstage. Meanwhile there was another album in the works, Linda's new photography book, a concert film and *Anthology*. In spite of everything that was happening in his life, McCartney found time to write Bob Harris a 'really sweet' letter when he lost his long-running Radio 1 show.

'Paul's a great guy. Very down to earth, with some iffy friends. The entourage, I mean. You just had to accept that.'

Early on Thursday afternoon, 26 November, members of McCartney's fan club began filing into North London's Black Island studio to act as extras on the promotional film for his new single. The cheers that had gone up when the doors were opened had long since turned to groans by the time Paul himself finally showed after a long Thanksgiving dinner at MPL. For most of the seven hours in-between, the crowd had been harangued by a perky young MC who could have doubled as a power-aerobics instructor; 'Havin' a good time?' she shouted into her fast-food-drive-through mike, while clapping her hands vigorously above her head. One Jason Hobbs was to record his experience of the day in *Beatles Book Monthly* magazine:

> The [wait] went on hour after hour . . . some people walked out in protest. Eventually, we were ushered on to the video set, which looked like a forest. Paul and the band then walked on to some disgruntled moaning from the tired and fed-up extras. Things didn't get much better, however. For the entire hour Paul was on the set, he only spoke once, and that was in reply to a fan who called out 'Say something, Paul.' Paul's reply was 'I don't speak until tomorrow.' After the shoot was over [he] just got in his car and drove off.

Two weeks later, McCartney was back in the old Ed Sullivan theatre to perform for the MTV series *Up Close*. Here the audience were asked to start with some 'simple warm-up moves – And *clap*, and *clap*, and *bounce* to the beat . . . Got it? That's what your parents did for the Beatles.' The actual show was flawless if, occasionally, a tad *too* impeccable, with Paul leafing through the Lennon-McCartney songbook and throwing in a snatch of Jingle Bells, a tune MPL were apparently keen to acquire.

After the gig, the McCartneys took a car over to the Capitol Records office on Fifth Avenue. Lee Eastman had died the previous summer, aged eighty-one, but his son John was still tending the family business. Paul's worldwide recording services, his brother-in-law reckoned, were worth some $100,000 a week until his seventieth birthday. A hundred million, Paul might well have reflected, recalling the time Epstein and Sullivan had argued over a couple of grand. He signed his new contract that Christmas.

One of McCartney's collaborators on *Off The Ground*, his eighteenth solo outing, explains how 'Paul wanted to connect the three chords of the Clash with the classical-lite vibe of the *Oratorio*.' This application of punk aesthetics to orchestral theory gave rise to one of his better albums since *Back to the Egg*. The single Hope Of Deliverance was smart and worthy, being adapted into an acid dance mix that spectacularly wrong-footed the critics. Bonuses included the take-one romp Biker Like An Icon, some leftovers from the Elvis Costello sessions and even a fade-out track Paul had written in India, twenty-five years earlier, entitled Cosmically Conscious. Deliverance's B-side, Big Boys Bickering – a protest, apparently, about 'things like a hole in the ozone, and people starving in Africa' – would earn a BBC ban for its seditious use of the word 'fuck'.

The lyrics were a problem elsewhere on *Off The Ground*, being occasionally wry but more often clichéd and mawkish. In the tune Winedark Open Sea McCartney would sing, 'We can be so loving/I feel love for you now/I feel love for you right now'. The first words on the album's first single were 'I will always be hoping, hoping/You will always be holding, holding/My heart in your hand'. Much as it was admirable in itself to still feel that way about Linda, there were those who yearned for the ironic snap of, say, 'She was just seventeen/You know what I mean'.

Off The Ground spent two months on the chart, reaching number five. Thirty years to the month after Please Please Me, the hits still kept coming.

For all the good vibes of the album, some things irritated

McCartney. He was rich but he was possessive, and he still missed his babies.

'I can't blame Michael Jackson for buying my songs,' he announced. 'But I've written to him three times. I'm the only living asset in the company, and he won't even reply.' Later that year, Jackson began talking publicly about a *Beatles Rap* album to feature artists such as the Beastie Boys and Run DMC. Paul told the Argentinian paper *Clarin* he thought Jacko was a victim of his own fame, with an alleged Valium habit that was 'very LA'.

Back home, McCartney was on *Top of the Pops* for the twenty-eighth time, miming to a low-key number called C'Mon People. It was evidently pre-recorded. On that same Thursday evening, 18 February, he and the band flew to Milan to start a seventy-nine-date tour that wound down, ten months later, at a soccer stadium in Chile. Three years before, Paul had taken the brave and quixotic decision to warm up his audiences with Richard Lester's Sixties rocumentary, complete with frantic blasts of Beatlemania. As foreplay went, it was genius; for many present, the sound of She Loves You or Yesterday was inseparable from memories of adolescent dating, dancing, lovemaking and loss. There'd been a noticeable pressure drop as Paul himself then hit the stage and trotted straight into his new single, the forgettable Figure Of Eight. This time around, McCartney ensured there was no such let-down. As they took their seats, concertgoers were greeted with a selection of tunes on the PA, ranging from Monteverdi's *Vespers of the Blessed Virgin* to Marlon Brando warbling Luck Be A Lady Tonight. At that stage Paul appeared and launched smartly into Drive My Car, the first of fully eighteen Beatles songs. Things went on from there, with a full complement of classic arena kitsch – strobes galore and dry ice. The *New York Times*, denouncing McCartney as an 'Elton John act-alike', remarked of his opening night in Giants Stadium, 'Entertainment was clearly the point . . . His stage was framed by huge cloth screens on which were projected all sorts of things, from anti-vivisectionist pleas to live pictures of what was happening onstage to Matisse-like graphics; it made the show seem like an adjunct to television . . . The sentimental Mr McCartney would turn the personal into a spectacle of amiability, hardly the original intent of the music.'

That particular date drew a capacity 53,000 audience and grossed $1,722,923, the best box office for any act in the world that year.

Those kind of figures allowed McCartney to insist on certain 'technical riders' to his basic tour contract. At each stop along the way, the local promoter was to provide twelve bottles of Johnnie Walker Red Label, along with Coca-Cola, non-French mineral water (in protest at their nuclear testing in the Pacific), sushi, vegetarian curries and rice. No one backstage was to be allowed to eat anything that contained meat or meat by-products; if a roadie happened to fancy a Big Mac, he was out of luck. Paul also made clear his views on dressing-room furniture, which was to be all white and not involve any animal skin or print, and insisted he wouldn't even travel in a car with leather seats.

On 19 March, between houses at the Entertainment Centre in Sydney, where 20,000 seats sold at the phone-melting rate of 2,500 a minute, Linda went on a local TV news show to discuss the tour ('I quite like the manic din of the crowd,' she allowed) as well as her photography collection and book, *Linda McCartney's Sixties*. After these pleasantries were concluded, she told the interviewer that she didn't care for the Australian prime minister, Paul Keating. 'He's a pig killer,' Linda said. 'People like him don't like us and I don't like them. The only way to be a good leader is to be kind and fair. And you're not kind and fair if you're butchering animals for profit.'

Linda and her photos got a tidal wave of publicity, although there was a downside to it. For the next week she was blinded by flashbulbs every time she stepped out of the couple's rented home, but also bombarded with questions: *Why did you insult the PM, Linda? Are you going to apologise, Linda? Do you fancy a burger, Linda?* Meanwhile, behind the scenes, Paul was '200 per cent supportive' according to Geoff Baker, who now acted as his client's publicist, drinking companion and confidant. Three days later, the cameras were on hand to record the McCartneys' 'strictly private' visit to the Greenpeace vessel *Rainbow Warrior*, docked in Sydney harbour. The *Herald*'s speculation that 'the wave of controversy following [Linda's] outburst might harm hubby and her' proved idle, as both *Off The Ground* and *Sixties* did a roaring trade.

When he got home in July, Paul went back to the old Abbey Road zebra crossing to pose for the cover of yet another live album. Later that month, Richard Ogden resigned after six years as managing director at MPL. According to *Music Week*, 'his departure was linked to disagreements over the high costs and poor publicity on the New World Tour.' Geoff Baker was to issue a terse rebuttal to this story, which ran in full: 'Bollocks'.

On 11 September, George Harrison was among the audience for McCartney's homecoming concert at Earl's Court. 'He came back afterwards' Paul recalled, 'and criticised the gig in a sort of professional way. "A bit too long", George reckoned. Well, fuck you. And the old feelings came up. But George is a great guy. Even with old friends, this shit happens.'

Nine days later, EMI released the CD versions of *The Beatles 1962–66* and *The Beatles 1967–70*, priced at £25 apiece. Back in March, George Martin had answered a question about the group's outtakes by telling *The Times*, 'I've listened to all the tapes. There are one or two interesting variations, but otherwise it's all junk.' Six months later, Martin and his co-producer Jeff Lynne were to use this same junk in the forthcoming *Anthology*. Meanwhile, Paul, Yoko and half a dozen law firms were debating the terms of her release of four John Lennon home demos to the cause. Towards the end of the year, the Rock and Roll Hall of Fame also got involved; they planned to induct John and to 'reunite [his] two creative partners, just as he would have wished', for the occasion. This proved a hard sell.

Between mid-November and the night of 19 January 1994, the organising committee wrote to and spoke with McCartney several times. First, he apparently told them he was busy. Early in the new year, he called to say he needed to know the exact wording of John's citation. Then a mutual friend alerted Linda to the fact that Phil Spector would also be at the event. Linda conveyed the news to Paul, who had a distinct response.

'I'm not going.'

Despite the threat, McCartney did go. And earned a standing ovation as he joined John's widow onstage at the Waldorf-Astoria. Yoko took the opportunity to hand him the lost tapes, before remarking to the press, 'I didn't break up the Beatles. But now I'm in a position where I could bring them back together, and I don't want to hinder that. It was a situation given to me by fate.'

In the midst of all the negotiations, Capitol put out *Strawberries Oceans Ships Forest*, not the sort of thing – one sales executive ruefully noted – fans associated with most fifty-one-year-old pop superstars. The album dashed even the slim hopes the label had had for it. On its first day, it sold less than 400 copies in the US, compared with the 60,000 *Off The Ground* managed. Not long after that, McCartney told Youth that he wanted to do a follow-up. When the producer asked him if he had a concept in mind, Paul handed him some notes reading, 'The Fireman brings bison for trancing in the streets. The Fireman knows a lemon's peal . . . The Fireman understands darsh walls & emerdeen sky. Do you?'

Just as *Strawberries* was released, the McCartneys brought their world tour to a triumphant conclusion at the Estadio Nacional in Santiago. There was an emotional Band On The Run/Hey Jude encore, with everyone joining in the final chorus. Nobody there was to know that Linda had heard the manic din for the last time.

A star-packed audience was on hand to witness Paul and Yoko apparently resolve their love-hate relationship by embracing fondly and waving to well-wishers at the Waldorf-Astoria. 'Shit' was how John himself had always characterised such affairs. The spirit of rock 'n' roll, he felt, couldn't reside at a $1,500-a-plate banquet, or in lachrymose speeches from middle-aged men wearing tuxedos. But Paul made a bold stab at it, giving his rap in the form of a 'Dear John' letter.

'The joy for me,' he concluded, 'after all the business crap was that we were actually getting back together and communicating once more . . . John Lennon, you've really made it. Tonight you're in the Rock and Roll Hall of Fame. God bless you.'

Following his speech, Yoko passed McCartney a small padded bag and said, 'Here are John's tapes.' Paul put the package in his briefcase and carried it back to London, where the producer Jeff Lynne eventually retooled Lennon's late-Seventies rejects to 1994 specifications. By early February, when America celebrated the thirtieth anniversary of the Beatles' coming, Paul was able to confirm that they were back in business.

On Friday morning, the 11th, McCartney, Harrison and Starr met at Paul's Sussex studio, the converted windmill known as Hog Hill, their first such collaboration since January 1970. The idea was to start from John's rough vocal for the skeletally thin Free As A Bird; the 'Threatles', as they called themselves, would then build the song layer upon layer, Spector-style, until the whole not only over-whelmed the parts but rendered them irrelevant. Instead of one piano, they used three; six guitars instead of two – plus various effects courtesy of Jeff Lynne, not to mention a new middle-eight, all smothered in reverb. As McCartney consulted a notably grumpy Harrison about filling in the demo's numerous blanks, a row erupted. 'We competed,' Paul noted, 'on who actually had the better lyrics to the unfinished Lennon song.' Four months later, the trio reconvened at George's place to run through a selection that reached back over the years to Love Me Do. After this exhilarating blast of bare-bones rock, the conversation turned to Lennon's *Double*

Fantasy reject Now And Then. Democracy required that McCartney and Starr listen politely while their host, perched on a red Moorish throne, held forth. George, he made clear, wasn't interested in wasting his middle age on John's outtakes; nor on a new version of Paul's Let It Be. Instead, the three men sat down in front of a small but emotional audience that included Geoff Wonfor and his film crew to reflect on their career, and more specifically their time in India twenty-six years earlier. This particular sequence would conclude with George playing his unreleased tune Dehra Dun on a ukulele.

The Genesis 1:1 of Beatles lore is the story of the teenage McCartney stumbling on the Quarry Men that summer's day in 1957. But, for sheer drama, nothing would top the moment, thirty-seven years later, when Lennon's familiar voice had first come over the speakers singing Free As A Bird. Standing in the wings, even the roadies had been moved to tears. Wearing headphones, Paul quickly picked up the harmony, closing his eyes, nodding when he heard John and himself hitting the note, smiling when George joined in the chorus. He looked up once, to briefly acknowledge Ringo, as the room filled with that distinctive, crisp beat.

And on they went for a couple of minutes – this spectral glimpse of the band that had it all.

On 12 March 1994, the McCartneys celebrated their twenty-fifth wedding anniversary. 'We have our barnies, like everyone else,' Linda would note, *Woman* trilling that they were 'so normal.' After all this time, however, they were 'still in love . . . Paul always stops off after meetings to buy flowers.'

That same night, in Hollywood, McCartney picked up the Doris Day Music Award for 'exemplary accomplishment in spotlighting animal issues with creativity and integrity.' Some of the on-stage tributes were repetitive ('Paul is such a classy guy,' said all the presenters) and some genuinely moving. The evening broke up to the sound of female squeals as the early Beatles appeared on a giant video screen.

Over quarter of a century, McCartney's ex-band had survived cultural mood shifts that had run the gamut from glam to grunge. A sign of their continuing lure was the boom market in Beatles memorabilia, a world where a blown speaker cabinet might as well have been a Rodin sculpture. If Paul, John, George or Ringo had worn it, touched it, or so much as seen it, you could sell it. In New York that summer, an autograph dealer named Gary Zimet charged $90,500 for a brief handwritten note from Lennon to McCartney, requesting him to sod off. When EMI announced that they were moving out of their old Manchester Square offices in London, the building's internal floor railings – on which the band had posed for the cover of the *Please Please Me* album – were haggled over like fragments of the true Cross. (The banisters and an entire EMI staircase would, in the end, become McCartney's property.) On 27 September, Paul himself donated a piece of whittled balsa wood, about six inches square, to a charity event called Little Pieces From Big Stars – it sold for £13,000, or twenty-six times its reserve estimate. Finally, on 30 November, the Beatles' back pages once again went gold with the release of *Live At The BBC*. Two thousand fans lined up all night outside the door of a London branch of Tower Records to buy the double album, which went straight to number one.

Fully a year after starting work on Free As A Bird, the trio were back at McCartney's home studio to eke out their virtual reunion. Harrison again took the opportunity to air his misgivings about Now And Then. Nor was he keen to revisit Paul's 'randomised freakout' Carnival Of Light. However, he agreed to perform on Lennon's 1979 Real Love, for which they dug out John's old Salvation Army harmonium. This time around, Geoff Wonfor's cameras were present for the full session, which proceeded under McCartney's donnish eye. Paul was later to say of the familiar Beatles dynamic,

'Ringo was great . . . George and I did agree we might work together, but the truth is, after Real Love, I think he had some business problems [notably, a pending $20 million lawsuit against his former film-production partner] and it didn't do much for his moods . . . He's been having a bit of a bad time actually, he's not been that easy to get on with. I've rung him up and he doesn't ring back.'

Just a month later, the whole reunion took a new and surprising turn when Yoko and her nineteen-year-old son Sean joined the McCartneys for a working weekend at the farm in Sussex. Paul would remark how odd it was to wake up to see his house guest in her bathrobe. That was nothing compared to the music that resulted – seven minutes of clumping bass and high-pitched Japanese rapping entitled Hiroshima Sky Is Always Blue. Five months later, on the fiftieth anniversary of the dropping of the atom bomb, Hiroshima received its first and only public airing, as part of a day-long commemoration by Japanese state radio. It was a characteristic genre-leap by Paul, the man who listed both Fred Astaire's *Funny Face* and Snoop Dogg's seminal *Doggystyle* among his favourite LPs, as was his use of the original Heartbreak Hotel double bass on the track. Sean Lennon told *Rolling Stone* that the song was the fruit of 'our reconciliation after twenty years of bitterness and feuding bullshit.'

But the feud wasn't quite over yet. The McCartneys and Onos were at it again just six months later, arguing about old song credits. Paul complained that 'the widow' was earning as much, or more, from Yesterday as he was. In April 2002, the press asked McCartney if he planned to invite Yoko to one of his concerts in New York. 'We're not friends,' he told them. 'I don't hold a grudge [but] life is short, and if I throw a party, I just invite who I wanna have there, people you're gonna have a laugh with.'

He sold out at Madison Square Garden, she stayed home in the Dakota Building.

*

May 1995: McCartney, Harrison and Starr finally wrapped Free As A Bird and Real Love, two slight songs with a baroque, Electric Light Orchestra production. Paul and George then attempted to combine on a track they called All For Love. This brought a fresh round of debate and muttered asides, until somebody again mentioned Now And Then. At that there was the noise of slammed doors, and soon Lynne found himself sitting alone with the Beatles' rhythm section.

'I think John would have liked Free As A Bird,' George later commented. 'In fact, I hope someone does this to all my crap demos when I'm dead, making them into hit songs.' On that note, the whole reunion limped to its close.

For ten months, from mid-January to 19 November, some 600 television executives, captains of industry, bankers, lawyers, accountants and publicists worked around the clock to launch *Anthology*, which would come to comprise a three-part miniseries (later released in an eight-video/four-DVD box) of old and new footage, three double albums and a coffee-table book. In spite of everything that was happening, the McCartneys found time for a life away from the Beatles. On 16 May, Linda opened a new £10 million factory in Fakenham, Norfolk, where her vegetarian pies were manufactured. Her latest cookbook was a runaway best-seller, and she was fortunate enough to be appointed *Anthology*'s official photographer. Between them, the couple were the directors of a dozen thriving companies. When the *Sunday Times* came to compile its annual Rich List for 1995, there was Paul's name alongside those of Getty and Rothschild, with a fortune of £420 million.

That same month, McCartney was the anonymous host of a seventeen-part North American radio series that went out under the title *Oobu Joobu*. According to the news release, this was a weekly collage of 'jokes and jingles', linked by 'nutty, Goon-type effects', with a regular Cook of the House slot and music from 'Rude

Corner'. The playlist tended to the avant-garde. Any Beatles fans tuning in might have been surprised to know that it was the composer of Yesterday behind the falsetto warbling and looped glass-smashing of Hot Soup – Jammin' Fools, a work premiered on *Oobu Joobu*.

The executives at Westwood Radio were thrilled by their famous presenter. 'Paul was a revelation,' says one of the few managers actually to meet him. 'He'd get up on a chair and announce, "Tea nearly ready" and he'd imitate a kettle. I mean, you'd never get anything as funny as Paul McCartney doing tea . . . Or he'd sing beautiful piano ballads with a Jamaican accent. One night he played forty minutes of music from the Baka tribe, who are pygmies from equatorial Africa. You never knew what you'd get. It was like working in the middle of a thunderstorm – these lightning bolts were all around you.'

A certain kind of critic had long assumed that McCartney was both professionally twee and personally tight-fisted – but there he was, anonymously plugging *Oobu Joobu* and quietly supporting dozens of friends and strangers behind the scenes. Back in their early Hamburg days, the Beatles had been taken under the wing of a nightclub bouncer and ex-West German featherweight champion named Horst Fascher. Thirty-five years later, McCartney would pay for a critical heart operation for Fascher's baby daughter. The League Against Cruel Sports, Friends of the Earth, War Child and Rye Memorial Hospital were among his other beneficiaries. While not some 'sad hippy', he once noted, he wanted to 'give something back . . . What you've gotta do is grab life by the balls and say we *can* work it out.' There seems to have been no question that Paul wanted anything, least of all publicity, in return.

On 4 October, Linda held a press conference in the ballroom of the Ritz-Carlton in Dearborn, Michigan, to discuss her vegetarian meals, and also drum up support for World Food Day. After her prepared remarks, she paused, glanced back, and apparently choked up, began, 'I'm so lucky . . .' Linda swallowed, unable to speak for a few seconds. 'You're the best. And I could never, never do this without you.' The room was spellbound.

Moments later Linda recovered. She concluded her remarks with the climax everyone had been waiting for. 'Let me introduce you to my husband, Paul,' she said.

That month *Anthology* fever gripped even Sotheby's, where McCartney's handwritten lyrics to Getting Better (dashed off one spring day in 1967) sold for a world-record bid of £161,000. Shortly afterwards, Paul joined the Beat poet Allen Ginsberg for a rare free-form concert at the Albert Hall, where they debuted a short piece called Ballad Of The Skeletons. This was described by its author as 'a political song with very definite statements about the far right, and the monotheist theocratic Stalinists.' It was also the closest thing of the evening to an emotional surge.

'I asked [McCartney] for advice on a young guitarist,' Ginsberg told the journalist Steve Silberman. 'And he said, "Why don't you try me, I love the poem . . ." and I said, "Sure" . . . So he showed up for the soundcheck, and he bought a box for his family. Got all his kids together, four of them, and his wife, and he sat through the whole evening of poetry, and we didn't say who my accompanist was going to be. We introduced him at the end, and then the roar went up on the floor of the Albert Hall, and we knocked out the song.'

McCartney played drums and piano on the recorded version of Skeletons, which became a surprise worldwide hit. The Mouth Almighty catalogue also lists him as a 'driving force' and co-composer of this 'contemporary protest that rails against today's heartless global political establishment.' By chance, just twenty-four hours after the song's release Paul was presented with an honorary fellowship of the Royal College of Music. He'd first been told of the honour some nine months earlier, on the occasion of the royal premiere of his classical piano prelude, A Leaf, held in the state apartments of St James's Palace. Following the recital, Prince Charles had taken the stage to acknowledge 'the remarkable talents' and 'contribution to British life' of 'my friend, Paul McCartney', before springing his announcement. It was the first time in the College's 113-year history that a pop musician had received the award.

'I'm more interested in the new thing,' McCartney had said in 1979. 'I'm not into Beatles repackages myself, because it seems like a second-class item to me.' Three years later, reflecting on the reunion hype of the mid-Seventies, he'd added, 'We generally thought if we did it, it would be a let-down. One of the things we'd been consciously aware of with the Beatles was to go and have a great career and leave 'em laughing and we'd done that, you know. We didn't want to come back as decrepit old rockers saying, "Remember us?"'

None of this deterred the build-up to *Anthology*'s release in November 1995, an event anticipated as something like an Eleventh Commandment or a book tour by J.D. Salinger. For several weeks that autumn, 'straight' and trade press alike ran headlines such as 'YEAH YEAH YEAH!' and 'COME TOGETHER!' about this pop equivalent of the unquiet dead. The band's revival from behind their marble slab swung to its zenith with ABC TV billing their first two-hour transmission 'the television event of a lifetime' and an on-screen clock counting down the hours, minutes and seconds to the 'new' songs. Meanwhile, huge billboards proclaimed the *Anthology 1* LP as 'RE-BEATLEMANIA!' And, as a more realistic slogan: 'Contains studio rarities and previously unreleased material'. Hairy and bedraggled, thin smiles pasted over their craggy features, Paul, George and Ringo squinted out from every possible cranny. They had a lot to live up to. In the week before Thanksgiving, more than two million American fans laid advance orders for the album; for its part, the first *Anthology* special was watched by an audience of forty-nine million, or some fifty per cent of all adult US television viewers.

Sadly, the material itself failed to match the marketing effort. In commenting on the 'avidly awaited Free As A Bird', the *New York Times* found only 'a ballad with a wistful, descending doo-wop chord progression and lyrics that don't get far from the title's cliché . . . T[his] posthumous electronic collaboration, an ornate edifice built on a shard of a dead man's music, can't help sounding creepy.' There were better reviews for the album and its two follow-ups, though even these contained 'leftovers only obsessed fans will want to hear: false starts, lacklustre renditions of oldies, dialogue from an English comedy show, a version of the Isley Brothers' Shout that turns it into a polka. Even when the Beatles were cranking out three albums a year, they didn't release such stuff.' In the end, the 'patch on an otherwise beautifully cut suit', as one rock critic calls it, enjoyed only mixed returns. British viewership figures for *Anthology* fell from an initial high of fourteen million to a sorry 2.7 million. Across the Atlantic, ABC's once upbeat charts and graphs had to be turned upside down once the final totals were in: these showed a loss of twenty-six million viewers, or some fifty-five per cent, over the three-part series, much the same ratings the Monkees reunion would enjoy twelve months later. Meanwhile, Free As A Bird entered the UK chart at number two. It was kept off the top spot at Christmas by McCartney's friend Michael Jackson.

For all that, everyone involved with *Anthology* made a tidy sum. They may have been on a par with the Monkees, but they weren't paid peanuts. McCartney saw to it that Pete Best, once dubbed the 'unluckiest man in showbusiness' received his full cut – a million pounds, apparently – for his drumming on the early tracks. Real Love would duly become the Beatles' twenty-ninth and final hit on its release in March 1996. Their second coming had been remarkable to behold, a return to public if not critical favour, but still not quite the 'event of a lifetime'. By pitching the PR a fraction above delivery, ABC and co. had virtually ensured the anticlimax – 'that faint *pfffft* of escaping air,' one executive now puts it – seen in the Nielsen figures. The band, too, were said to have had mixed emotions about their two-year ordeal, which had dragged on longer than anyone had expected and become the subject of a heated internal debate. At one point near the end, a red-faced Harrison had reportedly turned to McCartney, who was calling for 'just one more take', and sputtered, '*Anthology* is our Vietnam.'

Not long afterwards, Yesterday was voted the 'greatest song ever' (with some twelve million airplays) by a blue-chip panel of *The Times* and Radio 1 listeners. After thirty years, Paul's dream still had the power to stir strong emotions. Not least his own: later that winter, he again wrote to Yoko requesting that the song credit read McCartney-Lennon, if not McCartney. By all accounts, their subsequent discussions would present much the same lively spectacle as two ferrets trapped in a sack. 'He wanted to change the names – which isn't going to happen – and he was also venting his anger,' Yoko reported.

McCartney's frustrations continued when Michael Jackson took advantage of 'Re-Beatlemania' to set up a joint ownership of ATV Music with the Sony Corporation, who paid him $95 million. Jackson was said to have needed cash following lukewarm sales of his album *HIStory*, and to pay legal bills. The Sony executive who signed the deal was Richard Rowe, son of the late Dick Rowe – who once turned down the Beatles as uncommercial.

'Was it all worth it?' a reporter asked, referring to McCartney's distress about his 'babies' and the similar concerns of millions of fans around the world.

'Omigod, definitely,' said Jacko.

In the midst of all this, Linda had discovered a small lump on her breast, which was diagnosed as malignant. On 11 December 1995 she underwent surgery at the Princess Grace Hospital in London. 'We're very optimistic,' Paul emerged to tell reporters. 'Luckily, it was caught in time . . . the doctors have said she'll just need a couple of months of recuperation.'

That same night, someone acquainted with McCartney's schedule broke into Cavendish Avenue while he was five miles away, at his wife's bedside, and stole most of his clothes and guitars. Linda was able to leave the hospital for Christmas, Paul again stressing 'She's fine; she just needs rest.' A month later, he hosted the official press launch of the Liverpool Institute for Performing Arts. Repeated attempts to interview Linda (so visible during *Anthology*, for which she'd sold the photographs) were rebuffed, and all her agency said in a phone conversation was: 'God knows. She's under care. There's no comment.'

In the spring Paul was back in the studio with Ringo, working on a track called Beautiful Night. Some months later George Martin would give this a lush, Abbey Road makeover, after which it was released on the chart. (More attention was paid to the accompanying video, in which the actress Emma Moore took a leisurely skinny-dip.) 'It's very Beatley,' Paul announced. 'It sounds very Beatley . . . A very Beatley one, that . . . So very Beatles . . . You can almost hear a sort of very John Lennony voice in there.'

As well as McCartney and Starr, the song featured Jeff Lynne, several session players and a thirty-two-piece orchestra. George Harrison was notable by his absence.

McCartney was back in Liverpool on 7 June to usher the Queen around his old school. It was a 'proud and moving' moment to be standing on stage in the newly refurbished hall, now named after him, with his kids by his side. The triumph of perseverance and upward assimilation that had, almost incredibly, led to this scene had begun forty years earlier, when Paul picked up a guitar in a nearby semi.

On 4 July, Linda made her will. This eighteen-page document left her entire fortune (estimated at $200 million) in a 'qualified domestic marital trust' which was to pay Paul a quarterly sum for the rest of his life. In the week in which these arrangements were made public, Linda's first husband Joseph See, sixty-two, killed himself.

Later that summer, the hundredth performance of the *Oratorio* took place at the Philharmonic Hall in Liverpool. Geoff Baker was to tell the assembled press, 'You said it would never last. It's now played twenty countries and travelled 195,504 miles.' Paul himself listened and nodded as Baker assured everyone that 'Mrs McCartney' was doing fine.

Two weeks later, on 3 October, Linda began chemotherapy treatment at a hospital in Los Angeles. Baker was again on hand to confirm that she was 'do[ing] fantastically well; the doctors are amazingly pleased with her.' In the trying times ahead, McCartney's devoted spokesman – who talked on the phone an average of 120 times a day – would prove invaluable in suppressing the wrong kind of publicity as well as promoting the right kind. That same month, Paul began High Court proceedings against Mal Evans' widow Lilly over some handwritten Beatles lyrics she was trying to auction at Sotheby's. Most of the British press either ignored the unpleasantness, or were broadly sympathetic to the plaintiff, who insisted, 'I'd like to meet Mrs Evans and discuss this, [and] come to some arrangement to see that she's taken care of.' 'They stood a classic David and Goliath story on its head,' recalls one veteran showbusiness hack, admiringly. '[McCartney] had one of the two best images of anyone in the country at the time. Him and the Queen Mum.'

In November, Apple released the following statement: 'The end has finally come . . . The Beatles are no more. The official word is that Paul McCartney, George Harrison and Ringo Starr will never play together again as a group, and that they have decided that there will be no more singles issued from their back catalogue.' Despite falling audiences for the *Anthology* TV series, the three albums had all gone multi-platinum, making 1996 a bumper year both for Apple and MPL, with sales of some £42 million and £17 million respectively – thus relieving George and Ringo from financial worries for the rest of their lives. At least commercially, the Threatles had achieved every pop group's burning ambition to be 'bigger than the Beatles'.

On 17 December, the McCartneys appeared in public for the first time since *Anthology*, thanking an animal-rights group who were presenting them with a lifetime-achievement award. Linda was sporting a new close-cropped haircut. 'You're the greatest, and you've brightened my year up,' she announced in a televised message. There was more: a few days earlier, the palace had been in touch to ask whether Paul would accept a knighthood. Acknowledging that there were those who would deem it a sell-out, he promised to think carefully about his answer, which turned out to be yes. The announcement on 31 December was a shock only in that many papers expressed their surprise that he hadn't been honoured already. According to one leader, 'In the twelve years, eleven months and fifteen days' that had elapsed since his last pot bust, 'Paul McCartney's conduct has been exemplary, to the extent that anyone can expect of a rock star.'

McCartney went to the palace on 11 March 1997, accompanied by his three youngest children; Linda stayed home. 'This has to be the most popular gong of all time,' said the BBC court correspondent. 'No other person has brought such pleasure for so long to so many millions of people.' By the end of the month, MPL would receive some 12,000 letters and cards of congratulation. Among the well-wishers was George Harrison, who used the slightly expanded title of 'His holiness Sir Paul McCartney'.

Early May: Tony Blair was elected prime minister, and pop's new knight bachelor released his album *Flaming Pie*. McCartney's latest back-to-basics gambit was a high-wire act without a net. There was no obvious single, the lyrics didn't make immediate sense and most of the tracks were too slow, disjointed or weird for radio. The title tune's a good example: over a treated boogie-woogie piano vamp,

Paul wails the sort of Lewis Carroll-on-acid lines that are the flip side to all the sap: 'Tucked my shirt and unzipped my fly/Go ahead, have a vision/I'm the man on the flaming pie'.* Even the 'nice' songs withhold a conventional melody; on the rare occasions Paul lets rip, the anticlimax comes on fast. With the good-rockin' intro of the album's would-be knees-up, The World Tonight, McCartney wakes from a deep slumber and sets forth, hands clapping, voice and guitar full of resolve. Then he inexplicably turns around and climbs back under the covers. Ironically, in a record that strains for relevance, the one real standout is the ballad Somedays, where Paul and George Martin combine on the chamber-pop style they'd perfected thirty years earlier.

In a long notice, *The Times* called *Flaming Pie* 'the sound of rock and roll with its teeth in a glass of water by the bedside.' McCartney told the press he 'really didn't give a shit if it [was] a hit or not. I'm saying that and I mean it. Sure, everyone likes to have a hit – but not at the expense of having fun.' A week later, the album went to the top, providing Paul with his eighty-first gold disc.

On 17 May, VH1 broadcast *Paul McCartney's Town Hall Meeting*, a Q&A event aired live from Bishopsgate Memorial Hall in London. The station revealed that they received a total of 2,476,092 questions in advance, rather a lot for a sixty-minute transmission. President Clinton was one of those phoning in. Paul then repeated the exercise for Chris Evans' cult show *TFI Friday*. This time around, it was Ringo, taking a break from his new solo LP *Vertical Man*, who got past the call-screeners. 'Paul, who's your favourite Beatle?' he asked.

In late summer, McCartney went to the Suffolk home of Derek Taylor, the legendary Apple press officer and a moving force behind *Anthology*. Taylor, who had been suffering from lung cancer, passed

---

* The title came from John Lennon's droll account of how the Beatles got their name: 'A man appeared on a flaming pie and said unto them, "From this day on, you are Beatles with an *a*."'

away on 7 September. It may have been a coincidence, but there was a brief return to the herbally-scented days of 1967 and petitions in *The Times* when, later that month, McCartney again publicly called for the legalisation of pot. 'You're filling all the jails,' he argued, 'and yet it's when you're in jail that you really become a criminal. That's when you learn all the tricks.' He soon sparked another lively debate by placing an ad in the winter-fashion edition of the *New Yorker*, offering to send callers a catalogue of 'our frisky collection of fox, mink and raccoon.' Prospective customers received a video entitled 'Paul's Furs', which showed not runway models but graphic scenes of animals being tortured and killed. Between these various dramas, McCartney appeared on stage at the Albert Hall to raise funds for the island of Montserrat, an uncontroversial event.

On 6 October, McCartney released his second major classical work, *Standing Stone – A Symphonic Poem*. Paul explained time and again to interviewers that 'unlike the *Oratorio*, this relies entirely on colours and effects'; explained that the piece 'describes the way Celtic man wondered about the origins of life and the mystery of human existence.' The Radio 1 show *Evening Sessions* then talked to Liam Gallagher of Oasis about his roots, which gave him an opportunity to share some thoughts on McCartney's recent work. 'Sitting around with a bunch of old dykes writing doesn't sound classical to me,' Gallagher mused. 'I've written three classic albums.'

Ten days later, a reporter named Jim Repard, on assignment to cover the *Q* Awards ceremony at London's Park Lane hotel, encountered a 'puce-faced' McCartney hurriedly leaving the building through a side door, apparently miffed by recent events. 'Fucking hell,' he commented at intervals to his companions. '*Fucking hell.*' It appeared there was good cause for Paul's distress. Unbeknownst to him, the event's organisers had also thought to invite Phil Spector to speak. 'He rather suggested that that had been a *faux pas*,' Repard recalls. Paul claimed, however, that his reservations about the famed producer were strictly professional.

'He fucked up *Let It Be*, so I'm not going to fucking sit there clapping him.'

Ringo and his own producer, Mark Hudson, then drove to Sussex in order to record McCartney's contribution to *Vertical Man*. Paul, Hudson says, 'was the perfect Beatle when we were at his house. He took out his Hofner and said, "You've got to teach me the chords, man", and then he gave me John's guitar. So there I am standing back to back with Paul McCartney, reading my handwritten chord chart, looking at Ringo like, "Take a picture. Take a picture, Ringo. Take it now, Ringo . . ." I'm standing next to McCartney, holding John Lennon's guitar and playing. And the brilliance of Paul was, once he got it, and it was only two passes, he owned it. That was pretty magical.'

McCartney and Starr pursued, from that point on, widely divergent paths. Following his latest pop and classical hits, Paul was soon engrossed in two 'very alt' projects – the Fireman's second LP and a collection of Linda's original songs and early rock 'n' roll covers entitled *Wide Prairie*. The latter would bring a fresh round of debate and press controversy when the BBC banned one of its tracks, The Light Comes From Within. After due consideration, this was felt to contain inappropriate lyrical content. 'You say I'm simple/You say I'm a hick/You're fuckin' no one/You stupid dick' Linda sang, a reference to 'all the people who'd ever put [her] down, that whole dumb male chauvinist attitude.'

On 11 March 1998, Paul and Linda were in Paris, where they sat hand-in-hand at daughter Stella's catwalk show for the designer Chloe. 'Right now I'm feeling great,' Linda told reporters. 'I'm feeling fit and well and looking forward to having lunch together as a family before we go home.' It was hard to say why, even now, some people were still so uptight around Paul's wife. Though not a martyr to false modesty, she was usually warm and generous, with easy charm and a gentle yet highly focused manner. They just couldn't help it. When she posed for photos at Chloe, the shots showed a friendly Linda and Paul and a collection of rigid, unsmiling fans. The next day, in London, the McCartneys celebrated their twenty-ninth wedding anniversary.

It was at this point that rebellion could (and possibly should) enter the picture, but the couple's four eminently sane, down-to-earth children weren't having it. Linda's daughter with Joseph See, Heather, thirty-four, was a potter whose work was described by the Wedgwood company as 'among the most exciting by any young contemporary artist today.' Mary, twenty-eight, her mother's photographic assistant, had recently announced her engagement to TV director Alistair Donald. Stella, twenty-six, was reportedly earning £200,000 a year at Chloe, where her fashions tended to 'the hot, sexy and chic . . . skimpy frocks that will make all the men sweat.' James, twenty, played guitar and was studying sculpture.

All six family members opted to take a break that Easter; they discussed going to New York or Hollywood, but eventually agreed on the ranch in Arizona because it was deemed marginally safer there.

Linda died in the early hours of 17 April, with her husband and children at her side. She was fifty-six. A week earlier, a scan had determined that the cancer had spread to her liver, though this news was kept from her, and stronger medication was prescribed. After boarding the plane in London, Linda had apparently turned to Paul and admitted, with some frustration, she couldn't quite remember where they were going. It would be beautiful, Paul said. And he was right: from the sprawling, sand-coloured ranch they could see vast hazed tracts of American wilderness, tall cactus, and hills dried to the gold of the desert winter. This was the rugged terrain, more or less, through which John Wayne had travelled in *Stagecoach*. Behind the house was a small lake, from which a trail led up into the Catalina mountains where Paul and Linda had gone riding shortly before her death.

'In the end, she went quickly with very little discomfort,' McCartney told the press. 'The kids and I were there when she crossed over. They each were able to tell her how much they loved her.

'Finally, I said to her, "You're up on your beautiful Appaloosa stallion. It's a fine spring day. We're riding through the woods. The bluebells are all out, and the sky is clear blue."

'I had barely got to the end of the sentence, when she closed her eyes, and gently slipped away.

'She was unique, and the world is a better place for having known her. Her message of love will live on in our hearts forever.'

Linda was cremated on 18 April, and her ashes brought back to be scattered on the farm in Sussex. Paul and his son slept in the same room in the weeks that followed, both distraught after their loss. 'That's the way they are,' their friend Carla Lane would say. 'Paul told me, "We'll never get over this. But let's get through it."' One of the Eastmans adds, 'Talk about brave: he was comforting *me*.'

In an effort to protect everyone's privacy, Geoff Baker had waited some two days before breaking the news. For the same good reason, he also insisted that Linda had passed away 'while on holiday in California'. The delay inadvertently caused some distress, and left many of the McCartneys' friends cringing at a series of ill-timed gaffes. On the night of 18 April, BBC2 viewers had been treated to a clip of Paul hamming his way through a version of Yesterday that incorporated the Goons' Ying Tong Song, as part of a tribute to Spike Milligan. Nearly a week after her death, one news magazine was unable to pull its review of *Linda's Kitchen* and other writings, which it found 'unappetising' and 'sanctimonious in the extreme'. In conclusion, 'This will remind you just why so many people dislike Lady McCartney.'

For all the problems with lead times, most of the press were fulsome. This was one of those occasions of communal goodwill towards a given artist: virtues were suddenly discovered that had, somehow, previously failed to surface. The gap between how Linda was seen in her lifetime and how she was depicted in death wasn't just unusually wide, but risibly so. It was obvious now that pop commentators, in both Britain and America, of both sexes and all ages, took to this modestly gifted performer in a way which few had ever suspected. She was valued, liked and admired. With only a few exceptions, the media treated Linda with a respect that was as exaggerated as, a month earlier, it would have been astonishing.

'To be claimed by fame is to be pigeonholed,' wrote the *New York Times*. 'But Linda McCartney never seemed to feel fame's constraining effect on her life.' The paper's three separate obituaries dwelt at length on Linda's music, photography and cuisine. Reporting on the vegetarian meal she once prepared for the chef Pierre Franey, the *Times* noted that 'Ms McCartney was disarmingly earthy and outgoing', and that she cooked without regard to precise measurements. 'Everything [was] added in handfuls, pinches, smidgens. Her favorite measurement was "lots of".'

'I thought I might be dead by the end of the first year, it was just so unbearable,' McCartney told the press. Compounding his grief, perhaps, was the sheer scale of his loss. At a stroke, he'd been deprived of his wife, best friend and closest professional partner. It was genuinely distressing to learn that Paul could hardly trust himself to appear in public and that, even when he did, things would go wrong; the following spring, at a press preview of his 'McArty' paintings in Germany, he broke down and wept uncontrollably when Maybe I'm Amazed played in the gallery. For most of those initial twelve months, Paul would cope as he'd done in the days and weeks after Lennon was shot, and as he always had in a crisis: he worked. As a result, Linda's album and the Fireman's follow-up would both appear within a few days of one another, only to be consigned, shortly thereafter, to the obscurity of music reference books.

Linda's London memorial service took place at St Martin-in-the-Fields church early in June. McCartney gave the address, after which he ushered two of his wife's Shetland ponies, Schoo and Tinsel, up the aisle. 'She'd have loved this,' Paul informed the congregation. 'She was the toughest of women, who didn't give a damn what other people thought.' A similar ceremony followed in New York a fortnight later, complete with banner headlines insisting PAUL SNUBS YOKO.

By all rights it should have ended in a crack-up, or at the very least Norma Desmond-like seclusion. Instead, McCartney hired a therapist. 'He was great,' Paul told *USA Weekend*, 'particularly in helping me get rid of my guilt. Whenever anyone you care about dies, you wish you'd been perfect all the time you were with them. The guilt's a real bugger. But [we] were just human . . . That was the beautiful thing about our marriage. We were just a boyfriend and girlfriend having babies.'

As well as the outside assistance, there was also a fair amount of self-help involved. Most days eleven o'clock would pass, and then midnight and then, often, one o'clock, and two – and McCartney, pale and haggard under the lights, would still be slumped on a stool in the studio, guitar in one hand, notebook in the other, trying to do 'everything'. By late summer, he was preparing Linda's final book *On Tour* for publication, as well as working on his own poetry, painting and music. It was all intense, obsessive and a bit worrying. Paul was livid when *On Tour* got only fair reviews, and on turf well beyond that when Radio 1 and others banned The Light Comes From Within. In January 1999 full-page advertisements appeared in several British newspapers which shouted, 'PARENTS!! We need your guidance', and went on from there to engage in a lively, if one-sided debate on censorship. Released on the Beatles' old label Parlophone, Linda's single finally earned the McCartneys a Parental Advisory sticker.

Meanwhile, Paul's original draft notes for Hey Jude had been sold for £115,000 at Sotheby's; he was suing to prevent a similar fate befalling his lyric sheet for Sgt. Pepper, apparently stolen from

Cavendish Avenue. There were new songs and videos, and he remained a thrilling ranter on the topic of animal rights. Despite or because of all the activity, friends still recognised certain personal danger signals, notably his abrupt and untypical flashes of anger. Late one night in the studio, a hollow-eyed McCartney allegedly turned to a staffer and said, 'Get me a drink.' The underling returned two minutes later with an ice-cold Scotch and Coke with all the trimmings, including a variety of symmetrically cut fruit slices, fresh cherries and a silver spoon and fork, all of which, he says, 'looked good to me'. But Paul, setting down his guitar, glanced over the selection and said, 'Well, you've done it again.' His employee still couldn't see anything amiss.

'Come on,' McCartney said. 'C'mon! C'MON!!! I don't know what to make of you.'

'What's wrong?' his aide asked.

'There's no doily.'

On 2 October 1998, several thousand internet surfers tuned in to a 'cyber promotional party' for the Fireman album *Rushes*, a collection of rapping, animal tapes and phone sex with a light, chill-out accompaniment. They were entertained by the fireman himself, who dressed for the occasion in a yellow rain hat, black hood and sunglasses, singing a medley of free-form numbers which were looped and treated by the nearby Youth. The broadcast footage was liberally interspersed with rather full images of nude women. About halfway through the performance, the host sat down on a couch and took questions both from colleagues and the viewing audience, among them:

Q What does *Rushes*' music desire to symbolise to the people?
A *Rushes* desires only the fertility of the imagination.
Q What initially inspired these recordings?
A Inspiration is derived from the cosmic creative force of the universal fire.

Q How do you classify your music?

A Ambient dreams in rainbow arches describe the circles of the Fireman.

Q What is the significance of the naked woman on the inner sleeve of *Rushes*?

A The symbolism of the unknown nude is an ancient mystery. We do not have her number.

Q What moved you to do this album?

A Night skies, flowing streams and whipped cream fire extinguishers.

The fireman never actually revealed his identity, but there was a clue right at the end of the webcast when he looked up, smiled, and gave a familiar thumbs-up to the camera.

On 29 January 1999, a day early, the Building Societies Association organised a thirtieth anniversary rooftop concert at 3 Savile Row. The surviving Beatles all had other plans, and didn't attend. McCartney, in particular, had no use for any of this 'nostalgia bag'. He was keener to discuss his painting, on which he was 'obsessed', even if the results had remained private over the years. 'I know, with the way my celebrity works, the tabloids will pick up on the ones with tits in 'em,' Paul had told Barry Miles. 'I could hire a gallery, but I wouldn't want to do that because that's not what I'm into. I've always avoided exhibiting, because I'm trying to avoid the Tony Curtis actor-turned-painter syndrome. I was thinking something quieter, a little German [place] might be nice.'

Now McCartney was ready to go public, at the Kunstforum Lyz gallery, Siegen, downriver from where it had all started in Hamburg. Ringo, meanwhile, whose *Vertical Man* had left the chart after peaking at number eighty-five, was set to embark on yet another oldies tour with his All-Starr Band. George had been treated for throat cancer in 1997, and was fighting various court cases. Among these was a successful action to prevent one Edward 'Kingsize' Taylor from releasing a live Beatles album recorded 'with John Lennon's verbal permission' in 1962.

On 1 March, McCartney went back to Abbey Road for seven days of 'raw, untreated recordings', mixing in originals with rock 'n' roll covers. A fortnight later, he was in New York to be inducted into the Hall of Fame. Paul's acceptance speech, which raised the loudest cheer of the night, was enlivened by Stella's appearance in one of her own numbers, a snug, hand-embroidered vest. The slogan on it read: ABOUT FUCKING TIME. For Paul, the backstage fence-mending with Phil Spector may have been even more edifying than the satisfaction he took in joining his fellow inductee John Lennon.

'Life's short,' Spector had said. 'Why sweat it?'

The great producer had explained to the press how much he really loved his friend Paul, who was a sweetheart and a genius and a true gentleman, as he stood expressionless next to him and then reportedly muttered, 'OK, Phil. I'll see you.' That set the tone for a bittersweet year of changing moods and fortunes. McCartney became a grandfather on 3 April. The tabloids were on his case again about a woman named Sue Timney he was allegedly seeing – 'a pack of lies' Geoff Baker said. On the 10th, an all-star cast assembled for the televised *Here, There and Everywhere – A Concert for Linda* at the Albert Hall. Towards the end, the giant screens showed close-ups of Paul singing the Ricky Nelson ballad Lonesome Town, and these shots, of him struggling through Linda's favourite song, were the most devastating part of the whole night.

McCartney's first exhibition was considered a success: the gallery had planned for 20,000 visitors over ten weeks but welcomed twice as many. As they strolled between exposed aluminium tubes and vulcanite slabs to view the seventy abstract canvases, fans were greeted by a new composition – *Feedback*, in which Paul alternately played a guitar and a chainsaw, and sometimes apparently both at once. His next musical project followed in kind. This was Clean Machine, an instrumental tune recorded for an all-vegan cycling team Linda had sponsored shortly before her death. The title's allusion to Penny Lane was the one and only concession to 'classic' McCartney: the track itself dubbed funky drums and an assortment of abrupt cries and yaps in a throbbing, electronic mix.

Three weeks later, on 20 May 1999, McCartney was at the Dorchester hotel in London, on his first official home engagement since Linda's death. This was the annual Pride of Britain event, an opportunity to salute those disabled heroes and others overlooked in the official honours list. A tearful Paul climbed on stage to present the first Linda McCartney Award for Animal Welfare to Juliet Gellatley of the vegetarian pressure group Viva. He was 'visibly moved' according to newspaper reports, appearing 'shaky' and 'emotional', seemingly 'gutted' by the repeated mention of his wife's name. Following his speech Paul returned to his seat at the head table, where Tony Blair was seen to sympathetically pat his back.

It was into this already charged scene that Heather Mills strode. According to the official billing, she was the thirty-one-year-old 'activist, after-dinner speaker, motivator and Nobel Prize-shortlisted campaigner' whose modelling career had been shattered when a police motorcycle crashed into her and ripped off her leg when she was twenty-five. Mills, who was also a Pride of Britain presenter, had never previously met McCartney and was only faintly aware of his music. 'However, I remember thinking how nice-looking he was,' she recalled, 'and saying as much to my friend Verna when I left the stage and sat down next to her.'

Mills' back-story, even by rock and roll standards, was unusual. Her early life, with its Victorian mix of debt, crime and violence might not have disappointed Dickens himself. The Mills household had moved frequently around Tyneside in the early Seventies, somehow managing to keep one step ahead of the bailiffs but 'royally messing up' the children in the process (in their cups, the grown-ups were allegedly prone to a bit of 'domestic'). Even when things were relatively stable financially, there always seemed to be a fresh, or worse crisis on the horizon. When she was little more than a toddler, Heather had been abducted and molested by a swimming coach who held her and another girl hostage for three days. (Heather's parents later explained that they'd assumed she was safe and sound at a pool somewhere.) When the girls were finally rescued, the man jumped off a cliff and killed himself. In 2005, the other party sued Mills over the latter's published version of events, claiming that 'the private [material] was mixed with a substantial amount of false and invented information that served to sensationalise and distort.' The case continues.

After years of alleged abuse, Heather's mother Beatrice then ran off with an actor from *Crossroads* and supposedly didn't communicate with her three children for years to come. Her husband, Mark, was an advocate of the self-help school of child care. Heather, a latchkey kid whose one real attachment was to Sunderland FC, would note that if she didn't steal, they didn't eat. This put her in a pragmatic frame of mind, and apparently with Mark's tacit approval she became an expert shoplifter by the age of ten. 'I stole clothes, food, everything – to survive,' she notes. 'My old man would say, "Go get the food." He knew we had to nick it.'

When her father went to prison for fraud, Heather went to join her mother and her boyfriend in London. That arrangement also failed, and the fifteen-year-old girl resorted to sleeping rough, dragging her worldly belongings around with her in a bin bag. A concerned aunt and uncle then brought Heather back to the North-East and arranged for her to have a part-time job in a jewellery shop. Over the next few weeks, she stole £1,000 worth of gold chains (traded in for a moped), for which she was arrested, jailed overnight and placed on probation. Some years later, the shop owner reportedly complained that the thefts had been more extensive than Heather admitted, with losses of £20,000 in stock ultimately forcing him out of business.

Next, sex. Heather lost her virginity at sixteen and remarked, 'Lovemaking was incredible. It was everything I'd ever dreamed of.' After she matured into a striking, Playmate-scale woman ('Bloody hell, your tits are like *watermelons!*' she quotes one friend as enthusing) her ambitions turned to topless modelling. Several 'Page 3 Stunna' shots followed, as did a stint as a highly popular cocktail waitress. On 6 May 1989 Heather married Alfie Karmal, a half Greek, half Arab computer entrepreneur, who apparently grew alarmed at her mood swings and extreme sense of hyperbole. 'It got so bad,' he recalls, 'I told her [I'd leave] unless she saw a shrink to stop the lies and curb her temper.' In the event, the marriage floundered when Heather ran off with a Slovenian ski instructor named Milos. On her return to England she was to enjoy a notably brisk social life, before announcing her engagement to a City bond dealer named Rafaelle Mincione. Her accident took place on 8 August 1993, in London, in a scene reminiscent of Julia Lennon's death thirty-five years earlier. As Heather stepped off the curb at the corner of De Vere Gardens and Kensington Road, a motorbike came 'out of nowhere', swerving from behind a red double-decker bus. A witness named Andy Strauss turned at the blood-curdling scream to see Mills hurled 'ten or twelve feet' through the air. 'I still have nightmares about it. A white running shoe was in the road, and inside was someone's foot. The girl lay on her back, fully conscious.'

Heather was airlifted to Mount Vernon hospital, where surgeons were forced to amputate more of her injured left leg. She was said to have clinically 'died' four times during the procedure. The police motorcyclist involved later sued Mills for damages for 'stress and suffering', though the case ultimately collapsed. In the days ahead, representatives of the tabloid press called at the victim's bed, where she posed for photos and confirmed that she and her boyfriend were still 'doing it' despite her handicap. '"LOOK AT ME . . . I'VE GOT TWO LEGS AGAIN AND YOU CAN'T SEE THE JOIN! IF

MY LEG POPS OUT, I'LL POP IT BACK IN AGAIN" SAYS BRAVE HEATHER' ran a typically spry headline in the *Sunday People*. Discharging herself from hospital, Heather called off her engagement to Mincione on the day she was to have been fitted for her wedding dress. A month or so later she was involved with a tennis-tournament organiser named Marcus Stapleton. 'We are madly, madly in love,' Heather told the *News of the World*. There were four or five other short-lived fiancés, formal or otherwise, over the years, the tabloids dutifully reporting the lovers' highs – 'We're having sex with our minds and not just our bodies!' – as well as their inevitable break-ups. By the time of the Pride of Britain awards in 1999, Heather was planning to marry a BBC producer named Chris Terrill.

Meanwhile, there was an autobiography, with the toe-curling title *Out On A Limb*, and various charitable works that coalesced into the Heather Mills Health Trust. This would campaign tirelessly for the banning of landmines, as well as providing relief supplies in the form of medicine, crutches and prosthetic limbs to amputees in the former Yugoslavia and elsewhere. A slew of awards followed, including those from the Royal Association for Disability and Rehabilitation, the British Chamber of Commerce and *The Times*. Heather was fond of remarking that 'the girl who used to sleep in a cardboard box' was now among the most requested female speakers in England, and the seventh most popular worldwide. She was able to 'pick up the phone and ring presidents and prime ministers.' Due to the many calls on her time, for several years Heather seemingly never managed to register her Trust with the Charity Commission, which requires that any organisation raising more than £1,000 a year file an annual report. She eventually did so in 2000. Some time later, the *Sunday Mirror* agreed to pay £50,000 in damages for wrongly implying that Mills' handling of donations for victims of the Indian earthquake in Gujarat was being 'investigated'.

A gutsy crusader and champion of the needy, or a gold-digging minx? When Heather launched Adopt-a-Minefield in conjunction with the United Nations Association, the UN secretariat admiringly compared her to the late Princess of Wales. To others the template was Madonna, to whom Mills bore a passing resemblance, as well as sharing that great artist's gift for reinvention. Even detractors never questioned Mills' drive or legendary promotional flair. She enjoyed something of a makeover around 1998–9, emerging with a new, softer look, smaller breasts and a proper marketing plan for her charity. Yet again, the *Sun* noted, 'Heather was back'. The only question was: which one?

On the night of 6 June, Mills returned from filming a documentary in Cambodia with the Duchess of Kent to find a puzzling message on her machine: 'Hi, it's Paul McCartney here. Would you give me a ring?'

A few days later Heather went to MPL, where she was struck by the 'energy [McCartney] projected . . . he moved like Fred Astaire, almost as if he was dancing.' After discussing her charities and promising to be in touch again, he walked her to the lift. 'As I stepped in,' Heather recalled, 'I turned around and saw him peering at me round the corner. If it had been any other man I could have sworn he was looking at my bum.'

Later in the autumn, McCartney told Mills that he wanted to make a small donation to her Trust, which he handed her in a sealed envelope. Inside was a cheque for £150,000.

Shortly afterwards they began spending weekends together, often, in deference to Paul's children, in a rented cottage on the Cliveden estate. (The Beatles had filmed the climax of *Help!* there in 1965.) 'It evolved very slowly,' Heather notes. 'I was properly dated and properly wooed. I had flowers sent to me; I was sung to on the phone, sung to while I was making dinner. I thought, This is unbelievable! This is what people dream of!'

★

The three-year interval since *Flaming Pie* would lend McCartney's new album, *Run Devil Run*, a Garbo mystique. Advance details were scant, conjecture was rife, and the results sharply polarising. To some, the twelve covers and three McCartney originals came as a welcome blast of loud, propulsive rock. To others, this 'retro theme party' was the sound of a fifty-seven-year-old man 'rummag[ing] in the undergrowth for his roots', more for his own pleasure than his fans'. *Run Devil Run* peaked at number twelve on the chart. Two weeks later EMI released *Paul McCartney's Working Classical*, another fifteen tunes in very different vein. Finally, in late November, came Vo!ce, Heather Mills' debut single which featured some distinctive guitar and backing vocals. The accompanying video saw Heather boogieing around shouting 'I'm so flexible now, I can dance with Michael Jackson' – at which point her false leg came off and flew across the floor.

On 14 December, McCartney went back to the new Cavern club, thirty-six years after he last appeared on site, where he sang himself hoarse to a capacity crowd of 300. An overflow audience of 12,000 braved the bitter cold to enjoy the repertoire of 'straight, gutbucket rock' on a giant screen erected nearby in Chavasse Park. Fifty million more saw part or all of the concert on television.

'It's fantastic to be back here,' McCartney said. 'What better place to see out the century? I'm back here because I love Liverpool and I'm playing the music I love best in the city I love most.' When it was mentioned to him that the latter-day Cavern was much more clean and airy than the original, which had seemed shot through with the seedy charm of early rock and roll, he said simply, 'Well, that's showbusiness.'

CHAPTER 10

Heather

The lights were low, the music soft as guests arrived at the elegantly appointed farmhouse, deep in the Hampshire countryside, to celebrate Heather Mills' thirty-second birthday. It was Saturday 29 January 2000. As she circulated among a few old friends from Tyneside, and her new ones from the London arts crowd, Mills appeared radiant in a red dress cut to accentuate the figure which, despite surgery, remained quite generous. 'Heather looked incredibly glamorous,' her friend Pamela Cockerill would say. 'She outshone everybody.' An assortment of caterers, waiters and security personnel provided a steady hum of whispered gossip beneath the main drone, which rose to a crescendo when the guest of honour was delivered by a chauffeured Mercedes around 10 p.m. 'She just turned and suddenly said, "Oh, there's my man," and went outside,' Cockerill says. 'There was a big kiss on the lawn with their arms around each other, and it was perfectly obvious.'

Just as McCartney and Mills were no longer hiding their love away, Paul was also paying a moving homage to his late wife. On 10 January, he donated $1 million apiece to Arizona Cancer Research and the Sloane-Kettering Cancer Center in New York, where Linda had received treatment. (Paul made it a stipulation of the gift that no animals be used in any form of testing.) Meanwhile, Stephen Connock, chairman of the Ralph Vaughan Williams Society, and himself a cancer sufferer, had invited McCartney to co-compose a suite that would be part tribute, part charity fundraiser. The result was *A Garland for Linda*, which was released by EMI Classics on 7 February. McCartney's contribution was Nova, which he'd written in the days immediately following his wife's death. The shouted refrain in the first verse, '*Are you there?*' was answered by a voice calling, 'I'm here in every song you sing.'

A Garland for Linda was performed later that spring at small venues in England and on the American east coast. McCartney was in the audience for the New York premiere, held at Riverside Church, the site of Linda's US memorial service just two years earlier. He was dressed for the occasion in a formal black suit, open-necked shirt and blue shoes, and was not accompanied by Heather Mills.

The press always loves a spicy Beatle romance. John and Yoko, Paul and Linda, George and Pattie, even Ringo and Barbara Bach had all filled the bill at one time or another. But none of the above could compete with the headlines that started up in the spring of 2000. As well as celebrating her birthday, McCartney and Mills had already managed a brief sailing trip off the coast of New England and enjoyed a week's break in the Caribbean, both of which made it into the *National Enquirer*. But the feeding frenzy really began on the night of 13 March, when they were seen leaving a restaurant in St John's Wood with the Ringo Starrs. The next afternoon, Paul and Heather were out strolling with his daughter Mary and her baby son. A reporter from the *Daily Star* waylaid them and asked McCartney if by chance he had 'anything to say about [his] relationship with Miss Mills.'

'Yes, we're very good friends,' Paul replied. 'She's a very impressive woman. We're an item.' The day the news broke worldwide

marked the start of the worst year of even Mills' life. Some of Fleet
Street's best and brightest minds would be devoted to raking through
her recent past, with a bumper crop of 'Come Together'-type stories.
'She gives her men sex, sex, and then even more sex – anywhere and
everywhere,' noted one old friend. 'She says she's giving Paul the
best sex of his life, and as much of it as he wants – no wonder he looks
happy.' Not all the coverage was quite as high-minded. Mills herself
would characterise her press image around 1995 as 'POOR DISABLED
MODEL OVERCOMES ADVERSITY', and five years later as 'YOU'RE
AFTER OUR ICON, YOU BITCH'.

Meanwhile, in late March, McCartney exclusively assured the *Sun*
that 'Linda would approve of my love for Heather.' A few weeks later
he enlightened the press with the knowledge that the two women
were 'very different', that he was still talking to his late wife, and that
she was 'thrilled' by his new relationship. But Linda had apparently
added: 'If I was there, you'd be dead meat, sucker.'

That summer, Paul bought Heather and himself a million-pound
beachfront villa in Hove, East Sussex, roughly an hour's drive from
his farm. This seemingly innocuous move brought a fresh media
salvo, with 'relationship experts' trundled out to speculate on
whether Mills had refused to live in Linda's homes, while freely
offering advice couched in terms like 'sad . . . tragic . . . with his wife
dead less than three years, is Paul really ready to marry again?'

In July, McCartney and Mills flew to Reykjavik, where she was the
guest speaker at a conference on women's rights and disarmament
issues. Paul stayed in the background, but was seen to chat affably
with Eirikur Einarsson, president of the burgeoning Icelandic Beatles
Club. The couple's property-buying blitz continued in the autumn,
when they acquired a home reputedly furnished 'like a Sixties
Playboy club' with a wall TV, hot tub, jukebox and kooky artwork,
located a few miles from the Eastmans' estate on Long Island.

Linda's four children were said to have been perturbed by some of
these apparent lapses in taste. Publicly, however, goodwill reigned.

'We get on so well it's hilarious,' Mills told *Vanity Fair*. 'We get along brilliantly. I'm closest to Heather [McCartney]. We speak every day. We're so close she's like another sister!' Eighteen months later, both Heather and her half-brother James would reportedly decline to attend Mills' wedding. Patrons at a New York art gallery, meanwhile, were apparently startled to hear Stella McCartney turn to Paul and shout, 'You've chosen her over your own family!' before leaving the scene in tears.

McCartney's unlikely dalliance in such genres as prog, grime, industrial, techno and thrash continued, in August 2000, with the release of *Liverpool Sound Collage*. Among the titles on the five-track CD: Plastic Beetle (eight-and-a-half minutes of recycled drum loops, backward pianos and ambient traffic noise), Made Up (street interviews and snatches of sea shanties, on a bed of tinkling cymbals) and Free Now, a melange of swooping, rock 'n' roll guitar, angelic choirs and archival Abbey Road chit-chat, credited to McCartney, the Beatles and Super Furry Animals – the record retailer's nightmare when it was first announced ('Fabs Back in Business!'), then shelved as a single. *Liverpool Sound Collage* came packaged in a collage of its own: Paul's crucifix-shaped rendering of a screaming man, a corpse, a darkened corridor and a blonde woman not unlike Linda. The album died commercially, but proved a point. For every Bip Bop in the McCartney oeuvre there was something like this.

Bill Clinton's friend Denise Rich was in despair that summer, when the headline act cancelled on the eve of her annual New York charity ball, which was to be graced by both Clinton and Mikhail Gorbachev. McCartney, citing unspecified but well-founded 'concerns', was finally replaced by the one man Rich 'rank[ed] alongside him in the rock pantheon': Michael Jackson, who welcomed an opportunity to sit next to the president and first lady. Six months later, Clinton would issue an eleventh-hour pardon to Rich's fugitive billionaire ex-husband, Marc, who'd been facing sixty-five federal indictments regarding the biggest tax fraud in US history. Even in terms of a most elastic political morality – that of Clinton's White House – it was a bold decision, one which was followed by congressional subpoenas for all concerned. The blaring headlines – 'TRUTH BEHIND "CHARITY" FUNDRAISER: WHO CAME, PAID AND SANG FOR THEIR SUPPER' – seemed to confirm the wisdom of Paul's non-appearance.

Back home, the online subscription service MP3.com would testify to their admiration of McCartney's music by making it widely available on the internet. It was only the latest of several alleged piracies that he was to fight in court. There was also a long and, to some, unseemly spat with the one-time Quarry Men pianist John 'Duff' Lowe over the ownership of a forty-year-old demo tape of That'll Be The Day. The full majesty of the High Court would be required to rule that this barely audible recording, worth some £70,000, was rightfully Paul's. There then arose the question of how someone at a car boot sale managed to buy a second-hand PC 'containing 108 files relating to Sir Paul McCartney's private pecuniary affairs', as the legalese put it. 'Top merchant bankers Morgan Grenfell,' explained the Daily Express, had apparently 'failed to erase the memory contained on the computer's hard disc.' This matter, too, went to law. Very quickly, a defence counsel recalls, 'we realised you didn't trifle with Sir Paul, who had this strangely powerful organisation around him.' But to the staff at MPL, the most 'strangely powerful' person on the premises was the man in the penthouse suite. One giant in the recording industry, with seventy or eighty devoted employees of his own, regularly announced his arrival in the building by asking meekly, 'Where's God?'

Previously 'not worried one bit' by Third World privation, McCartney was also the most liberal of rock stars, notably towards sick children and animals. Some of his blunt views on product testing ironically pitted him against his friend Jane Asher, a patron of the group Seriously Ill for Medical Research. 'It's very hard to see how any rational person can object to carefully controlled experiments used to develop drugs and medical techniques,' Asher commented. 'I believe that some form of animal testing will be needed for many years to come, and we shouldn't have to apologise for it.'

The Beatles again took their past to the bank with *1*, the twenty-seven-track CD released in November 2000. In a tribute to the staying power of classic rock, it went gold at the same time as both the latest Elvis and *Bowie at the Beeb*, becoming the top-grossing album of the year. On its first day, *1* sold a total of 105,424 copies in the UK, compared with the 13,000 the Spice Girls' latest managed. Not long after that, McCartney confirmed that he was 'dead chuffed' and 'thrilled by the continued success.'[*]

Nor had the melody gods quite flown. That's what the heavyweight critics said. On a trip to New York, Paul had found himself back in the Carlyle hotel, 'a very des res . . . I was on the seventy-third floor and it was a fantastic big suite with a plate glass window overlooking Central Park. To the side there was a black Steinway piano, so it was like walking in Cole Porter's life . . . I thought if the neighbours could stand it, I'd try and write something.' They could; he did. Porter himself might not have been shamed by the result, a raw ballad of uncharacteristic vulnerability, called Your Loving Flame. Within an hour Paul was ready to perform the song to an audience, and so rang its subject, who happened to be at her desk in London writing a petition to world leaders. Hearing that distant but familiar voice, and the lines about their spending eternity together, Heather broke off from her appeal and wept.

Mills' main focus in 2001 was on her Adopt-a-Minefield charity, which would be launched in June. Paul's was on finding a band. This came to include the American guitarists Rusty Anderson and, later,

---

[*] He was apparently less pleased to see 'a large picture of John Lennon' next to the listing for Yesterday, and would soon resume his campaign for a credit change.

Brian Ray, the man-mountain drummer Abe Laboriel Jr and 'Wix' Wickens from the old firm. Once past the audition, they found him warm and witty – 'happy to get a round in', as one of them says, 'and not to swagger around with twelve minders.' (Paul also noted that he was partial to a pint, and 'loved taking the Tube home' instead of a car.) There were relatively few fifty-nine-year-old millionaires who still pushed themselves the way he did or slipped as easily into his persona as a kind of pop salesman, sometimes trying yet also touchingly sincere. By now he'd become that persona so completely that even the band playfully referred to him as 'Fab Wacky Thumbs Aloft', as *Smash Hits* had dubbed him in the Eighties. The total package, Paul McCartney, was like a tuned-up version of an old-fashioned Hollywood star with the added bonus of humour. His friend Grace Slick says, 'It's as though he's the son of Fred Astaire and the Marx Brothers' kid sister.' That's close.

Before Heather's arrival, McCartney's sometime 'image consul-tant' was more confined to ensuring that his client look 'very dignified – very regal' and, above all, that he appeared to age grace-fully. 'I'll be leaving the grey in,' Paul had assured *Rolling Stone* in 1986. 'My wife actually likes it. When you're past forty the game's up, you know?' Fifteen years later, McCartney not only dyed his hair a youthful chestnut but took to padding around in trainers, snugly cut jeans and a variety of bright red T-shirts. (He then added women's false fingernails in a bid to improve his guitar playing.) *New York* magazine was unimpressed. 'Sir Paul,' it wrote, 'is beginning to look like the Elvis of 1968: intact, more or less, but teetering on the precipice of something unbecoming. And Ms Mills, who seems to be cottoning to the role of McCartney's Colonel Parker, may be the last person he needs whispering in his ear.'

Meanwhile, Heather's refusal to kowtow to 'the great Fab' was a source of both mild concern and amusement to their friends. 'Paul, we *can't* go on the bus,' she once told him at Cavendish Avenue, it's said, when he suggested catching his beloved 189 to Oxford Street.

She broke off from another conversation when Get Back came on the radio by asking him, straight-faced, 'Who's that group?' A larger question concerned Heather's much-aired relationship with Paul's children. As Ruth McCartney had had cause to say, 'Bonding with a partner's kids is hard enough', even without the media, requiring a high degree of tact and passing familiarity with the concept of self-abnegation. It has to be said that Mills didn't quite conform to this ideal, but continued to insist loyally that 'I speak to Heather, Paul's eldest, forty minutes every day. Every day! And Stella and I get on brilliantly.' Just weeks earlier, Mills told *New York*, Stella had even issued a press release 'say[ing] how much the two women liked each other.'

This came as news to one Mesh Chibber, who was Stella's publicist. 'No,' he replied firmly. '*No*. Stella never discusses her private life, so a press release would never have been issued.'

The upside to having reporters 'literally dig through your rubbish', Heather would note, was the opportunity it brought to focus attention on her charity. On 12 June 2001, she and Paul appeared on the top-rated CNN programme *Larry King Live* to discuss her campaign against landmines. It was a pivotal moment. After forty years in broadcasting, King had long since become the self-styled 'Pope of Celebrityville', conferring instant ordainment on those politicians, reality-TV stars and lovable felons typically gracing his show. Mills would become something of a fixture in CNN's Studio 11C in years to come, apparently relishing the way in which King slips his guests into a hot tub of mutual reassurance and respect. After that, there was an anti-climactic meeting with the US Secretary of State, Colin Powell, who emerged to tell reporters: 'We had a good debate, and are very proud of our efforts to support the Adopt-a-Minefield program. We still have some concerns about the convention Mr McCartney and Ms Mills are so supportive of, [but] I'm very pleased to have a chance to exchange views with both of them. Now I turn them over to you, while I have to go back to work.'

In between the lobbying, McCartney and his group had gathered at Hollywood's Henson studios (the old Chaplin sound-stage) to record the album that became *Driving Rain*. The band loved it: they plugged in prompt at eleven every morning and went home by teatime. For years, Paul had gone in for long pre-production meetings and interminable rehearsals, but now he wanted to work at Beatle pace. 'We didn't fuss about it,' he reported. 'I didn't even tell them what we were going to do until the day we were going to do it. Nobody knew what I was going to pull out of the hat.'

On 14 June, Mills and McCartney hosted an Adopt-a-Minefield gala in Los Angeles. She gave a speech and presented some awards. He recited his poem Jerk Of All Jerks. (The title referred to John Lennon's killer.) By then Paul was back in the charts with *Wingspan*, a two-disc anthology and TV special of the same name, each of which plugged the other. It was a spectacular success: the CD sold 260,000 copies during its first week of release in the US, compared to the 40–50,000 typically enjoyed by most greatest-hits collections. Promotional *Wingspan* knickers were offered for sale on the website, while the musicians each got a form letter from MPL and a cheque – enough for that used car, in Henry McCullough's case. 'The great thing is,' Paul told *Mojo*, 'it vindicates Linda. I know she wanted to do the *Wingspan* thing . . . I know she always wanted the record put straight. And this does. You see her playing. You hear her singing beautifully . . . You see why *she had to be in the group.*'

On Monday morning, 23 July, Paul and Heather drove to the Lake District and registered at the Sharrow Bay hotel, where they took up residence in a two-storey waterfront suite, separated by a rose garden from the main building. They were there on a brief holiday before flying back to California. Just before dinner on the first evening, McCartney did something that was both in and out of character, falling to one knee to present Heather with a sapphire and diamond engagement ring that had cost him a whopping £18,000. Mills would record what followed in her hurriedly-to-be-revised autobiography, *A Single Step*:

> 'I love you, will you marry me?' he said.
> The room went all fuzzy. I wanted to cry, but couldn't. I wanted
>   to speak, but couldn't.
> 'Well?' Paul asked.
> 'Yesss,' I squeaked.

When the news broke on the 26th, certain friends would remark that Heather actually reminded them of the 'ballsy' Linda (whose own ring, incidentally, cost £12). To others, it was Mills' keen ambition, both for herself and Paul, that distinguished the two wives. 'From what I understand,' says McCartney's guitarist Rusty Anderson, 'Linda had always persuaded him to keep a low profile . . . That's in direct contrast to Heather, who tells him, "Go out there, flaunt it, do it, go" . . . I think spouses are very influential in the lives of musicians.'

Nor had Linda ever commented on her marriage in quite the terms Heather adopted in *Vanity Fair*: 'I'm really happy. It's incredibly passionate. It's intense all the time . . . I've met someone who's at the same level intellectually, but who's like a little boy, so I feel like I'm a grown woman and he's my little boy . . . I could eat him! When you love someone, you just like their smell, and he smells fantastic. I think when you find your soul mate, you could sleep under their armpits. I'm like a little dog. He says, "You're always sniffing me!"'

Paul bridled at the notion that he was in any way, shape or form ever henpecked, or that his fiancée might be – to quote the *Daily Mail* – 'hugely vain, bloody-minded, confident, combative and pushy.' By all accounts he was quite satisfied, like Mills, that 'landmines are the scourge of our time . . . They take or wreck three lives an hour, every hour of every day. We have to come together to stop that.' The issue was at the very top of the couple's agenda when they embarked on yet another publicity tour of New York in September 2001.

On Tuesday morning, the 11th, Paul and Heather were sitting in the first-class cabin of a BA jet scheduled to fly from Kennedy airport to Heathrow. After a long delay, the captain's voice came over the intercom to advise his passengers of an 'incident' at the World Trade Center. 'If you look out of the right side of the aircraft you can see the smoke,' he added. A few minutes later everyone filed back into the terminal building, stunned.

McCartney became something of a goodwill ambassador in the weeks ahead, visiting police and fire houses, moving about the city offering sympathy and helping organise the 20 October all-star concert at Madison Square Garden. The day of the show started badly when Paul somehow ricked his back while leaving his car. There was then a band to break in and an unreleased song to debut – both of which happened in front of a TV, radio and internet audience of eighty million, more than had watched the Beatles' first appearance on *Ed Sullivan*. Rusty Anderson recalls it suddenly dawning on him that he was part of an act headlining over the likes of Bon Jovi, the Who and Jagger-Richards. And it was another triumph: the new single, Freedom, went over so well that the band played it three times. When Paul saw the faces of some of the victims' families looking up at him from the front row, he started to cry.

A work with a title like *Ecce Cor Meum* doesn't raise high expectations of hit parade success. In the event, McCartney's latest classical venture was followed, just two days later, by the album *Driving Rain* – with Freedom added as a last-minute 'bonus track'. While it was good to hear that he'd rediscovered his knack of consoling America in times of crisis (he also made a substantial cash gift to the bereaved), the first fruits of this therapeutic exercise didn't bode well. 'I'm talkin' 'bout freedom' Paul twice announced in the song's chorus, which found him elaborating, 'I will fight/For the right/To live in freedom.' If that didn't exactly have the world singing along, the rest of the album was characteristically tuneful, in a low-key, almost worryingly mellow way. McCartney had been here before, of course, and certain tracks, albeit goosed by modern production techniques, could have come straight off *Ram*. The new work threw in some mournful synths, and the sleeve notes refer to such matters as being 'uploaded into Logic Audio', but the essential illusion of innocence remained.

Driving Rain came with a striking cover photograph of McCartney at a urinal, an image captured for posterity by his new Casio camera-watch. The album spent a week on the chart.

Paul wasn't doing much promotion that fall, just *Top of the Pops* and Jonathan Ross and a bit of Saturday morning television. Mostly he was back in New York, fundraising and visiting George Harrison. The latter's cancer had spread to his brain. A sometimes troubled relationship that had begun on the top deck of a green Corpy bus would be resolved forty-five years later, in a close, darkened room in the Radiosurgery Center of Staten Island University hospital. 'The best thing for me was seeing him for a couple of hours,' Paul said, 'laughing and joking and holding his hand. Afterwards, I realised I'd never, ever held his hand. We'd been to school together and on buses together and we didn't hold each other's hands. It was like a compensation; he was rubbing his thumb up and down my hand and it was very nice.' As Paul sat there reminiscing, the sound system built into the adjacent day room had begun playing its regular afternoon selection of muzak numbers, apparently programmed in chronological order. First piping in some Sinatra, followed by cocktail-lounge versions of Motown and surfing hits. As if on cue, the startlingly raw Love Me Do. And then just the Beatles. Just the Beatles.

George died on 29 November.

'He was a very brave man with a heart of gold,' Paul said, 'but also someone who didn't suffer fools gladly. I'll always remember that without him it all wouldn't have been possible.

'I'll miss him dearly and I'll always love him – he's my baby brother.'

On 11 December, McCartney closed the Nobel ceremonies by performing his song for Heather, Your Loving Flame, and Freedom. He said, 'The first one I wrote for my fiancée, and the second one I wrote for the American people after 11 September, but tonight I'd like to dedicate them both to my friend George.' In London, he signed copies of his book *Paintings* (1,700 customers) and made various appearances for animal-rights groups. When a hunting ban again came up before Parliament, Paul wrote Tony Blair an open letter, evoking the spectacle of 'packs of hounds chasing and savaging innocent animals, [an] activity that we, along with most British people, find cruel, unnecessary, unacceptable and outdated.' It followed on from a recent spate of such representations about GM foods, global warming and various foreign policy issues. Blair responded as best he could, with a statement, although he'd previously considered Paul a 'good mate'. At one stage, Cherie had even had his photograph up on the wall.

'We may have suffered the worst day in our history, but thank God there are still Beatles songs,' a former president had remarked of the Concert for New York. America had that much to console it when, after entertaining the crowd at Super Bowl XXXVI in New Orleans, McCartney announced his plans to go out on tour for the first time in nine years. Despite the layoff, he pronounced himself 'pretty hip'. Paul's horoscope and market research had both told him, several weeks in advance, of the success of the whole enterprise, thus sparing him the torments of self-doubt and first-night jitters other artists experience as they wait up till dawn to read the reviews. He was back in Hollywood in late March to perform Vanilla Sky, the theme to the film of the same name, at the Academy Awards; in the event, an

Oscar would be the one gong Paul, a sweep at the Critics' Choice and Golden Globes, failed to win.

Later that spring, the Public Record Office in London released the thirty-year-old transcript of *McCartney v Lennon, Harrison, Starr.* Long queues would immediately form to read the full contents of File J84/646, which confirmed that Paul had once thought Allen Klein a bit pushy. There was also yet another lawsuit involving the original lyric sheet to Hey Jude, which a judge ordered should be returned to its author. That meant a great deal to him, Paul said.

'None of us are here that long. This is the main event.' So saying, an energised McCartney hit the road: over the next eight months he'd play fifty dates in North America, Mexico and Japan, grossing $126 million, thus making the 1993 tour look like a whelk stall. There were heady scenes along the way, where the combination of Boomer nostalgia and musically-assisted post-9/11 therapy would make Beatlemania seem merely civil by comparison. This was a seller's market, and Paul and his management knew it. Ticket prices topped out at between $250 and $300, even before all the spurious handling charges. For real skinflints there were a few 'restricted view' bargains at sixty bucks. A couple earning $25,000 a year after tax would have had to spend a week's salary to watch the two-hour concert without the aid of binoculars. According to one trade paper, Paul had demanded and got a 90/10 split with the local promoters. No wonder he seemed to bow in thanks to those in the premium seats down front.

The actual show followed a bizarre bit of performance art as costumed characters wound their way through the stalls, with a variety of freaks and contortionists prancing wildly on stage. This striking warm-up act was accompanied by a pulsing, techno sound-track, never formally introduced, but by the same composer of such works as The Frog Chorus. (McCartney himself was behind the curtain, leading his musicians in a prayer.) This being America, and it being 2002, concertgoers were meanwhile subjected to lengthy security checks and a variety of exhortations appearing in either written or spoken form. Sit here. Don't stand up. Give us your cameras, phones and lasers. Don't smoke. No outside food or beverages. Don't disrespect the staff. Be courteous. Your patience is appreciated. No latecomers admitted. All rise for the national anthem. Have a nice concert. Eventually, there's a tribal drum beat on the PA and a puff of smoke. Just as dreamily as it appeared, the circus troupe vanishes, leaving behind a beaming McCartney and his men. The audience goes nuts.

After opening night, in Oakland, the whole spectacle settled into a groove. Paul's ad-libbed remarks were neatly done, as was the cherry-bomb moment in Live And Let Die, the acoustic interlude, the blistering *Abbey Road* finale. These crowds had come to be pleasured, and you could feel them willing the show on. He didn't disappoint: there were generous helpings of *Sgt. Pepper* and the White Album, and moving tributes to John, George and Linda. Yesterday ranked up there with the original. The entire, briskly paced programme was a glorious rebellion against the march of time, and well up with the main contemporary competition – the Stones, Elton John and Cher's interminable farewell tour.

On 6 April, McCartney became the highest paid entertainer even in Vegas history when he appeared at the MGM Grand for a flat fee of $4 million, part of a two-show gross of $5.6 million. A fortnight later, backstage at Madison Square Garden, he was made an honorary detective by the New York police department. Around one the following morning, he and Mills stopped at a Greenwich Village restaurant frequented by celebrities for a late supper. A minder went in first to get a table. As the couple was getting out of the car and walking towards the door, the bartender called out in a loud voice, 'Ladies and gentlemen, Sir Paul McCartney.' They left.

Back in Beverly Hills, McCartney enlivened the post-gig party at the Four Seasons by staging a mock drug bust, complete with uniforms, of his friend Geoff Baker. Everyone laughed at the time. In

Atlanta, Paul drove down to the Language Research Facility and, while the cameras rolled, jammed with two 500-pound bonobo apes. 'We found ourselves communicating with them easily,' he reported. 'The male played keyboards and his sister played drums . . . Music's in their blood.' McCartney's own need to perform transcended mere cash or his love of putting on a show. Later that night, following his sold-out concert at the Philips Arena, Paul sat down incognito and played the piano in his hotel lounge.

When all the numbers came to be added up McCartney was comfortably the year's top attraction, with the Stones in second place. A few cynics asked how such characters would have felt if in 1967, the year of *Sgt. Pepper* and acid trips, the big draws had been Rudy Vallee and others who crooned through a megaphone. Paul didn't care. Never one to miss a chance for cross-pollination, he went on to release a live album and video, various TV specials and a lavish, coffee-table book on the tour. 'I suppose I do already have a lot of money,' he allowed. 'And you know, I really don't mind earning it. I never have and never will. It's our capitalistic ethic.'

In between barnstorming American stadiums, McCartney appeared at the Walker gallery in Liverpool, Heather having loosened former inhibitions about exhibiting, for a 'Long-awaited retrospective' of his art. This included *Hottest Linda*, a nude of his late wife, and driftwood sculptures with such titles as *Running Legs with Penis* and *Large Cheetah, Small Cheetah*. Few of the reviews seemed prophetic of a glorious second career. 'McCartney is potentially better than a chancer,' the *Daily Mail* declared on 24 May. 'He has promise. That said, none of these works is there on any artistic merit.'

A week later, McCartney closed the show at the Queen's jubilee concert. It was a change: a few minutes of warm applause instead of hysteria. Paul bumped into Joe Cocker backstage and remarked that they were both 'lucky to be here' and 'blessed to be working'. 'He was gushing all night about it,' says another artist. '[McCartney] was saying, "This is what it's all about. I don't care if anyone buys the records. I have to do this.'"

Another kind of turn would follow. Paul and Heather were busy planning their wedding, among the most elaborate Busby Berkeley production numbers British showbusiness had seen, if not preparing quite as diligently to be a stepfamily. According to published reports, Stella either didn't offer, or wasn't asked to design the bridal dress. (Mills was quoted as saying that Stella's creations, which had featured strategically-positioned slogans such as 'Hot' and 'Wet', were 'too tarty'.) At one stage there had apparently been plans for Mary to take the official pictures and for James to perform a song, neither of which happened. Some of the apparent tensions surfaced one evening that spring during the course of a dinner at Simply Italian, a popular restaurant near the farm in Sussex. Heather McCartney was deep in conversation with Paul, who was heard urging her to 'wear that white dress your mother gave you. We'd like that.' Other diners listened, rapt, as Heather – who happened to be four years older than her namesake – replied, 'I'll wear *what I want*,' ('*fucking well want*', in some versions) before changing the subject.

'We were crazy,' McCartney said. 'We had a big argument the night before we got married and it was nearly called off. We were very up and down, quite funky . . .'

He was speaking about Linda, but it was a reasonable sketch of events thirty-three years later. At the end of May 2002, the British press reported an apparent lovers' tiff at the Turnberry Isle hotel in Miami, caused by Heather's request that Paul remove the wedding band given to him by Linda. Instead, Heather's own ring somehow took flight off their fifth floor balcony. According to a security guard, McCartney was then heard protesting, 'I don't want to marry you! The wedding's off!' For several minutes the suite appeared to be in Vesuvian eruption, bringing worried aides running from their rooms. Some of the other $1,000-a-night guests reportedly rang the desk to complain about Paul's language, which, in the assessment of one Dan Chernow, on the floor below, was 'ripe'.

After the ring was defenestrated, McCartney summoned the hotel staff to help look for it, to no avail. It was eventually located several days later, with the help of a metal detector, and hand-delivered to London. Heather later told an interviewer, 'We were playing a game – having a joke, doing catch with the ring.' Friends familiar with Paul's spending habits thought this version unlikely.

In the end the wedding took place as scheduled that 11 June, on the 1,000-acre estate of Castle Leslie in County Monaghan, Ulster. There were 300 guests, who were served champagne at £180 a bottle in two marquees erected beside a lake, watched over by sixty armed security guards, all part of a package reportedly costing £2 million. (Paul's wedding to Linda, by contrast, had totalled around £60.) Mills, swathed in an ecru lace dress of her own design, had entered the chapel to the strains of Heather, a tune Paul wrote for her on *Driving Rain*. 'She briefly faltered and wept while making her vows,' Geoff Baker reported. At the conclusion of the forty-minute ceremony, the newly-weds walked down the aisle as another McCartney number, Wedding March from the 1966 film *The Family Way*, played on the organ. At the groom's insistence, there was no prenuptial; the couple honeymooned in the Caribbean.

Heather was thirty-four, Paul turned sixty a week later.

In July, he showed the Queen around his etchings at the Walker gallery. 'I think she liked them,' McCartney would venture. 'She said they were very colourful, and I took that as a compliment.' He some-how managed to narrowly miss Yoko Ono, who was in town that week for the opening of John Lennon International airport. Nor would Yoko attend any of Paul's American concerts. 'We're just not the greatest of buddies,' he noted. 'Everyone has a family, and sometimes your Uncle Eddie is not your greatest friend. It's like that with us. Too many things have gone down.'

When the tour wound up in mid-November, McCartney turned to

the latest Beatles remix project, *Let It Be*. It had always been a wretched conclusion to the band's career, and had evidently nagged at Paul for thirty years. One of his last conversations with George Harrison had concerned the title track, on which George's original, muted solo had been replaced by a more florid one. Nor had McCartney ever quite come to terms with The Long And Winding Road being overdubbed (or, as he put it, 'totally fucked') by Phil Spector's orchestra.

The upshot? Everyone went back to Abbey Road and finally re-edited the album, which emerged a year later as *Let It Be . . . Naked*.

Whatever records McCartney broke or awards he potted, it was his home life that would engender the most headlines in years ahead. The puns ranged from 'LOVE ME GOO' to 'A DAY IN THE STRIFE', and touched on everything from Paul's art exhibitions to his wife's reproductive system, with some choice items in-between. At one stage, Geoff Baker would issue a formal statement after his boss was criticised first for failing to sign an autograph in B&Q one Sunday afternoon, and then for snubbing a fan named Vaseem Adnan who encountered him walking by the Thames.

'Paul's approach to preserving privacy in situations like this is as he's repeatedly said,' Baker explained. 'It's, "Sorry, I don't do signings when I'm in a restaurant or shopping, but I'll say hello, shake your hand and have a chat with you. I just don't always want to do autographs."'

This was a notable paraphrase. What McCartney actually told Adnan was, 'Fuck off. I'm a pedestrian on a private visit.'

The press were on his case again in May 2003, when Adur district council announced plans for a new lorry depot 'with substantial benefits for the local economy', near the McCartneys' home in Hove. After some months of delicate negotiations, during which a number of prominent local residents, among them Zoe Ball and Fatboy Slim, had agreed to lend their support, it was reported that 'a global icon' had queried the council's decision on the grounds of 'environmental integrity'. On 23 July, the protesters lost their case.

McCartney was back on the road that Easter, for his first European dates in ten years. As always, there was wild acclaim for the Beatles suite and polite acceptance of the new album, which, by comparison, sounded so safe and middle-of-the-road that it could have come packaged with promotional cat's eyes. On 10 May he played the first ever rock concert in Rome's Colosseum, a charity affair with a paying gate of just 300. Crowds roughly a thousand times larger lined up in the Via Appia for his show the following night. On 24 May Paul was in Moscow, where the tour took on all the trappings of a state visit, including a warm Kremlin welcome by Vladimir Putin.

'I wish to propose a toast,' the interpreter rumbled in McCartney's ear. 'In our country we have seen in years past perhaps too few Britons of Sir Paul's progressive stamp. We hope in the next few hours to hear from him much that is vital, and perhaps we may in turn inform him of our own proud culture. So let me at once, then, since there is a saying that too long a cooking spoils the stew, offer to drink, firstly to the success of the visit and, in the second place, to the mutual gain of international goodwill.'

After the vodka, McCartney and Mills enjoyed a few minutes alone with the president, with whom they debated landmines. On 16 June, Putin revealed that he had written to Heather to thank her for her views. Further consideration of the matter 'would require careful diplomatic and military expert analysis' and a 'thorough, fully informed dialogue,' the Tass agency added.

McCartney ended his tour that month, at the King's Dock in Liverpool. All 30,000 tickets sold out in four hours, though this prodigal return was somewhat marred by reports that 5,000 seats had been reserved for town-hall staff – 'as per standard Council practice.' The local Labour party leader Joe Anderson didn't care for it. He was 'appalled that we would give [our] workforce privileged oppor-tunities. We are all public servants and that doesn't mean we should be treated better than anyone else . . . Someone made a crap decision.' Despite that, it had been a triumphant fourteen months, with total box office sales of £128 million and rave reviews that dubbed McCartney 'Saint Paul' and 'one of only two men whose mere presence guarantees pandemonium on the streets – the other being the Pope.'

So wild new allegations that Mills was a 'complete fruitcake' who, according to her ex-husband, 'should have "Buyer beware" stamped on her forehead' were, while wide of the mark, a distinct comedown for the former Beatle. A pregnant Heather countered that the press had turned against her only because she 'rarely open[ed] up in public.' Speaking of McCartney's first marriage, she said: 'For me, what people don't realise is that I have a huge amount of respect for that relationship. She did a great job on him – she trained him up well.'

On 11 June, McCartney and Mills returned to Castle Leslie for a private ceremony, 'just to say a prayer of thanks for [their] good fortune.' They booked into the Red Room, where they spent their wedding night; it featured what was the first fully plumbed bath in Ireland, and a bed said somehow to be 'lucky'.

McCartney, certainly, was better off in his sixties than ever before. When he walked off stage at King's Dock, he was worth around £750 million – twice as much as Britain's next richest entertainer – just twenty years after his career, written off as 'slushy' and 'wince-inducing', had appeared to be in free fall. MPL now employed a staff of 140 full- and part-time managers, account handlers, secretaries, valets and PRs. But it wasn't just the money that kept those legendary thumbs aloft. 'I love what I do,' Paul revealed on his website. 'I love playing music and the intense feedback you get from the audience . . . It's all about the excitement of contact with people.'

Another man might have throttled back, but for McCartney much of the charm lay in 'prov[ing] it night after night.' Almost immediately one tour ended, the office was busy planning the next one.

After that, there was little to report but Mills' pregnancy, and the unvaunted ferocity of the couple's various third-party feuds. There was Yoko, for one, whose camp reacted badly to Paul's billing of nineteen songs on his *Back in the US* live double-album to 'McCartney-Lennon'. Yoko's long-time friend and spokesman Elliot Mintz would comment that 'Sir Paul ha[d] kidnapped Eleanor Rigby' while her attorney Peter Shukat called the move 'ridiculous, absurd and petty', before adding that he was 'actively exploring' the prospect of legal action. (At that stage, Ringo would remark that 'the way Paul did it was underhand. He's wanted to do it for years . . . It was the wrong way to go about it.') Yoko herself retaliated by calling McCartney 'distant' and 'two-faced', while removing his name from the credit for Give Peace A Chance on John's *Legend* DVD. Paul told her not to get her knickers in a twist.

The row bespoke a wider disenchantment on McCartney's behalf. After forty-two years, he'd never quite reconciled himself to the terms of the original Northern Songs deal, or to the impositions it put on his work. Early in 2005, Paul was to have released the 'definitive collection' of his love songs, including Yesterday. Due, it was alleged, to Yoko's veto, the album never appeared.

The word from both sides was that the whole 'Lennon-McCartney' or 'McCartney-Lennon' epic arose out of Paul's famously protective feelings towards his 'babies', and was the latest manifestation of the intense business and personal rivalry between two titans, a rivalry which had only been heightened by the events of autumn 1966. 'That's the subtext of everything,' says a well placed, neutral observer.

Mills never wavered in her belief that certain parties were out for the McCartneys, and noted bluntly, 'It's jealousy. What else would it be?' During the next year or two, she found plenty of articles in the press to buttress this claim. In her first British interview since her wedding, Heather told Michael Parkinson, 'Everything I've worked

for in my life, tried to do and overcome, it's just all been forgotten
. . . It's all just "She's the bird of Paul McCartney" and it's just
knock, knock, knock. That's affected me badly.'

As to why people had singled her out for such obloquy, Heather
always cited her own belief in the doctrine of 'brutal honesty . . . I've
admitted everything – give[n] them ammo – because I thought, "Oh,
that'll inspire someone to say that, you know, even if you've done this
in your life you can get past it."' She went on to tell Parky of the
romantic walks she shared with her husband, how he planted a tree
for her in the garden, and the breakfast in bed he brought her every
morning. Despite the rosy picture, Heather accepted that 'there are
always problems with stepmothers. Think of Cinderella, there's the
wicked stepmum.'

On 30 August Stella McCartney married magazine publisher
Alasdhair Willis on the Isle of Bute, in a million-pound ceremony
she was said to have paid for herself. Earlier in the day, the bride
had held a memorial service for her mother, and wore a creation
inspired by Linda's own wedding outfit. Unnamed sources told the
press that 'The kids aren't getting on very well with their dad since
the arrival of Heather, and it's fair to say that relations have cooled
further since she announced she was pregnant.' (McCartney
would dismiss all this as pure fiction.) A few weeks earlier, Mills
had apparently forgotten to invite Stella, her two sisters or her
brother to a surprise party she threw for Paul's sixty-first birthday.
The alleged cold war between father and daughter was highlighted
when Stella then labelled him a 'tight bastard' for having sent her
to a state school.

'It was a mum-and-dad decision,' McCartney responded, 'and she
hasn't done badly by it. I'm not really that tight. Just careful.'

Stella's own business acumen was considered modest: in
December 2003 it emerged that her new label had lost £7.2 million
over two years. Also aggravating family tensions was the fact that
Mills, as reported, felt her stepdaughter's designs 'tarty', where-

upon Stella allegedly replied, 'Doesn't she know lace is out of fashion?' There was even a second generation Beatles-Stones feud to savour, when Sir Mick Jagger's model daughter Lizzie announced, 'It's no good just rehashing old trouser suits . . . [Stella] treats me like her sister, but I hardly know her. I really hate that rock-chick thing.'

Good copy. Even in the drenching rain of the worst floods in memory, there was a permanent media watch at each of the McCartneys' six British homes. Mills rewarded their vigilance by appearing in a variety of glamorous maternity frocks, and being quoted as saying that 'she want[ed] her child to have the best of everything – including an expensive education.' (This reputedly came as news to Paul.) Later, when asked the baby's sex, Heather grew untypically coy; pressed, she told Larry King that 'we know what it is and we know the name. We know everything, but we ain't saying.' She did elaborate, however, on the day she had told Paul her news. 'I went upstairs and he was in a meeting,' Mills said. 'And I kept walking in and out of the meeting, because I'd done the test and it was positive . . . And then he came out and I showed him. We both broke down and started crying. It was just a miracle.'

Later that summer, Mills applied to the US Patent and Trademark Office to put her name on a line of 'quality prosthetic limbs', apparently wanting in the American market, to be launched in 2004. She showed a range of them to King, but declined to remove her own leg while on air, as she had the previous year. For Heather's admirers, this latest venture was proof of her dazzling skills as a businesswoman: her visionary leadership, her legendary drive and her willingness to do whatever it took. For critics such as the anonymous weekly *Review* correspondent, 'Lady McC has never cracked New York's elite and never will, because of too much hair gel, overconfidence and those grotesque interviews.'

*

On 20 September 2003, Britain awoke to the news that Paul McCartney was under police investigation. It followed a late-night outing to see David Blaine, the anti-escapologist, suspended in his glass box above Tower Bridge. Geoff Baker had taken the opportunity to tip off one Kevin Wheal, a photographer working for the *Evening Standard*, that 'someone very big' would be in the vicinity. McCartney, however, had no intention of having pictures taken of his visit after a meal out with friends, and was said to have lost his rag, shouting that he was there 'to see this stupid cunt' (Blaine) and shoving Wheal away. A member of the public chose that moment to stroll up and ask to shake McCartney's hand. He was invited to fuck off. Turning to his publicist, Paul observed, 'You're bang out of order. You're fired.'

By lunchtime the next day, Baker had issued a statement explaining that his sacking was all a joke. McCartney was a 'great guy and one of the lads,' he said. 'We pull each other's legs all the time.' The police, meanwhile, took details from Paul, his entourage and the paparazzo, and confirmed that they were dealing with 'claims and counterclaims of assault' from all parties. A spokesman for David Blaine added that he slept through the whole thing.

One Saturday in October, a boxer named Justin Newton took his two-year-old son Billy to the Hove branch of Toys 'R' Us, lost sight of the lad for a moment and then saw 'an old bloke' pick him up. Newton (career record: 37–2, with seventeen knockouts) approached the man and asked, 'What the fuck are you doing with my kid?' According to press reports, McCartney was 'full of apologies and clearly upset that his actions could have been misconstrued. Paul told Billy he was one of the most beautiful boys he'd ever seen and revealed he couldn't wait to be a dad again.'

On the 27th, McCartney drove Heather the 400 yards from Cavendish Avenue to St John and St Elizabeth, one of the leading private hospitals in England. Linda had been one of its many celebrity friends in the Seventies. Press stories soon circulated of

Paul 'review[ing] every charge to his bill' and 'negotiating a discount from the florists'. Beatrice Milly McCartney was born on the evening of the 28th, a month early but 'perfect and quite, quite beautiful,' her parents announced. 'I want to be a proper mum as much as I can,' Mills added. 'I want to be totally focused and spend some quality time with the baby.' The infant was named after Heather's late mother and Paul's aunt Milly, who died in 1993. One person not invited to the christening was Heather's father Mark, who had been estranged from her for twenty years. Speaking to the tabloids, Mr Mills drew on a range of footballers' superlatives. 'I'm over the moon,' he reportedly announced. 'It's a result. [But] it looks as though I'll never see my granddaughter. It hurts to say that, but after the relationship I've had with Heather over the years I think I'll be denied any rights.'

Forty-eight hours later, McCartney went into the studio and re-recorded Mother And Child, an outtake from the *Let It Be* sessions, which he lushed up with violins and harps. The gloss was in stark contrast to the rest of the album, which emerged as . . . *Naked* on 18 November. Under Paul's direction, the engineers had removed all traces of Spector's orchestrations, erased certain overdubs, dumped Lennon's Dig It completely, and employed a more dignified running order. (In the 1970 version, the title track had been bracketed between John trilling 'Now we'd like to do 'Ark the Angels Come' and a dockside knees-up about a whore.) Overall, most critics considered it a significant improvement on the original.*

For three months that winter, McCartney was on top of the world. After a year of personal and professional success, the Christmas party for members of the crew was apparently a particularly festive affair. A buffet was laid out, toasts given, gifts exchanged. In one version of events (the author wasn't invited), Paul was said to have made a short speech, then reached into the pocket of his tracksuit trousers

---

* *Let It Be . . . Naked* rounded off a poor year for Phil Spector, awaiting trial for the murder of his house guest, the actress Lana Clarkson.

and brought out a piece of paper. 'Almost forgot,' he said. 'Someone gave me this on the way in. It says, "one". For a second, I thought it was *Naked*'s chart position.' His audience smirked; they knew that the album had topped off at number seven. Flashing his familiar, cheeky grin, Paul continued: 'Well, I'm sorry to report it's not that . . . it's the number of candles on Bea's next birthday cake.'

Everyone laughed, the way people do when the boss cracks a good one. There was a generous bonus that year.

After four decades, McCartney was well aware that 'the media harass me [even] when I do fuck all,' as he put it at the time of the David Blaine incident. Even so, the coverage in early 2004 would mark a new low. On 23 January, the Associated Press reported that 'Heather Mills must undergo major pelvic surgery. Metal plates inserted in her following a road accident eleven years ago need to be replaced as a result of her pregnancy . . . "The weight of the baby caused them to tear apart", her spokeswoman said.' At that the tabloids cleared entire news pages for graphic accounts of Heather's obstetric problems, including an impassioned debate of the respective merits of caesarean and vaginal delivery. As Paul was allegedly to remark, 'That bugger [an editor involved] would have to be tranquillised if I wrote about his missus the way he does about mine.'

A few days later, McCartney placed a call to the offices of the *Sun*. 'I'm not some stupid old git who fell for someone who looks good,' he assured them. 'That's rubbish. I'm not dumb . . . All my wife does is good things. I see the other side of her that people don't see because I'm married to her. The truth is, Heather never seeks publicity for all the work she does with her charity. And yet all people do is knock her. They don't see all the stuff she does without asking for any thanks or recognition . . . We're just a normal family, trying to do normal things.'

In March, McCartney was in Hollywood's Ocean Way studio, home of sunny Sixties classics like Don't Worry Baby and California

Dreamin', among many others. While there he collaborated with Brian Wilson, whose music, he'd recently said, 'was so deep, [it] reached down in me and made me cry', on a track called A Friend Like You. Wilson then announced that the two men would cut an album together. The good vibes continued on a variety of fronts. Mills made a full recovery, in time to be awarded a Melvin Jones Fellowship by the Lions Club for 'philanthropic work in the tradition of Diana, Princess of Wales'. The club's Elliot Shubert told *Hello*, 'A lot of celebrities lead charmed lives and don't give their time to charity. They occasionally throw a little bit of money here and there, but that's not how Heather works. She devotes her time and energy to helping people and to travelling to places where people need her. She doesn't just talk about things; she does them.'

Later that month, McCartney released his animated film *Tropic Island Hum*, featuring the lovable antics of Wirral the Squirrel. It would be part of a chart-topping DVD collection that autumn. The same rodent also starred in an 'original work conceived and created by Sir Paul' (though fleshed out by the author Philip Ardagh) called *High in the Clouds*, a triumph at the Bologna Children's Book Fair. Meanwhile, pop's Renaissance Man somehow found time for his 'freeing exercises' – painting, poetry, classical music. He and Mills were soon back in Liverpool, helping counsel a teenage girl who had lost a leg in a rail accident. Heather, emerging from her various health crises, was again '110 per cent committed' to her humani- tarian causes and, wherever possible, to ensuring Paul was involved. The worse the press, the harder they worked for acceptance.

McCartney had always been realistic about his own fame, which he never underestimated. 'He said to me, "I'm about uniting people, and you can expect everyone from grandmas to screaming kids,"' says one Midwest concert promoter. 'Particularly after 9/11, he definitely saw himself as one of the "reassuring points of light".'

On 25 May 2004, McCartney began a five-week tour of Europe;

it would include his first visit to Prague, his first to St Petersburg (his 3,000th gig) and his first to the Glastonbury festival. Every account of the trip depicts it as a summer of frat-house antics, good cheer and frequent practical jokes, apparently involving strippers. The London *Evening Standard* caught a bit of the flavour when it reported, 'Hard-rocking Macca has been ordered to turn down the juice at Millennium Dome practice sessions after neighbours complained. The ex-Beatle's "booming" music is carrying across the river to their homes in the Isle of Dogs, they claim. Eric Pemberton, 67, said: "I'd love to invite him over here and make him listen to this racket" . . . Greenwich council hopes to review the situation with Sir Paul, [whose] spokesman was unavailable.' The real shocker, it emerged, was that Geoff Baker wasn't even taken on much of the tour – the first he'd missed in fifteen years. Sometime that spring, McCartney's PR brief was quietly given to the Outside Organisation, distinguished handlers of the Victoria Beckham account.

McCartney's first impression as he ran on at Glastonbury – a man of sixty-two – was that in doing so he'd raised the average age in the place to twenty-five. The concert that followed was vintage stuff. So strong was the material, it could sustain even relics such as Paul's 'psychedelic rainbow' piano, not to mention all the joss sticks and lava lamps. By Hey Jude, the fists shaken aloft stretched back to the Acoustic Tent, recently graced by the Rutles (of *All You Need is Cash* fame), and off-key audience participation nearly drowned out the band. As one new admirer put it, 'Despite [McCartney] throwing in a few comments your dad would make, the hits flowed and it was bloody fantastic . . . the ultimate Beatles karaoke.'

Eight months later, *New Musical Express*, a paper that had denounced McCartney throughout the Eighties as an old fart, presented him with its Best Event award for Glastonbury.

Altogether, *The Times* agreed, Paul was a 'pretty groovy grandad.' In his seventh decade he seemed to be flourishing; 'happier in myself than when I was twenty-one,' he noted contentedly. 'I'm a very tomorrow kind of guy.' As he also acknowledged, 'bits of the Cross' kept surfacing, and always would, old tapes and films truffled up out of the archives and hyped as the latest 'lost Beatles classic'. Despite his being dubbed the 'rockin' geezer' by *NME* and others, McCartney politically speaking was no fogey. Later that summer he was back campaigning against the fur trade, demanding a ban on 'criminal force-feeding of geese' among other items and pronouncing on the current situation everywhere from Warsaw to Washington DC. Like so many others, he felt the American-led coalition 'too hasty' in invading Iraq.

Mills' star also continued to rise, with her exclusive CNN interview (while guest-hosting for King) of Paul Newman. This gave Heather an opportunity to share some thoughts on Afghanistan. 'I do a lot of work there,' she confided. 'It's as if we're paying the price for interfering with another country's way of life.' But, even so, 'some of the women I've spoken with, they wanted the freedom of choice. So, you know, what do you do?' Never one to be overawed, Heather proceeded to probe Newman on a variety of subjects, such as his marriage and the death of his only son, that he apparently preferred not to discuss.

But even then, the grilling wasn't quite over. 'I think you're very handsome' Mills told her guest, in closing. 'I don't just think you're handsome, I think by now that you're seventy-nine and you're still looking great, you should accept it.'

Some time later, the McCartneys made a legal complaint over the apparently innocuous suggestion that the family might move to America for a year so that Heather could pursue what the *New York Post* called her 'burgeoning TV career'.

Shortly after leaving the stage at Glastonbury, McCartney had reportedly sat down for a heart-to-heart with Geoff Baker, with the result that Baker resigned. Since 1989, the hippyish but supremely capable PR had been more than a mere media wrangler. It was Baker who'd first loyally denied that Linda was terminally ill, then successfully kept her death a complete secret until the family were safely back home in England. After that he'd gone on to rubbish the 'daft story' that McCartney and Mills would marry, before overseeing both the press and security arrangements at Castle Leslie and deftly negotiating a settlement between Heather and her wedding-dress suppliers, who'd claimed she owed them £10,000. It was hard to see what more he could have done, short of staying to sweep up the confetti. But Baker, it was widely reported, never quite hit it off with his new mistress. It was said that Mills had disapproved of him from the moment they met, and allegedly deemed him a 'bad influence'.

After several weeks of tactful silence, Baker would drop a broad hint as to the reasons for his departure. 'I don't think Heather shares my liberal views on cannabis,' he noted. There was apparently fury in the McCartney camp as a result, and Paul felt moved to issue a long and tersely-worded statement of his own.

'I find it very sad that after years of friendship, Geoff Baker and I are parting,' he confirmed. 'Over the past few months, his behaviour has not reached the professional standards I had come to expect, and it's with regret that I am forced to end our relationship . . . It's particularly sad that he has chosen to implicate my wife Heather in this business, and I can say now that she has had absolutely nothing to do with it.' McCartney would go on to theorise that his formerly trusted adviser had grown 'unstable' of late.

Baker: 'If I'm unstable, maybe that's because somebody drove me to it.'

It may be only a myth that McCartney's wife had expressed her reservations about certain long-serving members of his entourage. At least one of Baker's friends would, nonetheless, speculate fancifully that 'Paul felt Geoff was to blame for some of the bad press [Mills] was getting.' Another source told the *Daily Mail*, 'The writing was on the wall as soon as Heather arrived. My feeling is that she was uncomfortable with Geoff because he was so much a part of Paul's old life.' Back in 1990, Linda had gone on record as calling the right-on, vegan Baker 'my kind of guy', and had frequently invited him to the family farm. In those days, she'd added, the McCartneys hadn't felt compelled to do rounds of interviews to promote their latest product. 'You didn't see Orson Welles flogging *Citizen Kane*, did you?' By 2004 that sort of attitude seemed hopelessly quaint, with Paul's recent US tour billed as 'a pop thanksgiving', 'now and forever', 'truly THE event of the new millennium'.

The age of the 'rockin' geezer' had met the age of the spin doctor.

McCartney saw out the year in high gear, obsessively recording and re-recording (in contrast to the 'raw' *Driving Rain*) at Ocean Way. Even by Hollywood standards, his work hours were impressive, extending through late nights and too many weekends. His studio nourishment (tea and tofu) was unvarying. He was also ferociously loyal to the band, at least up to the moment his producer booted them from the studio in favour of having Paul play virtually every instrument himself.

In-between sessions, McCartney announced a five-year sponsor-ship of the Conservation Awards, devised specifically to recognise 'excellence and innovation in safeguarding the UK's cultural heritage.' The one-time pop rebel was now a preservationist. Later that month, he auctioned his Epiphone Texan guitar – a mere replica of the one he'd used in the Sixties – on behalf of Mills' charity. The estimate: $7–10,000. The winning bid: $50,000. Paul and Neil Young performed, Heather spoke and fellow campaigner Pamela Anderson posed fetchingly at the gala Century Plaza event, which raised some million dollars for Adopt-a-Minefield.

A week later, the British tabloids reported that McCartney had broken off from 'express[ing] his concern for the plight of the starving in Africa' to scoff a £400 meal at the Feng Shang Princess floating restaurant near Regent's Park, North-West London. That Christmas, he was one of the troupe performing on Band Aid's reprise of its 1984 chart-topping single in aid of famine relief. After the final take, McCartney had reportedly slumped down on the studio floor, groaned, and mumbled, 'Enough.'

The strain of working round the clock on two continents, while also keeping up with a one-year-old child, proved too much. Paul closed his eyes and took a nap.

McCartney and Mills ended 2004 by appearing on a 'special Christmas celebrity edition' of *Who Wants to be a Millionaire*. They won £32,000, and donated £1 million to victims of the tsunami that struck overnight.

On 6 February 2005, McCartney once again provided the mood music at the Super Bowl, performing ecstatically-received oldies to an American viewing audience of 145 million. Rather justifiably, the organisers had been keen to erase the memory of Janet Jackson's infamous 'wardrobe malfunction' of the year before by engaging an artist felt unlikely to expose himself on national television. Their confidence was well placed. Paul used the occasion to perform a spirited, if somewhat raspy Drive My Car and three other numbers. The only disrobing came when he took off his jacket to sit down at a piano. Nothing malfunctioned. If, like Jackson, he wore any nipple jewellery, he mercifully kept it to himself.

'It was obviously a dream ticket,' says an interested National Football League official who prefers anonymity. 'The idea was to add a touch of class, and the history didn't hurt: [forty] years after the Beatles rocked Jacksonville, down the road, there's the magic again . . . It just doesn't get any better.' That's why, he adds, he and his colleagues were able to enjoy the highest Nielsen ratings, and the most lucrative advertising revenues in the event's own thirty-nine-year history. There were also several amenities 'we were delighted, under the circumstances, to furnish Sir Paul and his family': a police escort to his private lounge, equipped with a 'five star luxury toilet', apparently, part of a backstage village where staff hung modern

American oil paintings, which the official refers to as 'decorative stuff – you know, nothing over $50,000.'

Meanwhile, fans on both sides of the Atlantic had urged – actually begged – McCartney to resume his never-ending tour. The 2004 box office had generally 'stunk', the *Today* correspondent wrote. Springsteen's 'Vote for Change' shows had stunk. The whole industry stunk. And the primary cause was the lack of such talent as McCartney's. To refuse, the critic had argued, was selfish. It was Paul's duty to get back on the road.

When McCartney confirmed that he was hard put to resist – announcing gigs to start on 16 September, in Miami – it wasn't for lack of other projects. After a year, he was still putting the finishing touches to his Nigel Godrich-produced album, released that autumn as *Chaos and Creation in the Backyard*. Here Paul tugged on the handle of the old fruit machine – the folky Jenny Wren being one of several obvious Beatles homages – but it stubbornly refused to register three oranges. There was also a starring role at the London branch of Live8, that latest well-meaning effort to succour the various crooks, charlatans and top-of-the-range Mercedes owners governing much of Africa.

Although McCartney limited his formal charity appearances, his crusading spirit was always ready to be roused. His empathy was vast. The imprisonment of the Burmese dissident Aung San Suu Kyi spurred him into action, as did California state policies on a wide range of agricultural and husbandry issues – the subject of a 'sharp letter' to Governor Schwarzenegger. Other pet causes were less exotic, a campaign to save hedgehogs in Surrey being the most persistent.

The lavishly appointed American tour sold out almost the moment it was announced, with a few strategically placed interviews and studiously polite press conferences which resembled those quaintly deferential political debates of the early Sixties, where the 'moderator' kicks off by asking Senator Kennedy if he minds terribly answering a question or two. Once on stage, McCartney, now neatly groomed and a bit pudgier, had such a sober, businesslike air that his

Hofner might as well have been a briefcase. Indeed, he used the occasion not to evoke the counter-culture, but to pitch financial planning on behalf of Boston-based Fidelity Investments.*

Paul would also go on to develop a long version of *Tropic Island Hum* and yet again re-release We All Stand Together, his classic amphibian anthem. As he turned sixty-three he still proudly believed in 'family values, love stories [and] happy endings.' He sometimes used a bit of invective ('The fuckin' frog's wrong,' he'd apparently noted of one promotional flyer), but generally he was 'all for' the wonderful world of Disney. 'In animation,' Paul said of *Tropic Island*, 'I think it's good to have a bit of a youth[ful] quality about yourself. And I certainly have. It's just something that's in me. I'm still fascinated by things I was fascinated by as a boy: humour, romance, passion. All the things you like as a kid.'

Despite his claims to childlike simplicity, McCartney wasn't ascetic. As he'd made clear to the band, he was 'happy to get a pint in', even if his preferred tipple was more apt to be Château Lafite or something involving tequila. He clearly enjoyed being Beatle Paul, but wasn't willing to 'kick back and stew in all [the] acclaim.' He wanted to do what he'd always done – write songs, tell stories, make speeches, crack jokes, chair meetings, perform for his public and, in general, friends couldn't help notice, micromanage everything from his world tour down to the office party. As Derek Taylor had said, 'When [McCartney] set up MPL, I went to see what he'd made of it. It was on three or four floors and was exactly what he'd wanted Apple to be. It was beautiful, orderly, nice carpets, plenty of hush, nice modern paintings on the walls . . . Paul pays enormous attention to detail. This is a man who could be sitting on an island in the sun, but he loves hard graft.'

---

* Asked to comment on his legacy, McCartney informed one magazine, 'I'd like people to think I was . . . sensational. And that I was a damn good bass player and that I was a damn good singer, and a damn good writer, and I'd like them to wrap that all up in a little ball and swallow it.'

As usual, too, McCartney worked on a broad canvas. In 2005 he's spoken, in passing, to environmental groups (about global warming and CFCs), record company executives (about an album of his remixes, called *Twin Freaks*) and a party of schoolchildren (about Wirral). He's glad-handed in Soho Square. Signed copies of *Each One Believing*, a book of photographs based on the last tour. Sat for half-a-dozen interviews. Pushed his daughter around St John's Wood. Chatted to Ringo. Flown the Atlantic.

And that was just one day.

The Beatles were doing better than ever, a chain of independent, but dedicated shops selling 'new and original band memorabilia including T-shirts, posters, records, badges, buttons, mugs and collectibles new and old, plus autographs.' Liverpool itself was back from the brink, thanks in part to a thriving nostalgia industry. The 'Cavern quarter', once a ghetto of stress cracks and peeling paint, now boasted such attractions as Yesterdays and the Rubber Soul Oyster Bar. Six days a week, April to October, busloads of tourists descend on Forthlin Road, the double row of neat, semi-detached houses seemingly frozen in time since the Fifties. Sir Paul (Macca, still, in the city) regularly appears for some civic or semi-public event followed by a turn around the old neighbourhood, an occasion when fans like Rusty West are moved to unveil a specially themed tribute. 'One year we painted the car psychedelic,' he recalls with quiet pride.

McCartney's music has already survived forty years longer than most forecasts (including that royal New Year's wish for 'less moptops') made back in 1963. It's curiously tempting to bet on it lasting forty more. Nobody can say, with absolute conviction, if the same will apply to today's crop of aerobicised teens and tattooed cases from Jerry Springer's green room who've sidled through the door the Beatles opened, and whose very existence would be doubtful without them.

Instead of retiring, McCartney embarks on the most lucrative tour in pop history. It's clear that we don't want less of him. We want more.

CHAPTER 11

Coda

In May 2006, McCartney signalled the end of his four-year marriage to Heather Mills, raising the prospect of Britain's biggest ever divorce settlement.

In an official statement, the couple said that they were separating 'with sadness', leading lawyers to speculate that McCartney might face a divorce claim of £200 million. Mills herself roundly denied that she was a gold-digger, and went on to blame the split on the media's 'constant intrusion into our private lives.'

Some felt that there was a touch of irony, if not hypocrisy, about complaints of excessive press attention, particularly from a woman who had sold her story to the tabloids about having sex in her hospital bed immediately after having her leg cut off in 1993. But there was also sympathy for the couple's 'immensely stressful' ordeal, as they put it, as well as for their two-year-old daughter Beatrice.

Events seem to have come to a head in the early weeks of 2006. Following a joint appearance that March to protest against the Canadian government's culling of harp seal pups, the couple evidently decided to go their own ways. The woman known, not always fondly, as 'HM' took up residence in their beachfront home in Hove, while her husband favoured the old family farm at

Peasmarsh. Late in April, McCartney enjoyed a solo break in Beaulieu Sur Mer in the south of France, triggering headlines and accompanying photographs – showing a notably glum-looking Paul – the world over.

According to most sources, Mills had been keen to devote more time to her various campaigns and to her media profile, while McCartney was happy spending his time at home. The result was what one friend called a 'deep-seated resentment.' The friend said: 'She is angry that he gets so much adulation from fans and is one of the most famous people on the planet, while she feels she should get just as much respect for being a model and campaigner.'

Compounding the problem, perhaps, was Mills's obvious distress at enduring yet another operation on her injured limb, followed by a lengthy period of convalescence. 'The Leg' itself became something of a celebrity in the midst of all the media coverage of the breakup, with numerous colourful re-tellings of Mills's accident and the occasion, for instance, on which she waved her prosthetic around while live on TV with Larry King. In September 2005, the same leg was reportedly pulled off by security guards in New York when, followed by the media, Mills tried to enter the office of Jennifer Lopez in order to protest Lopez's decision to wear and sell fur products.

In a purely coincidental development, the news of the McCartneys' separation broke in the very week the Mills launched her work *Life Balance*, a self-help book revealing her secrets to finding 'spiritual, physical and emotional' health and happiness. The book contained many moving references to her 'open and loving' marriage.

Among Mills's insights in *Life Balance* was the information that 'Most of the disagreements in the world are due to misunderstandings, or failing to see the other person's point of view. Countless relationships could be healed through proper communication.'

Mills would go on to ruefully admit to 'holding back on what I wanted to say in case I hurt someone's feelings,' which had led to 'me becoming frustrated and expressing myself impatiently.'

Mills also appeared to offer a glimpse into the couple's domestic life when she wrote: 'It is all very well telling people to put their clothes in the laundry basket, but old habits die hard.' She advised imposing a set of house rules, such as 'everybody clears up after themselves.'

Meanwhile, the proceedings themselves contained a series of colourful allegations on Mills's part, including wife-beating, and details of rows over such matters as bedpans and breast milk. McCartney flatly denied every single claim.

When the dust settled, the general consensus was that Mills had – to put it no stronger – reservations about McCartney being back on tour, and had declined to accompany him on certain dates. There were also claims that, while Paul was happy to simply switch off when not on stage, Mills – twenty-six years his junior – harboured media ambitions of her own. The exact cause or causes of the breakup will probably always remain a mystery, perhaps even to the couple themselves.

Meanwhile the lawyers went to work, debating whether or not Mills might actually be due some £50 million for each year of her marriage. McCartney was said to have earned £48.5 million in concert fees and royalties in 2005 alone. In the early months of 2006, by coming off the road and pottering around the farm in Sussex, he was down to more modest earnings of some £650,000 a week.

While legal experts were trundled out in print and on air, the headline writers contented themselves with endlessly repeating the lyrics of McCartney's long-ago song, 'When I'm Sixty-Four'. The date in question fell on 18 June 2006. It must have been a particularly wretched birthday for him.

Bibliography

Badman, Keith, *The Beatles Diary Vol. 2*, London: Omnibus Press, 2001

Benson, Harry, *The Beatles in the Beginning*, Edinburgh: Mainstream, 1993

Benson, Ross, *Paul McCartney Behind the Myth*, London: Gollancz, 1992

Brown, Peter and Gaines, Steven, *The Love You Make*, London: Macmillan, 1983

Carr, Roy and Tyler, Tony, *The Beatles: An Illustrated Record*, London: Triune, 1978

Coleman, Ray, *McCartney Yesterday & Today*, London: Boxtree, 1995

Davies, Hunter, *The Beatles: The Authorised Biography*, London: Heinemann, 1968

Flippo, Chet, *McCartney: The Biography*, London: Sidgwick & Jackson, 1988

Giuliano, Geoffrey, *Blackbird: The Life and Times of Paul McCartney*, Updated edition, New York: Da Capo Press, 1997

Goldman, Albert, *The Lives of John Lennon*, New York: William Morrow, 1988

Harry, Bill, *Mersey Beat: The Beginnings of the Beatles*, London: Omnibus Press, 1977

Harry, Bill, *The Paul McCartney Encyclopedia*, London: Virgin Books, 2002

Hill, Tim and Clayton, Marie (eds.), *The Beatles Unseen Archives*, New York: Barnes & Noble Books, 2003

Lennon, John, *A Spaniard in the Works*, London: Jonathan Cape, 1965

Lennon, John, *Skywriting by Word of Mouth*, New York: Harper & Row, 1986

Lewisohn, Mark, *The Complete Beatles Chronicle*, London: Pyramid Books, 1992

Lewisohn, Mark, *The Complete Beatles Recording Sessions*, London: Hamlyn, 1988

McCartney, Paul (from interviews with), *Wingspan*, London: Little, Brown, 2002

MacDonald, Ian, *Revolution in the Head*, London: Fourth Estate, 1994

McGee, Garry, *Band on the Run*, New York: Taylor Trade Publishing, 2003

Miles, Barry, *Paul McCartney: Many Years From Now*, New York: Henry Holt, 1997

Norman, Philip, *Shout*, New York: Simon & Schuster, 1981

Peel, Ian, *The Unknown Paul McCartney*, Richmond, Surrey: Reynolds & Hearn, 2002

Sandford, Christopher, *Mick Jagger: Primitive Cool*, London: Gollancz, 1993

Scaduto, Anthony, *The Beatles Yesterday, Today and Tomorrow*, New York: Signet, 1968

Shepherd, Billy, *The True Story of the Beatles*, London: Beat Publications, 1964

Shipper, Mark, *Paperback Writer*, London: New English Library, 1978

Taylor, Derek, *It Was Twenty Years Ago Today*, London: Bantam, 1987

Whitaker, Bob, *The Unseen Beatles*, London: Conran Octopus, 1991

Williams, Allan, *The Man Who Gave the Beatles Away*, London: Hamish Hamilton, 1975

Sources and Chapter Notes

Author's Note: Endnotes are a necessary evil in a book like this. The following pages show at least the formal interviews, conversations and/or other source material mined in the three years beginning in July 2002. As well as those listed, I also spoke to a number of people who prefer not to be named. Where sources asked for anonymity – usually citing a healthy and well-earned respect for Paul McCartney's lawyers – every effort was made to get them to go on the record. Where this wasn't possible, I've used the words 'a friend' or 'a colleague', etc, as appropriate. Once or twice, I've resorted to the formula of an alias. No acknowledgement thus appears of the help, encouragement and kindness I got from a number of quarters, some of them, as they say, household names.

Chapter One

The events of 16–25 January and 8–9 December 1980 were exhaustively covered in papers and periodicals around the world. Among those consulted were *Billboard*, *Life*, *Newsweek*, the *New York Times*, *People*, *Rolling Stone*, the *Seattle Post-Intelligencer*, *Time*, *The Times*, *USA Today*, the *Washington Post*, the *Weekly*. I should particularly thank Bob Harris, Jeff Griffin and Andy Peebles, all latterly BBC, and Andy Partridge of the great XTC. It's a pleasure, too, to acknowledge Keith Badman's *The Beatles Diary Vol. 2*, Geoffrey Giuliano's *Blackbird* and Albert Goldman's *The Lives of John Lennon*; the last, albeit labouring under its author's note of simulated moral outrage, is particularly rich in detail.

Chapter Two

For events from 1942 until fame struck, exactly twenty years later, I'm grateful to a Mohin relative and also those who spoke to me about McCartney's childhood and/or postwar Liverpool, notably Allan Clarke, Rex Evans, the late Adam Faith, Max King, Tony Huss, Alan Lane, Dave Peters, Chris Rea, the late Dick Rowe, Tony Yeo. The Liverpool *Echo* was a mine of information, as was the city's Business Centre and Tourist Information – I'm grateful to Nichola Lee – as well as Companies House and the UK Family Records Centre. I visited the scene of McCartney's youth, and should acknowledge both Alan Foulder and the verger and others at St Peter's Church, Woolton. My thanks, too, to Stefan Hansen at the Federal Bundesministerium archive in Berlin, one of my favourite haunts. Secondary sources included Bill Harry's *The Paul McCartney Encyclopedia*, Barry Miles' comprehensive *Paul McCartney: Many Years From Now*, Philip Norman's *Shout*, and Allan Williams' *The Man Who Gave the Beatles Away*, the last a lively read even if McCartney himself thought the title a bit of a stretch.

McCartney's 'Stu and I used to have . . .' quote first appeared in Barry Miles' *Paul McCartney: Many Years From Now*; his 'I'll kill you, you bastard . . .' quote first appeared in Geoffrey Giuliano's *Blackbird*.

Lullaby Of The Leaves written by Bernice Petkere and Joe Young.

She Loves You (Lennon-McCartney)
© Northern Songs Ltd
Published by Sony/ATV Music Publishing.

Chapter Three
Interviews and/or taped conversations, some conducted at the time

of my earlier biographies, took place with the late Larry Adler, Ben Brierley, Allan Clarke, the Delafonts (arranged by Pete Dutton), Rex Evans, the late Adam Faith, Chris Farlowe, Judy Flanders, Lucy Gentry, Tom Keylock, Robert Mann, Dave Mason, Don Short, Pat Sims, Eric Stewart, Robert Stigwood, Kathy Ward. I'm particularly grateful to Angie and Ruth McCartney, both of whom have enjoyed notable success since the lean years following Jim McCartney's death. For secondary sources I should credit *Billboard*, the *Herald Tribune*, *Melody Maker*, *Mojo*, the *New York Times*, *Nova*, *Rolling Stone*, *The Times*, *Variety*, *Vogue*. It's a pleasure to acknowledge, as any McCartney author should, Mark Lewisohn's *The Complete Beatles Chronicle*, a testament to sheer dedication and original research, as well as Ross Benson's *Paul McCartney Behind the Myth*, Ray Coleman's *McCartney Yesterday & Today*, Ian MacDonald's *Revolution in the Head* and, of course, Hunter Davies' peerless *The Beatles: The Authorised Biography*. The Beatles' own *Anthology* (Chronicle Books, 2000) and *The Beatles: The First US Visit*, the pioneering film shot by the Maysles brothers, were both useful; a number of short quotes by McCartney, included here, first appeared in one or both of them. I should also thank the public affairs staff at Seattle's Key Arena and the secretary of the RN Officers Club, Portsmouth, for their help. My own memory is to blame for the account of the winter of 1962–3, Britain's worst in 200 years. I visited Wimpole Street.

McCartney's 'And that was the deal . . .' quote first appeared in Ray Coleman's *McCartney Yesterday & Today*; Cynthia Lennon's 'fell like a ton of bricks . . .' quote appeared in her *A Twist of Lennon* (Star, 1978); Tom Wolfe's 'There were hundreds of boys, high school students . . .' quote appeared in *Entertainment Weekly*'s special issue, Winter 1999; McCartney's 'You kidding?' quote appeared in Barry Miles' *Paul McCartney: Many Years From Now*.

Chapter Four

McCartney's purple patch was recalled by, among others, Allan Clarke, Micky Dolenz, Bob Harris, Alan Hazen, Dick Heckstall-Smith, the late Al Hendrix, Tom Keylock, Angie McCartney, Ruth McCartney, Mark Noble, Ken Pitt, Ravi Shankar (interview kindly arranged by Irfan Zuberi), Don Short, Grace Slick, Ed Strauss, the late Frank Thorogood, Adele Warlow. I should particularly acknowledge Noel Chelberg and Marshall Terrill for, respectively, helping deconstruct much of McCartney's music and kindly supplying a number of facts, figures and reference points, notably the excellent *Daytrippin'*. Francie Schwartz returned my e-mail.

Secondary sources included *Life*, *Metro*, *Melody Maker*, the *New York Times*, *Rolling Stone* (as from 1967), *The Times*, *Vogue* and, not least, Mark Lewisohn's *The Complete Beatles Chronicle*, best by far of a series of such blow-by-blow accounts.

McCartney's 'It was raining and we had a couple of bits of corrugated iron . . .' line, as paraphrased here, is a combination of two quotes that appear separately in the Beatles' *Anthology* and Barry Miles' *Paul McCartney: Many Years From Now*; McCartney's 'I felt it was a bit much . . .' quote is also from the latter. Joanne Newfield's 'Paul could get to Brian . . .' quote is from Philip Norman's *Shout*; Winona Williams' 'went into a pout . . .' quote is from Ross Benson's *Paul McCartney Behind the Myth*.

Penny Lane (Lennon-McCartney)
© Northern Songs Ltd
Published by Sony/ATV Music Publishing

Getting Better (Lennon-McCartney)
© Northern Songs Ltd
Published by Sony/ATV Music Publishing

Suicide (McCartney)
© Northern Songs Ltd
Published by Sony/ATV Music Publishing

All You Need Is Love (Lennon-McCartney)
© Northern Songs Ltd
Published by Sony/ATV Music Publishing

Why Don't We Do It In The Road? (Lennon-McCartney)
© Northern Songs Ltd
Published by Sony/ATV Music Publishing

Chapter Five
Comment on the Beatles' break-up and aftermath came from Randy Brecker, Dan Chernow, Chris Farlowe, Libby Fields, Jeff Griffin, Dick Heckstall-Smith, David Henshaw, Tony Huss, Lenny Kaye,

Tom Keylock, Angie McCartney, Ruth McCartney, Henry McCullough, Dave Mason, the late Mickie Most, Andy Peebles, Peter Perchard, Pat Sims, David Sinclair, Grace Slick, Kathy Ward, Mark Wilson, Robert Wise, Tom Wolfe. Some of my research into Allen Klein (for whom I have nothing but respectful awe) and his business dealings took place at the time of my earlier biographies of Mick Jagger and Keith Richards. Companies House and the Public Record Office also both provided limited but riveting archive material on the Klein-Beatles-McCartney debate. I should particularly acknowledge the help of the General Register Office in London.

Michael Lindsay-Hogg's 'When George left . . .' quote first appeared in *Entertainment Weekly*'s special issue, Winter 1999; Alistair Taylor's 'arranged flights, deflected paternity suits . . .' quote is from his and Stafford Hildred's *A Secret History* (John Blake Publishing, 2001); McCartney's 'I [was still] having a bad time . . .' quote is from Barry Miles' *Paul McCartney: Many Years From Now*; JoJo Laine's 'The place they expected . . .' quote is from Geoffrey Giuliano's *Blackbird*.

The End (Lennon-McCartney)
© Northern Songs Ltd
Published by Sony/ATV Music Publishing

Too Many People (McCartney)
© MPL Communications Ltd/Inc

Chapter Six
McCartney's personal and creative highs – and the nadir of Mary Had A Little Lamb – were crisply brought home by Ross Benson, Micky Dolenz, Jeff Griffin, Bob Harris, Angie McCartney, Ruth McCartney, Henry McCullough (and a second member of Wings, who prefers anonymity), Max Paley, May Pang, Eric Stewart, Willie

Weekes, Glen Woodman, Tony Yeo. I should also particularly thank Paul Rutherford, our man in Lagos. Secondary sources include the previously mentioned periodicals and books, notably Garry McGee's *Band on the Run* and Ian Peel's *The Unknown Paul McCartney*. Certain material relating to Jamaica and the *Papillon* shoot came from research for my earlier biography of Steve McQueen.

McCartney's 'Looking at it purely bluntly . . .' quote appeared in *Time*, 31 May 1976; his 'I'd ring John . . .' quote came from Barry Miles' *Paul McCartney: Many Years From Now*; his 'began to feel a bit odd . . .' and 'When we had parties . . .' quotes are from *Wingspan*; Ken Mansfield's 'I asked him how he was . . .' quote is from his *The Beatles, The Bible and Bodega Bay*, with thanks to Marshall Terrill; the 'McCartney's demeanour was entirely Beatlesque' line is from the marvellous *Seattle Times*, 11 June 1976.

Hi, Hi, Hi (Paul & Linda McCartney)
© MPL Communications Ltd/Inc

Live And Let Die (Paul & Linda McCartney)
© MPL Communications Ltd/Inc
Published by MPL Communications and EMI Unart Catalog Inc

Silly Love Songs (Paul & Linda McCartney)
© MPL Communications Ltd/Inc

Chapter Seven
The death throes of Wings were vividly recalled by, among others, Dan Chernow, Lol Creme, Rex Evans, Charlie Gillett, the late Bill Graham, Roger Greenaway, Jeff Griffin, Max King, Henry McCullough, Andy Partridge, Andy Peebles, Dave Peters, Jim Repard, Tim Rice, Eric Stewart, Ed Strauss, Kathy Ward, Alan Weyer. Published sources included *Billboard, Life, Melody Maker, New Musical Express*, the *New*

York Times, *Q*, the *Seattle Post-Intelligencer*, *Seattle Times*, *Sounds*, *The Times*, *Variety*, *Vogue*. I should again particularly mention the late Ray Coleman's *McCartney Yesterday & Today*.

The 'McCulloch's arm outstretched . . .', Denny Laine's '[McCartney] certainly tried to get rid of . . .', 'I think that [Paul] and Linda . . .' and 'Everyone was uptight . . .' lines are all from Geoffrey Giuliano's very fine *Blackbird*; the 'It was too much money . . .' quote appears in Chet Flippo's *McCartney: The Biography*; McCartney's own 'The first night I didn't sleep . . .' quote is from *Rolling Stone*, 26 June 1980; his 'Of course when I got home . . .' quote is from Ray Coleman's *McCartney Yesterday & Today*.

London Town (McCartney-Laine)
© MPL Communications Ltd/Inc

Chapter Eight
Primary sources included Jeff Griffin, Bob Harris, the late Nicky Hopkins, Max King, Alan Lane, Rita Latimer, Andy Peebles, Eric Stewart, Ed Strauss, Dick Taylor, Rusty West, Mark Wilson, Robert Wise, David Wood. A number of people put their reminiscences of Live Aid at my disposal, notably Matthew Seligman, who performed with David Bowie on the historic day. I should also particularly acknowledge and thank the staff at Companies House for their help in explaining the Central Television-ATV/Carlton connection.

McCartney's 'That's where our friendship suffered . . .' line is from Ray Coleman's *McCartney Yesterday & Today*; his 'The Beatles used to say . . .' and 'Britain's attitude toward apartheid . . .' quotes appeared in *Rolling Stone*, 11 September 1986; his 'It was cool that I'd started ringing John . . .' quote appears in *Mojo*, July 2001, the 'so close' being my own synopsis; Robbie McIntosh's 'It was never my place . . .' quote is from the always enjoyable *Daytrippin'*, issue 12.

Somebody Who Cares (McCartney)
© MPL Communications Ltd/Inc

Be What You See (McCartney)
© MPL Communications Ltd/Inc

Pretty Little Head (McCartney-Stewart)
© MPL Communications Ltd/Inc

Eleanor Rigby (Lennon-McCartney)
© Northern Songs Ltd
Published by Sony/ATV Music Publishing

Chapter Nine
Help in recalling the era came from Dan Chernow, Paul Du Noyer, Rex Evans, Judy Flanders, Jeff Griffin, Bob Harris, Alan Hazen, Jill Holmes, Peter Perchard, Jim Repard, Ravi Shankar, Don Short, David Sinclair, Grace Slick, Ed Strauss, Mark Wilson. I should particularly acknowledge both Terry Lambert and Marshall Terrill for their cuttings service, as well as the source at the Olympic Four Seasons hotel, Seattle, and my friends at the Rock and Roll Hall of Fame. I also read the *Daily Mirror*, the *New York Times*, the *Seattle Times*, the *Sun*, *The Times*, *USA Today* and the *Washington Post*. I should again credit Ian Peel's *The Unknown Paul McCartney*, which I warmly recommend.

Carl Davis' 'One day, Paul said . . .' quote appeared in the *Mail on Sunday*, 23 November 2003; the quotes from Ringo Starr's producer Mark Hudson are excerpted from an interview Marshall Terrill conducted for *Daytrippin'*; a number of short quotes or observations by Heather Mills McCartney first appeared in *Vanity Fair*, October 2002, which issue also excerpted her autobiography *Out On a Limb*, republished as *A Single Step*.

Chapter Ten
Parting comment from: Ben Brierley, Dan Chernow, Judy Flanders, Jeff Griffin, Bob Harris, David Jacobs, Henry McCullough, Dave Mason, Andy Partridge, Andy Peebles, Peter Perchard, Dave Peters, Pat Sims, David Sinclair, Grace Slick, Eric Stewart, Kathy Ward, Rusty West. I read accounts of the McCartneys' marriage in, among others, *New York*, *People* and the *Sunday Times*, and I should acknowledge the staff at both the Public Record Office and the US Patent and Trademark Office. I'm also grateful to the source, who preferred anonymity, at the Turnberry Isle club, Miami.

The account of Heather Mills McCartney's thirty-second birthday was drawn in part from *People*, 3 April 2000; Rusty Anderson's 'Linda had always persuaded him . . .' quote is from Marshall Terrill's interview with Anderson in *Daytrippin'*, with permission; McCartney's 'We were crazy . . .' quote appears in Barry Miles' *Paul McCartney: Many Years From Now*. More information on the London Beatles store, not a subsidiary of Apple but not far from the old headquarters in Baker Street, can be found on www.beatlesstorelondon.co.uk

Freedom (McCartney)
© MPL Communications Ltd/Inc

Index